NEW RESUMÉ NEW CAREER

Catherine Jewell
The Career Passion™ Coach

ALPHA

A member of Penguin Group (USA) Inc.

To all job seekers who honor that small, insistent voice within urging you to create your perfect work in a job you love. I admire your courage and marvel at your resilience, talents, and tenacity.

ALPHA BOOKS

Published by the Penguin Group

Penguin Group (USA) Inc., 375 Hudson Street, New York, New York 10014, USA

Penguin Group (Canada), 90 Eglinton Avenue East, Suite 700, Toronto, Ontario M4P 2Y3, Canada (a division of Pearson Penguin Canada Inc.)

Penguin Books Ltd., 80 Strand, London WC2R 0RL, England

Penguin Ireland, 25 St. Stephen's Green, Dublin 2, Ireland (a division of Penguin Books Ltd.)

Penguin Group (Australia), 250 Camberwell Road, Camberwell, Victoria 3124, Australia (a division of Pearson Australia Group Pty. Ltd.)

Penguin Books India Pvt. Ltd., 11 Community Centre, Panchsheel Park, New Delhi—110 017, India

Penguin Group (NZ), 67 Apollo Drive, Rosedale, North Shore, Auckland 1311, New Zealand (a division of Pearson New Zealand Ltd.)

Penguin Books (South Africa) (Pty.) Ltd., 24 Sturdee Avenue, Rosebank, Johannesburg 2196, South Africa

Penguin Books Ltd., Registered Offices: 80 Strand, London WC2R 0RL, England

International Standard Book Number: 978-1-59257-975-4

Library of Congress Catalog Card Number: 2009934673

12 11 10   8 7 6 5 4 3 2 1

Interpretation of the printing code: The rightmost number of the first series of numbers is the year of the book's printing; the rightmost number of the second series of numbers is the number of the book's printing. For example, a printing code of 10-1 shows that the first printing occurred in 2010.

Printed in the United States of America

Note: This publication contains the opinions and ideas of its author. It is intended to provide helpful and informative material on the subject matter covered. It is sold with the understanding that the author and publisher are not engaged in rendering professional services in the book. If the reader requires personal assistance or advice, a competent professional should be consulted.

The author and publisher specifically disclaim any responsibility for any liability, loss, or risk, personal or otherwise, which is incurred as a consequence, directly or indirectly, of the use and application of any of the contents of this book.

Trademarks: All terms mentioned in this book that are known to be or are suspected of being trademarks or service marks have been appropriately capitalized. Alpha Books and Penguin Group (USA) Inc. cannot attest to the accuracy of this information. Use of a term in this book should not be regarded as affecting the validity of any trademark or service mark.

Career Passion™ and Resume Billboard™ are trademarked terms.

Most Alpha books are available at special quantity discounts for bulk purchases for sales promotions, premiums, fundraising, or educational use. Special books, or book excerpts, can also be created to fit specific needs.

For details, write: Special Markets, Alpha Books, 375 Hudson Street, New York, NY 10014.

Contents

Introduction

Today, career changing is normal. Because of our tumultuous job climate, many people not only *want* to change careers but are also *required* to change careers. The new worldwide economic scene produces winners and losers every business day. Businesses once thought to be industry giants go bankrupt. Workers lose their jobs and find it difficult to find the same work with another company. Mergers and off-shoring make jobs once thought to be "secure" evaporate overnight.

On the other hand, emerging businesses create entirely new careers and job positions that couldn't have been foreseen just a few years ago. So today's job seeker is caught up in a constantly changing job landscape. Once thought to be an aberration or an exception, career changing has actually become the norm.

Career changing is logical. It is common today for the average adult to work between the ages of 20 and 70. So in a 50-year time span, you would expect that most people would want to apply their skills and talents to more than one industry—or at least several different jobs. Job seekers in their 40s and 50s now have diverse experiences in their job histories. Some have already had three different careers. It is easy to project that most workers starting their careers in the early twenty-first century will have not one career but three, five, or even seven!

Career changing is accepted. Today's employers are looking at career changers more favorably than ever because they bring capabilities, knowledge, and practical experience from other work environments. A large hospital chain might benefit by hiring workers who bring high-tech marketing techniques, or a solar energy company might benefit from production workers who understand the clean-room manufacturing of the semiconductor industry. In some cases, emerging industries are actually targeting job candidates in other industries that face similar challenges.

Career changing is also more urgent. The "finding passion" goal is often replaced in our shattered economy by "desperation" because workers *must* change careers for economic reasons. Their old jobs no longer exist or have been moved to another state or offshore. The reality of the two-income family makes career choices more complicated. Job seekers in this time feel the critical need to find a job—any job—because the family home and the welfare of spouses and children depend on it.

Getting a new job often means changing careers, too. This book is designed to help you do just that. By featuring the stories of 50 career changers, you can learn how to rethink and reposition your assets for a new career. The pivotal skill in career changing is marketing. It's all about a major makeover of that all-important marketing document called the resume.

I hope you can relate to these stories of career change and find inspiration in them. They are all based on real people who have real needs to retool their careers. All of them sat and faced a blank page, wondering how to write their next resume. All of them have used the resumes you'll find in this book to win interviews that eventually led to new jobs.

You will find the techniques in this book easy to understand and implement for yourself. As a career coach, I have helped more than 600 adults make career transitions. Each person I have worked with is a fountain of talent, experience, and knowledge. You are, too. You *can* make a career change by rethinking your current skills and experience. You can use these assets to lead you to the ideal job in your new career.

Let's explore together how your new resume can make that happen.

Catherine Jewell

www.CareerPassionCoach.com

Acknowledgments

Some say a book is a journey. You begin with a destination in mind, but you're never sure what kind of challenges you'll meet along the way. This journey has been short—about 90 days—and intense. It has been thrilling and tedious. It has also been exhilarating and rewarding.

I wish to acknowledge Nancy Faass and Bob Diforio, who both stood for my skills and encouraged me to take on this project. Your belief in me was sweet and powerful. It called forth something in me that been dormant too long. I thank my coaches, Stephanie Wood and Sara Kellner, who helped me face each challenge with grace and positive energy.

I so appreciate the panel of career experts and job seekers who rushed to my aid in writing some of the resumes and profiles in this book. I want to thank Nancy Bishop, Anna Gregerson, Christine Lambden, Sharon Williams, and Tracie Schatz, each of whom contributed with suggestions, writing, proofreading, and editing.

I thank my editors at Penguin/Alpha Books: Mike Sanders, Janette Lynn, and Lynn Northrup. Your patience and kind responses helped this new writer wade through the details with ease.

I appreciate my husband, Jay Taylor, and all my extended family members who asked constantly about my progress and provided encouragement at every turn.

I wish to acknowledge the readers of *Career Passion News*, who lent an ear to my ideas, provided helpful suggestions, and nominated career changers to feature in the book. Each time I asked for help, you flooded me with resources, ideas, and quotes for this book.

Without my clients and their career challenges, I would never have had the background and the courage to tackle this project. *You* have provided me with the training ground and the practicum I needed to formulate and refine the ideas in this book. I thank each of you.

Finally, I thank each of the career changers in this book. Thank you for providing your stories and career details. Thank you for allowing me to tell your stories in a way that helps other career changers. Your resilience, courage, talents, and tenacity inspire me.

Part 1

Strategies for the New Job Market

Chapter 1

Your New Job Is Out There— But Which One?

Your resume is the primary tool for marketing your skills, knowledge, and experience to prospective employers. Most resumes are 1 to 2 pages and just 300 to 900 words. Here's the picture: you are facing the most important task of your adult life—finding a way to make a living. And you have 300 to 900 words to capture the attention of a hiring manager with an overflowing e-mail box and a stack of resumes 3 inches deep. Is it any wonder that this task seems a bit daunting?

Now, let's add the ingredients of today's pressure-cooker job market—savings running low, unemployment benefits running out, a mortgage payment (or two) due, and credit card payments due at the end of the month. You can see why most people are just glad to add their last job title to the 1997 resume and put it "out there" in the marketplace, hoping for the best.

Writing a resume about yourself without having a specific job in mind is like jumping off a diving board without knowing how deep the water is. Your chance for success is small and you could even hurt yourself.

A smarter way is to see the resume for what it is: an advertisement for a wonderful, complex, intelligent, educated, hardworking individual who can contribute in a significant way to a company's success. As an advertisement, it can't possibly tell everything about who you are, however. How can you possibly communicate the complexity of the widget product launches at your last company? How could you accurately describe the persistence it took to get engineering and production to cooperate in order to meet the new government regulations? How could you tell about your role as referee when you managed that international team? The reality is that you can't.

The resume is just a sample—simply a taste of the challenges you have faced and how you have succeeded in your work life. What you put on the resume needs to be significant, positive, and effective. Each achievement, phrase, and word needs to be carefully selected to meet the goal: generating an interview.

Your resume will be more effective if it's written for a specific job in a specific industry. "Fine," you might be saying. "If I knew what *that* is, I wouldn't have bought this book. I'd be working already, with my mortgage paid and my credit card payments up-to-date!" Take it easy—we'll get to your perfect, target job. But first, let's look at the world of career changing and see how it applies to you.

Three Types of Career Changes

There are really three types of career changes: the industry switch, the functional switch, and the switch in both industry and function. Let's look at each scenario in detail.

Changing Industry

Changing industries is perhaps the simplest career change. If you think about it, you know that most businesses use the same functions to get work done. Most businesses have sales. They have a reception department, sometimes called traffic, which helps schedule the work or service. They have a production department—a group of people who perform the service or make the product. They have a customer service department, and these people work face-to-face, by telephone, or virtually with customers making sure that the product or service works and that they can benefit from it. Many companies that have a physical product also have a shipping department.

Of course, all companies need departments that help them stay organized, such as accounting to keep the books and human resources to screen, interview, and hire new employees. No business would be complete without management. So if you think about all of those functions and understand *your* function, you'll realize that changing industries is simply changing the *business* where you do your work.

This is the easiest of all career changes, because when you change industries you are simply moving into a new environment. Chances are that the business is organized similarly and that you will absolutely be doing the same activities daily. With an industry change, the biggest challenge may simply be learning the *language* of the business. There are literally thousands of terms that are distinct or distinctively used in any industry.

It can be overwhelming at first until you learn the context and priority of work. A nurse who moves from a school environment to a hospital emergency room will know the meaning of medical terms. In her new environment, she may have expanded her tasks—but chances are she received training in all of them. She will quickly see how the staff organizes its efforts and how it decides which tasks are critical and which ones can wait. This on-the-job, in-the-heat-of-the-battle training is all that's needed to help this nurse succeed in her new industry of the emergency room. Her tasks have not necessarily changed, but the pace and priority might have. She speaks the language of medicine; now she has also learned a new context and priority.

Learning the hundreds of terms that are distinctive to that industry is possible and even easy when you consider that the newly hired employee is quickly immersed in the jargon of the new industry.

When you make an industry switch, you have new customers who have different needs. You have new services or a new product line. In some cases when you change industries, there will be different techniques for selling and distributing the product. Your accounting technology may also change, in addition to new procedures. Many industries have stringent rules and regulations, and many of them are governmental in nature and absolute.

The changes experienced in an industry switch are manageable. Many career changers actually enjoy the process. They love the challenge, the learning, and the pleasure of becoming an expert in the new terminology. They also love discovering that two different industries have more parallels and similarities than differences. You can rest assured that your professional experience in one industry can easily translate to another.

Changing Function

The second kind of career switch is the functional change, which is a bit harder. Examples would be moving from shipping to sales, from production to accounting, or from customer service to human resources. This change is more difficult because most training is focused on function—managing, accounting, teaching, designing, writing, testing, and so on. Even if your college degree is in biology, psychology, or history, you were graded on the functions of learning, writing, presenting, and testing. A change in function often requires tasks and activities that are new to you.

When you make a functional shift, there is also a shift in skills. A finance professional who has expertise in tax accounting might make a shift to forecasting income for the company. That's a change in function within the function of accounting—a small shift, but a career change nonetheless. The tax accounting professional may have to brush up on computer modeling and interpreting reports. While both these skills were probably included in his or her accounting curriculum, some skills may be rusty.

If you basically enjoy what you do, the ideal shift might be changing to a similar function. One common change is from marketing to sales. Those who have a heart for promoting the business and for supporting salespeople may find it easy to move into sales. Marketing often supports sales, so marketing staff have a chance to observe the challenges of sales firsthand. They can make the change in function with their eyes open and knowing the key terminology of sales.

A functional shift also requires a shift in focus. You now must ask, "What is my new purpose or mission?" "What are the standards of success in my department?" In customer service, the standard of success might be how many customer calls you are able to handle in an hour or a day. The measure of success in sales will be very different. It's not going to be about how many calls you take; it's going to be about how much product you sell.

The functional switch is often executed by people who have no heart for their chosen field. Take the high school debater who wanted to be a communications major and train to be a professional speaker. When she went to college, her father thought there was no real money to be made in speaking for a living, so he insisted that she get a business degree with an emphasis in accounting. Years later, she made the functional switch from accounting to training. She had always had a heart for speaking, training, and teaching. She was easily able to take her expertise in accounting and her natural ability for speaking and create a new career for herself. She made a functional career shift from accountant to accounting trainer.

Functional career changes nearly always come about because a skill or talent has been dormant for a while. The individual is seeking expression of his or her natural ability. If the person can stay within the same industry, he or she only has to change the activities or skills—having already mastered the industry terminology and subject matter.

Changing Both Industry and Function

The third type of career change is perhaps the most difficult: changing both your job function and industry. What is interesting to me as a career counselor is that fully one third of the professionals I have worked with go for this type of change—even though it's what I would call a C-change, requiring a lot of adaptation and resilience.

It can be very satisfying, particularly if you are walking away (or running away) from a profession that no longer serves you. If the industry is close (such as health care to pharmaceuticals) or the function is close (sales to marketing), it can work very well. As I discussed earlier, you will have challenges on several fronts: learning new business activities and learning a new business. You could drown in the immersion of new technology, activities, and responsibilities—all in an environment that feels unfamiliar. People who do well in this type of career shift are usually going back to an industry or to skills they have learned in the past.

This multidimensional career change is just too difficult for some people to make in one leap. Planning your career change as a two-step process can make the transition easier. Let's say, for example, that you are in the software industry providing software support. You are tired of the frantic pace, the problems with implementation, or the sales goals that cause you so much stress you want to quit. Regardless of the reasons, a change to health care is going to be a big change. An easier way to make the transition is to find a software position in the field of health care. The health-care industry is constantly upgrading its technology, so there are a number of companies that specialize in health-care software. The two-step transition might go as follows: keep the same function, software support, and change industries. In a short time, learn the terminology—then change your function. That's a two-step career change: first industry, then function.

Here's another example directly from this book. Thomas Steinbach, featured in Chapter 8, has had a long career in retail and has several problems with it: the longer hours, being on his feet, and his ever-changing work schedule. His entire career is retail sales and retail management. He is currently working in a hardware store managing the flooring department. He wants to make a shift in industry and get away from retail.

The first step is to make a slight change in industry. Tom makes the decision to start applying for jobs in the wholesale flooring industry. He already knows the terminology and a lot about their product line. He knows about measuring, relating to customers, and a bit about sales. The change to flooring is a slight industry change, combined with a move into a new function—sales. Once established in commission sales, Tom can move into almost any industry or product. So the first step is to move into a side industry; the second is to move into another function—sales.

Lindsay Haines, who is featured in Chapter 28, was a loan originator when she lost her job due to the crash of the subprime market. So she knows mortgages—but she also knows that federal guidelines now require mortgage lenders to have additional certifications and training. She doesn't mind the idea of training, but no longer wants the stress of generating all her own business. Lindsay is networked with Realtors, title companies, and many real estate agents because they have been her partners as a loan originator. With their advice, she decides to apply for a job as a leasing agent of an upscale apartment complex. By taking a job as a leasing agent, she gets more regular hours and the customers come to her. Once she is established in a salaried sales position, she will probably gain the confidence she needs to move on to a commission-based sales position or perhaps become an independent real estate person full-time.

Andrea Galloway, who is featured in Chapter 36, wants to go from trade show specialist to executive director of a nonprofit. While she has managed a nonprofit and written grants, her experience is 20 years out of date. One way for her to get back into the nonprofit world is grant writing—especially now, when so many nonprofits are struggling to generate funding. She begins by brushing up on her grant writing skills by creating a course for the local community college. She also volunteers for several nonprofits and becomes familiar with the mission and the vision of these organizations. These activities provide her with dozens of new contacts in the nonprofit world—very targeted networking for her new job. Her first transition to grant writer may eventually lead to business developer or even an executive director position.

This kind of side-door or two-step career shift is also excellent for those who are not sure what they really want. Being *in* an environment for a few months will help you know whether it's the right place for you. It's also easier to execute a career move from within an industry. Just remember, career changing is more common now—and experimenting a little is expected and smart.

Separating the Job from the Work

Any time you experience a career loss, your first reaction is to escape the pain. You might have been forewarned about losing a job. You might have heard the rumors and seen the signs. It is still a huge emotional blow to lose your livelihood. In fact, it is one of the biggest blows adults will experience in their lifetimes. Many people express a desire to get out, escape, and completely change circumstances. A factory worker who loses her job might say, "I'll never work in a factory again." A software developer who is laid off might say, "I'm never going to write software again." But that attitude is like throwing the baby out with the bathwater. These job seekers are discarding all of their hard-earned skills, experience, and education. They are turning their backs on expertise that they may have gained over 20 or even 30 years.

Job Conditions

It's important to take a step back when you have had a job loss and separate the job from the work itself. The *job* is a specific set of responsibilities in a specific company or work setting. It includes your work duties, the environment, the physical circumstances, the emotional climate, the corporate culture, the politics, the time demands, the hours, the pace, the supervisor, the customers, and the congeniality (or pettiness) of your work associates. Many people have a bad work experience just because *one* of these factors is not pleasant. People tend to hate their jobs if just two or three of these conditions are unpleasant. Sometimes it's a tense relationship with one or several work associates. Sometimes it's a micro-managing boss or one who is unavailable and uncommunicative. Sometimes it's a specific customer or group of customers that are particularly difficult.

When workers think about all those issues associated with their *jobs*, they tend to throw out the idea of ever doing that *work* again. A better way to move forward is to separate the characteristics of that job from the work itself.

Work Responsibilities

To describe your work, it's helpful to look at your last position description and find a list of "-ing" words. Those are your job accountabilities, and they are the skills that you are building day in and day out. They might include going to meetings, writing e-mails, processing reports, creative writing, designing, analyzing, managing, and speaking to customers.

To create a list of work responsibilities, think about a full week at your job and how you actually spend your time. You will likely find that your *work* is a mix of 10 to 12 functions. As you work with the list, be sure to add a few words to create a phrase that applies to you. "Analyzing" might become "Analyzing new legislative rules." Or "Writing" might become "Writing the employee newsletter." These work phrases are your transferable skills.

☐ Analyzing	☐ Demonstrating
☐ Assembling	☐ Developing
☐ Budgeting	☐ Displaying
☐ Calculating	☐ Documenting
☐ Circulating	☐ Drafting
☐ Collaborating	☐ Editing
☐ Communicating	☐ Engineering
☐ Compiling data	☐ Forecasting
☐ Constructing	☐ Identifying
☐ Consulting	☐ Informing
☐ Contracting	☐ Inspecting
☐ Controlling	☐ Interviewing
☐ Coordinating	☐ Maintaining
☐ Counseling	☐ Managing
☐ Creating	☐ Marketing
☐ Debating	☐ Measuring
☐ Delegating	☐ Meeting

☐ Modeling	☐ Recruiting
☐ Monitoring	☐ Reporting
☐ Negotiating	☐ Researching
☐ Ordering	☐ Scheduling
☐ Organizing	☐ Screening
☐ Overseeing	☐ Selecting
☐ Paying	☐ Selling
☐ Persuading	☐ Serving
☐ Planning	☐ Strategizing
☐ Presenting	☐ Streamlining
☐ Processing	☐ Summarizing
☐ Programming	☐ Supervising
☐ Projecting	☐ Synchronizing
☐ Publishing	☐ Systemizing
☐ Quoting	☐ Tabulating
☐ Ranking	☐ Teaching
☐ Rating	☐ Training
☐ Recording	☐ Writing

As you look at this list, imagine yourself doing each of the activities. Check the ones that make you feel very capable. Now, go back and underline just five or six of these activities that actually please you—activities that you truly enjoy. The purpose of this exercise is to show you that the conditions of the job that you were doing may have been unsatisfactory, but the work itself may have been very pleasing and fun for you.

There are no perfect jobs. There will always be unreasonable demands, critical bosses, and unpleasant co-workers. While the job may not be perfect, the work could be perfectly suited to who you are. In each job there are activities, responsibilities, and structure that you resist, resent, or maybe even hate. This does not mean the work is not for you. You can simply change jobs and have a better situation. A career shift is changing the industry, the function, or both. Changing jobs is simply finding a new position with a different company. So it is important to see that you probably did enjoy parts of the work of even your most detested job. Focusing on what work you enjoyed will give you an idea of what to look for in your ideal new job.

Get a Clue: Discovering Your Career Successes

The first step in any career change (or any job change, for that matter) is to find out what you truly love to do. No one wants to make a career or job change with all its attendant effort and issues—only to find that that job is not suitable for them.

It's very difficult for many people to determine what they love to do. Why? Because they have been conditioned to dismiss what they truly enjoy because it might not generate income. For example, a young boy might dream of being a professional baseball player when he grows up because he loves the game of baseball. His parents might discourage him from this path, however, because they know so few people are actually able to fulfill such a dream. In actuality, there are many, many people in our economy who are employed by the sports industry, and there are many side careers that relate to sports. The young man who loves sports could become a sports writer or a salesman of sports equipment. He could study physical education and become a high school or college coach. He could study kinesiology and become a sports therapist or a personal trainer. There are numerous options.

The way to find out what you truly love to do when you're an adult is to discover your career successes. The first step is to remember a significant job you've held. You can consider your career in reverse and think first about your current job, then the one before that, and so on. Or you can begin with the first job you ever held. For each of these jobs, you want to ask yourself these five questions:

1. How did you do your job differently than others in the same job?

2. Did you create or bring innovations to your job, your process, your work duties, or your business tools in some lasting way?

3. What assignments did you volunteer for beyond your job responsibilities?

4. Did your co-workers look to you for special knowledge, talents, or abilities?

5. What did you enjoy about the work?

How did you do your job differently than others in the same job? helps identify your contribution. What was the special style that you brought to the role of customer service that other customer service representatives didn't bring? What special way did you do your job as secretary or administrative assistant that made you absolutely irreplaceable in your office? What made you stand out from all the other accountants? The answers to this question are usually quality and style answers. "I was more efficient. I was always looking for a better way." "I took more time to truly listen to customers. I solved their problems faster because I was solving the right problem." Or "I loved to find errors in the code. My programs ran better the first time."

Did you create or bring innovations to your job, the process, your work duties, or your business tools in some lasting way? identifies innovation. If you truly love your work, you will find a way to change it, upgrade it, or enhance it. You will make it go better. Because you love the work, you will want to find new and better ways to do it—new and better ways to innovate the work process, for example. You will create new business tools to help you accomplish the work more effectively. Employers are always looking at better ways to get the job done. Innovation isn't always accepted, but innovative ideas tend to flow from people who truly like their work.

What assignments did you volunteer for beyond your job responsibilities? gets at your initiative. When you truly love what you're doing, you will find yourself volunteering to lead a team, to be part of a multidisciplinary committee, or to create a software tool that will help many people in the office. What you volunteer for gives you a good idea of what you truly enjoy. One career changer loved computer networking so much that she volunteered to be the network administrator for her accounting office. At first, she struggled to figure out things on her own. Later, her company paid for her training as a certified network administrator. She used this training to make a career change.

Did your co-workers look to you for special knowledge, talents, or abilities? identifies your talents. Perhaps you had extraordinary patience with mechanical devices and were great at troubleshooting. Another example is the individual who brings calm and mediation to any situation. So she becomes the person in the office who always deals with the most difficult customer. Another example of special talent is writing. One administrative assistant was such an extraordinary writer that she was given the responsibility of writing the company newsletter distributed to more than 50,000 employees worldwide. She wasn't an administrative assistant for very long.

What did you enjoy about the work? is a very important question. It's easy for us to remember the difficult things about a job—the way we were micromanaged, the unreasonable deadlines, or the extreme stress every Friday when reports had to be submitted. Those memories often overshadow the moments when we truly felt successful. Take some time to look at what you truly enjoyed about your work. Was it a particular report that made you feel very satisfied when it came together? Was it a meeting you facilitated that made you feel powerful, influential, and effective? Was it meeting with new customers to discover their needs? What were the activities that actually gave you pleasure in your job?

These career successes are completely unique to you. When translated to achievement statements, each one makes your resume one of a kind. No one else can prepare the same resume that you would. Only *you* can provide your special brand of contribution to the company.

Documenting the Details: Your STAR Stories

Many professionals make the mistake of writing a resume that is little more than a list of position descriptions. In other words, they create a list of responsibilities that are common to the job. While this helps the reader understand what you were expected to do, it doesn't explain how you performed on the job. Remember your audience. Hiring managers have to read your resume, and they thoroughly understand job descriptions. They might even be responsible for writing position descriptions for their company. They are certainly not interested in reading them!

To make your resume powerful, you need to create a list of achievement statements. Achievement statements have four parts and can be remembered with the acronym S-T-A-R:

- **S stands for the *situation*.** This is the condition or set of circumstances that existed before you did your magic. You can paint a picture of a process that was incomplete or ineffective in some way. You can describe customer service scores that were not acceptable. Be careful not to paint the situation so darkly that you are seen as criticizing your former employer or co-workers, however.

- **T is for *thinking* or the *tactic* you took.** Professionals today are valued for the quality of their thinking. In an achievement statement, it's a great idea to give the reasoning behind the actions you took. You can also use the concept of tactic, which is the *way* you chose to solve the problem (in other words, the tool you used).

- **A is for *action*.** State the action you personally took to achieve the result. If you led the committee, *say* you led it. But if you were part of a committee, say you were *part* of a committee. Be as honest as you can about your personal actions, because this gives the hiring manager a sense for your level of responsibility and autonomy. As you go through your career stories, you might surprise yourself realizing how many times you took a leadership role.

- **R is for *results*.** No achievement statement is complete until there is some indication about what results were achieved. In business, the only results that really matter are time saved, money saved, income generated, or effectiveness improved. All of these can be presented in dollars, numbers, or percentages. When you state results in terms of achievement statements, add in numbers to the best of your ability. You may feel that you sincerely do not remember a number, but if you really think about it, you will remember an approximate amount.

  The idea is to help place the achievement in context, so the number is just an indication of the playing field. I once asked a career-changing client how much revenue was generated by the new product launch. She said, "I have no idea." When I asked her, "Was it $1 million or $10 million?", she immediately replied, "About $3.5 million." That is proof that you probably have a sense of what number is appropriate. It is not important that the number be perfect but that it is indicative of how large, how much, how long, or how well you achieved the results you were going for.

By taking the time to discover your STAR stories, you accomplish some very important things:

- You create a list of important achievements to add to your resume.

- You reconnect with the successes you have achieved and rediscover what you enjoyed about your work.

- You create one-of-a-kind stories that make your resume and your interviews more memorable.

- You help yourself prepare for the job interviews to come when you will be asked to talk about your work achievements.

What to Take with You: Transferable Skills

Knowing *how* to do tasks gives the industry changer more than half of what he or she needs to succeed. These job activities are often called transferable skills because they are common to the same job in several industries or several functions.

Here's an example: James is moving from marketing computer hardware to marketing professional services. His marketing degree and experience have allowed him to build skills in the areas of proposal writing, sales, creating presentations, writing brochures, researching client satisfaction, assessing market potential, and so on. If he moves to the industry of accounting, the term "marketing" may not even be used. He might be hired for business development, practice development, or even client relations. His first month on the job, however, he might be asked to write a brochure, create a presentation, develop a research questionnaire, or work on a proposal. So the language may change—but the basic skills haven't. That's why it is so important to understand which skills you have that are *transferable* from one industry to another.

If you compare your job skills with other job seekers, you will find your skills are similar even though your responsibilities are very different. For example, a project manager and an accounts receivable clerk could both have integrated a new software tool at their company. An administrative assistant and a marketing specialist could both have planned and staged a trade show. These are business activities that might be essential to two completely different businesses. There are literally dozens or even hundreds of these skills that you pick up during your career. You might be tempted to use just an action verb that you get from a resume book, such as "integrate," "plan," or "lead." Phrases help put those action verbs into context and present your skills more powerfully.

Transferable skills can be expressed in three- or four-word phrases that describe either the situation you have worked in, the activity you have mastered, or the business challenge you have encountered. Here are a few outstanding examples from the resumes in this book:

Situation

Multinational product launch

Coordination of e-commerce and phone sales

Inbound and outbound phone contact

Activity

Field training

Event planning

Workshop facilitation

Challenge

Multitasking in a call center environment

Building relationships with regulators

Powerful communication of complex ideas

Identifying your transferable skills will allow you to make any of the three types of career changes. To help you generate ideas, I've included a list of transferable skills in Appendix B. There is no limit to the number of ways to describe your unique abilities. The list is organized by function. Use it as a thought starter for your own unique resume.

Hot on the Trail: Sleuthing the Perfect New Job

Let's say you now know your successes, your STAR stories, and your transferable skills. All of this information is useless if you don't know what jobs to apply for. This is the big sticking point for most career changers. They know they want something different, but they don't know what.

So how do you find out what positions you want to apply for? You can conduct your research in three ways: by networking, by information interviewing, and by doing research on the Internet.

Networking and Information Interviews

Everyone recommends that you network to find a new job. In fact, I tell my clients, "If you're not networking, you're not looking for work." There are numerous opportunities for great networking—job clubs, church groups, professional association meetings, business leads groups, chamber of commerce functions, and so on. If you approach it directly, asking for job leads, you might discover that people run in the other direction because they feel they can't provide help. A better technique is to go to these meetings looking for information and introductions. Ask advice about your job search. Ask people to introduce you to hiring managers. Ask people about their work. Have a few great conversations. Focus on just three significant connections instead of trying to meet 10 people.

Once you have new contacts, meet one-on-one with a few people for an Information Interview. This technique is designed to learn about careers and companies. Meet with workers who are at your level, in jobs that you admire or are curious about. Because it's not a job interview, you can ask direct questions such as: "What salary would a person with my experience command?" Or "What are the educational requirements for that position?" Always ask for job titles in that company so you can focus your search on a specific target job. Later, if you have made a great impression, your contact might come across a job lead and give it to you. By expecting less, you will get more.

Remember that anyone can be a source of information and job leads. Talk to the cashier at your local grocery store or dry cleaner. Talk to complete strangers at the coffee shop or gym. Become a career detective, constantly asking people about their work and their companies.

Working the Internet

Today, the world is at your fingertips with the plethora of job boards and job information on the Internet. Sites such as the U.S. Department of Labor (www.dol.gov) tell you what industries are expanding in your state. You can even get a customized report for your metropolitan area at www.jobbait.com.

Another government site, online.onetcenter.org, can help you expand your career options in four distinct ways. You can search by occupation titles, skills, related occupations (called Crosswalk Search), and tools and technology. You can find a new occupation by typing in key words from your current occupation. You will soon see a list of related occupations, either by function or by industry. You can also take a quick skills assessment and find dozens of new occupations that fit your skills.

A third function, called Crosswalk Search, allows you to enter a title and see many related titles. Each summary report for a job title is rich with information. You will find tasks, tools and technology, knowledge and skill requirements, work activities, work values, and more. Finally, if you are particularly skilled at a tool such as Adobe Dreamweaver or Microsoft Frontpage, you can type those in and find a list of jobs that utilize such tools.

Perhaps most helpful is that many occupational titles are marked with a green "in demand" sign. The report will also give you numbers for projected growth in that occupation and median salaries. If you do not want to retrain, you can simply stay with jobs in the Job Zone 1 "little or no preparation" and so on. Other zones will show you how you might move up in the same career path with additional education or training.

If you are searching on Monster.com, CareerBuilder.com, Indeed.com, or any of the hundreds of job board sites, remember that websites reveal only a small percentage of job possibilities. To begin your search, type in key words that are job titles you have held in your career. Be sure to search nationally so that you get as many options as possible. When you type in a job title, you will see how many jobs with that title pop up by industry. If you are considering changing industry, check out how your old job might play out in another industry.

Sometimes typing a job title will yield the group of jobs in a particular industry. This is how you find careers that are close to what you used to do and yet different enough that they will provide you with a new challenge. For example, typing in the words "grant writer" generates a list of jobs that are open in many nonprofit organizations, such as "volunteer coordinator," "business development director," "CEO," and "director." These are all functional jobs within the industry of nonprofits.

If you're working in a hardware store as a manager and wish to change functions, you can type the words "hardware sales" and hundreds of jobs will pop up. If you are a nurse and want to move from the clinical setting to education, you would type the words "education" and "nurse" and see what job postings come on the screen.

Capture the Target Job Description

Once you find job descriptions on the Internet, your first inclination will be to discern whether a particular job is the one for you. Resist this temptation. When you put your discerning mind to work, you will immediately see all the things wrong with that position. "I wouldn't move there." "The company is probably too big and impersonal." "I don't have a Bachelor's degree." You will almost always be disappointed. The purpose of this exercise is not to find a specific job but to find a target job title that is right for you. You can't go looking for just any job; it has to be a precise job title. At this point, you are a career detective seeking job titles that might work.

You'll start to notice that job titles across industries are often similar. For example, the word "specialist" normally indicates an entry-level position in marketing, customer service, or sales. At a higher level, the job title "account manager" or "senior account manager" might be used.

Keep in mind your career successes, your STAR stories, and your transferable skills as you read job descriptions. When you find a job description that makes use of some or all of your skills, save and copy the description into a word processor document. (Many listings will be in table form, so make sure you capture the *name* of the job, which is at the top of the table.) Once you have several job descriptions, combine them and eliminate the redundant items. The result will be a succinct listing of the requirements for your target job. (For each of the 50 career changers featured in this book, you will find a target job description that inspired the resume makeover.)

Capturing your target job title will give your job search direction and focus. You can always adjust your direction and change your target—but having a clear target shortens your job search by weeks and even months. With your target job title and qualifications identified, you are ready to begin writing your resume.

Chapter 2

Build a Resume That Wins Interviews

When you are eager to find a new job, you want it to happen *now*. Your enthusiasm is high, and you're ready to move forward. In reality, however, when changing careers, it is likely to take a little longer. The good news is that you can shorten the search and increase your chances of success. How? Use that enthusiasm to write a new resume.

This is the point where you step back and take some time to create a resume that clearly presents who you are and how you fit into the job that you want. Remember, the purpose of a resume is to get you an interview. If you are screened out because of irrelevant or missing information, your resume has not done its job.

Think of your resume as a well-written advertisement for your services. In an advertisement, words and phrases are chosen very carefully. The advertiser is speaking directly to a targeted customer, giving only the information that will help sell to that specific customer. Your resume must be just as closely focused. At the least, it should be written with a specific function in mind. For best results, write your resume to a specific job description in a specific company.

Which Resume Format to Use?

The first big choice you will make is whether you should create a chronological, functional, or combination (also known as blended) resume. Today, each kind is acceptable—but you need to be strategic in choosing your format.

The **chronological resume** presents details in your work history, beginning with the most recent position and listing jobs in reverse chronological order. Each item includes the name of the company, city, your job title, dates of employment, and responsibilities. This is the most widely accepted and expected format. It works best for those who can show steady growth in their careers with a continuity of either functional or industry success.

The **functional resume** focuses on the professional skill sets related to the job you seek. Your skills and achievements are grouped into three to five broad categories and highlight relevant information about what you can do or have done, rather than detailing your previous job duties. This format is often used when a job seeker has a wide-ranging career and there are sharp detours to other professions, industries, or activities. This is the preferred format for those who have large gaps in their work history but still want to show what they know how to do. Hiring managers generally do not like this format, so it is *not* recommended if you have another choice.

The **combination (or blended) resume** combines the best of both of the other styles. It allows you the freedom to list important skills along with your achievements in each area. You can follow this list by briefly describing each of your significant jobs. By presenting your information twice, the reader can choose to scan either listing and then go back for the detail.

Answering the questions in the following table might help you make your decision about which resume format to use.

Choosing the Right Resume Style for You

	Chronological	Functional or Combination
1. Do you have a work history that shows steady progress in a function or industry?	X	
2. Have you changed careers or dropped out of the job market for more than two years?		X
3. Have your last 10 years been in the same department or function?	X	
4. Have you gained transferable skills that are needed in your new, targeted job?		X
5. Are you eager to showcase your past employers because they are recognizable, respected names in their industries?	X	
6. Have you been self-employed? Are your past employers small and unfamiliar to most hiring managers?		X
7. Are you proud of your consistent promotions?	X	
8. Did you take several detours in your career, working survival or part-time jobs, staying at home with children, or taking a sabbatical to help with family health issues?		X
9. Are the job titles in your history understandable outside your industry or used in your target industry?	X	
10. Do you want to include non-paid volunteer work because it has provided you with new skills?		X

As you can see, the decision isn't cut and dried. That's why most of the resume makeovers in this book feature a combination or blended approach.

Write to Win the Interview

Regardless of which format you choose, every line, word, and date on your resume should promote you—rather than hurt you—in getting an interview for that particular job.

When working with job seekers, I find that most people are scrupulously honest—sometimes to their own detriment. One job seeker was incensed when I asked her to remove her Master's degree in education from her resume. She was applying for work as an administrative assistant. This is a job that rarely requires more than two years of college and a few years of office experience. A Master's degree had no bearing on her current job search and would likely raise red flags in the screening process. I had to point out that in this case, her advanced degree would actually prevent her from getting interviews.

Eliminating extraneous information isn't lying; it's smart marketing. Do not include information that distracts from the message that you are a perfect fit for this job. Think of it this way: Would you feel the necessity to include a belly-dancing course on your resume just because you took it? There is no way you can sum up your life on two pages. That is why you select information carefully. Use information in a way that makes sense for your targeted job.

Special Issues—Age and Gaps

Be careful about how you address gaps in employment. In the following example, the job candidate has a six-year gap in her career because she stayed at home to raise two children. During that time she generated extra income by becoming a distributor for a multi-level marketing (MLM) health supplements company. She might just leave the gap of 2000–2006, but it would certainly generate a question in the interview. My advice is to include line items for gaps in your career history, along with simple and truthful explanations such as:

Marketing Manager	XYZ Company	2006–2009
Self-Employed/Sales	Acme MLM Company	2005–2006
Homemaker Sabbatical		2000–2005
Marketing Coordinator	ABC Company	1997–2000

This is straightforward and honest. Good marketing documents don't leave a lot of questions in the mind of the consumer. Good resumes should generate questions such as, "Tell me more about that marketing project you described," instead of, "What were you doing between 2000 and 2006?"

Another concern today is age discrimination. While companies are usually careful to operate within the law, hiring managers are people looking for the best fit for their team. Unfortunately, there are assumptions—both conscious and unconscious—about older workers. Hiring managers might be concerned about health problems, or that older workers might retire soon and not stay in the job as long. While both assumptions can be proven wrong statistically, the assumptions remain. A job history with 30 years of experience may reflect an established career professional—or, to a 35-year-old hiring manager, it may just seem dated.

It has often been advised that job seekers focus their resumes on the last 10 to 15 years of work history. These are usually the most critical years as they are thought to indicate what you currently can bring to the job. Beyond 15 years can be subject to stereotypes, including that older experience predates software innovations, the Internet, or even the computer!

While these are patently false, this is the screening process—and during the 12 seconds of resume review you don't get time to debate history. If the experience is more than 15 years old, it's critical to use clear achievement statements and relate them to the job. Even better, list continuing education, volunteer experience, or training that shows how you have kept them current or refreshed.

Education can also screen you out if it's dated. One way of dealing with this is to leave the date of graduation off the resume. When describing your skills and experience, be sure to use current and accurate terms, particularly in fast-changing fields such as technology, marketing, sales, and health care. This shows that you are current and knowledgeable in the latest tools and opportunities in your new field.

Create and refer to your profiles on social media sites such as LinkedIn, Facebook, and Google. Check out all the new courses being offered on how to use these tools to expand your job search. Make sure your online profiles are consistent with what you say on your resumes. Be cautious of what you put on your profiles—keep the information professional. (There's more about social media in Chapter 3.) Use professional e-mail addresses on recent popular services or your own website. Check out the examples of resumes in this book to make sure your resume is in a contemporary form.

All the information on your resume should be complete and true as stated. In most cases, any factual errors in your resume can later be cause for dismissal—even if you are an exemplary employee. Don't overstate or fabricate; just choose your facts carefully.

Find and Use Key Words

Most resumes today are read by scanners long before they are given any attention by a human being. Special Optical Character Recognition (OCR) programs can scan both digital and printed resume documents, looking for words that are included in job requirements, activities, or results. These so-called "key words" are considered by that company as essential to your success as a job candidate.

How can you know what key words are important in your target job? Many sites, such as CareerBuilder.com and Monster.com, actually list key words at the bottom of most job postings. What a relief! There's no wondering or guessing—just collecting. Highlight the words, copy them, and begin collecting them in a word processor document. Later, you can put them in a column and alphabetize them. You will immediately see the words that are repeated over and over. These are the words you *must* put into your resume.

If the words are not listed at the bottom of the job posting, look closely for the skills and requirements listed. Include these words both in the summary and in describing achievements. Take care to stick rather closely to the job description. For example, if the requirement is 3 to 5 years of experience, do not point out that you have 15. If you have had a job in marketing and you are applying for a job in business development, change the term "marketing" to "business development" every time it makes sense.

When you wrote term papers in school, the teacher would take points off for redundancy. If you repeated a word or phrase, it was considered poor writing. In the resume game, redundancy is not only good, it's necessary. Internet job boards use spider technology that rates your resume based on the number of matches with the job description key words. The more matches, the higher your rating. (This is the same technology that is used every time you do a computer search. The links on the first page of search results have more key words that matched your search words.)

Since most companies are inundated with job candidates, they appreciate receiving the top 10 candidates, instead of the 980 who posted. That is why the combination resume could be your best choice. It gives you a chance to use key words in your skills and achievement statements and then repeat those words in your career history. You can even create a table at the top of the resume called "Core Competencies" or "Selected Professional Skills" and load up the table with key words.

The more key word matches you have with the job description, the higher your placement as a job candidate. Just think of your last Google search. Did you look at all 10,000 results or just the first 25? You can guarantee better positioning by using the key words of the job description.

Link Your Resume to a Job Description

The task of a hiring manager is to find a near-perfect match between the job applicant and the job. With the deluge of job candidates on the market today, hiring managers are more selective than ever before. At the point of screening, the match of your capabilities to the requirements of the job isn't just the big thing: it's the *only* thing. Your resume must answer the question the hiring manager asks, "Can this candidate do the job?" That's why it's so important to have a target job in front of you when you write your resume.

In Chapter 1, I showed you how you can collect job descriptions from job sites on the Internet. It is probably best to find three to five descriptions that appeal to you and place them in a word processor document. Then, edit the statements until you have one concise job description in front of you. This is your target job. You may have to do more research to find a job title that most closely fits this description. Ways to do this include noticing common titles of job descriptions you are interested in and double checking with network contacts in the industry. When you have figured out what fits best, this will be your target job title.

As you speak to others in networking situations, be sure to use your target job title. It allows people to know precisely what you are looking for and prompts them to think of ways they might help you. Many job seekers are afraid that this kind of specificity limits their chances. In reality, it's just good marketing and communication. You can always *look* at other opportunities. Or you can even change your target job title as your search continues.

In linking your resume to a job, focus on the top third of the first page—a section I call the Resume Billboard. (You'll learn more about this a little later in the chapter.) This section will be read in the first 8 to 12 seconds and should tell the manager, simply and directly, that you can do the job. If you get this first 3 ½ inches right, chances are more of your resume will be read and considered.

Here is an example from Andrea Galloway's resume, featured in Chapter 36. The rest of Andrea's resume also used these key words as often as possible. While sticking with claims she can support, she has borrowed the language of the job description. The key words and phrases are underlined to show you how the job description and the Resume Billboard link up. (The underlining is for emphasis. I don't suggest underlining in your finished resume.)

Grant Writer

- Full-time grant writer to <u>create funding proposals</u> for <u>new and existing programs</u>

- Experience in proposal/grant writing; <u>budget preparation</u> and <u>needs assessment</u>

- One or more years experience and/or <u>training</u>; or equivalent combination of education and experience

- Careful reading of RFP's issued by <u>governmental funding</u> agencies, working with program staff to design new services, and preparing well-written proposals that are consistent with <u>RFP requirements</u>

- Familiar with a variety of <u>human services</u> (such as <u>developmental disabilities, mental illness, drug and alcohol rehabilitation, homelessness, and employment</u>), have a demonstrated ability to facilitate <u>decision-making</u> around questions of <u>program design</u>, and be able to work independently

- A writing sample (preferably a grant application) must be submitted along with a resume

- Proficient <u>computer, software, and organizational</u> skills

- Valid driver's license and insurability under the organization's motor vehicle policy

- Bachelor's degree from four-year college or university

DIRECTOR OF DEVELOPMENT/GRANT WRITER
Strategic Planning/Collaboration/Program Design

- Consistent achievement in creating <u>funding proposals</u> for <u>new and existing programs</u>
- Firsthand experience with <u>RFPs issued by governmental funding agencies</u>
- Significant management experience in <u>human services</u> including domestic violence, multicultural counseling, <u>mental health</u>, life transitions, <u>drug and alcohol rehabilitation</u>, and public affairs
- Effectively collaborate with corporate givers; ability to approach and influence community leaders
- Marketing savvy—capable of understanding ideas that will "sell" in the funding marketplace

Core Competencies

- <u>Grant/proposal writing</u>
- Facilitate discussion for program strategies
- Direct and indirect sales; influence key thought leaders
- Develop own leads for funding sources

- Community/<u>need assessments</u>
- <u>Training</u> design and delivery
- Powerful communicator
- <u>Excellent computer skills</u>

Director of Development Resume Billboard.

Components of a Resume

Today, resume design is wide open. Hiring managers are used to seeing new formats that present unique items in an unexpected order. You may be familiar with these traditional components of a resume:

1. Name

2. Contact information

3. Job objective

4. Opening statement

5. Summary of qualifications, including computer skills

6. Job history

7. Education

8. Other—interests, community work, certifications, testimonials, and so on

In many cases, the job objective is deleted because the same idea can be conveyed in just three words of a headline. If you are currently a marketing coordinator and want to go for a sales position, you can convey that idea by simply using a headline such as, "Marketing Professional." If you want to move into sales and can claim any experience in that function, you might use "Marketing/Sales Professional."

New items can be added to portray your special qualities. Some examples are "Professional Competencies," "Core Skills," "Special Qualifications," "Selected Projects," "Industry Experience," and so on. The list is endless.

A newer-style resume might have these components:

1. Name

2. Contact information

3. Headline and subhead(s) (matching the target job)

4. Opening statement

5. Summary of qualifications, including computer skills

6. Recent achievements by function

7. Professional work history

8. Education

9. Certifications

The sections you choose and the order in which they appear will be determined by your job target. The general rule: organize your information to put the most important information first. While you may use a two-page resume, the second page should always have less important information than page one. Also, the top of the page should be more important than the bottom. Sequencing the items of your resume is a marketing decision. Keep the hiring manager in mind, and determine what he or she wants to know most (and first) for filling the targeted job with the perfect candidate—you.

The Resume Billboard

Regardless of the format you choose for the rest of your resume, the first few inches are critical. Remember the hiring manager with an overflowing e-mail box and a stack of resumes three inches deep? He or she wants to glance at a resume and determine whether to put it in the "save" pile or the "round" file. Most experts estimate that your resume will get an 8- to 12-second look. So your first impression needs to be gold. You want to communicate in no uncertain terms that you are the right fit for the job.

I call this part the Resume Billboard because it acts as an executive summary, or billboard advertisement, for you. The billboard can be the most creative aspect of your resume. It usually is composed of three parts: the headline(s), the opening statement, and list of qualifications. Don't feel that you have to use these terms. It may be more powerful to use other words. There are lots of examples in the book to get you thinking.

Creating Headlines

Just as an advertisement begins with a larger-type statement called a headline, your resume has a headline to communicate in just a few words who you are and what you can do. If you have already held a job title that is near or similar to your job target title, use those few words as your headline. You can also add a subhead that gives three main skills, talents, or professional abilities. These elements work in the same way as a billboard on the freeway. In just a couple seconds, the hiring manager can see and understand what you have to offer. Here are some examples:

Service Support/Product Trainer

Energy Efficiency Strategist
Regulatory Influence/Industry Leadership/Power Source Expert

Sales Support/Graphic Design

Sales/Customer Service Specialist

Program Manager

Communications/Finance Professional

Senior Electrical Engineer
Electrical System Design/Equipment Installation/Construction Management

Announce Yourself: The All-Important Opening Statement

The opening statement is where you introduce your most important achievements that relate to the job description. This is often done as three to five phrases or incomplete sentences. For more visual impact, it is often better to use bullet points. The opening statement should provide data that proves you are capable of the job. If it makes sense, even more detail about these achievements can be included later in the work history or functional skill group.

The opening statement—plus your headlines—creates an advertisement that is unique to you. The Resume Billboard should be loaded with key words, and you want it to match, as closely as you can, the requirements of the job. If you have several versions of your resume, you might change only the billboard and leave the rest of the document alone.

Notice the contrast between a typical resume and one that markets the job candidate with the Resume Billboard. In the first version, the candidate, Ramona Snead, has used the first three inches to communicate only her personal information, education, and certifications. With her more than 10 years of experience, the last two items belong toward the end of the resume. In the second version, the headline immediately conveys both Ramona's experience and her job objective, "Security/Audit Professional." She follows this powerful headline with six statements that demonstrate how her skills as an auditor transfer to the qualifications of a security investigator.

Ramona Snead
1234 Chasewood Dr., Salem, OR 97200

email@email.com
(971) 123-1234

Education:

- **Master of Public Administration**—Arizona State University, Dec. 1999
- **Bachelor of Arts,** Political Science—Willamette University, May 1996

Certifications:

- **Certified Fraud Examiner, March 2007**

Snead Billboard before.

Ramona Snead

1234 Chasewood Dr., Salem, OR 97200 — (971) 123-1234 home — (971) 123-5678 cell — email@email.com

SECURITY / AUDIT PROFESSIONAL
Investigations/Risk Assessment/Loss Prevention

- Proven track record for identifying risks and operational inefficiencies, as well as completing assignments within budget.
- Successful leadership, development, and evaluation of team members.
- Adept at presenting recommendations to executive management, and building relationships with internal and external customers in public, private, and community environments.
- Over 8 years of effective communication and outreach in political, community, and professional settings.
- More than 7 years of data analysis, investigations, and problem-solving experience using Microsoft Office products.
- Subject matter expert in law enforcement, emergency management, credit card banking, health care, and call centers.

Snead Billboard after.

Who Are You? Make a List

A list of words can provide a quick read of what you want to communicate. Lists will also usually take up less space than a sentence and explain the same information. If you want to communicate breadth, there's nothing that works quite as well. Your resume will likely be read first by a machine using Optical Character Recognition (OCR) software. As I mentioned, redundancy can be to your advantage. A list allows you to use important key words the first time. Then, they can be used again in your functional skills section or work history a second or third time. Each instance puts your resume higher as a compatibility match. You can be creative in generating lists and name them to your advantage. Some resume experts are even advising candidates to include a list of key words on the resume and repeat important words, even if they are listed several times elsewhere in the resume. Here are some of the lists included in the resumes in this book:

- Core competencies
- Summary of qualifications
- Professional competencies
- Industry experience
- Computer experience/expertise
- Computer skills

- Related coursework
- Relevant skills
- Skills summary
- Skills profile
- Software
- Technical knowledge

Create a Marketing Document That Sells You

Because your resume is a marketing document, don't be afraid to sing your own praises. If you have taken leadership roles, make sure those are highlighted in your resume. Go back over your career successes and the STAR stories you created in Chapter 1. Use the top ones that apply to your targeted job. Make sure you include the times when you have volunteered, innovated, or created a unique solution. Like the STAR stories, state the results or difference that you made.

After creating the Billboard, the key decision will be whether to put your work history in reverse chronological order or to lead with a functional style, outlining three to five skills groups with achievements. The strongest resume will be reverse chronological, but this may not be an option if there are gaps in your work history and/or you can't show steady advancement in your career. If you use a functional style, lead with that and be sure to include an abbreviated work history. If you are using a combination resume, lead with the achievement statements that support the required skills and experience, followed by a brief listing of job history and education. There are examples of each of these in this book.

Turn Responsibilities into Achievements

Under each work history item, you will probably want to include a description of your former job responsibilities. Avoid the temptation to provide a laundry list of the stuff you had to do. Instead, find a way to turn your responsibilities into achievements. This makes for more interesting reading and markets you more successfully. The achievement statements also should be fleshed out if they appear under functional titles. The following table shows some examples.

Responsibility	Achievement
Training of order-entry specialists	Mentored and trained a team of five order-entry specialists, helping them reduce errors on more than 60 major orders per week with an average price of $30K and an average of 20 line items
Prepared lesson plans	Training and experience in preparing lesson plans that reflect accommodations for differences in student abilities and learning styles
Designed batteries	During fiscal years 1998 to present, designed, managed, and produced approximately 45 battery and power supply improvements, leading to 10 patent disclosures and 6 patents awarded at this time

As you can see, achievement statements sell the candidate more powerfully than simple lists of responsibility. By adding details about the size of the projects, how many people were involved, and the results of the work, you give information about how well you performed on the job. You also provide conversation points for the interview.

Using Action Verbs

No one expects your resume to be as interesting as the first page of the great American novel, but you can make it more dynamic to read if you focus on action verbs rather than nouns. Each statement in your billboard should begin with the same word form: adjectives, nouns, or verbs. Given the choice, it's best to start with verbs. These "action" words make you seem more of an action-oriented person. Using action verbs also allows you to provide the object—the thing or person you acted upon. In just a phrase, you can create the entire idea of a sentence. Just read these two lists and see which one appeals to you more. Also note how the results and thinking behind each item makes it come alive.

Training

- Software training to 75 customers per week

- Training design for specialized software

- PowerPoint presentations

Training

- Delivered training to 75 customers per week via Internet conferencing, reducing the need for onsite trainers and saving the company $2,000 or more per new installation

- Developed training for specialized software, standardizing content delivery and improving customer satisfaction

- Created PowerPoint presentations to maximize student retention of course content

Name Your Resume Versions

Years ago, we would slave over our one resume, print it, proof it carefully, then take it to the copy store and have 100 copies made. Now, resumes can be living, breathing documents. You can evolve your resume monthly, weekly, or even several times in the same day. That said, it's probably best to limit yourself to four or five versions of your resume. This makes it easier to track what you have submitted to each prospective employer.

Here's an example. James Templin (featured in Chapter 24) is an electrical engineer with a long history of designing batteries. He might apply for new battery design jobs that are cropping up in alternative energy companies. Or seek work as an energy efficiency strategist. He could also use his data center knowledge and go for a job as power supply consultant, or use his background to become a chief technical officer (CTO). Each revision involves fairly minor but significant changes. He might name the four resumes as follows:

Templin - Battery Design.doc

Templin - Energy Efficiency Strategist.doc

Templin – Power Supply Specialist.doc

Templin - CTO Candidate.doc

There are many benefits of doing this. First, James can easily decide which resume to send when he gets a new job lead. Second, the document title is distinctive and easily understood on the receiving end. The titles are future oriented; they indicate his career objective. Finally, they help the reviewer keep the resume connected with his cover letter and application. Hiring managers are often reviewing resumes for more than one job at a time. Resumes coming in through e-mail and job boards can often get mixed up. This naming convention keeps your name connected with your targeted job. Because file-naming conventions have been expanded and you're not limited to just a few characters, why not take advantage and put even your filenames to work for you?

What to Leave In or Out

The guidelines for what to include in your resume are changing all the time. Back in the 1970s, when most baby boomers started their careers, it was common to have a section called "Personal" on their resumes. Job seekers would include their age, height, weight, marital status, ethnic background, hobbies, and even the names and ages of their children! All of that information is considered taboo on today's resumes. Companies are trying very hard not to be accused of any type of discrimination. Your resume shouldn't include any information that is illegal for them to collect, such as ethnicity, age, marital status, health and parental status.

There are a few exceptions to this rule. If your resume is for acting or modeling jobs, where your physical characteristics and "look" will be a part of the hiring decision, it should include a photo. (Otherwise, never.) If you are applying for work as a firefighter, police officer, or construction worker, where good physical condition is a plus, you might want to include your weight, height, and physical accomplishments such as marathons or sports competitions.

In the contact information area, it is common today to include full name, one or two phone numbers, and e-mail address. In general, it is taboo to include a current work phone. (Keep your cell phone handy during your search and take any job-seeking calls in a private space, such as a conference room or your car.) Some people still like to include their address or at least the city where they live. In posting resumes online, it may be best to eliminate your address details because it gives identity theft criminals more details about you. Newer to the scene are your LinkedIn profile address, or your personal website, that direct hiring managers to your professional profile online.

Just know that today's hiring managers are Internet savvy and will do a search on your name at some point during the screening process. If you have any drunken photos from your friend's bachelor party on the Internet, now is the time to make sure they are deleted. The social websites such as Facebook.com and Match.com need to be made more professional in tone because it is likely these will be checked out, too. One way to strengthen your profile is to contribute thoughtfully and professionally to online discussion boards such as those found on LinkedIn or online special interest groups.

Academic information is pretty straightforward. Simply include the college or university, the degree (Bachelor's, Master's or doctorate) and the year(s) of graduation. More seasoned workers sometimes delete the year of graduation, because a quick calculation will reveal the applicant's age. Older workers with a recent degree can add the year of graduation to appear younger and more current in the field. It's better to have a graduation date, so think about it carefully before you delete it.

Whether to include your major is a marketing decision. If it adds to your story of experience, by all means include it. If you are currently working on an MBA or other advanced degree that applies to the job, you might even wish to include the coursework completed or the number of hours until graduation. If you are within 18 months of graduation, you can add that degree, then state "Expected Graduation—Spring 2012." It is not advised or necessary to include the high school attended unless the job specifically calls for a high school diploma and this is your highest level of education.

Certifications can be important to your job search. If they contribute to your story, by all means include them. If they show a detour away from the field you are applying in, leave them out. The same goes for the many training programs you may have received on the job. Remember, the resume is a marketing document; choose your information carefully!

Make Your Resume Easy to Read

It's important to remember that the reviewers are likely screening many resumes at once. If your typeface is small and difficult to read, your resume will be put aside and could easily be forgotten. As a general rule, serif typefaces (type styles that have little "hooks" on each letter) are easier to read than sans serif (without "hooks"). However, in recent years, sans-serif typefaces and other similar styles are very readable and can actually allow you to include more words in your precious two pages of space.

As a rule, I suggest using a font size no smaller than 10 points. If in doubt, it's better to cut words than to make the typeface smaller. (Remember the concept of the advertisement.)

Paragraphed copy makes the best use of the space but is harder to read than bulleted copy. Look at the following two examples. Which is easier to read?

Paragraph style:

Managed implementations of new computer systems, coordinating end-to-end activities including shipping, on-site installation, training, and post go-live follow-up. • Provided single point of contact for all aspects of implementation projects. • Maintained SharePoint database of more than 100 projects. • Conducted weekly status and issue resolution meetings. • Reported weekly to upper management overall progress of all implementations. • Developed training curriculum for new products. • Tested and refined training processes before distribution to training staff.

Bulleted style:

- Managed implementation of new computer systems, coordinating end-to-end activities including shipping, on-site installation, training, and post go-live follow-up.
- Provided single point of contact for all aspects of implementation projects.
- Maintained SharePoint database of more than 100 projects.
- Conducted weekly status and issue resolution meetings.
- Reported weekly to upper management overall progress of all implementations.
- Developed training curriculum for new products.
- Tested and refined training processes before distribution to training staff.

White space is the open space between the so-called "black type." This space actually makes the document look easier to read and guides the reader to the next line. Use white space carefully—enough to provide a distinction between items, yet not so much as to make the reader lose interest or wonder, "Why did he use two pages when one would do?"

With today's color printers, most of us have the resources to create a multi-color resume. Surprisingly, though, you will rarely see one. If you are a graphic designer, you probably *should* add graphics and color to your resume. For the rest of us, colored ink might be perceived as less than professional.

In the past, we were concerned about choosing a classy paper on which to print resumes. A plain white bond paper works best with plain black type, because it makes the resume easier to scan, fax, and photocopy. In general, you should try to deliver your resume electronically so that it can be forwarded to others. The days of the paper resume are almost over.

Style: Be Consistent Within Your Resume

If you're not in the publishing world, it's easy to miss what are called "style" errors. To a great extent, there are no hard-and-fast rules about capitalization, use of tense, and punctuation. You will make your own decisions about these items. Just be sure you are consistent within your document. Here are some examples:

Job titles—are they all capitalized or not? (Capitals seem to make the job more important. I prefer them.)

> Marketing Manager or marketing manager
>
> Office Nurse or office nurse

Phrases—are they headline style or sentence case? (Notice that headline style is harder to read.)

> Identify Fraud, Waste, and Abuse (headline style—all major words capitalized)
>
> Identify fraud, waste, and abuse (sentence case—just the first word capitalized)

Are all the verbs that begin phrases in the first person voice? In the same tense?

> Review and analyze federal and state laws (first-person voice; the "I" is missing—preferred)
>
> Reviews and analyzes federal and state laws (third-person voice; the "He" or "She" is missing)
>
> Presented findings to agency management (prefer past tense for former jobs)
>
> Present findings to agency management (prefer present tense for current job)

Use of commas, semicolons, and periods. These are choices; just make sure you are consistent:

> Completed substitute assignments in biology, chemistry, and language arts classes (serial comma—comma before "and")

Or

> Completed substitute assignments in biology, chemistry and language arts classes (no serial comma)
>
> Volunteered for and participated in a county-wide truancy reduction task force. (period)

Or

> Volunteered for and participated in a county-wide truancy reduction task force (no period)

Type style and size: Is it consistent for each item in the resume?

You can use up to two sizes and two typefaces in a document and still have a unified look. (In the following examples, notice that the type size increases in the second group of statements.)

Energy Efficiency Project

- Conceived, designed and led a project to reduce energy use of CC Computer Corporation's on-site desktop computers by more than 30 percent
- Saved the company $1.8 million per year in electrical power use, offsetting 8 tons of CO_2
- Worked with software vendor to private label their innovative product for company's use with clients

Regulatory/Design Achievements

- During fiscal years 1998 to present, have designed, managed and produced numerous (approximately 45) battery and power supply improvements, leading to 10 patent disclosures and 6 patents awarded at this time.
- Created an energy efficiency regulatory road map for delivering regulations ahead of schedule, while reducing the churn in the organization, maintaining total cost of ownership, and building market share
- Developed safety qualification process for Lithium Ion and Lead Acid batteries used in Computer Portable and Enterprise systems

A good way to check whether you're being consistent is to use the Print Preview function on your word processing program. Study the page for a while, and you can easily see errors in typeface and size, use of commas, capitalization of headlines, etc.

Check It Carefully

When you are finished with your resume, you will want to check it carefully. It's a good idea to have at least three friends or family members proofread it. New eyes will find unclear phrases and words that can easily be replaced to enhance your message. Don't expect your word processing program to find all your errors. If the wrong word is spelled correctly, your spell checker won't catch the wrong word choice. Imagine the shock and chagrin one public relations professional felt when a potential interviewer discovered the phrase "pubic relations" three times on her finished resume!

The Writing Process

You might be thinking "It all sounds easy, but where do I begin?" If you were going on a journey, you would have to get into the car to get the journey started. In the same way, you need to get *into* your resume process to start your new career journey. Here's a sequence of events that will help you organize the task:

1. Locate your old resume(s) and print copies that you can edit. Chances are you can use your current work history, with editing that sharpens your achievement statements.

2. Do your market research and choose *one* job target description. Combine several job descriptions to get a generic description that is packed with key words.

3. Think about your former jobs and create five to seven STAR stories.

4. Go through your old resume and rewrite as many responsibility statements as you can, adding results and other details from your STAR stories. Focus on statements that describe your contributions, innovations, initiatives, talents, and career passions.

5. Decide whether you need a chronological, functional, or combination resume. If you decide on a functional section, organize your achievement statements into three to five broad categories.

6. Choose a resume format (type size and style) that you like. There are dozens available through Microsoft Word. Or use one of the formats you find in this book. Any of them can be downloaded as Word documents from www. careerpassioncoach.com. (The resumes are filed by the headline in each of the profiles.) Simply create a "Save As" document and type over the headlines and other information. You will have a great look without a lot of design time.

7. Develop your Resume Billboard last, putting the most important five to seven achievements of your career into short statements. Choose statements that fit the requirements of your target job. Use as many terms from the target job description as you can. Include key words in your headline and subheads.

8. Develop several lists and determine where they should go in your resume. Some examples are as follows: Key Skills, Core Competencies, Computer Skills, Courses Completed, Industry Experience, Transferable Skills, and so on. (Check out Appendix B for a list of transferable skills.)

9. Determine the ideal sequence of the elements of your resume, putting the most important at the top followed by the next most important, and so on.

10. Go through your resume with a list of key words and try to incorporate those terms into as many statements and phrases as you can.

11. Spell check and proofread your resume several times, both on screen and on paper.

12. Save your resume in a special resume directory and name it using your last name and words from the target job title. E-mail your resume to two family members and ask them to save it for you as a backup.

13. Share your resume with three individuals and ask them to look it over for spelling, punctuation, and wrong-word errors. Be careful to make all the corrections on one final document. (You might save printed copies of your first drafts, just in case you want to go back to earlier versions. But don't save drafts with errors, as you might post or send one of these by accident!)

That's a huge job done! By following these process guidelines, you can build a resume that is uniquely yours while selling you clearly to the requirements of the job. A career change is indeed more difficult to sell than a logical, stepped progression in your career. Despite that, thousands of people make career changes every year.

You can, too. It takes strategic thinking. It requires time and care to craft your resume into your best marketing document that sets you apart from other candidates. Even if your experience isn't an exact match, the Resume Billboard and lists of qualifications can clearly show how you fit into your targeted job. Use the 50 before-and-after resume examples in this book to take you step-by-step through your own process. By following these ideas, you'll create a resume that wins interviews.

Chapter 3

Test Driving Your Resume

It's time to take your resume out for a test drive. Feedback from friends and family is usually where you will start—especially the three people who are proofreading for you (see Chapter 2). When you do this, be clear that the purpose is to support your new career choice. If you can do so, provide a sample job description for that job title. In this way, reviewers have some context. Also, be clear in your request. If it's only a review for typos or formatting, say that. If you want to know whether it makes sense for a given job, say that as well. Be wary of lots of advice at this point, because it is also likely your friends and family are *not* trained as career counselors! Thank them for their time, correct the mistakes, and proceed to the next step.

Networking events can be great places to hand-deliver a few resumes to appropriate people. Just as in any marketing campaign, focus thoughtfully and spend the most time and energy at those events that closely align with your target industry or job title.

Just as you would never leave home without a business card, you should always have your resume with you if you are actively job searching. Keep a notebook with you in the car with 5 to 10 copies of your resume. Wherever you go, you will be able to take notes and provide a copy of your resume. When you introduce yourself to someone, say that you are seeking an opportunity in a new career. Out of the 20 to 30 people who might attend an event, it is likely that at least a few people will have some insight or connection with your new job. See how the conversation goes. If they seem knowledgeable and willing, then ask whether they would take a look at your resume and give feedback. Offer to share the one you have with you, or send the file to them by e-mail. Again, be clear about what you want from them and how you'll use it. Networking is a two-way street, so listen carefully—because you might be able to help them out as well.

At first, you may want to push your new resume on complete strangers you have just met. You will want to give it to business contacts who know you are seeking work, in the hopes that *someone* will pass it along to someone who can give you a job. Resist this urge. You are really only interested in feedback and comments from people in the new field or who are connected to the job title. You are seeking ideas on how to put the final touches on your resume to show you are a good fit. You want to show relevant career successes, transferable skills, or ways to position yourself on paper (or screen) as a good candidate for that job. Find out what is critical, what is preferred, and what should just be left off. At this point, your resume is in the final stages of revision.

Advice: What to Use and What to Ignore

Understand that you will get advice from everyone who sees your resume. You will get as many opinions as the number of people who read it. Some advice will be good, some discouraging, some encouraging, and some just plain stupid. How do you sort the good from the bad?

Your mother wasn't wrong when she told you to "consider the source." My mother always said that when a jealous or hurtful comment came my way. I never fully understood what she meant until I was full-grown, giving the same advice to my son.

Think Enhancements, Not Revisions

People believe what they believe because of their perspective—from the experience and knowledge that's available to them. Always consider whether their experience and knowledge really apply to you and to your job search. If your aunt in another state, who cannot even spell semiconductor, tries to tell you how to describe your project experience, you might smile and say kindly, "Thanks for your input." Then ignore the advice. On the other hand, if your aunt in another state *works* for a semiconductor manufacturer and advises you to add key words to your achievement statements, thank her, add them in, and maybe even send her the revised resume to see whether you've gotten it right.

It is always easier to critique than to create. Think about revisions as enhancements, not corrections. If someone has a critique, ask immediately, "What do you think I could *add* to make the resume stronger?" You will feel more confident if you take the position that your resume might be *incomplete* than to think it is *wrong*.

Dealing with Reactions

Don't ever ask friends or family members, "Do you like my resume?" That is the wrong question. A better one might be, "When you read my resume, what impressions did you get about me? What statements made you want to learn more?" If you are generating confusion, you might want to rewrite. However, when you generate curiosity, you know you are on the right track. Curiosity could be just the hook you need to get an interview. Here are some comments you might get and what to do with them:

- **"Hiring managers won't like this resume format."** Consider whether the person *is* a hiring manager. If they are, ask a follow-up question: "What could I add that would make it sure to catch attention?" For example, if you have created a combination resume, they may suggest that you put something on the first page indicating that the chronological listing of your jobs is after the functional section.

- **"Why didn't you put your complete job history?"** Consider whether those jobs from 1970 to 1985 really matter in your job search. If they don't, forget this comment and move on. If they do, you may want to add a section called "Other Relevant Experience." If there are gaps in your recent job history, be prepared to address them in the cover letter, resume, or interview.

- **"Don't use that term. People will think you're (a liberal, a conservative, a Jew, a Catholic, an environmentalist, a tree-hugger, or whatever).** Leading with controversial beliefs might limit your opportunities. Purge your resume of all references to political, religious, and social beliefs. Save the soapbox for later, after you get the job. You might turn off a prospective employer with just one term or phrase.

This actually happened to a civil engineer getting back in the business after an 18-year hiatus. She used the term "environmentally conscious" on her resume. In her first information interview, a fellow engineer said he couldn't hire anyone with beliefs that strong—they might not be able to work with his clients. Because the comment came from the owner of a civil engineering firm, she took it seriously and changed the phrase to "experience with environmental issues."

If you are applying to a political, religious, or social welfare organization that works on those causes, you may be able to strategically leave them in. Always do company research first.

- **"The experience looks outdated**." Companies and industries change constantly. It is important for you to use the current language and references. For example, the terms "value-added" and "out-of-the-box thinking" were great 10 years ago but are now considered dated. Ask how to rephrase it, or check out company and industry websites and blogs to find the latest terms for key skills, concepts, and issues.

- **"I don't understand what you are looking for."** This is a serious issue. If you have a good Resume Billboard, the person reading your resume should see exactly what you are looking for. Consider a rewrite of that part of your resume.

- **"I don't like that list of personal characteristics. It looks boastful."** Generally, you might agree—but consider the purpose of the resume. You are trying to communicate who you are. If you back up those personal attribute words with achievement statements on the resume, go for it. It is also acceptable to include words from personality tests that you have taken. Some examples are: ambitious, competitive, diplomatic, enthusiastic, accurate, consistent, and methodical. Behavioral tests are generally considered scientifically reliable in predicting future behavior because they indicate your behavior *style*—a pattern that you routinely follow. Besides, if you get the interview, a skilled hiring manager can *see* and *hear* your behavior style within the first five minutes of meeting you.

- **"This resume looks too long."** This comment might be coming from the one-page-only school of thought. If you are not a new graduate and have been in the workforce three years or more, you *deserve* a two-page resume. It's hard enough to put all your important information into two pages. Get over that one-page thing! Please note that even three- or four-page resumes are sometimes appropriate. These are often called "curriculum vitae" or an "executive profile." The longer form is most appropriate for college professors, researchers, long-time engineers, or top executives. Even those individuals usually have a shorter version, limited to two pages.

Be sure the comment isn't being made because of the "look" of the resume. The type font should be easy to read and at least 10 points in size. Consider whether you can cut words without losing meaning. Use a thesaurus to see whether you can find more powerful words so you don't need as many. Be sure that there is a lot of white space. Margins should be one inch and no less than three quarters of an inch. Bullet points are easy to read and create the illusion of space.

The point is to consider deeply and factor in the comments that you think have real merit. Don't get insulted by comments or even take overly complimentary statements too literally. By now, you know what you have to offer and how that fits into your new career. Edit your resume according to what *you* think. The resume represents you, and you need to be proud of it.

Must-Have Tips from Hiring Managers

To find out what really matters to the most important group reading resumes, a group of hiring managers was asked: **"What elements of the resume must be present in order for you to consider the candidate?"**

In general, everyone asked for clear, detailed information that ties directly to the requirements of the job. The hiring manager needs to see a fit between your skills and the demands of the job. That's why we recommend a Resume Billboard that ties in directly to the job requirements. One manager said he wanted "relevant experience that indicates strong evidence this candidate can get off the ground quickly. I don't have time to build someone from the ground up." If you are changing function or industry, you will need to include any and all experience that shows your competence as it applies in the new situation.

One hiring manager said, "I look for evidence of demonstrated leadership and influence with people, aggressive results, and innovation." Finding those STAR stories and including the details in your achievement statements creates a picture of you as a valuable contributor at work. It's also important to be clear about your role in the task. Did you lead? Were you part of a four-person task force? Did you represent your department on a 10-person team?

In this economy, hiring managers can afford to be picky. One top executive who hires sales managers said he looked for "experience in our industry" and experience "driving revenue growth from $5M to $10M." Both of these comments show how critical it is to get as specific as you can about your achievements. It doesn't mean a thing to say you increased sales by 100 percent if you don't state the base. If you write "Increased sales from $10M to $20M," the hiring manager can gauge the achievement and how it relates to the job at hand.

Another hiring manager wrote eloquently about *coherence*. "What doesn't work is a form resume that is really off-target with the job offered. Do the answers and energy level match up with the work experience and education they offer? Do I get a coherent, consistent experience from them?"

This point speaks to the importance of expressing who you are with your resume. If you are expressive and passionate, you can use more flamboyant words and phrases. If you are more analytical and restrained, it is wise to have a more formal, logical presentation of information. When the hiring manager meets you, she can feel your energy. It is distracting and confusing if you are far different than what they were led to expect. It is important that your in-person presence reinforces and builds on the image created in your resume.

Focus is also key. "We look for a candidate who appears to be focused, career-minded, and goal oriented." Be strategic about what you include in your resume. If you are changing functions, only include experiences and skills that build your image as a qualified candidate.

If you limit your experience to what is relevant, you will give the impression of being focused and career-minded. If you are changing industries, you may need to clearly translate your experience to make the connection to the new field.

A consistent track record is important. "I look for a person who stays put for more than 1 $\frac{1}{2}$ to 2 years in a position. I don't want people who leave just when they're hitting their stride." This is bad news for people who have been downsized several times and can't show more than a few years in any position. You might want to include a mention of why you left those jobs in your cover letter. Paul Shankle, featured in Chapter 9, added "reason for leaving" to each of the jobs on his resume. He was moving from a relatively unstable industry (high-tech) to a more stable environment (government). He wanted to be sure he was not viewed as a job-hopper, since most of his jobs ended because of business conditions unrelated to his performance. It is a good idea to note that you now wish to bring your broad base of experience to make a long-term contribution to a stable organization.

Hiring managers also care whether you have done your homework. One said, "Why would I invest time and energy in someone who uses a one-size-fits-all cover letter and resume?" Customizing your cover letter and your Resume Billboard shows that you have taken the time to understand the job, the company, and the environment you are selling into. If you are willing to work harder and smarter to get a chance for an interview, you will stand out as someone willing to do the same in the new job.

Checklist for a Great Resume

When you have finished your resume editing, you can use this checklist to determine whether it is a great one. These measures are listed from the top to the bottom of the resume, in no particular order of importance:

- ☐ Is the overall look inviting? Can someone read the most important items in 10 seconds?

- ☐ Does your resume boldly state your name and contact details? Is your e-mail address professional? Are the phone numbers triple-checked for accuracy?

- ☐ Does your resume clearly sum up your most important career achievements and skills as they relate to a specific job you are targeting? Did you include enough details to portray the level and difficulty of your accomplishments?

- ☐ Can a hiring manager scan your resume for important details about your job history? Are the dates checked and factual? Have you accounted for gaps in your history?

- ☐ In your job history, did you include a brief description of each employer? Have you used job titles that are understandable to a person outside your business or industry? Are the titles true to the work you actually performed?

- ☐ When highlighting jobs held, did you lead with the company or your job title? Did you choose the one which sells you better?

☐ Have you explained or eliminated industry jargon so that the reader can truly understand your achievements? At the same time, have you used key words from the new job description to make as many connections as possible?

☐ Did you use a page-two header so that a company could reach you if page one was lost?

☐ Are type sizes and the use of tense, punctuation, italics, boldface consistent? Do all the statements begin with the same word form? (Verbs work best).

☐ Does the resume invite the reader to ask questions about your achievements?

☐ Do you believe that the resume best sums up who you are and what you can contribute?

☐ Are you so proud of your resume that you would post it on the Internet? That's great, because you should post it on numerous job sites and create a shorter version for social media site profiles.

Putting Your Resume to Work Online

At some point, you need to put your resume to the real test: using it to apply for jobs. Some job seekers are stingy with their resume—holding on to it unless they believe the job is perfect for them. Other job seekers push their resume on everyone they meet. Try to strike a balance. If you are freely seeking work, don't be shy about giving your resume to anyone who is genuinely interested. Chances are, your most important job lead will come from a friend of a friend.

As much as possible, present your resume online—on your own web page or as an e-mail attachment—so that it is easy to store, print, and forward on to others. (When e-mailing a resume to a recruiter or hiring manager, copy and paste the resume into the e-mail as text, and attach it to the e-mail as well. Some companies do not allow attachments to be opened due to virus threats.)

Of course, you'll also want to post and activate your new resume on Internet job boards. At the same time, you should update your personal profiles and job search criteria on each of these. For a list of job boards, including some specialized ones, take a look at Appendix A. You will find instructions in Appendix B for converting your resume to text for job boards and online applications.

Take the time to change your e-mail signature to reflect your job search. It's common for job seekers to put a link to their online resume in their e-mail signature along with a one-line message about what they are seeking.

Create a new business card to present yourself as a job candidate, including your desired job title. Use space usually allotted for fax and address information to direct people to your online resume URL. You can also put top key words about yourself to remind people what you offer. There are several ways to get full-color business cards for free from large-scale Internet printers. (You will pay for shipping and extras.) Just do an Internet search on "free business cards" to find one.

There are a number of ways you can use the new features of social media—such as LinkedIn, Facebook, Google, and Twitter—to assist you in your search. First, update your Internet profiles to be as consistent as possible with your resume. Make your profiles available to the public. Create a customized URL for your profile using the tool for this on your homepage(s) of social networking sites (for example, www.linkedin.com//your name).

Social networking sites also give you the chance to put in a lead message about yourself. Make use of this by writing something about your search. Update your message at least once a week to let your network know that you are still looking, or announce new developments in your search. You can even ask questions that will generate help from online contacts. For example, you might write: "I'm looking into a project manager job at XYZ Semiconductor. Anyone know the name of a hiring manager?" Or "I want to become a product manager for a high-dollar high-tech product. Can you provide some ideas?" Or "I'm an experienced builder of custom upscale homes. Anyone know of a company that is remodeling foreclosed properties?"

Be sure to post your resume on Google or another search engine using the profile feature. Limit contact information to name, city, and phone for security reasons. Recruiters and managers will usually do a search for you anyway, and this puts your resume at the top of the results with your online profiles nearby. When companies use job boards, they pay a fee to post the jobs and to receive your information. You can make it more cost-effective for them if you use some of these free Internet resources, and direct hiring managers to your resume.

If all these new online resources sound overwhelming, get help from friends or younger relatives who use these programs daily. Many job clubs or state hiring agencies conduct workshops to help you learn how to use the Internet to full advantage in your job search. The features and tools are changing quickly as these sites become more popular. Actively working with even one social media site will produce surprising results.

Don't get so caught up in the details that you delay your job search because your resume or profiles aren't "perfect" yet. Let your resume and all your marketing materials be living, breathing documents. Create new versions as you discover new target jobs of interest to you. Periodically make small revisions to your resumes posted on job boards so that they are perceived as "new" and fresh by the web crawlers. Most important, get your resume out of your hands and into the hands of someone who can hire you, or at least pass it along.

What's Your Resume Worth?

When you have finished your resume, take time to enjoy the fact that you have produced one of the most difficult pieces of literature ever written. Even though it's not the great American novel, your investment of time and energy will probably make you *more* money than if you had written a novel!

Know that your resume is going to land you a job worth $100,000 or even $1 million in income over the life of that job. If your new resume gets you a new career, just take those numbers times 10.

The rest of this book features 50 job seekers who are caught in today's ever-changing job landscape. The names of the job candidates and their companies have been changed, but the resumes and stories represent real people like you. As you read their stories, imagine how you can apply the ideas to execute your own career change. Look closely at the resume makeovers and see how easy it is to reposition and reframe your experience. You *can* change careers. These 50 examples give you the ideas and techniques to do it.

Part 1: Strategies for the New Job Market

Part 2

Career Transitions: Changes in Industry

Automotive to Renewable Energy

Leo Harper was one of the top salespeople at a Chrysler dealership before auto sales tanked during the recession. After his commissions steadily declined for six months, he began looking for ways to use his sales skills in other industries. As he surveyed prospects, he ran across opportunities at renewable energy companies.

Leo fit most of the qualifications, including experience in construction. Years ago, he worked for his father's residential construction business and later became a real estate agent specializing in upscale homes and condominiums. Leo hopes to get on the ground floor of an emerging industry and sees growth opportunities as government tax incentives entice more people to install solar panels and other energy-efficient products.

Challenges to Making the Switch

Leo finds few posted job openings and begins making cold calls to small renewable energy companies. He discovers that many company owners handle sales and don't need to add more people on the payroll. Leo broadens his search by offering to work solely on commission for a 90-day trial basis to prove that he can generate new business.

Leo's HVAC experience is limited to overseeing crews that install units in new homes and small businesses. He realizes he needs to be more knowledgeable about insulation, HVAC solar units, and other energy-efficient products. He begins learning all he can about the technical aspects of the business to use the proper lingo during meetings with potential employers.

Another concern is whether Leo can generate sufficient income by maintaining a quota of at least five sales each month. The basic residential solar system is $20,000, which Leo knows sounds expensive to homeowners who are cautious about making large purchases. Leo believes his previous real estate experience will help him because his target audience is the same group of wealthy people who are more likely to buy renewable energy products.

Transferable Skills

Sales

Cold calling

Business development

Outside sales

Marketing

Product presentations

Construction knowledge

HVAC knowledge

Job Description

Renewable Energy Consultant

- Outside sales, sales prospecting, cold calling, and/or face-to-face consulting experience

- Bachelor's degree

- HVAC or construction background; renewable energy product experience is great as well

- Field sales experience with commercial or consumer products

- Track record of selling on the road with lots of driving around and getting up on roofs or into an attic

- High energy and a record of success; preference for a salesperson who has achieved quota on a regular basis

- Must have a passion for the clean energy industry

- Home energy efficiency knowledge via education, seminars, and experience

Resume Makeover

Leo's resume is updated and changed to a combination resume to highlight his sales and construction skills and knowledge.

1 Leo's old-style resume needs an updated format to create a positive first impression. The self-assessment "strengths" on his first resume are deleted.

2 The exact job title is used as the heading in the Opening Statement.

3 The qualifications summary uses key words from the job description and highlights relevant skills and knowledge. No mention is made of unrelated industries.

4 A brief mention is made of Leo's Bachelor's degree because it is a key qualification, and more details are found in the Education section at the bottom.

5 A Relevant Skills and Experience section expands on his sales background and his familiarity with construction techniques. Both are important to the job he is seeking.

6 Leo's work history has brief descriptions of sales-related accomplishments.

7 The personal information and references are deleted from his new resume. Personal details such as marital status and family size are inappropriate in today's resumes. References are usually provided in a separate document.

LEONARD HARPER III

123 Stone Ridge Trail   Sarasota, FL 34232   941-123-4567

❶ STRENGTHS
Team Player
Honest
Loyal
Highest Customer Satisfaction
Unselfish
Patient
Positive
Thoughtful
Diligent
Tactful

EDUCATION
Florida State University, BBA, 1981

QUALIFICATIONS
Real Estate Sales
New Car Sales
Travel Agent
Construction

EXPERIENCE

1/2008 – Present   Dan Hardy Chrysler, Inc. – Inside Sales
1234 Clark Road, Sarasota, FL 34233
Supervisor: Rich Goldman 941-123-4567

3/1998 – 12/2007   Ultimate Source Realty – Real Estate Agent
1234 Bee Ridge Road, Sarasota, FL 34239
Supervisor: Brad Williams 941-123-4567

8/1988 – 2/1998   D.W. Choate Travel Agency – Outside Sales
1234 Airport Blvd., Pensacola, FL 32505
Supervisor: Milt Anderson 850-123-4567

2/1984 – 7/1988   Harper & Sons Construction, Sarasota, FL
1234 Stone Ridge Trail, Sarasota, FL 34232
Supervisor: Leonard Harper Jr.

❼ PERSONAL   Married: two children, one grandchild; Kiwanis, Choir, History

REFERENCES   Dan Mardy/618-1234; Lawrence Claypool/818-1234
Stewart Swift/589-1234

ADDITIONAL REFERENCES PROVIDED UPON REQUEST

LEONARD HARPER III

123 Stone Ridge Trail • Sarasota, FL 34232 • 941-123-4567 • email @email.com

❷ ## ENERGY EFFICIENCY CONSULTANT

Consultative Sales ~ Business Development ~ Construction Management

❸
- Proven sales consultant with a consistent track record of exceeding quotas.
- Passion for renewable energy products and the clean energy industry.
- Experience overseeing HVAC installation and residential construction.
- Created effective marketing campaigns that significantly increased sales.
- Frequently traveled throughout a three-state region to develop new business.

❹
- Bachelor of Business Administration degree.

RELEVANT SKILLS AND EXPERIENCE

❺ **Sales and Marketing**
- Recognized as the top salesperson for six consecutive quarters. Received cash bonuses and an expense-paid trip.
- Created a marketing campaign with print advertising and sales brochures.
- Made effective sales presentations, which helped increase business by 20 percent.
- Sold energy-efficient homes ranging in price from $500,000 to $3 million.

Construction Management
- Oversaw construction crews, including HVAC installation in residential homes and commercial businesses.
- Recommended proper insulation and other energy-efficient products to homebuyers.
- Supervised all aspects of construction and completed projects ahead of schedule.

❻ ## EXPERIENCE AND RECOGNITION

Dan Hardy Chrysler, Sarasota, FL *New Car Sales* 1/2008 – Present
- Received bonuses and a trip to Las Vegas for top sales in 2008 and 2009.

Ultimate Source Realty, Sarasota, FL *Real Estate Agent* 3/1998 – 12/2007
- Received the President's Award for condominium and single-family home sales.

D.W. Choate Travel Agency, Pensacola, FL *Outside Sales* 8/1988 – 2/1998
- Recognized for expanding an agency from a start-up to the largest in Pensacola.

Harper & Sons Construction, Sarasota, FL *Manager* 2/1984 – 7/1988
- Oversaw construction of homes ranging in price from $500,000 to $2M.

EDUCATION

Florida State University, Tallahassee, FL
Bachelor of Business Administration

Consumer Electronics to Retail Gifts

Kerry Adkins was devastated when her job as event marketing manager was cut. She is a dynamic, outgoing achiever who loved the intensity of coordinating up to 28 trade shows each month. She consistently outperformed her peers and quickly redefined her administrative job to one that involved overseeing the work of other trade show managers. She is especially adept at solving problems in a crisis, such as tracking down a display that wasn't properly delivered or giveaway items that were not shipped on time. She is also a creative person who enjoys being a makeup artist for movies and photo shoots. While the trade show business was fun and exciting, it didn't allow her to get out of the office or express her creativity.

The good news is that her experience with MediaMemory has given her hands-on training in displaying innovative, quick-turning consumer products, such as flash drives, memory cards for cameras, and MP3 players. She even had a chance to provide input to display designers, coming up with creative ways to get the company's products noticed. She has learned a lot about how to help store managers think and how they make display choices. She decides to pursue a job that will give her a creative outlet, allow her to call on store managers, and use her organization and management skills. She discovers a merchandising manager job that combines all these activities.

Challenges to Making the Switch

Kerry lacks specific experience in the gifts/stationery market and has never had a merchandising job title. She knows that the challenges will be very different from the ever-changing field of consumer electronics. She is not even sure of the distribution channels, so she will need to do some research if she wins an interview.

The job she seeks also involves recruiting, screening, hiring, training, and supervising hourly sales staff. While she is very proud of the team she created during her years as a cosmetic counter manager, she had that experience 10 to 20 years ago. She will need to convince a prospective employer that her expertise is both relevant and important to the challenge at hand.

She also lacks the five years required experience in sourcing and product management. She is hoping that her work with numerous vendors in the trade show business will give her the examples of resourcefulness and negotiation to show her abilities in this arena.

Another issue is the length of time she has been without full-time work—nearly 18 months. Although she has been doing some contract work as an administrative assistant, makeup artist, and bookkeeper, she feels that she has lost her professional edge and the "STAT-Kat" reputation for crisis solving that gave her so much pleasure in her last job.

Transferable Skills

Retail management	Training a field sales force
Merchandizing; product placement	Negotiation skills
Supervising, mentoring sales staff	Research, reporting, and trend analysis

Job Description

Divisional Merchandise Manager

- Promote diverse and exciting array of products including greeting cards, gift wrap, gift bags, stationery, note cards, journals, and unique gift products

- Report to the chief merchandising officer and responsible for all categories of products

- Deliver top- and bottom-line planned sales for total division

- Required: five to seven years management experience in a fast-paced retail environment

- Minimum five years experience in sourcing and product management and development

- Develop vendor vision and strategy, exit strategy, and markdown management

- Coach, supervise, and mentor buyers; develop staff career paths

- Build vendor relationships and negotiation guidelines

- Develop and manage a travel budget for the division based on the goals of the company

- Experience in managing hourly and contract staff

- Expertise in retail budgeting and the planning process and vendor and sourcing analysis; deliver month-end reports and trending analysis

- Proficient in Microsoft Office: Excel, Word, and Outlook

Resume Makeover

Kerry creates a resume that emphasizes her retail and merchandizing experience.

1 She adds the headline "Merchandising/Retail Manager" under her name.

2 The opening statements all relate to her recent successes in the trade show and merchandising fields.

3 Key words are added to her Core Competencies section, including sales planning, merchandising, product placement, and markdown management.

4 Her two relevant jobs in merchandising and retail management are presented first, even though this creates a six-year gap in her work history (1999–2005).

5 This "gap" is covered when her administrative role for the Temple Bethel Israel is presented last, under the title "Other Experience." Several administrative task descriptions have been eliminated to focus on her higher-level skills.

6 Her Relevant Skills area is enhanced with several software products used in retail, including Planograms.

Kerry "Kat" Atkins
1234 Any Street
Costa Mesa, CA 92627
714.123.4567
email@email.com

Executive Summary:

To work with a progressive company as a marketing manager pertaining to their products or services.

Experience:

MerchantForce, Inc. Laguna Hills, CA
Event Marketing Manager – MediaMemory Sept 2005 to Jan 2009

- Reported directly to Senior Manager, Field Marketing and Intelligence at MediaMemory Corp. and ChannelForce Account Director - MediaMemory
- MediaMemory is the world's largest supplier of innovative flash memory data storage products (memory cards, flash drives, mp3 players)
- ChannelForce, Inc. - dedicated to executing channel strategies and developing relationships to increase clients' market share
- Coordinated needs of PMMs, Business Units, Sales Groups
- Managed assigned accounts and established close working relationships with the client, sales, marketing specialists, and field team
- Wrote, designed, and produced PowerPoint presentations for training Field Reps, Department Managers, and Buyers for key products. Ability to produce in French and English.
- Created and emailed newsletter blasts to Field Reps concerning new products, sales tools, and customer feedback
- Instrumental in managing all aspects of Training Special Events, from tabletop to trade show — including reps, PMMs, swag, booth requirements
- Trained and managed up to 100 Field Reps on products for specific events — provided training materials for sales day programs
- Used forecasting and strategic planning to ensure the success of the event based on the products, lines, and services
- Managed a 20-person team in our booth for a RadioShack trade show messaging over 3,000 attendees
- Successfully handled crises as they arose, be it personnel unable to make show, lost booths, swag misdirected
- Structured and maintained logs of the following: all events, costs, personnel, swag/materials in distribution center, shipping materials
- Conferred with legal staff to resolve problems, such as copyright infringement and royalty sharing if involved with event

Temple Bethel Israel Newport Beach, CA
Administrative Assistant to Cantor Dec 1999 to June 2005

- Performed general office duties such as ordering supplies, maintaining records management systems for Bar/Bat Mitzvah students and Choirs.
- Executed daily operations of producing study packets, Torah portions, customized CDs, and scheduling of students
- Wrote, designed, and produced programs for concerts
- Instrumental in managing volunteers and Junior Choir for Community Chanukah Concert and Israel Day at the JCC
- Successfully managed in conjunction with volunteers Cantor Grand Concerts and special guest concerts — sent emails, postcards, letters asking for donations of time or money
- Purchased and maintained inventory of Siddurs, certificates, bookplates, blank CDs, music for both choirs

Nordstrom Costa Mesa, CA
Cosmetic Counter Manager – Chanel July 1998 to Aug 1999

- Executed daily operations of Chanel Counter with yearly retail sales of $1.1 million — monitoring sales, inventory, schedules
- Supervised 7 employees, scheduled work hours, resolved conflicts, determined sales goals
- Successfully managed the West Coast premiere of the "Behind the Scenes Runway" event with 7 sales associates and 10 makeup artists to schedule customers every 1/2 hour per artist for 5 days producing over $25,000 in retail sales
- Displayed merchandise and suggested selections that met customer's needs

Nordstrom – Macy's – Robinson's Sacramento & Orange County, CA 1989 to 1999
Cosmetic Counter Manager – Chanel

- Inventoried stock and reordered when inventories dropped to specified levels
- Trained and managed up to 3 sales associates and resident makeup artist on sales skills; achieved significant improvements in productivity
- Recognized for customer service, sales, and counter manager of year
- Coordinated sales promotion activities, prepared merchandise displays and advertising copy
- Planned and prepared work schedules
- Listened to and resolved customer complaints regarding services, products, and personnel

Education:

Ohio State University Columbus, OH
B.A. – History of Art 1986

Lorain County Community College Lorain, OH
A.A.S. – Medical Lab Technology 1979

Skills:

OS- XP, Vista
Software: Microsoft Office Suite (Word, Excel, Outlook, PowerPoint, Publisher) — 2003, 2007; Adobe Professional 2007; DavkaWriter; SDL Desktop Translator

KERRY "KAT" ATKINS

1234 Any Street ■ Costa Mesa, CA 92627 ■ 714.123.4567 ■ email@email.com

MERCHANDISING / RETAIL MANAGER
Vendor Strategy / Relationship Management / Product Line Expansion

(2) 14+ year record of achievement in merchandising, event management, store field training, and gaining favorable placement (Planograms) for consumer products including digital memory, MP3s, and cosmetics
Tenacious in building new business through existing and new product lines, securing customer loyalty, and forging strong relationships with external business partners
Known as "STAT-Kat" — Thrive in a fast-paced, high-energy, demanding environment
Proven track record in recruiting, mentoring, and retaining retail staff
Influential with all levels of the decision chain — worked collaboratively with client contacts at VP level
Adept at working independently — solving problems, dealing with crises, meeting customer expectations

(3) Core Competencies

- Sales Planning
- Merchandising
- Product Placement
- Markdown Management
- Managed 6-Figure Event Budgets
- Product Evangelist
- High-Impact Sales Presentations
- Cool in Crisis Situations
- Nurture Executive Relationships
- Field Rep Training
- Multi-Tasking Wizard
- Eager to Learn

RELEVANT EXPERIENCE

(4) TRADESHOW / MERCHANDISING MANAGEMENT
Event Marketing Manager — MerchantForce, Inc. (Client: MediaMemory) 2005-2009
Laguna Hills, CA
Dedicated to executing channel strategies and developing relationships to increase clients' market share

Accountabilities
- Reported directly to Senior Manager of Field Marketing and Intelligence at MediaMemory Corp. (MediaMemory is the world's largest supplier of innovative flash memory data storage products — memory cards, flash drives, mp3 players)
- Managed accountability to MediaMemory Product Marketing Managers, Business Units, and Sales Groups
- Managed assigned accounts and established close working relationships with the client, sales, marketing specialists, and field team
- Structured and maintained logs of the following: all events, costs, personnel, giveaways, materials in distribution center, shipping materials

Selected Achievements
- Expanded my job description, taking more responsibility for booking, managing, PowerPoint presentations, and giveaway management. Increased my personal productivity from 9 events per month to 28 (311%).
- Requested by Best Buy Canada to present to Sales Managers — successfully revised a 45-minute presentation with 10 minutes' notice
- Wrote, designed, and produced PowerPoint presentations for training Field Reps, Department Managers, and Buyers for key products. Ability to produce in French and English.
- Created and emailed newsletter blasts to Field Reps concerning new products, sales tools, and customer feedback
- Instrumental in managing all aspects of Training Special Events, from tabletop to trade show — including staffing, giveaway distribution, and booth requirements
- Trained and managed up to 100 Field Reps on products for specific events - provided training materials for sales day programs
- Used forecasting and strategic planning to ensure the success of the event based on the products, lines, and services
- Managed a 20-person team in our booth for a RadioShack Trade Show — scheduling training in four separate stations, messaging over 3,000 attendees in 4 days
- Successfully handled crises, such as personnel unable to make show, lost booths, product misdirected
- Conferred with legal staff to resolve problems, such as copyright infringement and royalty sharing

Kerry Atkins ■ www.LinkedIn.com/in/name
1234 Any Street ■ Costa Mesa, CA 92627 ■ 714.123.4567 ■ email@email.com

---

KERRY ATKINS

RETAIL MANAGEMENT

Cosmetic Counter Manager – Chanel 1998–1999
Nordstrom, Costa Mesa, CA
- Successfully managed the West Coast premiere of the "Behind the Scenes Runway" event with 7 sales associates and 10 makeup artists, scheduling customers every 1/2 hour per artist for 5 days, producing over $25,000 in retail sales
- Executed daily operations of Chanel Counter with yearly retail sales of $1.1 million — monitoring sales, inventory, schedules
- Supervised 7 employees, scheduled work hours, resolved conflicts, and determined sales goals
- Displayed merchandise and suggested selections that met customers' needs

Cosmetic Counter Manager – Chanel 1989–1998
Nordstrom – Macy's – Robinson's, Sacramento & Orange County, CA
- Recognized for customer service, sales, and Counter Manager of Year
- Inventoried stock and reordered when inventories dropped to specified levels
- Trained and managed up to 3 sales associates and resident makeup artist on their sales skills and achieved significant improvements in productivity
- Coordinated sales promotion activities, and prepared merchandise displays and advertising copy
- Planned and prepared work schedules, and assigned employees to specific duties
- Listened to and resolved customer complaints regarding services, products, and personnel

OTHER EXPERIENCE

(5) Administrative Assistant to Cantor, 1999–2005
Temple Bethel Israel – Newport Beach, CA
- Was instrumental in managing 50 volunteers and Junior Choir for Community Chanukah Concert and Israel Day at the Jewish Community Center
- Successfully managed, in conjunction with volunteers, Cantors' Grand Concert, to raise $10,000–15,000 to support music program for the year
- Promoted special guest concerts — designed and sent emails, postcards, letters asking for donations of time or money

EDUCATION & SKILLS

(6) BA – History of Art – Ohio State University, Columbus, OH
AAS – Medical Lab Technology – Lorain County Community College, Lorain, OH

Relevant Skills
- Operating Systems — XP, Vista
- Microsoft Office Suite — Word, Excel, Outlook, PowerPoint, Publisher, 2003, 2007
- Adobe Professional 2007
- Planograms
- DavkaWriter
- SDL Desktop Translator

Kerry Atkins ■ www.LinkedIn.com/in/name
1234 Any Street ■ Costa Mesa, CA 92627 ■ 714.123.4567 ■ email@email.com

Credit Cards to Pharmaceuticals

Vanessa Devereaux has had a long career in the market research field. She has rarely had to look for a position because she has been active in her local American Marketing Association (AMA) chapters and has always networked effectively with other market researchers. She even brags to friends about how each of her job changes have come about from a phone conversation with a close friend in the business. She is stunned when she loses her job as market researcher for a credit card company. The issuing bank has failed, and all operations are shut down with no notice.

With the financial industry in such turmoil, she knows that market research jobs are rare in banking. She also wants to take her market research skills and apply them to an industry that makes a difference in people's lives. "I no longer *care* if market research can show whether Tinkerbell belongs on the front or the back of the card," she tells a friend. Vanessa hopes to land a job in pharmaceuticals or health care, because those industries are either stable or growing despite the economic downturn.

Challenges to Making the Switch

Vanessa's career in market research stretches back to 1998, and most of it has been in financial services. Except for some project work, she can claim little knowledge of the key issues in pharmaceutical research.

Her job history appears a little spotty over the last 10 years; she has stayed just 1 to 3 years with her last seven employers. Because her resume is so detailed, she isn't able to include on just two pages her eight-year term with a Fortune 500 Financial Services company. She will need to give reasons for her short terms in the last decade.

Transferable Skills

Qualitative research design

Managing research projects

Training staff

Moderating focus groups

Designing research questionnaires

Presentation skills

Branding and product strategy

Job Description

Manager, Market Research

- Provide strategic guidance to the marketing teams and other functional areas, utilizing primary and secondary resources and advanced analytic techniques

- Help marketing develop a strategic vision via in-depth portfolio and brand-specific market analyses

- Oversee the management of qualitative and quantitative marketing research projects, associated budgets, timelines, and relations with outside consultants

- Design, execute, and analyze custom qualitative and quantitative marketing research projects with actionable recommendations in development/support of brand/portfolio strategy and tactics

- Develop holistic and comprehensive market assessments and perform other ad-hoc analyses to proactively address issues in support of business objectives

- Support the planning process via market-based situation analysis to identify issues/opportunities and associated strategies/actions to address

- Play a leadership role through interactions with internal stakeholders to provide evidenced-based guidance for product lifecycle planning

- Consult with brand teams on proper focus and prioritization of marketing research resources against brand needs

- Develop presentations with clear storylines, communicating key conclusions and recommendations

Resume Makeover

Vanessa's resume needs a complete rewrite to make it more reader-friendly. It is now so content-dense that it is daunting to review.

1 Vanessa's original resume begins with a lengthy paragraph about her. It is written in the third person and is an old-style way of introducing the candidate.

2 Her new resume begins with the headline "Market Research" and is followed by seven key achievement statements.

3 The typeface is changed to Arial, and the size is increased to 11 point in order to make the entire resume easier to read.

4 The Core Competencies match, as nearly as she can, the requirements in the job description.

5 Each job listing begins with her title, emphasizing her role rather than the company.

6 Each achievement statement is edited, eliminating as many words as possible.

7 Less detail is included in her role as human resources director because it doesn't apply to her current job search.

8 Her educational listing is simplified. The term "Magna Cum Laude" is left in while her grade point average is left out. (It is generally considered proper to include grade point average only in the first few years after graduation.)

9 Her professional leadership roles are included in order to show her dedication to the profession of market research.

Vanessa Devereaux
123 Any Street
West Chester, PA 19300
Cell (215) 123-5678

Home (484) 123-1234   email@email.com

Vanessa Devereaux has worked in the research field for 20 years and is recognized as a master at her craft and a consummate professional. Ms. Devereaux employs a truly consultative approach in working with clients. Throughout her career, she has consulted on, designed, implemented, directed, and analyzed primary strategic marketing study initiatives for the pharmaceutical, biopharmaceutical, financial services, and professional services fields. These studies cover virtually all product categories in both pharmaceuticals and financial services, conducted among nearly all potential target audiences. Upon completion and presentation of research results, Ms. Devereaux is frequently called upon to continue her engagements in providing additional strategic consulting and guidance on implications and implementation of findings.

WORK EXPERIENCE

A-Bank Credit Card Services Wilmington, DE—Sr. Group Manager Market Research-Partnerships
October 2007 to present

- Serving as an internal consultant to key senior marketing decision makers. Identifying research needs of internal clients and determining the most effective and efficient way to meet these needs. Directing all research efforts within the Partner CoBrand Division to leverage research to improve business results. Working directly with senior leadership of the company. Manage activities of multiple suppliers toward the accomplishment of meaningful and timely results within budget. Effectively communicate to management and clients via presentations, reports and proposals.
- Provide coaching and counseling in developing direct reports.
- External Partnership clients include: Disney, United Airlines, Marriott, Continental Airlines, Southwest Airlines, AARP, and BP.

Researched Medical Communications West Chester, PA—Director of Qualitative Research
December 2006 to October 2007

- Responsible for leading all aspects of qualitative studies from proposal design to delivery/presentation of final results, including development of recruiting screeners, topic guides, overseeing all aspects of recruiting/fieldwork; analyzing and writing summary and detailed reports of results infused with conclusions and marketing implications.
- Moderates/conducts all forms of qualitative research interviews. Additional responsibilities include: overseeing Field Director training, budget preparation, recruiting updates; lead development of internal processes and procedures for tracking costs, methodologies, and project database; training of Business Development Specialist on principles of market research.

Triangle Research & Consulting, West Chester, PA—Senior Director of Qualitative Research
November 2004 to December 2006

- Designs and creates customized methodologies to meet clients' most urgent information needs, while personally managing and coordinating all day-to-day operational requirements of studies: developing all research materials, monitoring recruiting of participants, conducting research and analysis, presenting results to end-client as needed or requested.
- Interviewing an expansive variety of medical professional respondent-types, as well as patients, caregivers, public health officials, and therapeutic category thought leaders. Equally comfortable and proficient in conducting in-person depth interviews, telephone depth interviews, web-based interviews, triads, as well as leading focus groups in a variety of therapeutic areas.

Independent Market Research Consultant, Philadelphia, PA
November 2001 to November 2004

- Developed relationships with, and consulted for, national financial services and pharmaceutical strategic research agencies in conducting qualitative and quantitative studies.
- Designed and created targeted project methodologies to gain actionable insight into clients' pressing business issues, while responsible for all operational aspects of study management and coordination: developed all research materials, conducted research and analysis, presented results to end-client as needed or requested.

Britney & Winchester, Market Research Inc. Philadelphia, PA—Director Human Resources/Quantitative Research
January 2001 to November 2001 (laid off due to decline in international qualitative work after 9/11)

- Developed the company's first Human Resources role, charged with assessing staffing needs, conducting staff recruiting, selection, hiring, firing, and lay-offs, while effectively resolving all HR issues for the organization. Additionally, developed industry-standard position descriptions and performance evaluation protocols and tools.
- Established new Quantitative Department protocols to be implemented throughout qualitatively oriented company. Created, managed, and developed projects through all phases: client consultation, research design, data collection monitoring, data tabulation design and analysis, report writing, and presentations.

Mathew Harper & Associates/National Research, Washington, DC—Assistant Vice President
April 1999 to January 2001

- Marketed, proposed, designed, conducted, and managed clients and projects for all phases of financial services market research assignments on qualitative and quantitative studies. Created, developed, and implemented the first plans for: Marketing, Strategic Planning, and Business Development.
- Established new Marketing function by implementing: Customer Relations Manager Roles for senior staff, scheduling press releases, updating customer mailings, sales training for less experienced senior research staff.
- Identified and developed highly effective new internal systems and measures to enhance project management to ensure financial success. Increased company profits by 15% annually.

Roper Starch/Response Analysis Corporation, Princeton, NJ—Account Executive
April 1998 to April 1999

- Created and implemented marketing and sales strategy to reach out to financial service company prospective and neglected customers by developing marketing letters, conducting on-site marketing presentations, selecting key industry meetings for business development.
- Developed marketing database of 1,000+ existing customers and prospects for use in target marketing calls and meetings.
- Sold, designed, and executed all phases of qualitative and quantitative market research projects for financial services and health-care companies. On target to meet annual sales goal of $1m.
- Created and implemented the Knowledge Management Taskforce to assist in the merger transition to educate all employees worldwide on the resources available within the new, combined organization.

ACADEMIC YEARS

Drake University, Des Moines, IA
Majored in Speech Communication-Small Group Dynamics, BFA; minor in Marketing

- Graduated *Magna Cum Laude.* Major GPA: 3.93 out of 4.00; overall GPA: 3.75
- U.S. Senator Tom Harkin's Congressional Office in Washington, DC - US Congressional Press Intern

PROFESSIONAL MARKETING AND RESEARCH ACTIVITIES

- **American Marketing Association,** Member 1986–present: Advisor to Market Research Sub-Committee
- **Project Management Institute,** Charter Member, and Secretary of Iowa Chapter
- **American Institute of Business,** Business College Curriculum Advisory Committee
- **Insurance Advisory Board,** Founding Member
- **Veteran's Administration,** Program Research Advisor
- **American Institute of Business (AIB),** Market Research Methods Lecturer
- **Drake University,** Market Research Lecturer
- **US-AID, Citizen's Network for Foreign Affairs,** Volunteer Marketing Advisor in Nakhodka, Russia
- **Society of Insurance Research,** Board of Directors, VP Annual Conference Planning

VANESSA DEVEREAUX

123 Any Street • West Chester, PA 19300 • email@email.com • 484-123-1234 Home • 215-123-5678 Cell

MARKET RESEARCH

Primary Research / Qualitative / Strategic Focus

- 20 years experience in designing and directing primary strategic marketing studies
- Known for focusing research on pressing business needs and strategic decisions
- Provide strategic consulting for research clients on the implementation of findings
- Experience in pharmaceutical, biopharmaceutical, financial, and professional services
- Expert moderator for qualitative research interviews
- Created internal processes to track budgets, recruiting of respondents, and projects
- Train and mentor staff in leading-edge market research techniques

Core Competencies

- Brand-specific market analysis
- Product lifecycle research & planning
- Focus on strategic business issues
- Clear, focused presentations of findings
- In-depth phone, in-person interviews
- Web-based interviews
- Focus groups – moderate and manage
- Managing multiple research projects

PROFESSIONAL EXPERIENCE

Senior Group Manager – Market Research-Partnerships   October 2007 to present
A-Bank Credit Card Services, Wilmington, DE

- Direct all research efforts within the Partner CoBrand Division to leverage research to improve business results, working directly with senior leadership.
- Manage activities of multiple suppliers toward the accomplishment of meaningful and timely projects to develop strategic brand positioning.
- Effectively communicate to management and clients via presentations, reports, and proposals.
- Provide coaching and counseling in developing 13 direct reports.
- External Partnership clients include: Disney, United Airlines, Marriott, Continental Airlines, Southwest Airlines, AARP, and BP.

Director of Qualitative Research   December 2006 to October 2007
Researched Medical Communications, West Chester, PA

- Responsible for leading all aspects of qualitative studies from proposal design to delivery/presentation of final results.
- Developed and recruited screeners, topic guides, oversaw all aspects of recruiting/fieldwork.
- Analyzed and wrote summary and detailed reports of results infused with conclusions and marketing implications.
- Moderated/conducted all forms of qualitative research interviews.
- Additional responsibilities: overseeing Field Director training, budget preparation, recruiting updates; led development of internal processes and procedures for tracking costs, methodologies, and project database; training of Business Development Specialist on principles of market research.

Senior Director of Qualitative Research   November 2004 to December 2006
Triangle Research & Consulting, West Chester, PA

- Developed customized methodologies to meet clients' most urgent information needs.
- Developed all research materials, monitored recruiting of participants, conducted research and analysis, presenting results to end-client.
- Interviewed an expansive variety of medical professional respondent-types, as well as patients, caregivers, public health officials, and therapeutic category thought leaders.

VANESSA DEVEREAUX

215-123-5678

Independent Market Research Consultant, Philadelphia, PA   November 2001 to November 2004

- Developed relationships with, and consulted for, national financial services and pharmaceutical strategic research agencies.
- Designed and created targeted project methodologies to gain actionable insight into clients' pressing business issues.

Director HR/Qualitative Research   January 2001 to November 2001
Britney & Winchester, Market Research Inc., Philadelphia, PA
(Laid off due to decline in international qualitative work after 9/11)

- Established new Quantitative Department protocols; managed projects through all phases — client consultation, research design, data collection monitoring, data tabulation design and analysis, report writing, and presentations.
- Developed the company's first Human Resources role: assessed staffing needs, developed industry-standard position descriptions and performance evaluation protocols and tools.

Assistant Vice President   April 1999 to January 2001
Mathew Harper & Associates/National Research, Washington, DC

- Marketed, proposed, designed, conducted, and managed clients and projects for all phases of financial services market research for qualitative and quantitative studies.
- Established new Marketing function by implementing Customer Relations Manager Roles for senior staff, scheduling press releases, updating customer mailings, sales training for less experienced senior research staff.
- Identified and developed highly effective new internal systems and measures to enhance project management to ensure financial success. Increased company profits by 15% annually.

Account Executive   April 1998 to April 1999
Roper Starch/Response Analysis Corporation, Princeton, NJ

- Created and implemented marketing and sales strategy for financial service prospective and neglected customers. Developed marketing letters, on-site marketing presentations, and key industry meetings.
- Developed marketing database of 1,000+ existing customers and prospects for use in target marketing calls and meetings.
- Sold, designed, and executed all phases of qualitative and quantitative market research projects for financial services and health-care companies. Met annual sales goal of $1M.

EDUCATION

Drake University, Des Moines, IA
BFA – Speech Communication-Small Group Dynamics, minor in Marketing; graduated *Magna Cum Laude*

PROFESSIONAL

American Marketing Association, Member 1986–present; Advisor to Market Research Sub-Committee
Project Management Institute, Charter Member and Secretary of Iowa Chapter
American Institute of Business, Business College Curriculum Advisory Committee
Insurance Advisory Board, Founding Member
Veteran's Administration, Program Research Advisor
American Institute of Business (AIB), Market Research Methods Lecturer
Drake University, Market Research Lecturer
US-AID, Citizen's Network for Foreign Affairs, Volunteer Marketing Advisor in Nakhodka, Russia
Society of Insurance Research, Board of Directors, VP Annual Conference Planning

Financial Services to Nonprofit

Guy Logan resigned from his job as a call center supervisor to care for his wife while she was undergoing chemotherapy for lung cancer. After she died, Guy took a few short-term contract positions and then began applying for call center management jobs, which are scarce because of the economic downturn. He had a few interviews but no job offers and was told by one employer that he seemed to lack enthusiasm.

This feedback helped Guy re-evaluate his career path. He admits that he has reached a crossroads in his life and wants to pursue more meaningful work. Guy considers different options and feels an immediate attraction to a position he sees on the Internet for a Quitline intake specialist with the American Cancer Society. In this job, he would counsel individuals wanting to quit smoking. Based on his own experience, he knows how important it is for cancer patients and their families to receive support and information.

Challenges to Making the Switch

Guy's biggest challenge is convincing an interviewer that he has a long-term commitment to nonprofit work. He is prepared to take a lower-level position at a reduced salary as long as he can make a difference in people's lives. To increase his chances for an interview, Guy downplays his higher-level experience and expands on his volunteer activities.

Guy knows how to work effectively in a call center and has exceptional communication skills. What's lacking is prior nonprofit experience. His previous demanding work schedules left him little time for volunteer work; however, he's now using a portion of his time to get involved with organizations. One of his activities is the American Cancer Society's Relay for Life.

Another challenge for Guy is transferring his customer service skills to become a telephone counselor. He knows how to be an active listener and responds well to people who are under stress. To help him learn more about the counseling process, he volunteers at a local hospice. The experience helps him through his own grief process, and he receives training that he can use in other settings.

Transferable Skills

Call center background

Effective communicator

Counseling

Problem-solving

Technology skills

Customer service

Active listener

Emotionally composed

Job Description
Nonprofit Call Center Counselor

- Previous counseling experience, including intake and dealing with diverse needs

- Exceptional customer service skills and the ability to treat each person with respect and empathy

- An active listener who is skilled in assisting clients over the telephone

- Ability to guide people through the intake process using a series of scripted questions

- A problem-solver who can provide assistance and resources within a short time frame

- Amenable to structure and direction in a call center environment

- Knowledge of the American Cancer Society and the fight against cancer

---

Resume Makeover

Guy's resume is revised and shortened to downplay his managerial experience and focus on what he can do in a nonprofit call center.

1 The resume is more focused and effective as a one-page resume rather than two pages with unrelated information.

2 The objective uses the exact job title and the name of the nonprofit organization.

3 The qualifications summary includes keywords and information that accentuates customer service and downplays higher-level management skills.

4 A brief mention is made of nonprofit volunteer service.

5 Work experience is shortened to highlight customer service and call center skills.

6 The Professional Experience section is moved before Education to put it in order of importance.

GUY LOGAN
1234 Timberline Lane
Cedar Park, TX 78613
512.123.4567 email@email.com

Commitment to Customer Satisfaction

Proven Team Leader with over 12 years of customer service experience as a Contact Center Supervisor, Sales Coach, Team Lead, and Account Manager. Participated in the successful launch of two Contact Center Operations. Genuine ability to manage and passionately motivate Sales, Customer Service, and Call Center Teams.

HIGHLIGHTS OF QUALIFICATIONS
- Experience with MS Office Suite, CRM, CCPulse, and various mainframe applications.
- Ability to work with conceptual ideas and possess an innovative thinking style.
- Strong presentation, coaching, and interpersonal management skills.
- Self-starter with the ability to handle multiple projects and achieve objectives in an environment with changing priorities.
- Responsible for training staff and evaluating user access needs.

UNIVERSITY OF TEXAS AT AUSTIN   May 1983
Bachelor of Arts
Major: Economics

Texas Department of Insurance, Group I License

PROFESSIONAL EXPERIENCE

EDUCATION PARTNERSHIP, Austin, TX   01/07 – 08/08

Contact Center Supervisor

Managed the daily performance of up to 15 agents in Document Processing, Inbound and Outbound Contact Center Teams. Facilitated customer service escalation action items as needed. Assisted upper-level management in the planning and implementation of startup Contact Center Operations. Demonstrated teamwork and the ability to integrate with other operational teams and personnel to resolve issues and implement process improvements. Monitored individual employee attendance, productivity, and quality assurance.

- Held weekly team meetings.
- Documented, trained, and communicated company policies and procedures via MS Word, Excel, and PowerPoint.
- Delivered annual employee performance reviews.
- Conducted 1:1 coaching sessions with individual employees to reach quantity, quality, and incentive goals.
- Scheduled interviews and made new hire decisions as needed.
- Motivated three Operations teams to achieve department and individual goals.
- Evaluated and tested new software and made recommendations to management about CRM user access.
- Permanently laid off when the company ceased operations.

Guy Logan   512.123.4567   email@email.com

KELL FINANCIAL SERVICES, Austin, TX   09/97 – 01/07
Account Manager   FY05 – FY08
Public Group Lead   FY03 – FY05
Inside Sales Representative   FY01 – FY05
Sales Coach   FY98 – FY01

MAJOR ACHIEVEMENTS
1st President's Club (154% quota attainment)
Multiple Inside Sales Representative of the Quarter awards
Customer Experience Bronze award

Generated revenue from new lease agreements and renewals in an Inbound/Outbound environment. Used strong program management skills to meet deadlines and facilitate deliverables from key contributors in Credit, Special Pricing, Legal, and Operations Support during Master Lease Agreement negotiations. Handled customer service escalation action items as needed. Managed client expectations effectively and partnered with my Account Executive to be the 1st point of contact for lease originations in the Northeast Education Territory. Attended Executive Briefing Conferences to develop key large accounts (including K-12 and HIED) within my assigned territory.

- Negotiated, marketed, and sold the company's products via the telephone, e-mail, and Internet.
- Conducted account set-up meetings for Master Lease Agreement customers.
- Tracked the monthly/quarterly territory sales process through MS Excel forecast reports.
- Leveraged financing as an effective sales growth technique to Kell Sales personnel in team meetings and individual presentations.
- Mentored and coached new Inside Sales Representatives.
- Participated in the successful startup of the Kell-DFS Home Sales leasing department.

U.S. STUDENT LOAN CORPORATION Austin, TX   02/91 – 07/97

Production Control Specialist
- Acquired MS Office application skills in MS Word, Excel, and PowerPoint.
- Experienced with New Dimension's Integrated Operations software: Control-D.
- Demonstrated knowledge of data center automation, problem and change.
- Developed problem and change management/control techniques.

Retrieval Technician
- Reported monthly statistics and documented department policy and procedures.

Additional Work History and References Provided Upon Request

GUY LOGAN

1234 Timberline Lane
Cedar Park, TX 78613

512.123.4567
email@email.com

❷ OBJECTIVE: A Quitline Intake Specialist with the American Cancer Society

❸ QUALIFICATIONS SUMMARY

- Diverse call center experience includes guiding callers through an intake process, answering questions and providing information.
- Committed to the American Cancer Society mission and Relay for Life volunteer.
- Provide weekly volunteer counseling at Hospice Austin.
- Received recognition and bonuses for providing exceptional assistance to individuals.
- Skilled in using Microsoft Word, Excel, Access, and customized software programs.
- Bachelor of Arts degree. Completed training in counseling and communication skills.

❻ PROFESSIONAL EXPERIENCE

❹ COMMUNITY VOLUNTEER and Contract Work   Aug. 2008 – Present
- Volunteered to chair a Relay for Life committee and recruited other volunteers.
- Provide counseling each week for families and hospice patients.
- Completed counseling training at Hospice Austin.
- Worked a five-month temporary assignment in a call center for Vince Services at Lincoln Office Solutions. Assisted and resolved issues with more than 125 customers per day.

❺ EDUCATION PARTNERSHIP, Austin, TX   Jan. 2007 – Aug. 2008
Contact Center Supervisor
- Coordinated activities in an education financial service call center and initiated changes that improved customer service.
- Resolved escalated issues by using good listening skills and problem-solving ability.
- Used multi-tasking skills to handle a variety of functions, including addressing employees' and customers' concerns while documenting action taken.

KELL FINANCIAL SERVICES, Austin, TX   Sept. 1997 – Jan. 2007
- Advanced from entry-level sales to account manager in a call center with 350 agents.
- Received the Gold Award for providing the highest level of customer service.
- Successfully handled customer service escalation action items.
- Negotiated, marketed, and sold the company's products via the telephone and e-mail.

U.S. STUDENT LOAN CORP., Austin, TX   Feb.1991 – June 1997
Referral Specialist
- Monitored incoming and outgoing data exchanges between employer and vendors.
- Communicated with Accounting, Account Adjustments, Production Control, and Outside Collection Vendors to resolve issues.

EDUCATION

❻

UNIVERSITY OF TEXAS AT AUSTIN
Bachelor of Arts – Major: Economics

Hardware to Wholesale Flooring

Thomas Steinbach has been working in retail since he was in high school. He has always been hard-working, loyal, and eager to learn the business. With just a high school education, he has managed either departments or stores with some of the nation's largest chains. His job at an independent hardware store was a departure for him. He had been hoping to move up the ranks and perhaps even get an equity position when the store owner retired. Because the store couldn't compete with the large chains in pricing, it went out of business and Tom lost his job.

Tom has been ready for a change for a long time. His divorce left him as the primary caretaker for three children, ages 10, 8, and 5. He is hoping to make a career change that will allow him to work five days a week with a regular schedule. In addition, he is hoping to get off his feet, because a back injury five years ago is worsened by long hours of standing and walking (required in most retail positions).

Because he was flooring manager of the store, he starts his job search by talking to vendor companies and subcontractors. He becomes aware of a wholesale flooring sales position.

Challenges to Making the Switch

Tom has little proven sales experience. While he considers helping customers at the store a sales function, it might be viewed differently by a sales manager. While he understands flooring and the product lines of several retail vendors, he is unfamiliar with pure commercial flooring installations. Luckily, he has an interest in computers and has personally installed software at the store to create blueprints for flooring installations.

His lack of education may hold him back because he has completed just one year of college. Tom is hoping that his many years in management, coupled with the customer service and intense problem-solving of his last few jobs, will win over the hiring manager.

Transferable Skills

Sales skills

Communication skills

Detail-oriented

Commitment to quality

Problem-solving

Accurate measuring and ordering

Vendor relationships

Reading and creating blueprints

Managing hourly workers

Job Description
Flooring Sales Representative

- Call on homebuilders, owners, contractors, and commercial clients
- Apply retail/wholesale career experience and achievements
- Utilize a state-of-the-art design center showcase for design, maximizing sales, and serving customers
- Coordinate activities of vendors and subcontractors to ensure the best possible customer service
- Take personal accountability for delivering results
- $1 million annual sales record
- More than one year selling flooring and associated products
- Reading and interpretation of blueprints plus basic computer use
- High school diploma required; college and building industry experience a plus

Resume Makeover

Thomas's resume needs a makeover to reduce redundant information and replace responsibilities with achievement statements.

1. "Retail Management Professional" replaces the vague "Career Objective."

2. Special qualifications are brought to the top of the resume.

3. Emphasis is placed on commercial installations, and reading blueprints is added because it's part of the job description.

4. Each job listing emphasizes his title rather than the store name. He is building a picture of increasingly responsible positions.

5. His most current job responsibilities are stated in the present tense. This technique makes it appear that Thomas is still employed. All past jobs are stated in the past tense to give them the sense of accomplishment, rather than responsibilities.

6. Achievement statements are added to the most recent jobs, citing dollars and numbers wherever possible.

7. A Computer Software section is added. Many sales candidates can't claim this level of computing skill. This should give Tom an edge in the interview.

8. In the Education section, he clarifies the RMS training as being unique to Best Buy. His high school graduation is removed because he can claim some college work.

Thomas Steinbach
1234 Any Street
Woodward, IA 50276
(515) 123-1234 Cell
(515) 123-5678 Home
email@email.com

CAREER OBJECTIVE

To obtain a sales or sales management position with a company interested in training and maintaining loyal employees who are dedicated to the sales management field.

RELATED PROFESSIONAL EXPERIENCE

- **Independent Hardware, Des Moines, IA**
  - Dates Employed- 2006-2009
  - Position- Department Manager, Flooring
  - Responsibilities- Maintaining customer satisfaction
    Assist customers in retail and wholesale
    Managing internal personnel issues
    Training new employees in all phases of operations
    Organizing employee schedules, store inventory and equipment
    Analyzing consumer data and merchandise purchases

- **Seven Eleven, Waukee, IA**
  - Dates Employed- 2005-2006
  - Position- General Manager
  - Responsibilities- Maintaining customer satisfaction
    Assist customers in retail and wholesale
    Managing internal personnel issues
    Training new employees in all phases of operations
    Organizing employee schedules, store inventory and equipment
    Analyzing consumer data and merchandise purchases

- **Krispy Kreme Doughnuts, Clive, IA**
  - Dates Employed- 2005-2006
  - Position- Assistant Manager
  - Responsibilities- Maintaining customer satisfaction
    Assist customers, both retail and wholesale, with selection, delivery, and arrangement (box, rack, and load)
    Managing internal personnel issues
    Training new employees in all phases of operations
    Organizing employee schedules, store inventory and equipment
    Manage setup and delivery of wholesale accounts
    Analyzing consumer data and merchandise purchases

1

Thomas Steinbach
1234 Any Street
Woodward, IA 50276
(515) 123-1234 Cell
(515) 123-5678 Home
email@email.com

- **Best Buy, Ames, IA**
  - Dates Employed- 1997-2005
  - Position- PC Area Manager/Sales Manager
  - Responsibilities- Maintaining customer satisfaction
    Managing internal personnel issues
    Training new employees
    Organizing employee schedules and store inventory
    Analyzing consumer data and merchandise purchases
  - Achievements- 2004-2005 Achievers Award
    1999-2001 Top Gun Award

- **Blockbuster Video, Des Moines, IA**
  - Dates Employed- 1996-1997
  - Position- Assistant Manager
  - Responsibilities- Operating general store procedures
    Managing sales of merchandise
    Training new employees
    Organizing employee schedules

- **Pizza For Less, Little Rock, AR**
  - Dates Employed- 1992-1996
  - Position- General Manager
  - Responsibilities- Managing overall store operations
    Maintaining customer satisfaction and superior food standards
    Organizing store inventory

SPECIAL QUALIFICATIONS

- 18 years of experience:
  - Managing others
  - Working on a team
  - Maintaining a positive and smooth-operating work environment
  - Boosting company sales
  - Communicating with the public
  - Advertising merchandise and services

EDUCATIONAL BACKGROUND

- Completed Retail Management System (RMS) Training Course
- Attended the University of Arkansas
- Graduated from Oak Grove High School- Little Rock, AR 1994

Thomas Steinbach

1234 Any Street, Woodward, IA 50276 — (512) 123-5678 home — (512) 123-1234 cell — email@email.com

RETAIL MANAGEMENT PROFESSIONAL
Serving the Public/Managing Hourly Employees/Boosting Sales

(1)
- Proven track record – 18 years experience as a store or department manager

(2)
- Successful in leading teams, smooth scheduling, and creating a positive work environment
- Train new employees in all phases of the operation

(3)
- Plan and coordinate large installations, bringing vendors, materials and manpower together just-in-time. Take personal accountability for customer satisfaction
- Boost store revenue through on-the-floor sales, special orders, attention to customer needs
- Read and interpret blueprints; use proprietary design software

CORE COMPETENCIES

Logistics for commercial installations	Customer service
Analyzing sales data & managing inventory	Setup and delivery of large wholesale orders
Team and project leadership	Daily management of hourly personnel
Problem solving	Vendor/subcontractor relationships
Store computer troubleshooting	Proprietary design software

PROFESSIONAL EXPERIENCE

Department Manager, Flooring — 2006–Present
Independent Hardware — Des Moines, IA

(4)
- Assist customers in retail and wholesale

(5)
- Manage internal personnel issues; resolve scheduling conflicts
- Train new employees in several departments
- Assist the store manager in implementing a new online inventory system
- Analyze customer data to purchase just the right inventory

General Manager — 2006
Seven Eleven — Waukee, IA

(6)
- Built store sales from $25,000 to $40,000 per week
- Managed and purchased inventory of more than 33,000 items
- Screened, hired and trained a staff of 10-15 part-time hourly employees
- Achieved turnover reduction of 50% from 75% to 25% during my 12 months there

Assistant Manager — 2005–2006
Krispy Kreme — Clive, IA

- Managed internal personnel issues
- Setup, production and deliveries of huge wholesale accounts representing 70% of store's volume
- Maintained stock and forecasted materials use; responsible for ordering perishable foodstuff

PC Area Manager/Sales Manager — 1997–2005
Best Buy — Ames, IA

- Managed 11 directly; 90 indirectly
- Responsible for sales in ever-changing, highly competitive PC and digital products
- 2004-2005 Achievers Award for highest sales in region
- 1999-2001 Top Gun Award for highest sales by department

Assistant Manager — 1996–1997
Blockbuster Video — Des Moines, IA

- Operated general store procedures
- Managed sales of merchandise
- Trained new employees
- Organized employee schedules – 15-20 part-time workers

General Manager — 1992–1996
Pizza For Less — Little Rock, AR

- Managed overall store operations
- First given this responsibility at the age of 17
- Maintained customer satisfaction and superior food standards

COMPUTER SOFTWARE

(7)
- Microsoft Office Suite – Word, Excel, PowerPoint, Access
- 20/20 and Deck Designer planning software
- A+ Certified 2002

EDUCATION

(8)
- Completed Best Buy's Retail Management System (RMS) Training Course
- Attended the University of Arkansas

High-Tech Hardware to Government

Paul Shankle has worked in the high-tech industry in sales, proposal writing, and buying. He has especially enjoyed his most recent job as a production buyer and planner for a high-tech engineering company. Through a series of events beyond his control, each high-tech job has ended after only a short time. The fast-paced, ever-changing high-tech world no longer appeals to him, and he would like to move into the public sector. Although Paul realizes that making a switch to a government position could mean losing status, autonomy, and pay, he feels the tradeoff in longevity and the ability to make plans based on consistent employment and predictable income make this choice a good one.

Challenges to Making the Switch

Hiring managers in the public sector often look for experience in that arena when making hiring decisions. They know that government work is not glamorous and that the pay scale is lower, and they are reluctant to hire someone who may leave after only a few years. Paul's varied work history may also make them nervous. Unlike employees in high-tech and hospitality companies, where Paul has worked in the past, county and state employees do not change jobs often. He has to overcome this reluctance by showing that he is exceedingly qualified for the job on his resume so he can have an opportunity to explain his reasons for making the transition in an interview. Paul must also go back and add detail to his employment history, required by the state's application process. Luckily, he has an old resume showing the month/year dates for all his jobs.

The rewrite of Paul's resume into a more traditional job-focused format will allow him to cut-and-paste the information into an online government application. The printed resume will only be used as a tool in the interview process.

Paul has an advantage over other candidates who have worked exclusively in the public sector because he has experience with current tools and practices that may not yet have been adopted by government agencies.

Transferable Skills

Place, track, and expedite purchase orders

Vendor evaluation and negotiation

Cost-reduction skills

Process improvement

Produce accurate documentation

Word, Excel, PowerPoint, and Visio skills

Job Description
Government Buyer/Planner

- Purchase and expedite material based on demand forecast and inventory min-max reporting

- Compile information and records to prepare purchase orders for procurement of materials; verify nomenclature and specifications of purchase

- Negotiate pricing and contracts

- Evaluate and report vendor performance and enforce contractual requirements

- Manage prices, lead times, and safety stocks in online material tracking system

- Participate in process improvement activities to improve purchasing performance and service to the organization

- Prepare "invitations to bid" forms and send them to suppliers or for public posting

- Compile records of items purchased or transferred between departments, prices, deliveries, and inventories

- Compare prices, specifications, and delivery dates and award contract to bidders or place orders with suppliers

- Coordinate with all departments to procure quotes on required material and evaluate those quotes to determine best total value base on quality, price, delivery, and previous vendors' bidding

- Serve as point person for all aspects of production/purchasing, including planning, forecasting, shortages/late orders, cost discrepancies, and so on

Resume Makeover

Paul's resume needs to be converted to the more traditional reverse chronological format. It includes too much information about his early work and not enough detail about his relevant buyer/planner performance.

❶ Eliminate the Industry Experience section.

❷ Include his degree in public affairs in the summary at the top of the page because it shows an interest in government work during his college years.

❸ List each job in reverse order, including month and year dates and reason for leaving. Move the accomplishment statements under each job listing, adding specific details and metrics when possible.

❹ Add "reason for leaving" to all positions to address the hiring manager's potential concern about whether he is looking for long-term employment.

❺ Take off the inside sales representative jobs because sales experience is less relevant to his desired job of planner/buyer.

PAUL SHANKLE

1234 Parkfield Drive, Champaign, IL 61820 • (217) 123-4567 • email@email.com

PROFESSIONAL PROFILE

Experienced Buyer/Planner with strong skills in purchasing, customer/sales support, and project coordination. Is an excellent liaison between vendors, company staff, and customers. Is detail-oriented to create bottom-line results by being proactive in resolving issues.

INDUSTRY EXPERIENCE

Semiconductor   Telecommunications   Hospitality   Real Estate

RECENT ACCOMPLISHMENTS

Purchasing
- Place and expedite purchase orders to meet ever-changing project timelines and production schedules.
- Provide material commits and re-commits for all jobs under my planner codes.
- Work with Quality to process DMRs, expediting the repair or replacement of defective materials.
- Reduced Cisco product lead-time from six to two weeks for Port of Seattle airport project.
- Have experience negotiating prices, shipping, and delivery services with vendors and customers, for both stock and custom-made products.

Proposal Writing
- Researched and managed the collection of information from various internal and external groups, to create multi-million dollar proposals for customers.
- Wrote company proposals, Statements of Work (SOWs), and templates supporting both the Austin and UK offices, writing UK documents in British English.
- Proofread and edited company proposals before submission.
- Contributed to the company database of proposal information and visuals.
- With sales representatives, created sales strategies for writing proposals.

Consultative Sales
- Built a "cold territory" into a **$1 million/year** territory within two years.
- Enlarged territory by creating approximately **50** new accounts per year from customer referrals.
- Sold to and serviced over **300** accounts, ranging in size from bed & breakfasts to **150**-room hotels.
- Earned **1995 Winner's Circle Award** for top producing insurance agents.

Counseling/Customer Service
- Processed, expedited, and tracked customer orders to meet project timelines.
- Achieved insurance renewal rate of **over 90%**.
- Worked as a **Peer Advisor** in the Indiana University (I.U.) Overseas Study offices, helping students find information on programs and consulting on curriculum decisions.

Promotions/Advertising
- Served as team representative on the **Promotions Committee**, working with vendors to create monthly sales promotions and strategies.
- Represented sales office on six-member **Sales and Marketing Team**, which evaluated and updated company-marketing materials.

PAUL SHANKLE

Computer Skills
- Proficient in **Word, Excel, Outlook, Visio**, and using the **Internet** for research.

CAREER EXPERIENCE

Production Control Planner, Buyer/Planner, Fox Engineering, Inc., 2004-2009
A producer of customer-specific gas delivery systems and cleaners for the semiconductor industry. **In Production Control, worked as a liaison between purchasing, production, and management. Created work orders, scheduled the kitting of jobs, corrected inaccurate inventory quantities, escalated and filled material shortages.**
As a Buyer/Planner, purchased and expedited materials based on daily reports in Visual Enterprise, providing material commits to production, reducing inventories and material costs, obtaining vendor commits for the return of RMA (DMR) materials.

Opportunity Manager, Concurrent, L.L.C., 2002
Fast-growing contractor of HP Computer Corporation, providing managed deployment services and ongoing asset management tools for HP's corporate customers. **Supported Concurrent and HP sales teams by writing and creating proposals, Statements of Work (SOWs), and project change orders.**

Sales & Marketing Representative, Kendall Electronics Corp./Avnet, Inc., 2000-2001
Large value-added reseller (VAR) of computer networking equipment and services, creating end-to-end solutions for customers. Is a Gold Partner of Cisco Systems, Inc. **Supported field representatives by creating quotes and proposals, placing and expediting orders, and developing solutions working with engineers and customers.**

Sales Agent, CC Computer Corporation, Interim Personnel-contractor, 1999-2000
Largest and fastest-growing computer manufacturer in the U.S. **In Large Corporate Accounts (LCA), sold and processed PC orders for the Excel Communications program and for LCA's Employee Purchase Program (EPP). Promoted to Enterprise to work on the newly formed EPP for Enterprise, Global, and Large Corporate Accounts.**

Inside Sales Representative, US Hotel Supply Company, 1996-1999
Largest hospitality products supplier in the U.S. **Sold to and serviced over 300 hotel accounts throughout the country with frequent telephone contact and presentations.**

Package Sales Representative, AAA-Motor Club, 1994-1996
A membership-based provider of property, casualty, life, and health insurance. **Responsible for selling and servicing of insurance products to clients through prospecting, face-to-face presentations, and account management.**

EDUCATION & HONORS

Indiana University, Bloomington, Indiana, 1993
School of Public and Environmental Affairs
B.S. in Public Affairs, Concentration in Management
Erasmus University, Rotterdam, The Netherlands, study abroad semester, 1992
Member of **Pi Alpha Alpha**, National Honor Society for Public Affairs and Administration, requires minimum **3.5 G.P.A.** and be in **top 10%** of graduating class

PAUL SHANKLE
Buyer/Planner
1234 Parkfield Drive, Champaign, IL 61820 ♦ (217) 123-4567 ♦ email@email.com

Experienced Buyer/Planner with strong skills in purchasing, material planning, vendor evaluation and negotiation, and material coordination. Excellent liaison between vendors, company staff, and customers. Detail-oriented to create bottom-line results by being proactive in resolving issues. B.S. in Public Affairs, concentration in Management.

PROFESSIONAL EXPERIENCE
Production Control Planner, Buyer/Planner
Fox Engineering, Inc.   December 2004 to June 2009
A producer of customer-specific gas delivery systems and cleaners for the semiconductor industry.

- Place and expedite purchase orders to meet ever-changing project timelines and production schedules.
- Manage outside vendor that supplies over **$100,000/year** of floor stock parts and materials.
- Reduced overall material costs by more than **5%** on a **$2.1 million** project for our customer Axcelis, obtaining quotes with quantity price breaks from several vendors.
- In 2006, saved the company over **$30,000** by using recalibrated excess materials in jobs.
- Work with Quality to process DMRs, expediting the repair or replacement of defective materials.
- Reduced Cisco product lead-time from **six to two weeks** for Port of Seattle airport project
- Have experience negotiating prices, shipping, and delivery services with vendors and customers, for both stock and custom-made products.
- In Production Control, worked as a liaison between purchasing, production, and management. Created work orders, scheduled the kitting of jobs, escalated and filled material shortages.
- As a Buyer/Planner, purchased and expedited materials based on daily planner code reports in Visual Enterprise, provided material commits to production, reduced inventories and material costs, obtained vendor commits for the return of RMA (DMR) materials.
- Reason for Leaving: Economic downturn resulted in company-wide layoff.

Buyer (Contract Employee)
Custom Test, Inc.   February 2004 to December 2004
A leading designer and manufacturer of custom electronic test equipment.

- Following a Bill of Materials (BOM), placed, tracked, and expedited orders of electronic components to be used in the production of custom equipment for projects.
- Reason for Leaving: Contract assignment ended.

Paul Shankle   page 2

PROFESSIONAL EXPERIENCE continued
Launch Coordinator (Contract Employee)
Williams Shaffer Realty International   January 2003 to December 2003
The fastest-growing real estate company in the U.S.

- As a System Administrator, provided support to new franchises and current associates for the company's computer technologies (intranets, websites, and e-mail accounts).
- Reason for Leaving: Pursue career in Purchasing and Vendor Management.

Proposal Specialist
Concurrent, L.L.C.   March 2002 to November 2002
A contractor of HP Computer Corporation, providing managed deployment services and ongoing asset management tools for HP's corporate customers.

- Supported the sales teams of Concurrent and HP by writing and producing proposals (RFPs, RFIs, RFQs), Statements of Work (SOWs), and project change orders.
- Reason for Leaving: Temporary assignment ended.

Sales & Marketing Representative (Contract Employee)
Kendall Electronics Corp./Avnet, Inc.   July 2000 to December 2001
Large value-added reseller (VAR) of computer networking equipment and services, creating end-to-end solutions for customers. Avnet is a Gold Partner of Cisco Systems, Inc.

- Supported field representatives by creating quotes and proposals, placing and expediting orders for projects, and developing solutions working with engineers and customers.
- Reason for Leaving: Contract ended.

Sales Agent (Contract Employee)
CC Computer Corporation   June 1999 to June 2000
Largest computer manufacturer in the U.S.

- In Large Corporate Accounts (LCA), sold and processed PC orders for an Excel Communications program and for the Employee Purchase Program (EPP).
- Promoted to Enterprise to work on the newly formed EPP for Enterprise, Global, and Large Corporate Accounts.
- Reason for Leaving: Contract ended.

EDUCATION & HONORS
B.S. in Public Affairs, Concentration in Management
Indiana University, Bloomington, Indiana
Erasmus University, Rotterdam, The Netherlands, study abroad semester
Member of **Pi Alpha Alpha**, National Honor Society for Public Affairs and Administration

COMPUTER SKILLS
Proficient in **Word, Excel, PowerPoint, Access, Outlook, MAS90, and Visual Enterprise.**

High Tech to Solar

Patrick Richter had a long and productive career with ABC Microsystems, utilizing his substantial engineering and program management skills. He was known for understanding the technology at a micro level, designing a slight modification, then finding a client that could use the technology. In the high-tech industry, this is called "strategic customer development," because it is literally creating customer business by anticipating their needs. His personal efforts yielded huge new revenue streams for the company. That nine-year career ended when ABC's sales plummeted with the economy.

As an electrical engineer, Patrick is intensely curious about the latest technology, so he has directed his job search to an emerging industry: solar. To prepare, he takes a college-level advanced photovoltaic class delivered by one of the nation's top experts. As a class project, he designs the solar system for the Laura Bush Library. This design project gives him the advantage he needs to compete with other engineers seeking the new, prized positions in solar companies.

Challenges to Making the Switch

Patrick's major challenge may be his wide breadth of experience. During his career, he has been both a designer and business executive. He has led many teams as a program manager and related at the highest client levels. However, his role has been technology expert, not sales. Most of the jobs advertised in solar companies are either design jobs (for which he doesn't have the photovoltaic design expertise) or sales positions (which he probably doesn't want). He also lacks the MBA requirement for this specific position.

Because Patrick has served as a general manager and had profit-and-loss responsibilities, he will need to convince a prospective employer that he would be happy in a product manager position. He will be looking for the blend of business development and product design. This is what energizes and thrills Patrick.

Transferable Skills

Design and launch of new products

Opening new markets

Creating strategic customers

Customer requirements and communication

Multicultural program management

Product road mapping

Executive interface

Job Description
Senior Product Manager—Solar

- More than five years of successful experience in product and/or program management, including execution of marketing strategies, implementing customer requirements, and product-launch processes

- Define and prioritize product requirements, develop a product road map, and recommend product direction; work with engineering to develop functional specifications

- Work with development groups during the complete development cycle to ensure the product meets market/customer requirements

- Demonstrate ability to work with the sales and business development organizations to drive designs and develop strategic customers

- Run beta and pilot programs with early-stage products and samples; develop and manage the customer support process and protocol

- Work with manufacturing operations and supply chain management on logistics management on final configuration and shipping and packaging specifications

- Requires a Bachelor's degree in science or engineering combined with an MBA

- Excellent communication skills including presentation experience to large and diverse audiences

- Prefer two or more years direct solar industry experience (production, development, supply chain, and implementation sectors), experienced user of Microsoft SharePoint, and experienced user of Primavera Enterprise V5 or later

Resume Makeover

Patrick's resume is excellent. It requires a slight rewrite and a new Resume Billboard to emphasize his interest in solar technologies.

❶ The headline tells where he is coming from ("Program Manager") and the job he is applying for ("Product Manager"). The subhead includes the term "Strategic Customer Development," which will be the challenge for any photovoltaic company.

❷ The opening statements sum up Patrick's experience and dedication to the profession. He includes continuing professional education units because he consistently takes twice the required units each year. In addition, he adds the course he has recently taken in photovoltaic design along with the course instructor, who is a recognized expert in the field.

❸ The Core Competencies section is written to reflect the requirements of the job description.

❹ His professional experience entries all begin with the company name because he wants to detail different job responsibilities during his long tenure with the company.

❺ His achievement statements are copied directly from his old resume—each one focused on significant business results that are easy for the reader to comprehend.

❻ Under Education & Affiliations, he has spelled out his degree, electrical engineering, and added "honor society" to the Eta Kappa Nu item.

❼ His professional and civic roles are grouped under the title of "Professional & Community Leadership." It is a personal choice whether to include a presidency of the local homeowners association or being a volunteer at school. These items give the impression that he has a balanced life and serves his community.

Patrick Richter, P.E.

1234 Any Street
Austin, TX 78749

512-123-1234 / 512-123-5678
email@email.com

Senior engineering leader recognized for design creativity and the ability to lead teams to produce excellent results. Responsible for eliciting customer requirements and establishing systems-level design within each of the three constraints – schedule, cost, and technical requirements. Functional areas of accountability span technology direction and strategy, process and quality improvement, budgeting, business analysis, partner management, consulting, collaboration, and detailed system, control, logic and software engineering.

**Cross Functional Teamwork ~ Design and Launch New Products ~ Open New Markets
Accelerate Product Development and Growth ~ Customer Requirements and Communication
Multicultural Program Management ~ Executive Interface**

CAREER HISTORY

ABC MICROSYSTEMS, Austin, TX   1999 – 2008
Senior Engineering Product Program Manager (reporting to VP of engineering) **(2004 – 2008)**
Led teams to define product architecture and strategy, develop requirements, obtain business plan approval, implement, deliver and support from initial production to end of life. Provided system-level and detailed implementation-level customer technical consulting, including software / hardware trade-off analysis, to enable these servers and derivatives to be embedded into customer products to support real time applications, including ship-board applications for the Navy. Primary systems-level contact for technical customer consulting, presentations, technical proposals.
- *T6320 CMT blade server* – first quarter shipments exceeded forecast by 50%.
- *B125 server* – to date has produced $12M, all incremental revenue to the original plan. Four months from concept to production, enabled by innovative development processes.
- *B215/245 servers* – to date have produced more than twice the projected revenue.
- *B210/240 servers* – at $2B, exceeded original revenue projections of $1.4B.
- Reduced the cost of the V210/240 by 20% after transferring products from the UK.
- Merged UK-based ABC products into the U.S. organization to increase efficiency 50%.
- Detected and corrected a long-standing silent data corruption issue without any significant customer impact.
- Created B125 server in four months - $12M incremental revenue beyond original plan.

Senior Development Manager (1999 – 2004)
Consulted and managed teams to create products and expand customer base.
- Consulted to win Lucent as a customer and make ABC the telco platform of choice.
Primary systems-level contact for technical customer presentations, technical proposals and porting. This was key to winning several billion dollars telco and embedded business.
- Led and managed the design of the Vetra HA software suite.
- Created the B1600 blade concept, ABC's first entry into the blade server market.

Site Leader (1999 – 2001)
Host-managed Local Teams / Recruited Talent / Managed Site Services / Led Site Council
- Established the ABC Austin Engineering site — grew from 3 to 300 employees in one year.

Patrick Richter, P.E.   512-123-1234 / 512-123-5678   email@email.com   Pg. 2

ABC -TEL, Austin, TX   1997 – 1998
Senior Development Manager
- Developed ABC-based system-level products to support present and future demands.
- Led teams to define systems from high-level customer requirements to detailed systems, board and component level design.

LONE STAR INSTRUMENTS, Austin, TX   1982 – 1997
Deputy General Manager (1996 – 1997)
Primary business and systems-level technical interface managing 125 employees.
- Sold Lone Star Telecom Systems (125 employees) intact – excellent value for LONE STAR, ABC-TEL, and the employees — saved each company millions of dollars and maintained jobs for employees.

Senior Member Technical Staff / Senior Development Manager / Systems Engineering Manager
- Consulted with a wide variety of customers to bring Lone Star Instruments speech technology into the telco marketplace. Enabled voice dialing in the telco marketplace.
- Managed the third-party design of a SPARC processor to replace a Motorola processor in a Nubus system and ported the entire system to Solaris with the assistance of a lone software engineer. The move to current industry standards decreased software development and maintenance efforts by 30%.
- Systems architect for a geographically distributed DSP-based speech recognition system, including one of the largest distributed online databases of the time.
- Principal designer for the DSP-based system.
- Contributed to LONE STAR DSP internal architecture.
- Built the LONE STAR Telecom Systems team to address the emerging multimedia market. Defined the system architecture, established engineering and manufacturing processes, and managed media server design teams. Managed third party design and manufacturing partners.
- Designed the bidirectional fiber optic monitor interface – Explorer LISP workstation.
- Chairman of the test strategy team and new product introduction team.
- Designed power supplies, infrared LAN links, and process control systems.
- Production engineer for a variety of products at Lone Star Instruments.

EDUCATION AND CERTIFICATIONS

BSEE, Rice University, Eta Kappa Nu
Licensed Engineer Texas #75053
U.S. Patent # 5457786 Serial Data Interface with Circular Buffer

COMMUNITY AND PROFESSIONAL AFFILIATIONS

Former President of the Board – West Creek HOA
Past Chairman IEEE Acoustics, Speech and Signal Processing Society
Volunteer science lab manager – West Creek Elementary
Sunday school teacher – West Hills Presbyterian Church

PATRICK RICHTER, PE

1234 Any Street • Austin, TX 78749 • email@email.com • 512.123.5678 cell

PRODUCT / PROGRAM MANAGER

Registered Engineer / Strategic Customer Development / Solar Expertise

- Recognized for design creativity and ability to lead multicultural product launch teams
- Elicit customer requirements and establish systems-level design
- Led six blade-server product launches, exceeding business forecasts by 20–50%
- Tenacious in building relationships with strategic customers, creating slight technology upgrades that yield huge revenue streams
- Consistently complete 30 units yearly of continuing education as professional engineer (15 required)
- Successfully completed "Advanced Photovoltaics" Course led by John Hopper at Austin Community College; designed solar system for the new Laura Bush Library

Core Competencies

- Design and prioritize product requirements
- Develop strategic customers
- Multicultural team leadership
- Patent Holder – Serial data interface
- Program road-mapping
- Contact for system-level technical proposals
- Beta testing of early-stage products
- Coordination with supply chain, logistics, shipping
- Microsoft SharePoint
- Primavera Enterprise V5
- P&L responsibility
- Embedded servers and derivatives

--- **PROFESSIONAL EXPERIENCE** ---

ABC MICROSYSTEMS, Austin, TX
Senior Engineering Product Program Manager (reporting to VP of engineering) **(2004 – 2008)**   1999 – 2008
Led teams to define product architecture and strategy, develop requirements, obtain business plan approval, implement, deliver, and support from initial production to end of life. Provided system-level and detailed implementation-level customer technical consulting, including software / hardware trade-off analysis, to enable these servers and derivatives to be embedded into customer products to support real time applications, including ship-board applications for the Navy. Primary systems-level contact for technical customer consulting, presentations, technical proposals.

- *T6320 CMT blade server* – first-quarter shipments exceeded forecast by 50%.
- *B125 server* – to date has produced $12M, all incremental revenue to the original plan. Four months from concept to production, enabled by innovative development processes.
- *B215/245 servers* – to date have produced more than twice the projected revenue.
- *B210/240 servers* – at $2B, exceeded original revenue projections of $1.4B.
- Reduced the cost of the V210/240 by 20% after transferring products from the UK.
- Merged UK-based ABC products into the U.S. organization to increase efficiency 50%.
- Detected and corrected a long-standing silent data corruption issue without any significant customer impact.
- Created B125 server in four months — $12M incremental revenue beyond original plan.

Senior Development Manager (1999 – 2004)
Consulted and managed teams to create products and expand customer base.
- Consulted to win Lucent as a customer and make ABC the telco platform of choice.
- Primary systems-level contact for technical customer presentations, technical proposals and porting. This was key to winning several billion dollars telco and embedded business.
- Led and managed the design of the Vetra HA software suite.
- Created the B1600 blade concept, ABC's first entry into the blade server market.

Site Leader (1999 – 2001)
Host-managed Local Teams / Recruited Talent / Managed Site Services / Led Site Council
- Established the ABC Austin Engineering site – grew from 3 to 300 employees in one year.

512.123.5678

ABC-TEL, Austin, TX   1997 – 1998
Senior Development Manager
- Developed ABC-based system-level products to support present and future demands.
- Led teams to define systems from high level customer requirements to detailed systems, board and component level design.

LONE STAR INSTRUMENTS, Austin, TX   1982 – 1997
Deputy General Manager (1996 – 1997)
Primary business and systems-level technical interface managing 125 employees.
- Sold Lone Star Telecom Systems (125 employees) intact – excellent value for LONE STAR, ABC-TEL and the employees — saved each company millions of dollars and maintained jobs for employees.

Senior Member Technical Staff / Senior Development Manager / Systems Engineering Manager
- Consulted with a wide variety of customers to bring Texas Instruments speech technology into the telco marketplace. Enabled voice dialing in the telco marketplace.
- Managed the third party design of a SPARC processor to replace a Motorola processor in a Nubus system and ported the entire system to Solaris with the assistance of a lone software engineer. The move to current industry standards decreased software development and maintenance efforts by 30%.
- Systems architect for a geographically distributed DSP-based speech recognition system, including one of the largest distributed online databases of the time.
- Principal designer for the DSP-based system.
- Contributed to LONE STAR DSP internal architecture.
- Built the LONE STAR Telecom Systems team to address the emerging multimedia market.
- Defined the system architecture, established engineering and manufacturing processes, and managed media server design teams. Managed third party design and manufacturing partners.
- Designed the bidirectional fiber optic monitor interface – Explorer LISP workstation.
- Chairman of the test strategy team and new product introduction team.
- Designed power supplies, infrared LAN links, and process control systems.
- Production engineer for a variety of products at Lone Star Instruments.

--- **EDUCATION & AFFILIATIONS** ---

BS, Electrical Engineering, Rice University, Eta Kappa Nu Honor Society
Licensed Engineer Texas #75053
U.S. Patent # 5457786 Serial Data Interface with Circular Buffer

--- **PROFESSIONAL & COMMUNITY LEADERSHIP** ---

Past Chairman IEEE Acoustics, Speech and Signal Processing Society
Former President of the Board – West Creek HOA
Volunteer science lab manager – West Creek Elementary
Sunday school teacher – West Hills Presbyterian Church

Homebuilder to Government Construction

Construction of new homes in the United States is in a slump, and Kent Tyndall has had trouble finding work. He is tough and not afraid of a challenging environment, so he has decided to look for work in construction overseas. He is particularly interested in work in Iraq or Afghanistan with an international construction company because of the high pay rates. His plan is to work overseas for a couple years while he saves his pay and waits for the construction industry in the United States to pick up again.

Challenges to Making the Switch

International construction jobs require leadership and flexibility in addition to the specific skills required to build a house or office building. Kent has demonstrated these skills in his work, but he needs to emphasize them on his resume and during the interview process.

His employer will spend time and money just getting him to the job site to start work, so they will want some assurance that he is capable of enduring heat, unfamiliar environments, and diverse workgroups. His experience working in construction in both Florida and Texas are valuable evidence of this.

Transferable Skills

Master carpenter

Plumber

Construction supervisor

Field supervision

Reading blueprints

Drywall installation

Planning/calculating material needed

Vendor/supplier relationships

Job Description

Government Construction Carpenter

- Knowledge of residential construction and remodeling trades, practices, procedures, techniques, tools and equipment, materials, specifications, quality control, cost control, and safety

- Proficient in the following tasks: stain-grade trim work, hang doors, drill and set door hardware, set windows, layout for stairs and common rafters, and utilize appropriate math skills

- Able to read blueprints

- Mathematical skills and analytical skills necessary to perform material estimates

- Requires ability to perform tasks in all areas and aspects of construction project; requires ability to climb ladders for heights of up to 60 feet and crawl for distances of 50 feet

- Job requires ability to work with tools, lumber, and materials; ability to lift and manipulate objects of up to 80 pounds for 50 feet is required

- Adept at establishing relationships with all parties involved in the construction process that facilitate harmonious working relationships during the project; permit prompt resolution of problems and conflicts as they occur

---

Resume Makeover

Kent's original resume requires the reader to be familiar with a carpenter's tasks on a job and does not list any specific responsibilities or experience beyond the job description.

1 At the top of the resume, add a professional profile that shows his years of experience and highlights his background as a supervisor. He includes mention of a security clearance, which may be important to being hired for overseas government work.

2 After the Professional Profile section, his specific construction skills are listed to demonstrate his versatility and the extent of his abilities.

3 For each job, include details of supervisory and leadership activities, specific tasks performed, and unique challenges associated with the work.

4 His certification as a carpenter is separated from his Education section to call attention to it.

5 His computer knowledge is listed to further demonstrate his ability to live overseas and communicate as needed.

Kent Tyndall

1234 Any Road, Georgetown, TX 78628
(512) 123-4567
email@email.com

Experience:

Self-Employed Carpenter	Austin, Texas	2006 – Present
Lead Carpenter	Atlantic Framing Virginia Beach, VA	1992 – 2006
Field Supervisor	Snap Contracting Norfolk, VA	1989 – 1992
Self-Employed Carpenter	Norfolk, VA	1986 – 1989
Carpenter	Brian Fiske Design Build Foxboro-Sharon, MA	1985 (Six Months)
Field Supervisor, Carpenter	Surfside Builders Norfolk, VA	1981 – 1985
Carpenter	Superior Services Virginia Beach, VA	1980 – 1981
Carpenter	Seacoast Builder Newport, RI	1978 – 1980
Form Carpenter	Water & Utility Contractors Jacksonville, FL	1978 (Six Months)
Self-Employed Carpenter	Brevard County, FL	1976 – 1978
Truck Driver	Hudson Refuse Ft. Walton, FL	1975
Laborer, Rod Man	Evans & Mitchell Industries San Destin, FL	1973 – 1974

EDUCATION

Rhode Island Junior College – Liberal Arts, Completed 12 hours
GED – State of Florida 1977

Certified Carpenter, State of Florida - 1977

Kent Tyndall

1234 Any Road, Georgetown, TX 78628
(512) 123-4567 • email@email.com

❶ PROFESSIONAL PROFILE

Seasoned master carpenter with 30 years experience in residential, commercial, and industrial construction and renovation. Field Supervisor for crews of up to 15. Received security clearance to work on U.S. Naval base and port facilities.

❷ CONSTRUCTION SKILLS

Cabinets – installation & trim
Concrete – forming, placement, finish
Electrical – wiring
Plumbing – minor repairs
Flooring – vinyl, wood, ceramic, V.A.T., laminate
Framing – residential & commercial, custom and tract homes
Trim – interior trim and cornice
Roofing – shingle, roll roofing, terra cotta, slate
Painting – interior and exterior; roll & brush
Landscaping – tree trimming, planting
Wallboard – hang, float & finish; and some texture
Windows and doors – hang, trim, retrofit

❸ PROFESSIONAL WORK HISTORY

Self-Employed Carpenter   **2006–Present**   **Austin, TX**
Projects: Residential remodeling including window and door replacement; wallboard installation, tape and float; laminate flooring; interior trim; deck construction; ceramic tile; concrete; painting; minor electrical work

Atlantic Framing   **1992–2006**   **Virginia Beach, VA**
Lead Carpenter
Responsibilities: Residential framing, supervised crew of carpenters

Snap Contracting   **1989–1992**   **Norfolk, VA**
Field Supervisor
Responsibilities: Supervised crews of 2-15 people on Federal Contracts for residential renovation and industrial construction – Naval Operations Base, Norfolk; Coast Guard Base, Portsmouth; Oceana Naval Air Station and Damneck Training Facility, Virginia Beach; Ft Eustis, Newport News; Norfolk Naval Ship Yard, Portsmouth; NADEP, Norfolk (36-seat theatre, 4 conference rooms)

Self-Employed Carpenter   **1986–1989**   **Norfolk, VA**
Projects: Remodeling, renovation, office construction, interior trim

Brian Fiske Design Build   **1985 (Six Months)**   **Foxboro-Sharon, MA**
Carpenter
Responsibilities: Swedish interior trim, framed apartment buildings in Providence, RI

Kent Tyndall Resume – page 2

Surfside Builders   **1981–1985**   **Norfolk, VA**
Field Supervisor, Carpenter
Responsibilities: Remodeling, renovation, new construction. Field supervisor for a crew of four on government contracts such as Norfolk Naval Shipyard – firewalls, stairwells; Little Creek Amphibious Naval Base – movie theaters; Ft Story Army Base – remodeled barracks, installation of storm windows

Superior Services   **1980–1981**   **Virginia Beach, VA**
Carpenter
Responsibilities: Insurance work – repair of fire, water, storm damage

Seacoast Builders   **1978–1980**   **Newport, RI**
Carpenter
Responsibilities: Restoration, renovation of historical homes; new construction and remodeling

Water & Utility Contractors   **1978 (Six Months)**   **Jacksonville, FL**
Form Carpenter
Responsibilities: Erection of forms, placement of concrete for city sewage plant, culverts, curbs and gutters

Self-Employed Carpenter   **1976–1978**   **Brevard County, FL**

Hudson Refuse   **1975**   **Ft Walton, FL**
Truck Driver
Responsibilities: Driving, removal of refuse

Evans & Mitchell Industries   **1973–1974**   **San Destin, FL**
Laborer, Rod Man
Responsibilities: Shooting grades on roads and building sites

❹ EDUCATION

Rhode Island Junior College – Liberal Arts, Completed 12 hours
GED – State of Florida 1977

❹ SPECIALIZED TRAINING

Certified Carpenter, State of Florida – 1977

❺ RELEVANT SOFTWARE

- Email – Yahoo, AOL
- Internet Use

Hospitality to Government

California's declining hospitality industry forces Meghan Goldsmith to look at other industries. She wants to continue in the accounting field but longs for a work/life balance that is missing from her demanding schedule with hotels and casinos. After making a list of what she values most in a job, she surveys possibilities and determines that crossing over to a public agency would be ideal. Meghan is willing to take a pay cut for the opportunity to have more time with family and friends. In addition, the state benefits and pension plan are especially attractive because Meghan's retirement portfolio has taken a beating during the stock market decline. Meghan pinpoints auditing positions because of her extensive experience in that area and highlights her many transferable skills on an expanded resume that she submits with a customized state application.

Challenges to Making the Switch

Meghan has not worked in the public sector before and is concerned that she may appear overqualified for a junior-level auditor position. She fears that her high salary will eliminate her from serious consideration because friends have told her that government agencies are reluctant to hire people who may leave for better-paying jobs when the economy improves. Meghan tries to overcome the stigma of being overqualified by carefully tailoring her resume and application to highlight qualifications and keywords found in the job description. She downplays references to higher-level experiences.

Public agencies are a magnet for mid-career professionals who do not want to continue working long hours under stressful conditions found in declining industries. Meghan gathers as much information as she can to make her submission more attractive and follows up on recommendations from friends at state agencies. She decides to change her functional resume back to a chronological format with details of her work history so that it can be copied to online applications required by the state. (Functional and chronological resume styles are discussed at the beginning of Chapter 2.)

Transferable Skills

Auditing	Reviewing and analyzing records
Accounting	Training
Computer skills	Interpersonal skills

Job Description

State Agency Auditor

- A minimum of two years auditing or accounting experience

- A degree from an accredited university with a minimum of six units in accounting or auditing

- Experience in gathering and tabulating data, reviewing prior audit records and reports, and analyzing records in accordance with established policies and procedures

- Knowledge of rules and regulations administered by the Financial Services division

- Knowledge of personal computers and familiarity with Word, Excel, and other computer programs

- Work well under pressure

- Communicate well both orally and in writing

- Good interpersonal skills

- Willingness to accept additional responsibilities

Resume Makeover

1 An Objective Statement pinpoints the job title and agency, which is key in understanding the focus.

2 The Qualifications Summary section pulls together key skills and experiences stated in the job description.

3 The Computer Skills section is moved up and given its own table because computer skills are key qualifiers for this position.

4 The Professional Experience section is revamped to a chronological style with details about job duties.

5 Auditing and related accounting experiences are highlighted; management experience is downplayed.

6 The Honors section is dropped because the references to school and hospitality are not relevant.

Meghan B. Goldsmith
77 East James Street, Thousand Oaks, CA 91360 • Home: (805) 123-4567 • e-mail: email@email.com

PROFESSIONAL EXPERIENCE

Regional Controller
- Responsible for overseeing the month-end process for up to 12 full-service hotels concurrently.
- Created financial statements and reports utilizing multiple software packages; trained others in the use of this software to enhance overall company productivity.
- Reviewed and approved budgets and forecasts for multi-million dollar properties.
- Submitted all State/County/City Sales/Use, Gross/Transaction Privilege & Transient Occupancy taxes for the following states: California, Arizona, Colorado and New Mexico.
- Provided key support to the planning and implementation of acquisitions and divestitures.
- Traveled on an as needed basis for training and development of property controllers and their staff.
- Locations included: San Diego Resort & Golf Club (AZ), Huntington Hyatt (NY), Napa Valley Fairfield (CA), Pueblo Sunrise (CO), and Santa Fe Hyatt (NM).

Revenue Accounting
- Trained and supervised 14 revenue audit clerks for 11 daily audits.
- Responsible for accounting of all revenues received for a $550 million hotel and full-service casino.
- Reconciled accounts for fiscal and calendar month-end.
- Created and maintained spreadsheets for all audit areas, tax reporting, and financial analysis.
- Complied with state and federal government regulations and reporting requirements.

Financial Accounting
- Managed and directed all financial activities for a 357-room hotel and casino.
- Advised management regarding desirable financial and operational activities.
- Responded to accounting-related inquiries from state and federal government agencies.
- Safeguarded over $12 million worth of assets.
- Built spreadsheets to streamline the auditing process.
- Oversaw maintenance and troubleshooting for all computer hard/software systems and vendors.

Office Manager
- Controlled all office functions including payroll, human resources, accounting, credit and collection, customer service, accounts receivable, and accounts payable.
- Installed and managed integrated computer accounting system.
- Solicited and published advertisements for an annual listing of all contractors licensed in the state of Nevada.

EMPLOYMENT HISTORY

Sunrise Hotel Properties, LLC, San Clemente, CA	Regional Controller	January 2007 – Present
Skinner Gaming Corp., Las Vegas, NV	Revenue Accounting Manager	July 2000 – January 2007
Newton Inn – Town Hall Casino, Las Vegas, NV	Controller	August 1997 – July 2000
Governesis, Las Vegas, NV	Office Manager	January 1997 – August 1997
Newton Inn – Town Hall Casino, Las Vegas, NV	Auditor	August 1994 – January 1997

EDUCATION
Currently preparing for **CPA** exam
UNIVERSITY OF NEVADA, LAS VEGAS, **MBA** courses
UNIVERSITY OF NEVADA, LAS VEGAS, **B. Sc., Accounting**, 2000
MOORPARK COLLEGE, Moorpark, CA, **A. Sc., Accounting and A. A., Liberal Studies**, 1991

COMPUTERS
MS Office, Best Enterprise Suite, FRX Reporting, FrontPage, Unifocus, Quick Books, Peachtree, Basic

HONORS

Outstanding Business Student Award – The Wall Street Journal
❻ Hospitality Financial & Technology Professionals

the Kil Kostner Memorial Scholarship
Dean's List – multiple semesters

Meghan B. Goldsmith

55 East James Street • Thousand Oaks, CA 91360 • (805) 123-4567 • email@email.com

OBJECTIVE: An Auditor/Evaluator position with the California State Auditor

QUALIFICATIONS SUMMARY

- More than eight years of auditing and accounting experience
- Bachelor of Science degree in accounting and currently preparing for the CPA exam
- Diverse experience in gathering and tabulating data, reviewing prior audit records and reports, and analyzing records according to government regulations and corporate policies
- Accepted additional responsibilities for training audit clerks to update them on new state regulations and tax reporting procedures
- Accustomed to working under pressure and meeting daily deadlines while frequently traveling in California and throughout the U.S.

COMPUTER SKILLS

MS Office	Best Enterprise Suite	FRX Reporting	FrontPage
Unifocus	QuickBooks	Peachtree	
Visual Basic			

PROFESSIONAL EXPERIENCE

Sunrise Hotel Properties, LLC, San Clemente, CA   Jan. 2007 – Present
Regional Controller
- Oversee the month-end process for up to 12 full-service hotels
- Create financial statements and reports utilizing multiple software packages
- Submit all State/County/City Sales/Use, Gross/Transaction Privilege & Transient Occupancy taxes for California, Arizona, Colorado, and New Mexico
- Train others in the use of this software to enhance overall company productivity
- Review and approve budgets and forecasts for multi-million-dollar properties
- Travel to train and develop staff at locations in California, Arizona, New Mexico, Colorado, and New York

Skinner Gaming Corp., Las Vegas, NV   July 2000 – Jan. 2007
Revenue Accounting Manager
- Oversaw accounting of all revenues received for a $550 million hotel and full-service casino
- Created and maintained spreadsheets for all audit areas, tax reporting, and financial analysis
- Complied with state and federal government regulations and reporting requirements
- Reconciled accounts for fiscal and calendar month-end
- Trained and supervised revenue audit clerks for 11 daily audits

Meghan B. Goldsmith/Page 2

Newton Inn – Town Hall Casino, Las Vegas, NV   Aug. 1997 – July 2000
Controller
- Oversaw financial activities for a 357-room hotel and casino
- Responded to accounting-related inquiries from state and federal government agencies
- Built spreadsheets to streamline the auditing process
- Advised management regarding desirable financial and operational activities
- Troubleshot computer hardware/software systems problems for vendors

Governesis, Las Vegas, NV   Jan. 1997 – Aug. 1997
Office Manager
- Controlled all office functions including payroll, human resources, accounting, credit and collection, customer service, accounts receivable, and accounts payable
- Installed and managed integrated computer accounting system
- Updated, published, and solicited advertisements for an annual listing of all contractors licensed in the state of Nevada

Newton Inn – Town Hall Casino, Las Vegas, NV   Aug. 1994 – Jan.1997
Auditor
- Audited, balanced, and reported on all food and beverage outlets, cash and credit operations, house charges, promotional materials, and postings
- Audited, balanced, posted, and reported on the front desk, including room charges, phone calls, zero balance folios, corrections, adjustments, taxes, disputed charges, and deposits
- Prepared and input statistics and income journal sheets for preparation of daily reports
- Balanced and closed all bank ticket codes on a daily basis
- Ran night audit finals after ensuring all revenues were in balance

EDUCATION

Currently preparing for CPA exam

MBA courses, 2006
University of Nevada, Las Vegas

Bachelor of Science, Accounting, 2000
University of Nevada, Las Vegas

Associate of Science in Accounting and Associate of Arts in Liberal Studies, 1991
Moorpark College, Moorpark, CA

Internet Advertising to Software as a Service (SaaS)

Lorraine West had been a successful software-as-a-service (SaaS) sales manager when her company went through a corporate reorganization. She was transferred to another company and expected to work her same magic in Internet sales. For months, she learned everything she could about Internet marketing but found the medium extremely challenging. She couldn't cultivate the same strong relationships with clients, and despite working harder than ever, her commission sales salary steadily declined. The day the company vice president called her in to let her go, Lorraine felt a sense of relief. Now, she realizes that she has been shifted to the wrong industry and decides it is in her best interest to return to the arena where she excels.

Challenges to Making the Switch

For two years, Lorraine has been away from her specialty of SaaS sales. She begins rebuilding her network and finds that some of her former clients and coworkers have moved away. The good thing, however, is that the SaaS industry is hot now, and she finds multiple job opportunities in the Raleigh, North Carolina, area and other cities where she considers relocating. She hopes to accentuate her past success and downplay her lack of recent experience.

Many of the SaaS jobs require a Bachelor's degree, and Lorraine only finished 30 hours at a community college. She decides to apply for all positions—whether they require a degree or not—believing her seven years of experience should be counted as the equivalent of a degree. Lorraine recalls that many of the top salespeople she knows didn't finish college, and she hopes to be given fair consideration.

Although Lorraine is relieved to be out of Internet sales, she is concerned about the stigma of being let go from a company. She has glowing letters of recommendation from former employers and clients; however, she's concerned about whether her reputation will suffer because of her recent bad experience. She prepares damage control by planning positive ways to discuss her last job and checks with her former company's human resources director to find out what will be disclosed when companies do a reference check.

Transferable Skills

Consultative sales	Account planning
Prospecting	Leadership
Negotiating	Account forecasting
Cold-calling	Pipeline management
Closing	

Job Description

Internet Advertising to Software as a Service Sales Specialist

- Directly related previous work experience and demonstrating achievement of progressively higher quota and diversity of business customer

- More than seven years of advanced sales experience and a BS/BA degree

- Deep knowledge of software-as-a-service offering as well as competitive offerings and ability to integrate this knowledge into consultative selling

- Client engagement skills to collaborate with account leads to develop creative solutions to meet customer needs

- Demonstrating leadership and initiative in successfully driving specialty sales in accounts

- Account planning and accurate account revenue forecasting skills

- Prospecting, negotiating, and closing deals

- Ability to collaborate with management and sales teams in shared accounts to ensure the seamless integration of specialist sales with other sales activities

Resume Makeover

Lorraine's resume is revised to accentuate her qualifications and especially her record of success in her former field.

1 Subtle format changes are made, including increasing the font size of the body copy from 10 to 11 pt.

2 The Career Objective section specifies SaaS sales executive.

3 The name for this section is changed from "Profile" to "Qualifications" because the content focuses on SaaS skills and is not a general career overview.

4 The Qualifications section uses keywords and information that is directly related to her desired job.

5 Her impressive technical skills are moved from the bottom of her original resume to the Qualifications section.

6 Minimal information is included about her last job, and no reference is made to Internet sales.

7 The Professional Experience section is shortened to highlight skills that transfer to the new industry.

LORRAINE WEST
919-123-4567

123 Any Lane, Raleigh, NC 27605
email@email.com

CAREER OBJECTIVE
Results-driven professional and known hunter looking to contribute directly to the bottom line.

3

PROFILE
- Dynamic communication, presentation, relationship-building, solution-selling, and problem-solving abilities.
- Offer extensive lead generation and business development experience, with comprehensive management background.
- Effectively define, develop and implement targeted action plans to maximize operational productivity, efficiency and profitability.
- Proactive leader who successfully recruits, trains, develops mentors, and leads top-performing teams committed to providing superior service.
- Exceptional ability to research and evaluate industry trends and competitor products and use findings to design and execute innovative strategies to boost company leveraging in a saturated market.
- Excel at interacting with broad populations, including senior management, sales and customer service staff, as well as clients and external contractors.

KEY ACHIEVEMENTS
- Exceeded sales quota by applying solid presentation and interpersonal skills. Key clients included Nielsen NetRatings and Vantage Media.
- Innovatively designed, developed and implemented a Lead Generation program. Leads generated accounted for 60% of new revenue within 6 months and surpassed quota by 110%.
- Successfully leveraged partners' client base to maintain the #1 ranking territory for 8 consecutive quarters and produced 50% of the company's revenue.
- Directly collaborated with key clients, including Wachovia First Union, Calpine Energy, Reliant Energy, Valero, Verizon, WorldCom, and other major accounts.
- Generated over $250K in revenue by independently developing key customers, leading to the first enterprise-level accounts purchasing *NetBox* Enterprise solution products.

PROFESSIONAL EXPERIENCE
AdEvolution – Raleigh, NC   2007-2009
National Sales Executive
- Developed sales funnel from prospecting through development and close for an Internet advertising company.
- Contacted and nurtured pipeline, attended trade shows, and educated prospects on product.
- Executed and negotiated contracts.

Data Media – Raleigh, NC   2004-2007
Sales Director
- Attained 115% of $2M quota. Earned commissions in excess of $100K.
- Sold software and services packages with an average sale of $200K and up.
- Introduced responsible list management and performance marketing, demonstrating creativity and interpersonal relationship skills.

7

Activa – Raleigh, NC   2003-2004
Inside Sales/Lead Generation Manager
- Spearheaded diverse administrative activities, including staffing, training, and development for all aspects of the lead generation team, exhibiting solid leadership qualities.
- Sold SaaS services and attained 110% of $750K quota.
- Independently created compensation structure and definition of leads instrumental to boosting productivity and efficiency.

NetBox Inc. – San Diego, CA   2000-2003
Western Sales Manager
- Applied sales expertise and strong analytical skills toward successfully cultivating Western territory through cold calls, prompt client follow-up, and targeted project plans.
- Sold hardware and enterprise software solutions averaging in price between 75K and 250K. Exceeded quota 8 straight quarters and developed the first multi-million-dollar revenue-producing territory.
- Actively developed a strong enterprise-level client-base, including Wachovia First Union, Verizon, and WorldCom.
- Conducted comprehensive industry research and analysis to initiate and implement successful sales strategies, generating optimal results.

Apple Computer – Cupertino, CA   1999-2000
Apple Education Specialist, New York City Board of Education
- Contributed dynamic strategic marketing, cold-calling, and presentation skills toward successfully penetrating competitive markets and capturing 4 accounts within Queens high school district that had previously not used Apple technologies.
- Effectively planned, coordinated, and facilitated sales functions to optimize performance, exceeding $39M quota.

Sunset Marketing – San Diego, CA   1998-1999
Solutions Specialist/Team Leader
- Produced $9M in lead generation per quarter and closed $4M, working both direct and channel markets.
- Consistently chosen to be a member of the company's "Top Ten" performers computed by number of closed sales, qualified leads, and contacts, demonstrating exceptional project management and sales abilities in achieving operational goals and timelines.

EDUCATION & PROFESSIONAL TRAINING
Select Courses – Antelope Valley Junior College (Palmdale, CA)

Enterprise Storage Training – Amdahl
Outsource Messaging Solutions – Allegro
Infowave – Remote Access for Email
L & H Voice Express
Flow Charting – Micrografx
Exchange – Microsoft
Meeting Maker – On Technologies
Browser Security – Surf Control
Sony
Live Security – Watchguard

5

TECHNICAL SKILLS
Mac and PC environments; Microsoft Office, FileMaker, Outlook, GoldMine, Act, Saleslogix, Salesforce, PowerPoint, Pagemaker, Photoshop, GroupWise, Exchange, MIMEsweeper

90

❶ LORRAINE WEST

123 Any Lane • Raleigh, NC 27605
919-123-4567 • email@email.com

❷ CAREER OBJECTIVE

SaaS Sales Executive position utilizing experience contributing directly to the bottom line

❸ QUALIFICATIONS

⋏ More than seven years of advanced Software-as-a-Service experience with a record of surpassing quotas and developing multi-million-dollar territories.

⋏ Use consultative sales approach to develop new customers by sharing in-depth knowledge of Software-as-a-Service offerings.

❹ ⋏ Exceptional ability to research and evaluate industry trends and competitor products and use findings to design and execute innovative strategies to boost profits in a saturated market.

⋏ Proactive leader who successfully recruits, trains, develops, mentors, and leads top-performing teams committed to providing superior service.

❺ ⋏ Skilled in account planning and accurate account revenue forecasting.

⋏ Technical Skills: Mac and PC environments; Microsoft Office, FileMaker, Outlook, GoldMine, Act, Saleslogix, Salesforce, PowerPoint, Pagemaker, Photoshop, GroupWise, Exchange, and MIMEsweeper.

KEY ACHIEVEMENTS

⋏ Innovatively designed, developed and implemented a Lead Generation program. Leads accounted for 60% of new revenue within 6 months and surpassed quota by 110%.

⋏ Successfully leveraged partners' client base to maintain the #1 ranking territory for 8 consecutive quarters and produced 50% of the company's revenue.

⋏ Exceeded sales quota by applying solid presentation and interpersonal skills. Key clients included Nielsen NetRatings and Vantage Media.

⋏ Directly collaborated with key clients, including Wachovia First Union, Calpine Energy, Reliant Energy, Valero, Verizon, WorldCom, and other major accounts.

⋏ Generated more than $250K in revenue by independently developing key customers, leading to the first enterprise-level accounts purchasing NetBox Enterprise solution products.

❻ PROFESSIONAL EXPERIENCE

AdEvolution – Raleigh, NC   2007 – 2009
National Sales Executive
• Developed sales funnel from prospecting through development and close.
• Contacted and nurtured pipeline, attended trade shows and educated prospects on product.

Data Media – Raleigh, NC   2004 – 2007
Sales Director
• Attained 115% of $2M quota. Earned commissions in excess of $100K.
• Sold software and services packages with average sales of more than $200K.
• Introduced responsible list management and performance marketing, demonstrating creativity and interpersonal relationship skills.

Activa – Raleigh, NC   2003 – 2004
❼ Inside Sales/Lead Generation Manager
• Sold SaaS services and attained 110% of $750K quota.
• Independently created compensation structure and definition of leads instrumental to boosting productivity and efficiency.
• Managed diverse activities, including staffing, training, and development for all aspects of the lead generation team.

LORRAINE WEST

NetBox Inc. – San Diego, CA   2000 – 2003
Western Sales Manager
• Sold hardware and enterprise software solutions averaging in price between 75K and 250K.
• Exceeded quota eight straight quarters and developed the first multimillion-dollar revenue-producing territory.
• Successfully cultivated Western region through cold calls, prompt client follow-up, and targeted project plans.
• Actively developed a strong enterprise-level client-base, including Wachovia First Union, Verizon, and WorldCom.
• Conducted comprehensive industry research and analysis to initiate and implement successful sales strategies, generating optimal results.

Apple Computer – Cupertino, CA   1999 – 2000
Apple Education Specialist, New York City Board of Education
• Contributed dynamic strategic marketing, cold-calling, and presentation skills toward successfully penetrating competitive markets and capturing four accounts within Queens high school district that had previously not used Apple technologies.
• Effectively planned, coordinated, and facilitated sales functions to optimize performance, exceeding $39M quota.

Sunset Marketing – San Diego, CA   1998 – 1999
Solutions Specialist/Team Leader
• Produced $9 million in lead generation per quarter and closed $4 million, working both direct and channel markets.
• Consistently chosen to be a member of the company's "Top Ten" performers computed by number of closed sales, qualified leads, and contacts.
• Demonstrated exceptional project management and sales abilities in achieving operational goals and timelines.

EDUCATION & PROFESSIONAL TRAINING

Select Courses - Antelope Valley Junior College (Palmdale, CA)

Trainings include:
Enterprise Storage Training – Amdahl
Outsource Messaging Solutions – Allegro
Infoware – Remote Access for Email
L & H Voice Express
Flow Charting – Micrografx
Exchange – Microsoft
Meeting Maker – On Technologies
Browser Security – Surf Control
Sony
Live Security – Watchguard

Law to Lobbying

Laura Lawson had been working as a legal secretary for the last 11 years. She had the bad luck of being assigned as secretary to a pool of new attorneys who were let go from the firm when business demanded a cut in staff. She was also laid off with a small severance package for her six years of excellent service to that firm. Laura is an extremely outgoing person who thrives in a hyper-busy office environment. She is eager for a new challenge that includes a wider variety of tasks, and she is hoping to escape the law firm environment, where she is in front of a computer generating legal documents all day.

Laura has met some very interesting people through her law firm work and has always admired a high-profile lobbyist who is friends with the firm's partner-in-charge. She decides to go for a job in public affairs or lobbying, using her legal background as a foot in the door. With the new administration, lobbying efforts are expanding—and she is excited about the prospect of working for a cause.

Challenges to Making the Switch

For years, Laura's primary responsibility has been to revise, update, and proofread legal documents. Her skills as a personal assistant haven't really been put to the test since 2002. She knows the personal assistant role will revolve around excellent communication skills, being resourceful, making decisions, and working at a much quicker pace. She has been bored with the isolation of creating documents all day. The trick will be convincing an employer that she is up to the challenge.

Laura also has learned all her secretarial skills while in high school and on the job. She is concerned that her lack of a degree might shut her out in the highly charged political atmosphere of a busy lobbying enterprise. She has not included her legal studies on her resume up until this time because she was unable to complete the two-year program. She knows that she will be competing with young political science graduates who want to get their feet wet in public affairs.

Transferable Skills

Planning, scheduling, and cross-checking calendar dates

Event planning

Coordinating high-level meetings

Liaising with legislative staff

Editing, revising, and proofing legal documents

Billing, invoicing, and tracking expenses

Administrative support

Client correspondence

Customer/client communication

Job Description
Personal Assistant—Lobbying

- Seeking highly intelligent, multitasking, and resourceful person to provide close support for our highly energetic principal of a public affairs company

- Standard office duties: managing a very busy calendar, making travel arrangements, creating documents, liaising with the staff, sending e-mails, and screening calls

- Personal help: assisting the principal's family, running errands, managing the social calendar, purchasing, scheduling doctor's appointments, and coordinating with his wife about home responsibilities

- Event planning: invitations, facilities, catering, entertainment, sound and video equipment, and so on for several high-profile events each quarter

- Familiarity with legal documents and concepts; ability to proofread for discrepancies and omissions

- Light accounting: paying bills and processing insurance claims

- Occasional travel with the principal for work in Washington, D.C.

- Managing day-to-day surprises

- Computer skills: Word, Outlook, PowerPoint, Excel, and the Internet

- Creating and revising PowerPoint presentations

- Excellent writing and proofreading skills

- Minimum of 70 words per minute typing rate

- Requires flexibility, especially with late notice; some 12- to 14-hour days and weekend work

---

Resume Makeover

Laura updates her resume by adding her phone numbers, e-mail address, and LinkedIn Profile to show that she is Internet savvy. The new resume highlights her experience as an executive assistant.

❶ The Capabilities Profile section is replaced with a direct and focused headline: "Experienced Executive Assistant."

❷ Her opening statement emphasizes her ability to work with multiple priorities and to check and recheck details. These traits are especially important in an executive assistant.

❸ The Core Competencies section mirrors the tasks in the job description.

❹ Because Laura lacks formal education, she uses a personal statement to outline her talents and her passion for assisting top-level executives.

❺ The Legal/Business Documents bullets allow her to show, at a glance, that she is familiar with corporate law, lobbying, and even stockholder issues.

❻ Her Professional Career section is picked up from her last resume as is. The only changes are cosmetic. She eliminates semicolons at the end of each bulleted item. This is legal style and not necessary in a resume.

❼ Although she did not complete legal secretary certificate training, she includes what she has completed to show her dedication to her profession.

Laura Lawson
1234 Pearwood Street
Atlanta, GA 30301

CAPABILITIES PROFILE

Experienced Executive Assistant maintaining a positive, friendly attitude; dependable and trustworthy; outstanding communication skills and follow up; flexible with an ability to quickly adapt; professional demeanor in working with extremely sensitive and confidential information.

EXPERIENCE

❻ **ARMSTEAD, PC (Atlanta, GA) 2003 – 2009**
Executive Legal Assistant
- Assisted Attorney/Lobbyist in water law consulting and lobbying; as well as Partner and Associate in the firm's corporate and real estate practice;
- Managed scheduling for heavy business development and client interaction; scheduled and coordinated travel plans; responsible for planning meetings and events with outside contacts;
- Maintained and submitted monthly lobby reports to Georgia Ethics Commission; created invoices and followed up on client payments; prepared correspondence; managed attorney billing documentation; coordinated new client information processing; created and revised legal documents.

WEDDING CAKES UNLIMITED (Atlanta, GA) 2002
<u>Contract Personal Assistant to the President, Sharon Herald</u>
- Reorganized business and home offices to assist owner upon her return from medical leave;
- Responsible for client correspondence, billing, customer/vendor communications;
- Coordinated employee benefits needs, evaluated employee productivity, and advised owner;
- Responsible for daily bank deposits from business as well as personal bank transactions;
- Managed and purchased supplies for business office to meet daily needs of staff;
- Maintained calendar and schedules for employees' task list of production and deliveries;
- Scheduled sales appointments and conducted product sales meetings with customers.

CLM PETERS Law Firm (Atlanta, GA) 1999 – 2001
<u>Legal Secretary</u>
- Assisted three full-time attorneys in the Corporate and Securities Group;
- Scheduled meetings, managed appointment calendar, and coordinated travel arrangements;
- Created, revised, and edited legal documents; prepared client correspondence;
- Maintained attorney billing records and reports.

WOODE & WINCHESTER, LLP (Dallas, TX) 1998 – 1999
<u>Legal Secretary</u>
- Assisted Corporate and Securities Partner, who is head of the Corporate Section;
- Created, revised, and edited documents; prepared correspondence; attorney billing records; conflict checks; new client information processing;
- Managed appointment calendar, meeting planning and travel arrangements.

WORLDWIDE INDUSTRIAL PRODUCTS, INC. (Dallas, TX) 1992 – 1998
<u>Executive Assistant</u>
- Executive Assistant to President and Chief Financial Officer;
- Acted as liaison between Executives, Board, Executive Staff, Stockholders, and Analysts;
- Preparation of confidential documents relating to corporate issues, board of directors, scheduling appointments and meetings, travel coordination;
- Managed confidential files, expense reports, and client correspondence;
- Assisted General Counsel as needed with board meeting preparation and worked with news wire sources in issuance of press releases.

AMERITRUST, INC. (Dallas, TX) 1986 – 1992
<u>Executive Assistant</u>
- Executive Assistant to the Senior Vice President of Trust Operations; Liaison between Senior Vice President and Executive Staff and Operations Managers;
- Scheduled appointments, meetings, travel, confidential files;
- Managed expense reports and client correspondence and interaction;
- Human Resource Coordinator/Liaison for the Operations Division.

LAURA LAWSON

1234 Pearwood Street, Atlanta, GA 30301

H 404 123 1234 • C 404 123 5678 • email@email.com

Profile: www.linkedin.com/name

EXPERIENCED EXECUTIVE ASSISTANT

Seasoned legal secretary with a background of personal support to high-level executives. Capable of managing multiple priorities in fast-paced environments. Extremely conscientious about details and achieving project outcomes. Professional demeanor working with sensitive and confidential information.

CORE COMPETENCIES

- Organizing projects, office files
- Checking and clearing schedule conflicts
- Travel arrangements
- Event planning
- PowerPoint presentations
- Liaising with legislative & admin staff
- Press conference arrangements
- Drafting, proofing, editing documents
- Typing 70 wpm
- Outlook, Word, Excel, QuickBooks
- Email screening, writing
- Social, family calendaring

PERSONAL STATEMENT

My strongest professional attributes are personal talents and characteristics that cannot be taught. These characteristics differentiate me from other candidates with similar skill sets:

- **Excellent communication skills:** Responsible for drafting correspondence for bank presidents and top-level executives. My legal background gives me a finely tuned sense of the appropriate way to communicate difficult messages.
- **Event planning:** Work with three prominent law firms and several large corporations has given me the opportunity to plan and execute client appreciation and charity events that were elegant, cost-justified, and effective in winning the favor of our clients.
- **Personal support:** Enjoy supporting executives in coordinating their many obligations, both personal and professional. I consider these activities to be fun, stimulating, and challenging.
- **Flexibility:** Legal secretary work has demanded supreme flexibility to accommodate the needs of the moment. I thrive on this ever-changing landscape of priorities.
- **Street smarts:** Proud of my ability to do research, learning what I need to know in the moment. I am quick, adaptable, and resourceful in tracking down necessary resources and information.

LEGAL / BUSINESS DOCUMENTS

Have generated and worked with the following types of documents

- Real Estate
- Corporate Contracts
- Water Rights
- Lobbying Ethics
- Performance Appraisals
- Executive Compensation Contracts
- Securities
- Stockholder Communication
- Board Meeting Agendas
- Board Minutes
- Press Releases
- Stock Analyst Reports

PROFESSIONAL CAREER

ARMSTEAD, PC (Atlanta, GA) 2003 – 2009
Executive Legal Assistant

- Assisted Attorney/Lobbyist in water law consulting and lobbying, as well as Partner and Associate in the firm's corporate and real estate practice
- Managed scheduling for heavy business development and client interaction, scheduled and coordinated travel plans, responsible for planning meetings and events with outside contacts
- Maintained and submitted monthly lobby reports to Georgia Ethics Commission, created invoices and followed up on client payments, prepared correspondence, managed attorney billing documentation, coordinated new client information processing, created and revised legal documents

---

Laura Lawson   email@email.com

WEDDING CAKES UNLIMITED (Atlanta, GA) 2002
Contract Personal Assistant to the President, Sharon Herald

- Reorganized business and home offices to assist owner upon her return from medical leave
- Responsible for client correspondence, billing, customer/vendor communications
- Coordinated employee benefits needs, evaluated employee productivity and advised owner
- Responsible for daily bank deposits from business as well as personal bank transactions
- Managed and purchased supplies for business office to meet daily needs of staff
- Maintained calendar and schedules for employees' task list of production and deliveries
- Scheduled sales appointments and conducted product sales meetings with customers

CLM PETERS LAW FIRM, LLP (Atlanta, GA) 1999 – 2001
Legal Secretary

- Assisted three full-time attorneys in the Corporate and Securities Group
- Scheduled meetings, managed appointment calendar, and coordinated travel arrangements
- Created, revised, and edited legal documents, prepared client correspondence
- Maintained attorney billing records and reports

WOODE & WINCHESTER, LLP (Dallas, TX) 1998 – 1999
Legal Secretary

- Assisted Corporate and Securities Partner, who is head of the Corporate Section
- Created, revised, and edited documents, prepared correspondence, attorney billing records, conflict checks, new client information processing
- Managed appointment calendar, meeting planning, and travel arrangements

WORLDWIDE INDUSTRIAL PRODUCTS, INC. (Dallas, TX) 1992 – 1998
Executive Assistant

- Executive Assistant to President and Chief Financial Officer
- Acted as liaison between Executives, Board, Executive Staff, Stockholders, and Analysts
- Preparation of confidential documents relating to corporate issues, board of directors, scheduling appointments and meetings, travel coordination
- Managed confidential files, expense reports, and client correspondence
- Assisted General Counsel as needed with board meeting preparation and worked with news wire sources in issuance of press releases

AMERITRUST, INC. (Dallas, TX) 1986 – 1992
Executive Assistant

- Executive Assistant to the Senior Vice President of Trust Operations, Liaison between Senior Vice President and Executive Staff and Operations Managers
- Scheduled appointments, meetings, travel, confidential files
- Managed expense reports and client correspondence and interaction
- Human Resource Coordinator/Liaison for the Operations Division

EDUCATION

 Legal Secretary Studies, Brown Mackie College, Atlanta, GA 1999 – 2001
(Completed all but 4 credit hours) Coursework: Criminal Justice, Contracts, Securities

Manufacturing to Oil and Gas

Faith McMaster has survived three major layoffs at the manufacturing company that produces payment equipment for gas stations. She hopes to increase her chances of staying with the company by finishing her Bachelor of Science degree in information technology and transferring to a department that isn't downsizing. Unfortunately, her best-laid plans fail five months after graduating, when she and 150 others at her company are laid off.

Faith feels betrayed the day she receives her pink slip because she has been such a dedicated employee for 20 years. It takes her several months to recover and begin her job search. Friends persuade her to set up profiles on LinkedIn, Facebook, and other social networking sites—and through that she reconnects with former clients who work for major and independent oil companies. A couple of them let her know about upcoming openings at their company that haven't been posted on any job boards. They remind her that she has valuable oil industry knowledge from the years she worked for a manufacturer that produces gasoline pumps and other automated fuel equipment. With help from these contacts, she applies for jobs.

Challenges to Making the Switch

Faith's biggest challenge is being underqualified for some IT positions that require not only a Bachelor's degree but at least two years experience. On the flip side, she is concerned that some companies may see her higher salary on applications and be concerned that she won't stay at a company where she is paid less. In addition, Faith is in her early 50s and wonders whether she will be unfairly passed over because of age discrimination.

The last time Faith worked for an oil company was 25 years ago, when she completed a three-month internship in Alaska. She still makes reference to that experience and her extensive knowledge of the business obtained from maintaining daily contact with oil company customers.

Faith realizes she may be perceived as a generalist rather than a business analyst specialist because she has handled so many duties, including sales, training, sales support, and market analysis. She recognizes the importance of focusing on the skills that transfer rather than offering an overview of everything she has done.

Transferable Skills

IT hardware, software, and programming

Process design

System modeling

Technical support

Planning and analysis

Coordinating cross-functional groups

Help Desk experience

Job Description
Oil Company Business Analyst

- Minimum of two years experience as a business analyst and legal authorization to work in the United States

- IT-related degree or business analyst certification

- Two or more years experience in requirements gathering, process design, system modeling, and testing in the trading or oil downstream business areas

- Knowledge of Oracle PL/SQL

- Ability to understand high-level technical requirements and identify appropriate tools to meet those requirements

- Collaborate with groups to design, develop, and administer computer-based training applications

- Strong communication and teamwork skills

- Must be able to multitask effectively and take on different business analyst roles as the project evolves

Resume Makeover

Faith's resume is refocused to highlight her IT skills and extensive knowledge of oil companies.

1 The Business Analyst Qualifications heading indicates her new target occupation.

2 The qualifications summary includes key skills, knowledge, and education that transfer from manufacturing to oil company business analyst work.

3 Technical skills are listed in a separate section to make them stand out.

4 The Education section is moved up to draw attention to the recent degree. Unrelated certificates have been omitted.

5 The Professional Experience section is shortened to highlight skills that transfer to the new industry. The paragraph style of her former resume has been changed to bulleted, easy-to-read achievements.

6 Older employment dates are deleted by using a general heading: "Work experience prior to 1989."

Faith McMaster

1234 Mountain Ct.
Houston, TX 78660
(713) 123-4567 email@emailcom

Summary

Strong technical aptitude. Creative and solution-oriented. Skilled at computer-assisted analysis, documentation, and presentation development. Flexible. Able to adapt and thrive in settings as diverse as headquarters office work and Alaska's primitive North Slope oil fields. BS degree in Information Technology.

Five years successful outside sales experience. Excellent communication skills. Work well independently or as member of team.

Over twenty years product support experience, helping customers fully benefit from product capabilities, and helping company benefit from customer input in developing new products. Trained end-users, customer in-house trainers, field service technicians, and outside contractors. Supported 3rd Party software engineers in interface development. Wrote and/or revised product documentation. Participated in market needs analysis and the design and development of next-generation product. Managed development of XML interface to POS platform. Drove development of SQL tool to print site-specific programming report.

Experience

⑤ DRACOR, INC., Houston, TX   **03/89 – 05/09**

Third-Party Interface Specialist (07/08 – 05/09)
Managed exchange of specifications and lab equipment with industry partners in the design, manufacture, and sale of customized gasoline station automation. Provided technical support for interface development, lab equipment, and field issues. Lab-tested new dispenser and card reader software and authorized release for field testing. Industry partners included other dispenser and point-of-sale manufacturers, tank level monitor, car wash, loyalty, and back office system vendors.

Sr. Technical Trainer (04/06 – 07/08)
Responsible for web-based and instructor-led course development, classroom seminar delivery, and training room equipment maintenance. Trained contract technicians and in-house Help Desk, Regional Service, and Service Group technicians to install, service, and maintain Wayne Point-of-Sale and Dispenser equipment Maintained course content per new software enhancements. Developed new courses for new product introductions. Restructured the Nucleus course from 5 days to 4 days by creating a web-based prerequisite, resulting in savings of travel costs and lost technician field time for our customers.

New Product Support Technician (09/04 – 03/06)
Responsible for field beta test of new POS software and hardware. Oversaw contract technicians who performed software upgrades and installations. Wrote first draft of installation/upgrade manuals. Primary contact for all beta field problems for assigned projects (24/7). Escalation point for post-beta field issues from product Help Desk.

POS Systems Analyst (10/96 – 08/04)
Managed 3rd Party companies that interfaced to Wayne POS products. Primary duty was to support Back Office inventory and accounting system vendors in interface development. Position required extensive knowledge of POS system database. Interface types include direct SQL database, XML, and flat file interfaces. Participated in an industry task force responsible for the development of a Standard XML Data Exchange specification. Provided beta site installation and follow-up support. Escalation point for field issues from product Help Desk.

Marketing Analyst, Control Systems (06/95 – 09/96)
Assisted in company's effort to develop Nucleus, a totally redesigned comprehensive gas station automation system. As Marketing Analyst, duties included contributing to features specification, interaction analysis, prioritization, and performance testing. Prepared trainers for system roll-out. Conducted system demonstrations for headquarters visitors and at tradeshows.

Product Trainer, Southeastern Region (05/92 – 05/95)
Developed and implemented Train-the-Trainer seminar for large customers' in-house training staffs. Trained and certified technicians and trainers for Authorized Contractors. Followed up training with on-site monitoring and support. Also supported salespeople with product demonstrations for customers, handled service departments' overflow, and served as resource for headquarters customer Help Desk.

Customer Trainer (03/89 – 04/92)
One of five Customer Trainers who, working individually, traveled up to 70% to install and configure new systems and train new end-users. Group training took place over several days. Trainees usually comprised six separate end-user groups, each requiring certain customization. Sole responsibility for equipment and meeting room logistics and program implementation. Wrote resource documents, including user Training Manual. Translated highly technical product documentation to improve usefulness to lay readers.

ARCTIC TECHNOLOGY, Anchorage, Alaska   **08/83 – 02/89**
Sales Engineer
Arctic Technology was a distributor and manufacturers representative for process instrumentation for oil and oil-related companies. Worked successfully with technicians, engineers, and purchasing managers. Responsible for entire Alaska territory. Increased revenue by 73% in one year.

ARCO, North Slope Operations, Alaska (Summer 1983)
Intern, Process Instrumentation Calibration

Education & Training

Phoenix University Online
Currently enrolled in Bachelor of Science program, Information Technology
Kenai Peninsula College, Soldotna, Alaska
A.S., Industrial Process Instrumentation
3.8 GPA, ARCO Scholarship

Certificates: Sybase SQL Anywhere 5.0, Dallas, TX
Val-Tek Control Valves, Springville, UT, ranked #1 in class
Magnitrol Level Control, Oakbrook, IL, 1984
Parker-Hannifin Instrumentation Fittings & Valves, Huntsville, AL

Computer Skills: MS SQL Server, XMLSpy, WORD, Excel, PowerPoint, various DOS utility programs

Faith McMaster

713-123-4567 • email@email.com
1234 Mountain Ct. • Houston, TX 78660

① BUSINESS ANALYST QUALIFICATIONS

- 5+ years relevant experience, including planning, leading, coordinating, and conducting business analysis.
- Diverse experience in requirements gathering, process design, system modeling, and testing.
- Participate in market needs analysis and the design/development of next-generation products.
- Adapt and thrive in settings as diverse as corporate headquarters development work, and Alaska's primitive North Slope oil fields.
- Drove development of SQL tool to print site-specific programming report.

③ TECHNICAL SKILLS

Databases: Oracle, MS Access, SQL

GUI/Tools: MS Project, Visio, Access, Word, Excel; DOORS 7.1, TrackWise, Crystal Reports

Industry Standards: HIPAA, SOX, CFR 21 Part 11, CFR 21 Part 820, ISO, Six Sigma, CMM

Platforms: Windows NT/2000/XP, MSDOS, Mainframe, Linux

Testing Tools: WinRunner, LoadRunner, Quick Test Pro (QTP)

EDUCATION

④ Bachelor of Science Degree, Information Technology   December 2008
Phoenix University   4.0 GPA

Associate of Science, Industrial Process Instrumentation
Kenai Peninsula College, Soldotna, Alaska
3.8 GPA, ARCO Scholarship

PROFESSIONAL EXPERIENCE

⑤ DRACOR, INC., Houston, TX

Third-Party Interface Specialist   July 2008 – May 2009

- Served as the key contact with major oil companies during the design, manufacture, and sale of customized gasoline station automation.
- Provided technical support for interface development, lab equipment and field issues.
- Lab-tested new dispenser and card reader software and authorized release for field testing.

Sr. Technical Trainer   April 2006 – July 2008

- Developed web-based and instructor-led courses for contract technicians and in-house helpdesk, regional service, and service group technicians.
- Updated course content during three software enhancements.
- Developed new courses for product introductions.
- Restructured the nucleus course from five days to four days by creating a web-based prerequisite, resulting in savings of travel costs and lost technician field time for customers.

New Product Support Technician   Sept. 2004 – March 2006

- Conducted field beta tests for new point-of-sale software and hardware.
- Oversaw contract technicians who performed software upgrades and installations.
- Wrote first draft of installation/upgrade manuals.
- Served as the primary contact 24/7 for all beta field problems for assigned projects.
- Resolved post-beta field escalation issues from product Help Desk.

POS Systems Analyst   Oct. 1996 – Aug. 2004

- Managed third-party companies that interfaced with company's POS products.
- Supported back office inventory and accounting system vendors in interface development.
- Position required extensive knowledge of POS system database and interface types, including direct SQL database, XML, and flat file interfaces.
- Participated in an industry task force responsible for the development of a Standard XML Data Exchange specification.
- Provided beta site installation and follow-up support. Resolved escalated field issues from product Help Desk.

Marketing Analyst, Control Systems   June 1995 – Sept. 1996

- Assisted in company's effort to develop Nucleus, a totally redesigned comprehensive gas station automation system.
- As Marketing Analyst, contributed to features specification, interaction analysis, prioritization, and performance testing.
- Prepared trainers for system roll-out. Conducted system demonstrations for headquarters visitors and at tradeshows.

Product Trainer, Southeastern Region   May 1992 – May 1995

- Developed and implemented train-the-trainer seminar for customers' in-house training staffs.
- Trained and certified technicians and trainers for Authorized Contractors. Followed up training with onsite monitoring and support.
- Supported sales staff with product demonstrations for customers, handled service departments' overflow and served as a resource for headquarter's customer Help Desk.

Customer Trainer   March 1989 – April 1992

- One of five Customer Trainers who traveled up to 70% to install and configure new systems and train new end-users. Group training took place over several days.
- Wrote resource documents, including user training manual. Translated highly technical product documentation to improve usefulness for lay readers.

⑥ Work Experience Prior to 1989

ARCTIC TECHNOLOGY, Anchorage, Alaska
Sales Engineer

- Sold process instrumentation in the entire Alaska territory. Increased revenue by 73%.
- Worked successfully with technicians, engineers, and purchasing managers.

ARCO, North Slope Operations, Alaska
Summer Intern

- Assisted engineers and technicians with maintaining equipment at the second-largest oil field in North America.

Manufacturing to Health Care

Mitchell Harrison is tired of riding the manufacturing roller coaster after being laid off three times during the last 10 years. When he decides to pursue a purchasing position in a more stable industry, health care appears to be his best choice. He's familiar with this field after serving as an Army medic. Numerous family members work in the medical field as well, including his father who is a radiologist. Originally, he had planned to be a physician assistant—but after treating soldiers on the battlefield during Operation Desert Storm, he didn't think he was suited for patient care. When he left the Army, he finished his business degree and worked his way into a well-paying high-tech purchasing job. Now that manufacturing opportunities are limited, Mitchell decides to change industries.

Challenges to Making the Switch

Mitchell has an impressive track record as a purchasing manager; however, he realizes he will need to take a lower-level position to break into health care. He's willing to take a reduction in pay and learn about the industry. As Mitchell begins his job search, he encounters many others who want to cross over into health care. The consensus is that it's challenging to make this switch, but Mitchell believes he will have an advantage because of his prior Army medic experience.

Mitchell asks his family members and friends to help him arrange information interviews with people they know in health-care purchasing. Through these meetings, he gains insight into how to apply through the official channels and network with people who can put in a good word for him. One of his contacts takes his resume directly to a purchasing manager.

Making an industry switch often lengthens the job search, and Mitchell needs supplemental income to help sustain him. He takes a weekend PRN patient care tech job at a local hospital and meets more people who offer advice. He still has time during the week for his job search and interviews, and he hopes current health-care experience will help his efforts.

Transferable Skills

Purchasing

Sourcing

Negotiating

Scheduling

Planning

Relationship-building

Medical terminology

Computer software skills

Job Description
Purchasing Assistant

- Advanced knowledge of purchasing/contracts management

- Experience in a purchasing environment, including prior supervision

- Strong communication and relationship-building skills with all levels of employees and management

- A blend of management skills with technical expertise proven by superior planning, decision-making, negotiation, leadership, and financial management skills with a focus on adding value to the bottom line of the business—fostering a preeminent health-care environment

- Experience with Supplier Relationship Management (SRM) practices in order to develop and manage strong supplier relationships

- Knowledge of business applications with experience in logistics or inventory management

- Proficiency in Microsoft Word and Excel

- Bachelor's degree in operations, finance, or a related field

---

Resume Makeover

Mitchell's resume is updated, and the billboard section is streamlined for the health-care field.

1 A heading replaces the objective statement to convey his new industry focus.

2 The Qualifications bullets use keywords for health-care purchasing and note his medical experience.

3 Columns of keywords make it easier to spot the essential skills that transfer from one field to the next.

4 Months are added to the start and end dates because employers prefer to see a more complete time reference.

5 His different job titles at his last job are simplified to avoid confusion.

6 More information is added about his Army Medical Specialist Corps experience.

MITCHELL HARRISON
123 RANDALL ROAD, Fort Wayne, IN 46802
(PHONE) 260-123-4567 (EMAIL) EMAIL@EMAIL.COM

OBJECTIVE

Senior purchasing or purchasing manager position in a manufacturing and/or corporate environment.

SUMMARY

Goal-driven **Senior Sourcing/Contracts Analyst** and **Buyer/Planner** with expertise in managing the purchasing and contract negotiations of MRO/commodities/services for manufacturing and corporate headquarters. Perform regional and global, cross-functional project management. Proactively implement continuous cost-reduction measures. Develop, monitor, and manage supplier relationships. Review and negotiate contract terms, conditions, and pricing. Extensive Oracle experience. Strong team player who also works well autonomously. Proficient computer skills in MS Office applications. Excels in writing procedures and training personnel. Bachelor of Business Administration Degree.

PROFESSIONAL EXPERIENCE

TITAN PHOTOMASKS, INC., Fort Wayne, IN   2000-2009
Senior Sourcing/Contracts Analyst II (2006-2008), Senior Sourcing/Contracts Analyst I (2003-2006), Sourcing/Contracts Analyst (2000-2003)
Purchased $30 million in commodities/services for a top supplier of photomasks used by semiconductor makers to transfer circuit patterns onto silicon wafers. Negotiated contract terms and conditions, non-disclosure agreements, pricing, and leases with strategic and tactical suppliers.
- Negotiated reduced overall supplier costs of goods and services by $1M in 2008.
- Implemented global chemical contract with standard costs for all sites.
- Achieved annual savings of $100k over three years by managing and negotiating U.S. contract for clean room supplies.
- Captured annual savings of $800K to $1M by leading cross-functional team that grew the use of corporate business credit card (Procard) through improved policies and implementation.

HILLCOM NETWORK SYSTEMS, Phoenix, AZ   1999
Buyer/Planner/Scheduler
Directed purchasing, planning, and scheduling of approximately $2M per month for printed circuit boards and chassis. Planned incoming products. Scheduled shipments for sales orders. Responsible for inventory cleanup and efficient utilization of existing inventory through revision upgrades.
- Decreased on-hand inventory by auditing, inventorying, and writing off obsolete printed circuit boards.
- Saved $600K in four-month period by working with manufacturing to upgrade boards to current revisions.

MITCHELL HARRISON/PAGE 2

ADVANCED MATERIALS, Phoenix, AZ   1994-1998
Buyer/Planner/Master Scheduler (1995-1998)
Oversaw purchase of customer engineering special parts and electronic components. Directed master scheduling for process and consumable parts/systems related to semiconductor equipment production. Provided parts support for down systems, non-conformances, engineering, and spares.
- Managed $1.4M of inventory using MRP and other applicable databases.
- Minimized parts problems or delays in schedule by effectively coordinating engineering change orders with Engineering, clean room personnel, and Buyers/Planners.

Senior Manufacturing Technologist (1994-1995)
Assembled complex semiconductor systems that make integrated circuits. Responsible for all parts, engineering changes or problems, training of personnel, meeting schedule, and testing.
- Reduced time to learn 20%, compared to one-on-one training by using digital camera and concise instructions. Wrote complex assembly procedures for several system parts.

MILITARY

United States Army Medical Specialist Corps

EDUCATION

Bachelor of Business Administration, *North Central College,* Naperville, IL

MITCHELL HARRISON

123 Randall Road • Fort Wayne, IN 46802 • 260-123-4567 • EMAIL@EMAIL.COM

HEALTH-CARE PURCHASING PROFESSIONAL

- Experienced Purchasing Agent with strong skills in contract management.
- Achieved substantial savings of up to $1M annually through skilled negotiation.
- More than four years medical experience with broad industry knowledge.
- Experience with Supplier Relationship Management (SRM) practices.
- Extensive Oracle experience. Proficient in Microsoft Word, Excel, and Access.
- Bachelor of Business Administration Degree. Additional skills include:

Supervision	Buying	Scheduling
Training	Planning	Inventory
Logistics	Negotiating	Relationship-Building

WORK EXPERIENCE

TITAN PHOTOMASKS, INC., Fort Wayne, IN   Jan. 2000 – June 2009
Advanced from Sourcing/Contracts Analyst to Senior Sourcing/Contracts Analyst II.

- Purchased $30M in commodities/services for a top supplier of photomasks used by semiconductor makers to transfer circuit patterns onto silicon wafers.
- Negotiated contract terms and conditions, non-disclosure agreements, pricing, and leases with strategic and tactical suppliers.
- Reduced overall supplier costs of goods and services by $1M in 2008.
- Implemented global contract with standard costs for all sites.
- Achieved annual savings of $100K over three years by managing and negotiating U.S. contract for clean room supplies.
- Captured annual savings of $800K to $1M by leading cross-functional team that implemented improved policies for using the corporate business credit card.

HILLCOM NETWORK SYSTEMS, Phoenix, AZ   Jan. 1999 – Dec.1999
Buyer/Planner/Scheduler

- Directed purchasing, planning, and scheduling of approximately $2M per month for printed circuit boards and chassis.
- Completed Supplier Relationship Management (SRM) training and followed practices to streamline and build more effective processes with suppliers.
- Scheduled shipments for sales orders. Oversaw inventory cleanup and efficient utilization of existing inventory through revision upgrades.
- Decreased on-hand inventory by auditing, inventorying, and writing off obsolete printed circuit boards.
- Saved $600K in four months by working with manufacturing to upgrade boards to current revisions.

ADVANCED MATERIALS, Phoenix, AZ   March 1994 – Nov.1998
Buyer/Planner/Master Scheduler   Oct. 1995 – Nov 1998

- Oversaw purchase of customer engineering special parts and electronic components.
- Directed master scheduling for process and consumable parts/systems related to semiconductor equipment production.
- Provided parts support for down systems, non-conformances, engineering, and spares.
- Managed $1.4M of inventory using MRP and other applicable databases.
- Minimized parts problems or delays in schedule by effectively coordinating change orders with engineering, clean room personnel, and buyers/planners.

Senior Manufacturing Technologist   March 1994 – Sept.1995

- Assembled complex semiconductor systems that made integrated circuits.
- Tested parts, made engineering changes, and scheduled meetings.
- Reduced time to learn by 20 percent by using digital camera and concise instructions to create group training sessions.
- Wrote complex assembly procedures for several system parts.

MILITARY

Four years of service in the United States Army
Medical Specialist Corps

Served as the primary Medical Officer of an
airborne infantry battalion during Operation Desert Storm

EDUCATION

Bachelor of Business Administration
North Central College, Naperville, IL

Real Estate to Public Utility

Rick Simms' electrical engineering career has taken several hits in the last few years. His 13 years with a major pharmaceutical company ended in a reorganization when a production line was moved to a plant in another state. He picked up a construction management job with a food processing plant, but that assignment lasted just one year. He most recently worked as a project manager for a real estate company. The downturn in the economy has cooled all construction plans, so he is out of work again.

Rick is unsure what type of engineering to pursue. His diverse experiences in the last few years could allow him to do more construction management work or be a site engineer in almost any type of manufacturing. He could specialize in control panels, conveyors, water/wastewater systems, HVAC, or even piping. Each of these specialties is within manufacturing, where jobs are scarce. He would rather be part of an in-house team of engineers in a stable industry, with a steady stream of familiar projects on the same campus. Rick has been looking online and finds a job lead for an electrical utility that is just 40 miles from home.

Challenges to Making the Switch

Rick's resume shows the duration of his career and lists responsibilities going back to 1975. Responsibilities are not as telling as achievement statements could be. He will need to flesh out each of these job descriptions in order to show his level of expertise and responsibility. Rick is concerned about his lack of direct experience with a public utility and the job he is seeking also includes nuclear design. He decides to list a nuclear design course he completed when studying for a Master's degree some years ago. Another challenge is Rick's age. A hiring manager can do a quick calculation and determine that he is probably 58 or older. Age discrimination is not legal, but it certainly could put him at a disadvantage.

Finally, Rick is wary of making any decision. Losing his long-term job back in 2004 still hurts, and while he longs for the team atmosphere of a large company, he is also wary. He decides to update his resume, positioning himself as a senior electrical engineer. Chances are that the utility may have more than one opening; perhaps he can be hired without nuclear experience.

Transferable Skills

Electrical system design

Construction management

Preparation and review of designs

Substation power plant systems

Bid/analytical calculations

Interfacing with vendors

Equipment selection and installation

Instrumentation

Job Description
Senior Electrical Engineer

- Project team environment involved in the design, modification, and analysis of power plant electrical systems

- Electrical system design; preparation and review of complex calculations

- Preparation and review of design inputs

- Preparation of reports and studies that present technical information in a clear and concise manner and meet client expectations

- Bid evaluations including calculations to support economic evaluations and interface with vendors

- Requires BSEE degree with experience in project engineering, preferably dedicated to nuclear power plants

- Experience with power plant electrical system design, including medium- and low-voltage distribution systems, communication systems, equipment selection, and analytical calculations

- PE license preferred

- SmartPlant experience desirable

Resume Makeover

By enhancing his resume with engineering terms, Rick is broadening his potential for different types of engineering positions. This one is loaded with power plant terminology to gain the attention of the utility hiring manager.

1 Early jobs from 1975 to 1990 are left off his resume. These experiences are less relevant—and by eliminating them, he takes 15 years off his age.

2 The headline "Senior Electrical Engineer" matches the title of his desired job.

3 He leads with his three primary competencies, in order of importance: electrical system design, equipment installation, and construction management.

4 The Professional Competencies section allows him to show his breadth as an engineer. He includes the keywords SmartPlant and PE Certification directly from the job description.

5 His professional experience leads with electrical site engineer because he prefers this role and it's his longest-tenured job. The simplified list of duties is revised into achievement statements.

6 The work history emphasizes his titles by placing them first and putting them in bold. These are more important than the company name, city, and dates of employment.

7 The date is taken off his Bachelor's degree. His Master's degree studies, although not complete, are added to show that he is committed to his profession.

Rick Simms
Home: **(847) 123-4567**
Cell: **(847) 123-5555**

ABBOTT LABORATORIES (*continued*)

- Managed money flow and schedules to keep multi-million-dollar construction on target and within budget.
- Managed $60M to $100M new construction and upgrade projects in chemical production facilities.

REIMERS INDRAMAT – Itasca, IL   1989 – 1990
Testing and Field Installation Engineer
- Calculated tuning set-ups and performed field spectrum testing on servo motors and installations.

DANFORD MACHINE CORP. – Cicero, IL   1988 – 1989
Design Engineer
- Designed press control systems for high and medium speed stamping presses.

ROCKWELL GRAPHIC SYSTEMS – Cicero, IL   1980 – 1988
Systems Design Engineer
- Designed and corrected electrical schematics for double-width printing presses.
- Worked with installation teams to correct flaws in the design packages.
- Assembled press-build packages.

①

KELSO ENGINEERING – Chicago, IL   1975 – 1980
Design Engineer
- Designed and programmed electronic control panels for manufacturing and food service applications.
- Programmed and field tested microprocessor-based control panels for automation.

EDUCATION

BS Electrical Engineering – University of Illinois, Champaign, IL – 1975

Rick Simms
1234 Anywhere Drive - Gurnee, IL 60031
Home: (847) 123-4567 - Cell: (847) 123-5555
email@email.com

ENGINEERING PROFILE

Skilled problem identifier and solver with more than 20 years of experience with a BS in Engineering. Detail driven construction management and electrical expertise from PLC to substations.

PROFESSIONAL HIGHLIGHTS

- Efficient, organized leader with experience in supervision and labor relations, including cost control and progress billing.
- Earned Abbott Laboratories President's Award for completing $100M project on time and on budget in 2001.
- Eligible for professional engineer certificate.

PROFESSIONAL EXPERIENCE

DTEL, Inc. – Dallas, TX   2005 – 2009
Project Manager Development and Operations
- Structured multiple projects in real estate development for commercial and residential properties, as well as developing and maintaining the flow of work processes.
- Managed the technical and administrative aspects of client projects in accordance with timelines, budgets, specifications, and project requirements.
- Assisted with marketing and sales development activities.

MIDDLE, Inc. – Oak Brook, IL   2004 – 2005
Construction Manager
- Responsible for $8M expansion at food processing facility.
- Coordinated piping runs without drawings.
- Coordinated electrical shutdown to pull feeders for two switchboards and 20 MCC sections.
- Coordinated installation of three 15,000-gallon, four 1,000-gallon, and four 600-gallon tanks.
- Set 150' x 18' stainless steel work platform.

ABBOTT LABORATORIES – North Chicago, IL   1991 – 2004
Electrical Site Engineer
- Liaison between project engineers/designers and contractors.
- Resolved design problems in the field to include, but not limited to, underground duct banks, sewer/chemical waste lines, concrete pours/testing, certified welding, steel erection, electrical issues from instrumentation to substations and HVAC.

RICK SIMMS
SENIOR ELECTRICAL ENGINEER

1234 Anywhere Dr   Gurnee, IL 60031   Home 847-123-4567   Cell 847-123-5555   email@email.com

ELECTRICAL SYSTEM DESIGN / EQUIPMENT INSTALLATION / CONSTRUCTION MANAGEMENT

- Efficient, organized leader with more than 20 years' experience in electrical system design
- BS in Engineering with some graduate coursework in nuclear energy
- Detail-driven construction management with expertise ranging from PLC to substations
- Well-rounded engineering background – 13 years as Site Engineer called for solutions and oversight of electrical, mechanical, and civil engineering

PROFESSIONAL COMPETENCIES

- Electrical system design
- Construction management
- Clean room construction
- Installing MCC motor control centers
- Sterile manufacturing environments
- MS coursework in nuclear energy
- Eligible for PE certificate

- Instrumentation
- Tank installation & platforms
- SmartPlant knowledgeable
- Underground duct banks
- Underground remediation
- Sewer/chemical waste lines
- Concrete pours/testing

- Conveyor systems
- Cost control
- Progress billing
- Labor relations
- Piping
- Certified welding
- Steel erection

INDUSTRY EXPERTISE (YEARS)

Pharmaceuticals (13)	Food Processing (6)	High-Speed Stamping (1)
Real Estate (3)	Servo Motors (1)	Large-Scale Printing (8)

PROFESSIONAL EXPERIENCE

Electrical Site Engineer
Abbott Laboratories, North Brook, IL

- Successfully managed the construction of 7 buildings for various uses – research laboratories, clean room manufacturing, and offices.
- Managed money flow and schedules to keep multi-million dollar construction on target and within budget.
- Designed and solved electrical issues from instrumentation to substations and HVAC.
- Managed $60 to $100M new construction and upgraded projects in chemical production.
- Resolved design problems in the field to include, but not limited to: underground duct banks, sewer/chemical waste lines, concrete pours/testing, certified welding, and steel erection.
- Liaison between project engineers/designers and contractors; experienced in supervision and labor relations.
- Earned Abbott Laboratories President's Award for completing a $100M project on time and on budget.

Construction Management
Middle Inc., Oak Brook, IL

- Responsible for an $8M expansion to an 85,000 sq. ft. food processing facility. Complex installation of piping, huge tanks, conveyors, and more than 20 MCC (Motor Control Centers).
- Coordinated the activities of 6 electricians, 12-15 welders, and 6 millwright laborers.
- Coordinated the installation of three 15,000-gallon, four 1,000-gallon, and four 600-gallon tanks.
- Managed the construction and setting of 150' x 18' stainless-steel work platform.

RICK SIMMS   EMAIL@EMAIL.COM

Construction Management continued…
Middle Inc., Oak Brook, IL

- Successfully coordinated the one-day staged shut-down of a 150-person plant. During that time our team successfully pulled feeders and reinstalled lines for two switchboards and 20 MCC sections.
- Working with the foreman of welders, we found a way to reuse stainless-steel piping for 15% of the project, saving the client approximately $30,000.

Real Estate Development Manager
DTEL, Inc., Dallas TX

- Structured multiple projects in Florida for Real Estate developer. Inspected sites for suitability of planned single family, commercial, and nursing home projects.
- Developed and maintained the flow of work processes.
- Managed the technical and administrative aspects of client projects in accordance with timelines, budgets, specifications, and project requirements.
- Created and delivered reports to up to 50 investors on a weekly teleconference.

WORK HISTORY

Real Estate Development	DTEL, Inc., Dallas, TX	2005–2009
Construction Manager	Middle Inc, Oak Brook, IL	2004–2005
Electrical Site Engineer	Abbott Labs, North Brook, IL	1991–2004

EDUCATION AND PROFESSIONAL DEVELOPMENT

Bachelor of Science – Electrical Engineering, University of Illinois, Champaign, IL
Master of Science – 12 coursework hours completed, including Nuclear Design

Self-Employed to Politics

Theresa Stehle is self-employed as a virtual assistant. With her husband's recent job loss and the current economic climate (slowing economy and rising prices), Theresa is looking for a steadier income.

The elections of the last nine years have sparked a real interest in politics and working for a cause, and with her administrative background, Theresa could easily work for a political action committee (PAC), a legislator, or some other politically based organization.

Theresa is a real go-getter and a great networker. With her broad experience in marketing, event planning, and administrative management and her community and volunteer work, she could potentially qualify as a political director, communications director, or executive director. Because she really likes working with people, she is focusing her work search on community liaison. While going from a self-employed virtual assistant to politics may seem like a big leap, the skills and experience that Theresa brings are perfectly suited to the job she is targeting.

Challenges to Making the Switch

Theresa lacks a degree, so she will have to play up her many years of experience and show how her experience can be translated into community outreach.

While political experience may not be mandatory for her desired position, she would do well to gain some knowledge about the organization and its goals and find a way to demonstrate her passion for its issues.

Transferable Skills

Customer service

Marketing—print and web

Presentation skills

Influence skills

Problem resolution

Organization

Job Description

Community Liaison

- Serve as an information resource to the community about our mission, goals, and/or services
- Develop and implement a strategic outreach plan in alignment with organizational goals
- Plan and execute meetings and events, including educational briefings, community-wide events, parlor meetings and outreach to new prospects, and annual fundraising events for major donors
- Participate on community boards of organizations complementary to our agency's mission and cause
- Identify community needs pertinent to our organization
- Develop and maintain a network with community organizations, businesses, and agencies
- Develop and make available information and materials to businesses, professional groups, associations, and government leaders
- Encourage active participation and interest in our organization through partnerships, volunteering, and donations
- Convey positive and negative feedback to the organization's management
- Work in partnership with other departments of the organization, meeting regularly to ensure consistency and cohesiveness in the organization's efforts
- Regularly meet with supervisor to go over goals, objectives, focus, and effectiveness
- Develop written reports and performance metrics as needed and in the required/requested format

Resume Makeover

Theresa's resume is completely revised to emphasize her organizational and marketing skills.

1 By enlarging the font and eliminating large paragraphs of text to create more white space, her resume becomes much easier to read.

2 A functional format highlights her pertinent experience and core competencies and separates her accomplishments from her work history. This is important because she has no college degree.

3 Her core competencies are organized and highlighted toward the top so a prospective employer can see her strengths and skills at a glance.

4 Theresa's Accomplishments and Work History section are separated into two distinct sections. Under Work History, months are removed—leaving just years.

5 Under the Qualifications/Education section, only the most pertinent education remains. The rest is removed, many of which are obsolete or provide information that gives a hint of her age.

6 Under the Activities section, only those activities that show her community outreach and leadership skills are retained under the heading "Professional Affiliations."

7 A short testimonial in a text box adds punch and lets a prospective employer know that this woman is good at what she does.

Theresa Stehle
123 Any Drive, San Diego, CA 92169
Cell: #619-123-4567 Email: email@email.com

In all my endeavors, my focus has been to provide outstanding customer service. I am a self starter and able to accomplish my goals without direct supervision. I'm prepared to take a pro-active stance on any challenge that may present itself. My strengths include: dependability, enthusiasm, organization, detail-oriented, highly motivated, strong work ethic, troubleshooting and problem solving abilities.

ACHIEVEMENTS:

- Launched virtual assistance business – www.ClearYourDeskNow.com, Founder/owner (Mar. 2009)
- Implemented first monthly newsletter marketing program for brokerage – City Properties, Licensed Assistant (Nov. 2006 – April 2008)
- Team award member - Top 5% in sales, company wide – Coldwell Banker Realty, Licensed Realtor (July 2004 – Oct. 2006)
- Developed successful female owned and operated pool service company – Cabana Pool Service - Owner (Jan. 1997 – Jul. 2004)
- Created support position to facilitate goal accomplishment outside scope of daily activities – Hugh Black, DMD, Administrative Assistant (Oct. 1990 – Sept. 1996)
- Developed zero base sales territory to 500 customers in five years
- Seminar speaker/facilitator at client meetings with an audience of 20 to 200 client attendees – Safeguard Business Systems, Independent Distributor (1979 – 1984)
- Instructed weekly software training classes for clients in groups of 5-15 individuals

SKILLS & ABILITIES:

- MS Office * Standard Office Machines * Information Processing * Organization Skills * Research Projects * Sales Support * Lead Management * Client Relationship Management * Desktop Publishing * Contact Management Software * Direct Mailings * Customer Surveys * Word Processing * Newsletters * Web - Blog site updates * Event Planning * Meeting Facilitator * Invoicing * Accounts Receivable Management * Accounts Payable * Reminder Services

TESTIMONIALS:

"When it comes to client care, follow-up, and tracking transactions from start to finish, Theresa is the consummate professional. Whether it's dealing with a tricky situation, tough client, or just putting out newsletters, Theresa handles things confidently and tirelessly. She's been my right and my left hand!" (H. Warner, Broker, San Diego, CA)

"Theresa has a rare combination of intelligence, humor, compassion, and a dedication to success. She has a great talent for working with other team members in a supporting role, or directing specific projects in a leadership role." (H. Black, DMD, Lake Arrowhead, CA)

QUALIFICATIONS / EDUCATION:

(5) Green Valley High School / California Professional College / Orange Coast College, Xerox Courses: Professional Selling Skills I & II / Time & Territory Management / Professional Telephone Techniques Safeguard Bus. Systems Accounting I & II, Licensed Realtor 1988 - Present

ACTIVITIES:

San Diego Community Foundation: Adopt-a-Garden, Chairman * Team Zen * San Diego Inclusive Networking Group * Soroptomists International * Women Business Owners Assoc. * Vice President – San Diego Toastmistress Club * SD Parks & Recreation Youth Basketball * AYSO Soccer Coach * Den Leader – Boy Scouts

❶

Theresa Stehle

619-123-4567 ~ 123 Any Drive, San Diego, CA 92169 ~ email@email.com

COMMUNITY LIAISON

❷ **LEADERSHIP / OUTREACH / SERVICE**

- Skillful networker with strong community connections
- Award-winning sales experience
- Effective communications
- Professional planning and organizing
- Firsthand know-how starting and developing small businesses
- Service on various boards and committees

❸ **CORE COMPETENCIES**

- Strategic planning
- Training and facilitation
- Proficient at marketing and public outreach (newsletters, direct mailings, websites, blogs, customer surveys, and events)
- Strong interpersonal skills
- Lead and client relationship management
- Excellent oral and written communication skills
- Superb computer skills – word processing, desktop publishing, CRM software

❹ **ACCOMPLISHMENTS**

- Launched and built several successful businesses
- Implemented a monthly marketing newsletter for a real estate brokerage (City Properties)
- Developed a zero-base sales territory to 500 customers in five years
- Served as seminar speaker and facilitator for audiences of 20–200 client attendees
- Instructed weekly software training classes for client groups of 5–15 people
- Received awards for sales achievement and client retention

❹ **WORK HISTORY**

2009 – 2009 Founder/Owner www.ClearYourDeskNow.com (virtual assistant), San Diego, CA
2008 – 2009 Chairman, San Diego Community Foundation: Adopt-a-Garden, San Diego, CA
2006 – 2008 Administrative Assistant, City Properties, San Diego, CA
2004 – 2006 Licensed Realtor, Coldwell Banker Realty, San Diego, CA
1997 – 2004 Owner/Operator Cabana Pool Service, San Diego, CA
1990 – 1996 Administrative Assistant, Hugh Black, DMD, Los Angeles, CA

❺ **EDUCATION**

California Professional College
(Sales Skills, Time and Territory Management, and Accounting classes)

❻ **PROFESSIONAL AFFILIATIONS**

Vice President – Toastmistress Club
Women Business Owners Association
San Diego Inclusive Networking Group
Soroptomists International

❼

"Theresa has a rare combination of intelligence, humor, compassion, and a dedication to success. She has a great talent for directing projects in a leadership role."

H. Black, DMD

Semiconductor to Health Care

Ellen Percy had a great 10-year run with a major semiconductor company. She was promoted from engineer technician to customer service manager overseeing an important part of the plant. She enjoyed working with all her internal customers in the plant, improving the quality of her department's output and saving the company money. She was known for her solid relationships at work and her unwavering commitment to quality. Because of lower sales worldwide in semiconductors, however, nearly 20 percent of the company was laid off. Losing her job was a huge shock and disappointment.

In thinking back over her career, Ellen remembered how much she enjoyed her early years as a dental assistant. She had managed to turn her high school work-study experience into a five-year career, assisting in root canals, fillings, crowns, and other complex dental procedures. Ellen wants to get back into the dental business as a salesperson.

Challenges to Making the Switch

Ellen has virtually no sales experience, and her experience in dental work ended 25 years ago. She holds an Associate's degree in a technical field. Her research on job sites shows that minimum requirements for most dental sales jobs are a Bachelor's degree plus sales experience of at least three years. She realizes this may be too big a career move for her.

In addition, Ellen's resume is filled with her technical and high-tech achievements. If she includes her dental assistant jobs, she will have a 10-year gap in her work history.

With persistence and a little research, Ellen finds a job that will allow her to get back into the dental business: dental treatment coordinator. This job position is focused on patient contact and education. She would also be responsible for calculating and recording costs and working out payment issues with insurance companies. She feels she is well qualified for this role, because her work as customer satisfaction manager involved constant communication with both external and internal customers. She applies for this position, hoping her switch to the dental industry will allow her to find a sales position in a few short years. By putting herself back in the industry, she will refresh her industry knowledge and have access to many more job leads.

Transferable Skills

Customer focus

Communication skills

Influence

Detail orientation

Commitment to quality

Problem-solving

Accurate documentation

> ### Job Description
> # Dental Treatment Coordinator
>
> - Conduct patient consultations on all types of dental procedures, including surgeries, tooth extractions, root canals, crowns, implants, and so on
>
> - Calculate fees for treatment based on various fee schedules
>
> - Assist patients with financing options, insurance questions, and treatment concerns
>
> - Educate patients concerning treatment, procedures, insurance benefits, pre- and post-treatment responsibilities, and so on
>
> - Call patients to schedule appointments and then follow up with reminder calls
>
> - Assist billing clerks with posting diagnosis and treatment as needed and directed by management
>
> - Answer telephones and schedule appointments as needed
>
> - Comply with all safety, emergency, hazard, OSHA, HIPAA, sterilization, clinical, quality assurance, and administrative plans, policies, guidelines, protocol, and standards

Resume Makeover

Ellen's resume needs a complete rewrite to show her dental background.

1 Her current resume has a one-liner about "five years dental assistant experience." This is expanded into a full section under Career Highlights.

2 Ellen reframes her objective into a clear statement of her primary skills in customer service. She also specifically mentions that she is able to consult with patients.

3 The Core Competencies section is loaded with functions that are true for her in her last position and that translate to the dental-patient environment. For example, "improving business processes" could be very appealing to a large practice trying to save time and money. "Client consultation and influence" relate directly to the job description for treatment coordinator.

4 Her dental experience is expanded from one line to an entire functional section. She describes the work without saying that the experience dates back to 1979 to 1984. She contacts her former employers, several of whom are already retired, and asks each to serve as a reference.

5 Job history is simplified to play down the high-tech companies and to emphasize her job titles.

6 She includes her Associate's degree, because two years of higher education is better than none.

Ellen Percy

email@email.com

1234 Big Drive, Fairfield, CA 94533 Home 707-123-4567 Cell 707-123-4567

Objective: To work as a Dental Sales/Account Representative so that I can apply my experience as a Dental Assistant and Customer relations. I really enjoyed dental assisting and working face to face with the customer. I believe that this would be a great fit for me. I am a self starter, detail oriented, have strong mechanical ability, can be aggressive, and am excellent working with people.

Work Experience:

SEMICONDUCTOR MATERIALS   1999-2007
Customer Satisfaction Manager for Etch Final Test Group   2001-2007

- Worked to improve any issue from the field and customer to factory, reduced cost, and made a better quality product. Started with an average of 150 non-conformances and reduced them to an average of 10 a month, resulting into an over 90% reduction in non-conformances.
- Worked on quality improvement teams: Field Communication Team, 200mm NC (Non-conformance) Reduction Team, Rapid Response Team, Corrective Action Team, which realized over $900,000 in savings.
- Ship Document Preparation.
- Reduced errors in system paperwork completion from 50% to 100% before shipment (no systems returned from warehouse), which reduced cost by over $500,000 a quarter.
- Made shipping more efficient by improving communication: having one on one with customers (Project Manager, Test Tech, Shipping dock, and Management).

Lead Customer Satisfaction Manager of the completed system (four major parts made up a system, each one was made in a different department of manufacturing, Final Test was the only place in the factory to see the complete system). Responsible to assign field issues quickly and to the correct department to resolve issues as quickly as possible.

Worked with Final Test Tech one on one and final test as a group. Responsible for making everyone aware of the issues that were reported and assigned to our group, so that we worked as a team. Interfaced with QA, the field, and customer to let them know what our group did to improve quality.

Engineer Tech II   1999-2001

- Etch Final Test 200mm Centura systems, troubleshoot system errors, and ordered parts as required.
- Shipment to customers were delivered 100% on time.

Emergency Response Team (ERT) 2002-2007 in addition to my customer satisfaction position.

NOV-CO, Fairfield, CA   3/98-9/98
Quality Control Inspector
Inspected workmanship quality of electrical and mechanical assemblies. Reviewed schematics for the latest engineering change notices. Performed set up of rental computers and identified unknown parts.

XYZ LAPTOP TECHNOLOGY, INC., Vallejo, CA   1995-1998
Hardware Repair Technician
Serviced high end laptop computers, board level repairs and upgraded systems.
Customer hardware support, system level testing, supported data base integrity, tested new products, and conducted monthly internal audits.

Skills: Basic machine language programming, AC/DC circuits, telecommunications, MSDOS, Unix, and Brick, Microcomputer hardware, Hydraulics/Pneumatics, Advanced peripheral devices, Solid state devices, Technical writing, Professionalism training, MS Office: Word, Excel, PowerPoint, Oracle, and SAP.

❶ 5 years dental assistant experience.

Education: **ELECTRONICS INSTITUTE - KANSAS CITY, MO**
Associate Degree in Applied Science - Electronics Technology - 1993 to 1994
2,160 acquired hours, GPA 3.0

Ellen Percy

1234 Big Drive ◆ Fairfield, CA 94533 ◆ (707) 123-4567 ◆ email@email.com

SALES/CUSTOMER SATISFACTION

❷ Customer satisfaction manager seeking entry-level sales or patient service position in the dental industry. Self-starter, detail-oriented, committed to superior customer service. Ability to understand new technological advances in dentistry, and explain them effectively to patients. Five years experience in dental assisting, working directly with patients, office managers, and dentists.

CORE COMPENTENCIES

❸

Quality client relationships	Strong technical skills
Resolving service issues quickly	MS Office, Oracle, SAP
Improving business processes	Technical communications and writing
Improving client satisfaction scores	Client consultation and influence

❶
CAREER HIGHLIGHTS

❹ Dental Assistant – Five Years

- Expanded my job from a work-study program to a full-time professional position, which I held for four years. Worked as a chairside assistant for three dental practices.
- Responsible for assisting with fillings, root canals, crowns, and other procedures.
- Personally took x-rays and impressions, sterilized instruments, kept patient records, made reminder calls and appointments, ordered supplies, and calculated patient invoices.
- Enjoyed one-on-one contact with patients, providing assistance to the dentists, keeping accurate records, ordering and using the latest dental supplies.
- Dentist references available on request.

Customer Satisfaction/Communication

- Lead Customer Satisfaction Manager for the Final Test team of a major semiconductor company. Interfaced with customers and colleagues in all areas of the plant.
- Responsible to assign field issues quickly and to the correct departments, and to correct problems as soon as possible.
- Decreased the average non-conformances by 90% (from 150 to 10 per month) in my first 12 months as manager.
- Made shipping function more efficient by improving communication with internal customers – project managers, test technicians, shipping personnel, and management.

Quality

- Worked on several quality improvement teams, which realized more than $900,000 in savings for our plant in the first year.
- Reduced errors in paperwork completion from 50% to 100% before shipment, which reduced costs by over $500,000 per quarter.
- Inspector for workmanship quality of electrical and mechanical assemblies.
- Reviewed schematics for latest engineering change notices.

❺
RECENT CAREER HISTORY

Customer Service Manager	Semiconductor Materials, Fairfield, CA	1999–2009
Engineer Tech II	Semiconductor Materials, Fairfield, CA	1999–2001
Quality Control Inspector	Nov-Co, Fairfield, CA	1998
Hardware Repair Technician	XYZ Laptop Technology, Inc., Vallejo, CA	1995–1998

EDUCATION

❻ Electronics Institute – Kansas City, MO
Associate Degree in Applied Science – Electronics Technology
2,160 acquired hours, GPA 3.0

Software to Medical Devices

Christopher Kramer is a sales champion at heart. He enjoys the "thrill of the kill" and is completely at home in the sales role. When he loses his position in a software integration company, he knows he wants to return to sales. This time, he'd like to get a position selling medical devices in a clinical setting. Because his first ambition was to become a veterinarian, he has a strong minor in medical sciences, having completed the entire premed curriculum. Christopher is also a consummate athlete who has personally experienced several orthopedic procedures to repair sports injuries. He is hoping his strong sales background will overcome his lack of clinical sales experience.

Challenges to Making the Switch

Christopher's medical background is limited to undergraduate courses more than 10 years in the past. While his sales achievements are impressive, he lacks the direct experience of selling to hospitals, doctors, or clinics. Most job postings in this arena specifically ask for clinical sales experience or a background as a nurse or medical technician. He decides to include his medical studies at the beginning of the resume and to include his passion for medicine in his cover letter.

Integration software sales is quite complex and requires a team effort to produce. As a medical device salesperson, he will be working on his own to build relationships and provide solutions.

Transferable Skills

Sales

Presentation skills

Partnering with clients

Developing complex solutions

Prospecting

Relationship building

Sales administration

Product training

Job Description
Clinical Sales Representative

- Become a clinical expert across all primary operating room (OR) procedures to position yourself as a partner in the development of surgical teams

- Work with senior hospital staff and key surgeons in the development and execution of a plan to effectively integrate our orthopedic devices at new customer sites

- Drive continuous expansion of the user base by working with key hospital staff and thought leaders to develop a qualified lead funnel

- Plan and conduct formal presentations, informal events, and get-togethers

- Effectively convert high potential leads and drive training activities

- Drive sales of instruments and accessories through new product introductions and solution selling

- Responsibly manage administrative tasks: reporting of sales/procedures, outcomes of sales activities, submission of expense reports, and so on

- Must have a proven track record in sales, preferably with a surgical device company

- Success in introducing new technologies to the market is a plus

---

Resume Makeover

Christopher revises his resume to highlight his sales skills and medical background.

1 The headline "Proven Sales Leader" is more powerful than "Summary" and is generic to any kind of sales.

2 The subhead "Account Manager/Consultative Selling/New Technologies" contains keywords taken from the job description.

3 The list of six achievements is filled with keywords: "relationships," "thought leaders," "high-potential leads," and "solutions." The last bullet paraphrases the seventh item in the job description.

4 The Core Competencies section is also loaded with keywords. In many cases, he simply rephrases achievements in his "before" resume.

5 Medical courses are included to show a knowledge base that could give him an edge over other sales candidates. If the medical device sales job doesn't work out, he can remove this section and have a very strong generic sales resume.

6 His Professional Experience section is basically repeated from his "before" resume, which is excellent. We lead with job titles, because these are common to all sales positions, and decrease the emphasis on company names.

7 The Relevant Skills/Sales Training section includes his impressive array of sales training—a real perk of working for large sales organizations.

Christopher Kramer
1234 Wyatt Way, Waltham, MA 00240
email@email.com
(781) 123-4567

SUMMARY

Seasoned account manager with proven experience of consistent overachievement of revenue goals. Deep expertise in management of highly complex technical selling situations to include product, consulting services and maintenance agreements. First-hand experience in contract negotiation for both direct and indirect clients OEM/Independent Software Vendors and complex procurement cycles.

XZY Software, Waltham, MA   *2007 – 2009*
XYZ Software provides budget-conscious enterprises, Independent Software Vendors (ISV), and systems integrators with a feature-rich and highly configurable product for data integration design, deployment, and management.

Account Manager
Responsible for selling XYZ Integration products to the ISV vertical
- Presidents Club FY08
- National Accounts such as ADP, Unica, Softrax, Micros-Retail, Progress Software
- Focused on signing new technology partnerships
- Coordinated Partner Enablement
- Prospected for new business with an ISV focus
- Strengths for developing strong relationships with customers and potential customers

XYZA Technologies, Waltham, MA   *2004 – 2007*
XYZA is the leading provider of high performance enterprise integration software. XZYA's customers include many of the world's Fortune 200 financial and telecommunications companies.

Account Manager
Responsible for direct and indirect sale of infrastructure software, services, and maintenance products in the West and South West territories.
- Consistently overachieved revenue targets
- President's Club 2006
- First Inside Account Manager to sell our new Service Oriented Architecture product
- Coordinated with Finance, Legal, and Operations to start, work, and close new business revenue
- Negotiated and closed new business contracts for OEM/ISV customers
- Monitored and managed distribution of existing OEM/ISV contracts
- Quota attainment at 1H 2007: 58% of annual number 1.2M
- Organized and delivered WebEx presentations to customers
- Responsible for detailed Account Plans

IBM (Rational Software Group), Lexington, MA   *2001 – 2004*
IBM Rational is the leading provider of application development software that lets companies build and deploy programs both internally and externally. Rational Software, an industry leader, was purchased by IBM in February of 2003.

Inside Sales Representative - Major Accounts Team
Responsible for generating new license revenue for several territories over the years including Federal Accounts and DOD.
- Drive consistent revenue via sales of new licenses and up-selling to more current versions and Rational suites.
- Consistently exceed quota
- Developed and maintained detailed spreadsheets used in monitoring performance and territory success for entire team
- Continually fine-tuned exceptional organizational skills in highly detailed, strategic closure of deals in Major Accounts. (i.e., General Electric, BAE Systems, Pitney Bowes, Motorola, Genuity)

Christopher Kramer   Page 1 of 2

- Attained high team honors and recognition through consistently exceeding quota and through acknowledgement as a team leader – often mentoring new members of the team
- Succeeded in adverse conditions in which a team member was unexpectedly out of work and covered open territory and still achieved highest quota achievement for both territories allowing for smooth transition upon their return
- Member of Founders Club 2001, 02 & 03: highest award given to sales individuals who consistently attain high quota achievement and display those characteristics held to be exemplary for success and continued improvement within the role

AmeriGas UGI, Houston, TX   *1998 – 2000*
AmeriGas is the second largest propane retailer in America

Transportation Coordinator
Directly managed the daily activities of 30 operations employees.
- Coordinated smooth operation of delivery services, acting as liaison between customers, delivery staff, and management
- Managed and reported on all Profit and Loss statements for each account
- Responsible for overseeing and maintaining customer inventory
- Established more secure hiring methods through creating method of thorough background checks of potential employees
- Fostered excellent working relationships with other large energy management companies, often acting as liaison between corporate executive staff and front line team members

Relevant Skills/Training
- Karrass Negotiation Training
- Participated in and completed SPIN Selling and Solution Selling, each was a 5-day course
- Completed one week of one-on-one Geoffrey Alexander Sales Training
- Exposure to the Socratic Selling Method
- Signature Selling Method
- CRM experience with Salesforce, ACCPAC, and Vantive

Education:
Texas A&M University, College Station, TX   **December 1997**
- Bachelor of Science, Business Administration and Business Management
- Minor in Medical Sciences

Christopher Kramer   Page 2 of 2

CHRISTOPHER KRAMER

1234 Wyatt Way, Waltham, MA 00240 • email@email.com • 781-123-4567 cell

PROVEN SALES LEADER

Account Manager/Consultative Selling/New Technologies

- ◆ Consistent overachievement of revenue goals in a highly competitive sales environment
- ◆ Firsthand experience with contract negotiations and creating continuing relationships
- ◆ Skilled at building relationships with thought leaders to launch new technologies
- ◆ Significant experience in new product introductions and customized solutions
- ◆ Effectively convert high-potential leads through persistent contact and developing personal relationships
- ◆ Responsibly manage administrative sales tasks – reporting, sales outcomes, expenses, etc.

Core Competencies

- Complex technical selling
- Business prospecting through indirect channels
- Direct and indirect sales; influence key thought leaders
- Develop own qualified lead funnel
- New technology partnerships
- Contract negotiations
- Strong relationships with customers
- Powerful communicator

Medical Courses Completed

- Biology I & II – 14 semester hrs
- Physics – 8 hrs
- Chemistry I & II – 8 hrs
- Organic Chemistry – 4 hrs
- Immunology
- Microbiology
- Biochemistry
- Human Physiology
- Cell Physiology

PROFESSIONAL EXPERIENCE

ACCOUNT MANAGER   2007 – 2009
XYZ Software – Waltham, MA
Provides budget-conscious enterprises, Independent Software Vendors (ISV), and systems integrators with a feature-rich and highly configurable product for data integration design, deployment, and management.

Responsible for selling XYZ Integration products to the ISV vertical market
- Presidents Club FY08
- National Accounts such as ADP, Unica, Softrax, Micros-Retail, Progress Software
- Focused on signing new technology partnerships
- Coordinated Partner Enablement
- Prospected for new business with an ISV focus
- Strengths for developing strong relationships with customers and potential customers

ACCOUNT MANAGER   2004 – 2007
XYZA Technologies – Waltham, MA
The leading provider of high-performance enterprise integration software. XZYA's customers include many of the world's Fortune 200 financial and telecommunications companies.

Responsible for direct and indirect sale of infrastructure software, services, and maintenance products in the West and Southwest territories.
- Consistently overachieved revenue targets
- President's Club 2006
- First Inside Account Manager to sell our new Service Oriented Architecture product
- Coordinated with Finance, Legal, and Operations to start, work, and close new business revenue
- Negotiated and closed new business contracts for OEM/ISV customers
- Monitored and managed distribution of existing OEM/ISV contracts
- Quota attainment at 1H 2007: 58% of annual number $1.2M
- Organized and delivered WebEx presentations to customers
- Responsible for detailed Account Plans

CHRISTOPHER KRAMER

781-123-4567

INSIDE SALES REPRESENTATIVE – MAJOR ACCOUNTS TEAM   2001 – 2004
IBM (Rational Software Group), Lexington, MA
The leading provider of application development software that lets companies build and deploy programs both internally and externally. Rational Software, an industry leader, was purchased by IBM in February 2003.

Responsible for generating new license revenue for several territories over the year including Federal Accounts and Department of Defense.
- Drove consistent revenue via sales of new licenses and up-selling to more current versions and Rational suites. Consistently exceeded quota.
- Developed and maintained detailed spreadsheets used in monitoring performance and territory success for entire team.
- Continually fine-tuned exceptional organizational skills in highly detailed, strategic closure of deals in Major Accounts. (i.e. General Electric, BAE Systems, Pitney Bowes, Motorola, Genuity).
- Attained high team honors and recognition through consistently exceeding quota and through acknowledgment as a team leader – often mentoring new members of the team.
- Succeeded in adverse conditions in which a team member was unexpectedly out of work and covered open territory and still achieved highest quota achievement for both territories allowing for smooth transition upon their return.
- Member of Founders Club 2001, 2002, & 2003: highest award given to sales individuals who consistently attain high quota achievement and display those characteristics held to be exemplary for success and continued improvement within the role.

TRANSPORTATION COORDINATOR   1998 – 2000
AmeriGas UGI, Houston, TX
The second-largest propane retailer in America.

Directly managed the daily activities of 30 operations employees.
- Coordinated smooth operation of delivery services, acting as liaison between customers, delivery staff, and management.
- Managed and reported on all Profit and Loss statements for each account.
- Responsible for overseeing and maintaining customer inventory.
- Established more secure hiring methods through creating method of thorough background checks of potential employees.
- Fostered excellent working relationships with other large energy management companies, often acting as liaison between corporate executive staff and frontline team members.

RELEVANT SKILLS/SALES TRAINING

- Karrass Negotiation Training
- Solution Selling – 5-day course
- SPIN Selling – 5-day course
- Geoffrey Alexander Sales Training – one week
- Socratic Sales Method
- Signature Selling Method
- CRM Experience with Salesforce, ACCPAC, and Vantive

EDUCATION

Texas A&M University, College Station, TX   December 1997
- Bachelor of Science, Business Administration and Business Management
- Minor in Medical Sciences

Part 3

Career Transitions: Changes in Job Function

AutoCAD to Kitchen Designer

Prade Mateja has been an AutoCAD draftsman for many years—most recently in residential construction. Unfortunately, the economic downturn has brought with it a decline in new home construction, and Prade was laid off in 2008.

Prade has only been in Chicago, his current home city, about two years and does not know a lot of people except through his last job. He is not familiar with the networking techniques that many job seekers are using today. He has a wife and two children to support, so he feels the pressure to find a new job quickly.

Challenges to Making the Switch

Prade has been doing AutoCAD and architectural drafting his entire career. He has been primarily an assistant to architects and construction managers, so his contact with customers is fairly limited. He feels frustrated that there are no AutoCAD jobs advertised and doesn't feel like he has any options. By changing his function slightly, however, he discovers that he *does* have options. While few people are buying new homes in the current economy, many are choosing to remodel. If Prade can translate his skills into some facet of home remodeling, he has a good chance of finding work.

Prade soon finds a job opening for a design assistant in a company that specializes in kitchen and bath remodeling. The job description fits him perfectly because it requires AutoCAD experience—and Prade studied cabinet making at the university. He revises his resume to a functional format, shortens his work history, and eliminates unnecessary information.

Transferable Skills

Knowledge of construction

Design knowledge

Needs assessment

Customer service

Supervision of drafting staff

Scheduling

Planning

Project management

AutoCAD

Hand drafting

Cabinetry knowledge

Oral and written communication

Interpretation of drawings

Record and file maintenance

Job Description

Kitchen Design Assistant

- Use AutoCAD systems to create, modify, and release drawings under supervision of a senior designer

- Use AutoCAD to draft cabinetry floor plans and elevations; plot drawings and file on our computer network

- Work with senior designer to measure jobsite spaces, add information to current drawings, and create Excel-based factory orders

- Attend client meetings in showroom and on site with senior designer

- Work closely with the order processing department in the factory to ensure that drawings are accurate; self-check own work for completeness and accuracy

- Liaise with clients, general contractor, or representative to ensure understanding for all parties and to execute an efficient installation

- An Associate's degree or completion of a technical trade school in AutoCAD, drafting, or a related field, plus one to three years of related work experience

- Demonstrate proficiency in both oral and written communication; read and interpret drawings; prepare accurate, detailed drawings using information from Designer

Resume Makeover

Prade's resume is reformatted into a combination of functional and chronological to emphasize his knowledge and skills for this specific job.

❶ Prade's target job is specified at the beginning of his resume, along with a short statement of his qualifications.

❷ He immediately follows with a list of competencies, including those mentioned in the job description.

❸ His significant drafting and computer skills are brought closer to the top of the resume. He includes SureTrak and Lotus because these are likely to be needed in his next job.

❹ His most pertinent experience is highlighted and divided into three primary categories.

❺ His Education section is added after his Experience section to show up front that he has the educational qualifications.

❻ Prade's Work History section is added toward the end of the resume. Employers from more than 10 years ago have not been included, and dates are listed with years only.

❼ The Other Information listed in his "before" resume is either incorporated into prior sections of his resume (such as his computer skills) or left off (such as salary range and career level).

❽ "References Available" is left off completely because it is assumed that references are available if requested.

❾ Because Prade's education and work history in the West Indies are red flags that he may not be a U.S. citizen, his work status is included at the end of his resume.

Prade Mateja

1815 Kaffe Circle, Chicago, IL 60664
email: email@email.com

(h) 773.123.1234   (c) 773.123.5678

OBJECTIVE: To become an Architectural or Structural Cad Designer in a Consulting or Contracting firm that will provide a rewarding yet challenging work environment.

EXPERIENCE:

Mar 2007 – Oct 2008   Premier Homes Inc.   Chicago, IL
Cad Operator
Prepare master construction drawings of floor plans, exterior & interior elevations, and electrical layouts from architect sketches or hand drafts for single-family homes. Incorporate architect redlines into the master set of drawings. Update, maintain, and publish a master set of floor plans and sales brochures. Prepare complete set of drawings for homes to-be-built as per buyer specifications. Resolve any drawing objections by Building Dept on permit issues.

Jan 2000 – Dec 2006   Benson Building Engineering   Richmond Hill, NY
Office Manager / Senior Draftsman
Supervise a CADD staff of six full-time and three part-time employees. Prepare architectural and structural drawings in AutoCAD for residential and commercial buildings and submission to the NYC Dept of Buildings for approval and permits. Check all permit applications for compliance to the NYC Zoning and Building Code. Maintain and upgrade the computer systems, network, and software.

Jan 2001 – May 2001   ACE Construction Corp   Richmond Hill, NY
Structural Draftsman
Prepare structural steel erection and shop fabrication drawings in AutoCAD for industrial and commercial buildings from engineer mark-ups.

Feb 1994 – Oct 1999   Capricorn Caribbean Ltd.   Trinidad W.I.
Dec 1997 – Oct 1999 Planner / Scheduler
Assist the Projects Controls Manager in scheduling, planning, and monitoring on-site progress in the construction of a new petrochemical plant. Prepare weekly reports in Microsoft Access, Primavera P3, and Suretrak.

May 1996 – Nov 1997 Engineering Technician
Prepare structural steel and reinforced concrete drawings in AutoCAD 95 for offshore oil rigs and refinery upgrades. Measure and report on field construction progress of roads and bridges in Microsoft Project. Prepare Bill of Quantities for project estimating/budgeting and for submission of tenders on public housing, schools, and office complexes using Microsoft Office software.

Feb 1994 – April 1996 Planning and Progress Technician
Measure on-site progress of civil, mechanical, piping, instrumentation, and electrical work for oil and gas refinery projects. Prepare weekly progress reports in Microsoft Excel for labor, equipment, and material. Update CPM and Gantt charts by hand.

Nov 1993 – Jan 1994   Implementation Group Ltd.   Trinidad W.I.
Architectural Draftsman
Prepare architectural, civil, and structural drawing using MiniCAD and other Macintosh software for hotels, schools, and housing projects.

Page 1 of 2

Apr 1988 – Oct 1993   Mallard Contractors Ltd.   Trinidad W.I.
Architectural Draftsman/Junior Estimator
Prepare architectural, civil, and structural drawings using MiniCAD and other Macintosh software for hotels, schools, and housing projects. Prepare Bill of Quantities for project estimating/budgeting and for submission of tenders on hotels, schools, and housing projects in Lotus spreadsheet. Measure and report on on-site progress of construction work in Lotus spreadsheet.

May 1984 – March 1988   Self-Employed   Trinidad W.I.
Architectural Draftsman
Design and prepare all necessary drawings by hand and obtain construction approval for various residential buildings for private clients.

Aug 1980 – Apr 1984   John Williams Caribbean Ltd.   Trinidad W.I.
Structural Steel Fabricator / Checker
Laid out, marked, and measured structural steelwork during and after fabrication in the shop for multi-story buildings, stadiums, and industrial projects.

EDUCATION:

Sep 1987 – Jun 1990   San Fernando Technical Institute
Diploma in Construction Engineering

Sep 1983 – Jun 1985   University of the West Indies, Extra Mural Studies
Four GCE Ordinary Level and Two Advanced Level subjects

Sep 1978 – Jun 1983   San Fernando Technical Institute
Diplomas in Woodwork and General Drafting

OTHER INFORMATION:

7 **Personal**

Career Level	Intermediate architectural or structural draftsman.
Years of relevant work	26 years
Work Status	US - Authorized to work in this country for any employer
Salary Range	Negotiable
Summary	Quick learner and self-taught in most areas. Motivated to experiment with new ideas and technology. Team player and follows instruction, policies, and procedures.

3 **Computer Software Experience**

Apple MacIntosh	April 1988 to January 1994
Microsoft Windows	April 1990 to Present
Microsoft Office Applications	January 1994 to Present
AutoCAD	May 1996 to Present
Primavera P3 & Suretrak	December 1997 to October 1999
Internet	January 1995 to Present, Advanced user

Target Company

Company Size	No Preference
Category	Architectural or Structural Engineering
Industry	Building Construction
Location	Austin - Round Rock, TX

8 References Available Upon Request

Page 2 of 2

Prade Mateja

(h) 773.123.1234   (c) 773.123.5678   email@email.com   Chicago, IL 60664

Design Assistant

Master AutoCAD designer with 24 years experience in translating customer needs to architectural designs. Excellent communication skills and customer focus. College degrees in construction engineering, cabinetry, woodwork, and general drafting.

AREAS OF EXPERTISE

- Drafting
- Design
- Construction
- Needs assessment
- Customer service
- Management
- Scheduling
- Planning
- Project management
- Cabinetry
- Reading/Interpreting drawings
- Record and file maintenance

DRAFTING / COMPUTER SKILLS

AutoCAD systems	Microsoft Office	Primavera
Apple Macintosh	Microsoft Project	SureTrak
Microsoft Windows	Lotus spreadsheets	Plotters
Hand-drafting		

EXPERIENCE

Customer Service
- Worked with clients to determine needs and to ensure accurate design specifications
- Maintained regular communication with clients during progress of projects

Supervisory/Project Management
- Supervised CADD staff of six full-time and three part-time employees
- Prepared weekly reports on labor, equipment, and material
- Assisted with scheduling, planning, and monitoring on-site progress of construction projects
- Measured and reported progress of construction projects using Lotus spreadsheets and MS Project
- Prepared Bill of Quantities for project estimating/budgeting using Lotus spreadsheets

Technical
- Prepared architectural, civil, and structural drawings using AutoCAD, MiniCAD, and other Macintosh software for residential and commercial buildings, including floor plans, exterior and interior elevations, and electrical layouts
- Ensured drawings were in compliance with local laws and ordinances, revising as needed
- Experienced at updating CPM and Gantt charts by hand

EDUCATION
San Fernando Technical Institute, Trinidad, W.I.
Diplomas in Construction Engineering, Woodwork, and General Drafting

---

Prade Mateja   (h) 773.123.4567   (c) 773.123.4567   email@email.com   Chicago, IL 60664

WORK HISTORY

Cad Operator
Premier Homes Inc., Chicago, IL (residential builder)   *2007 – 2008*
- Prepared master construction drawings of floor plans from architect sketches or hand drafts.
- Incorporated architect redlines into master drawings.
- Updated, maintained, and published a master set of floor plans and sales brochures.
- Prepared complete sets of drawings for homes to-be-built per buyer specifications.
- Resolved drawing objections on permit issues from Building Dept.

Office Manager / Senior Draftsman
Benson Building Engineering, Richmond Hill, NY (building and remodeling services)   *2000 – 2006*
- Supervise CADD staff.
- Prepare architectural and structural drawings for residential and commercial buildings for submission to NYC Dept of Buildings for approval and permits.
- Checked all permit applications for compliance to the NYC Zoning and Building Code.
- Maintained and upgraded the computer systems, network, and software.

Structural Draftsman
ACE Construction Corp, Richmond Hill, NY (commercial construction)   *2001 – 2001*
- Prepared structural steel erection and shop fabrication drawings in AutoCAD for industrial and commercial buildings from engineer mark-ups.

Planner/Scheduler
Capricorn Caribbean Ltd., Trinidad W.I. (single-family home contractor)   *1997 – 1999*
- Assisted the Projects Controls Manager in scheduling, planning, and monitoring on-site progress in the construction of a new petrochemical plant.
- Prepared weekly reports in Microsoft Access, Primavera P3, and Suretrak.

Engineering Technician
Capricorn Caribbean Ltd., Trinidad W.I. (single-family home contractor)   *1996 – 1997*
- Prepared structural steel and reinforced concrete drawings in AutoCAD 95 for offshore oil rigs and refinery upgrades.
- Measured and reported on field construction progress of roads and bridges in Microsoft Project.
- Prepared Bill of Quantities for project estimating/budgeting and for submission of tenders on public housing, schools, and office complexes using Microsoft Office software.

Planning and Progress Technician
Capricorn Caribbean Ltd., Trinidad W.I. (single-family home contractor)   *1994 – 1996*
- Measured on-site progress of civil, mechanical, piping, instrumentation, and electrical work for oil and gas refinery projects.
- Prepared weekly progress reports in Microsoft Excel for labor, equipment, and material.
- Updated CPM and Gantt charts by hand.

WORK STATUS
Authorized to work in the United States for any employer

Auditor to Security Investigator

Ramona Snead has worked for the state auditor's office for nearly five years. Oregon state agencies are tightening their belts, just as private industry is. While experienced as an auditor, Ramona does not have the academic credentials required for a financial audit. In addition, she has recently suffered some political setbacks at work, when several audits she was leading went substantially over budget. Rather than cutting her from staff, Ramona gets word that she will no longer be allowed to lead audit teams. She is removed from several teams and is reduced to picking up simple tasks from coworkers she used to supervise. She knows it is just a matter of time before she is laid off.

Ramona's degree is in public administration. She considers going back into law enforcement or perhaps work for a political candidate, but those extremely stressful environments no longer appeal to her. She decides to pursue a job in security because the industry is literally exploding. There are federal jobs with the Transportation Security Administration (TSA) and Homeland Security. Retail stores have also added security personnel in recent years, and credit card security is growing daily.

Challenges to Making the Switch

Ramona's last documented job in security ended nearly 12 years ago, so there are a lot of techniques and developments to catch up on. She will also have a challenge showing the relationship between audit assignments and security investigation.

On the plus side, her auditing experience involves the same analysis required for secure financial transactions and store inventory. She has a real knack for seeing discrepancies that most people would miss. In this respect, her audit background will serve her well.

She is also hoping that her leadership experience at the state auditor's office will allow her to make a lateral move, rather than starting at the bottom of the security field.

Transferable Skills

Fraud investigations

Data analysis

Problem solving

Accurate record keeping

Supervision of personnel

Presentations to management

Recommending corrective actions

Report writing

Emergency management

Audit procedures

Job Description
Investigations and Security Manager

- Development and management of corporate security program consistent with regulatory requirements and company standards

- Conduct and oversee investigations of fraud, theft, and other client- and associate-related matters—maintaining accurate records

- Coordination and oversight of our company's Red Flags Program

- Supervision of outside contracted security services and management of related contract terms

- Respond to robberies, kidnap/hostage, and bomb threat situations

- Primary liaison with law enforcement; make court appearances on company's behalf

- Oversight of Suspicious Activity Report (SAR) filings and board-level reporting

- Develop and conduct training on security-related topics: fraud, physical security, identity theft, robberies, and so on—both inside and outside the organization

- Administer card access, DVR (camera) system, and security alarm systems

- Daily oversight and management of several security associates

- Assist with examinations and audits by regulatory and outside accounting bodies

---

Resume Makeover

Ramona creates a resume that is easier to read and highlights her applicable work experience.

❶ Her title, "Security/Audit Professional," allows her to link her former work history with her current objective.

❷ She rewrites her opening statement achievements into security language. She also shows that she can handle oral presentations to high-level executives.

❸ Her Core Competencies section mirrors the requirements set out in the job description.

❹ The paragraph format in the first resume is converted into easily readable bulleted points. For her current job, she reports both achievements and responsibilities.

❺ Her Professional Experience section goes back to 1995 so that she can show she was promoted into loss prevention at a retail store. In the interview, she will talk about how security has long been a fascination for her.

❻ Her Education and Affiliations section moves to the end of the resume. This is an appropriate place for a professional with nearly 15 years experience.

Ramona Snead
1234 Cedar Dr. Salem, OR 97200

email@email.com
(971) 123-4567

Education:

- **Master of Public Administration**—Arizona State University, Dec. 1999
- **Bachelor of Arts, Political Science**—Willamette University, May 1996

Certifications:

- **Certified Fraud Examiner, March 2007**

Work Experience:

State Auditor's Office—03/05 – Present
Audit state agencies, higher education institutions, call centers, and private entities receiving state funding; develop risk assessments and audit programs, conduct interviews, investigate fraud, collect evidence; review and analyze laws and regulations, policies and procedures, revenue, expenditure, and program related data; analyze data; perform audit work/assessment of input and output controls and user access for information systems; train new employees in audit process and fraud techniques, review audit working papers, and supervise/evaluate other team members, including new employees; draft audit proposals; write audit reports for Legislative Audit Committee and public; present findings to management/executives; follow up on the implementation status of Information Technology project at a state health agency; conduct Federal compliance audit; assist in the preparation of Legislative Workforce Summaries; monitor legislative hearings as needed.

Potential fraud/waste/abuse noted on projects: altered documents (same name/different signature; copied signature/manual form completion); quantity change (reduce quantity of Rx without cause/amount owed by vendor decrease); material misstatement on financial record (record items as pass-through expenses to improve outlook of financial viability; ghost clients (reimbursement sent to non-client using eligible client data/created fictional clients).

City of Portland, Portland Police Department—01/02 – 12/04
Prepared performance measure/budget reports; implemented performance measure tracking program, including calculation methodology; conducted budget and performance measure processes training; prepared performance measures/budget documentation in accordance with business plan; created program goals and objectives for employee performance review process; evaluated program compliance and conducted quality assurance/performance measure assessments and audits; identified staffing needs and implemented new operating procedures; recommended and implemented patrol shift schedule changes and deployment strategies using Staff Wizard software; gerrymandered the city from 7 to 9 police sectors and realigned patrol districts using GIS software; presented program evaluation results and recommendations to Executive/Command Staff and City Management; performed extensive data analysis; provided consultative service and technical assistance to monitor patrol program efficiencies. Recommended service delivery improvements; wrote monthly crime and calls for service reports; evaluated criminal activity and provided data to support operational changes; analyzed service delivery to newly annexed areas; participated in county-wide Truancy Task Force in efforts to reduce juvenile crime.

Ramona Snead

City of Portland, Neighborhood Planning and Zoning—6/01 – 12/01
Completed five neighborhood planning projects simultaneously; represented city regarding neighborhood improvement projects; performed demographic and service delivery research and analysis; completed needs assessments (community improvement goals) and recommended action plans to meet goals; recommended changes in city policy to meet community improvement goals; prepared reports for Planning Commission and City Council; coordinated and facilitated neighborhood meetings and maintained relationships with community leaders; attended Conflict Resolution and Meeting Facilitation training; managed mediation agreement between city and plaintiff group and developed policies and procedures for meeting terms of agreement; processed payments to plaintiffs; monitored plaintiff accounts and maintained plaintiff files; ensured plaintiffs and city complied with terms of mediation agreement. Recommended termination of program participation for non-complying plaintiffs.

City of Beaverton, Communications and Information Technology—6/00 – 11/00
Revised Standardized Emergency Management System (SEMS) manual; assisted in emergency preparedness drill and evaluated compliance; assessed emergency needs and developed action plans to improve emergency readiness; represented city at Disaster Management Meetings; implemented emergency awareness program and provided supplies to each department; coordinated Neighborhood Beautification and Volunteer Awards programs; coordinated Public Safety Youth Outreach program; obtained sponsorships from amusement parks, sports teams, museums, and local merchants; liaised with Contract Services (cable, utilities) regarding service delivery complaints; performed grant research for refuse management; prepared news articles for release in local newspaper and city magazine; maintained effective relationships with city council, city management, and community leaders.

United States House of Representatives, Congressman Henson—5/99 – 5/00
Prepared Strategic Management Plan and Operational Policies and Procedures for District Office; delegated constituent inquiries to responsible staff; liaised between constituents and Federal agencies; performed Federal grant research on behalf of constituents; provided assistance to Legislative Aides as needed; managed Internship/Training Program; created Intern Reference Guide and internal newsletter; developed intern recruitment plan and recruited interns; implemented annual high school "job shadow" day; supervised and evaluated interns; maintained effective relationships with public and elected officials; represented the Congressman at events.

Chase Manhattan Bank—10/97 – 6/99
Started in inbound/outbound collections and promoted to Skip Trace/Collections Division in a call center environment; investigated and reviewed delinquent credit card accounts for possible fraud; top performer 13 consecutive months; familiar with Automated Call Distribution Systems and reviewed metrics reports for call center and staff performance; used investigation techniques to locate delinquent cardholders, including credit bureau reports, FastData, and contacts at other banking institutions; recommended skip trace and collection process improvements to enhance team performance.

Macy's—6/95 – 9/97
Started as a Sales Associate and promoted to Loss Prevention Agent. Conducted internal and external investigations, including surveillance; tracked overages/shortages associated with cash register transactions; performed cash and inventory audits; analyzed journal tapes and computer-generated reports to identify cash and inventory related discrepancies; interviewed customers and employees suspected of fraud, embezzlement, and theft; prepared investigation reports, collected and stored evidence, and recommended customers and employees for arrest or termination; responsible for opening/closing store and responding to alarm calls. Monitored employee compliance with policies and procedures; trained new employees; documented successful surveillance and investigation processes for management use.

Ramona Snead

1234 Cedar Dr. Salem, OR 97200 — (971) 123-4567 home — (971) 123-5555 cell — email@email.com

SECURITY / AUDIT PROFESSIONAL

Investigations/Risk Assessment/Loss Prevention

❶
- Proven track record for identifying risks and operational inefficiencies, as well as completing assignments within budget.
- Successful leadership, development, and evaluation of team members.
- Adept at presenting recommendations to executive management, and building relationships with internal and external customers in public, private, and community environments.
- Over 8 years of effective communication and outreach in political, community, and professional settings.
- More than 7 years of data analysis, investigations, and problem-solving experience, using Microsoft Office products.
- Subject matter expert in law enforcement, emergency management, credit card banking, health care, and call centers.

Core Competencies

❷
- Identify fraud, waste, and abuse
- Data analysis and problem solving
- Coordination and oversight of audit process
- Team and project leadership
- Conduct training on audit techniques and standards
- Daily management of audit personnel

❸

------PROFESSIONAL EXPERIENCE------

Senior Auditor—2005 to Present
STATE AUDITOR'S OFFICE—Salem, OR

Selected Achievements

❹
- Conducted audit work and wrote audit reports for high-profile, legislative, and public interest projects.
- Recognized altered documents (same name/different signature/copied signature).
- Noted irregular changes in records which reduced the amount of rebates owed to the State of Texas.
- Identified ghost/fictional clients where reimbursements were sent to non-clients using eligible client data.
- Volunteered to develop audit proposals, monitor legislative hearings, and prepare Legislative Workforce Summaries.
- Developed innovative course materials, conducted audit sampling training to 15 new auditors, received positive feedback.
- Trained 3 employees who were promoted within their first 2 years of employment with the agency.

Current Accountabilities
- Audit state agencies, call centers, and private entities receiving state funding, including audits for federal compliance.
- Lead, supervise, and evaluate audit teams, and review work papers in an automated work paper environment.
- Review and analyze federal and state laws and regulations, including client policies and procedures.
- Develop risk assessments and audit programs, conduct interviews, collect evidence, and perform audit testing.
- Evaluate revenue, expenditure, and program data, including input /output controls and user access for information systems.
- Present findings to agency management and client executives, as well as follow up on audit recommendations as needed.

Neighborhood Planner to Police Planner—2001 to 2004
CITY OF PORTLAND—Portland, OR

- Developed performance metric tracking, training, calculation, quality assurance, and reporting methodologies.
- Identified operational inefficiencies and implemented revisions to police officer deployment strategies citywide.
- Created 9 new patrol sectors using GIS software, and presented improvements in police response to executive city leaders.
- Analyzed crime data, service data to newly annexed areas, calls for service, and wrote monthly reports.
- Volunteered for and participated in a county-wide truancy reduction task force.
- Worked on 5 neighborhood planning projects requiring demographic and service delivery research and analysis.
- Facilitated community meetings, completed needs assessments, and prepared recommendations for Planning Commission.
- Managed mediation agreement requiring payment approval and termination of benefits for non-compliance with terms.

Communications and Technology Intern—2000
CITY OF BEAVERTON—Beaverton, OR

- Assisted in emergency preparedness drill, evaluated compliance, and created action plans to improve emergency readiness.
- Revised Standardized Emergency Management System (SEMS) manual and attended disaster management meetings.
- Initiated emergency awareness program and volunteered to provide supplies to each city department.
- Coordinated Neighborhood Beautification and Volunteer Awards programs.
- Organized Public Safety Youth Outreach program, and obtained sponsorships in the amount of $10,000.
- Liaised with contractors and resolved service delivery complaints from residents.
- Prepared news articles and performed grant research for refuse management program.

District Office Manager—1999 to 2000
U.S. HOUSE OF REPRESENTATIVES—Scottsdale, AZ

- Prepared strategic management plan and operational policies and procedures for District Office.
- Delegated constituent inquiries to responsible staff and liaised between constituents and federal agencies.
- Performed federal grant research and provided assistance to legislative aides in Washington, D.C.
- Managed recruitment, training, and supervision of interns, and documented procedures in Intern Reference Guide.
- Implemented annual high school "job shadow" day, which had over 75 applicants for 10 positions.
- Maintained effective relationships with public and elected officials, and represented Congressman Henson at events.
- Initiated internal newsletter, highlighting staff accomplishments at all 4 offices.

Inbound/Outbound Collector to Skip Trace Collector—1997 to 1999
CHASE MANHATTAN BANK—Tempe, AZ

- Excelled in inbound/outbound call center collections by exceeding call handling time and dollars collected performance targets.
- Promoted to Skip Trace Collections and investigated delinquent credit card accounts for possible fraud.
- Located delinquent cardholders using credit bureau reports, FastData, and contacts at other banking institutions.
- Achieved top performer 13 consecutive months, receiving monthly and quarterly bonuses and awards.
- Recognized for compliance with federal collection law, including Fair Debt Collection Act.
- Recommended skip trace and collection process improvements to enhance team performance.

Sales Associate to Loss Prevention Agent—1995 to 1997
MACY'S—Mesa, AZ

❺
- Achieved sales goals by serving customers, opening new credit accounts, and recommending "add-on" purchases.
- Conducted internal investigations, including surveillance and interviews, for theft, fraud, and embezzlement.
- Tracked overages/shortages associated with cash register transactions and performed cash and inventory audits.
- Analyzed journal tapes and computer-generated reports to identify cash and inventory related discrepancies.
- Collected evidence, prepared reports, and terminated 52 employees during tenure.
- Monitored employee compliance with policies and procedures and reported violations.
- Documented successful surveillance and investigation processes for management use and trained new employees.

------EDUCATION AND AFFILIATIONS------

❻

Master of Public Administration (M.P.A.) 1999 (Dec)—School of Public Affairs, Arizona State University, Tempe, AZ
Bachelor of Arts Political Science (B.A.) 1996 (May)—Willamette University, Salem, OR
Certified Fraud Examiner (C.F.E) 2007 (March)—Association of Certified Fraud Examiners
Arizona State Alumni Association Member
Forgotten Friends of Mixed Breed Rescue Volunteer

Bookkeeper to Math Teacher

Melinda McAdams enjoyed being a full-time parent for 10 years and supplemented her family's income by doing bookkeeping for small businesses and working as a substitute teacher. Her husband was the primary breadwinner until he lost his job at a semiconductor company and took a pay cut when he accepted a temporary position with another manufacturer. Melinda needs to boost her income and wrestled with the option of applying for staff accounting positions, which were easy to find. However, she knew she would not be happy "crunching numbers" all day.

What she loves to do is teach children. She did not expect her substitute work to be that enjoyable, but she has a gift for making math more understandable and has special success with at-risk students. With her Bachelor's degree in accounting, she is eligible for an alternative certification program through Texas State University and has passed the TExES exam for middle school mathematics.

Challenges to Making the Switch

Although she has more than three years of substitute teaching experience, Melinda is concerned about the difficulty of landing her first permanent job and competing against experienced teachers and those who obtained their teaching degree through traditional university programs. Melinda needs a teacher-style resume that emphasizes her education and instructional experience. She applies for positions through school district websites and attends job fairs. The large turnout at job fairs indicates that competition is stiff. She talks to teachers at her children's school and follows their recommendation to drop off her resume and cover letter at middle schools within a 20-mile radius of her home.

Although secondary school teachers are in demand nationwide, some of the best school districts have an abundance of applicants. Melinda recognizes she needs to apply through the traditional online channels and also present her resume— as well as follow up—with principals who will be involved in the hiring process.

Transferable Skills

Teaching

Lesson planning

Math knowledge

Behavior management

Motivating special-needs students

Grading tests

Record keeping

Verbal and written communication skills

Job Description
Middle School Math Teacher

- Bachelor's degree in education or equivalent with certification as required by the state

- Knowledge of core academic subject assigned

- Plan, develop, and implement lesson plans that fulfill the requirements of the district's instructional program

- Prepare lessons that reflect accommodations for differences in student abilities and learning styles; coordinate with special education teachers to modify curricula as needed for special education students according to guidelines established in individual education plans

- Help students analyze and improve study methods and habits; conduct ongoing assessment of student achievement through formal and informal testing; assume responsibility and sponsor extracurricular activities as appropriate

- Create a classroom environment conducive to successful student learning and appropriate for the physical, social, and emotional development of students; manage student behavior

- Skill in working with various forms of equipment, including personal computers, calculators, projectors, and printers

- Establish and maintain effective, open communication with students, parents, teachers, and administrators

---

Resume Makeover

While Melinda is making a major career shift, she is taking a subject matter knowledge that she already has and finding a way to transfer it to her goal career.

1 The headline, "Middle School Math Teacher," conveys the new focus on teaching.

2 The seven bullet points address teacher qualifications and contain key words from the job description. References are made to education, along with relevant paid and unpaid work experience.

3 The Education and Special Programs section is moved up and expanded to include the certification program, Bachelor's degree, and relevant coursework.

4 Substitute teaching experience is added to highlight key experiences and successes, including a special project and success with at-risk students.

5 School volunteer and related experience is added to reflect relevant work with young people.

6 A page 2 header is added so that Melinda's name and phone number appear on both pages.

7 The Additional Professional Experience section is de-emphasized and placed on the second page.

1234 Clearlake Loop
Austin, TX 78729

(512)123-4567
email@email.com

Melinda McAdams

Objective	To perform accounting-related work at home.		
Experience	1999–Present	McAdams Accounting Service	Austin, TX

Bookkeeper/Business Owner

- Processed payroll and payroll taxes.
- Processed customer invoices and handled receivables.
- Wrote checks.
- Maintained and reconciled checking accounts.
- Processed reports.
- Completed other tasks as requested.

	1995–1999	Texas State University	San Marcos, TX

Accountant II

- Set up and maintained research funding accounts.
- Reconciled bank and credit card accounts.
- Reconciled university records with federal government records.
- Entered journal entries.
- Processed invoices.

	1994–1995	The Forest Group	Brownsville, TX

Fleet Manager

- Processed payroll.
- Researched and maintained titles for all vehicles.
- Set up data system for titles.
- Communicated with insurance companies.

	8/1994–12/1994	Temporary Agencies	Brownsville, TX

Various

- Reconciled bank accounts.
- Processed journal entries.
- Entered data.

	1992–1994	Branco Marketing, Inc.	College Station, TX

Billing Clerk

- Produced customer invoices.
- Maintained inventory records.

Education	1989–1992	Texas A&M University	College Station, TX

- B.B.A. in Accounting

Qualifications	Current CPA license
	Experience with various software packages

References	Duane Smith 123-4567 Classic Auto Trim
	H.R. Schmidt 123-4567 H.R. Schmidt Tax Service
	Tommy Collins 123-4567 Texas State University
	Greg Edwards 123-4567

Melinda McAdams
512-123-4567 • email@email.com
1234 Clearlake Loop • Austin, TX 78729

❶

MIDDLE SCHOOL MATH TEACHER

❷
- Passed TExES 115 exam for Mathematics grades 4 to 8 and eligible for teaching assignment after completing Southwest Texas Alternative program coursework
- Regularly substitute in middle school math classes for more than three years
- Extensive experience teaching and conducting programs for adolescents during summer camps, scouting programs, and as a school library volunteer
- Training and experience in preparing lessons that reflect accommodations for differences in student abilities and learning styles
- Effectively manage student behavior and commended by middle school principal for special work with at-risk students
- Administered tests and assisted teachers with grading and keeping records
- Computer Skills: Microsoft Excel, Word, Access, and Outlook; QuickBooks, Peachtree, Ross, and Business Objects. Use projector, copiers, and other equipment

❸

EDUCATION AND SPECIAL PROGRAMS

Enrolled in the Southwest Texas Alternative Certification Program 2009
Completed courses in Effective Teaching, Assessments, Lesson Design, Classroom Management, and Reading/Cooperative Learning

Bachelor of Business Administration in Accounting 1992
Texas A&M University, College Station, TX
Completed 30 credit hours in math and 6 hours in education

TEACHING EXPERIENCE

❹
Austin Independent School District   *Substitute Teacher*   **2005 – Present**
- Completed long-term substitute assignments in middle school math classes, along with filling in short-term in biology, chemistry and language arts classes
- Assigned a special project to coordinate individual and group study sessions to improve math skills, resulting in improved grades for 95 percent of the students
- Followed lesson plans and effectively managed classes with diverse needs.
- Received commendation letter from principal for work with at-risk students.

❺
School Volunteer and Program Coordinator   **2001 – Present**
- Regularly volunteer at Carter Middle School in the library, lunchroom, and office
- Serve as an Assistant Girl Scout leader and help prepare weekly programs and accompany troop during overnight campouts and field trips
- Prepare lesson plans and materials for educational programs at a youth camp

---

ADDITIONAL PROFESSIONAL EXPERIENCE

❻

McAdams Accounting Service, Austin, TX   *Bookkeeper*   **1999 – Present**
- Sole proprietor of a business specializing in processing payroll and payroll taxes
- Write checks, process customer invoices, and handle receivables
- Maintain and reconcile checking accounts

❼

Texas State University, San Marcos, TX   *Accountant II*   **1995 – 1999**
- Set up and maintained research funding accounts
- Reconciled bank and credit card accounts
- Reconciled university records with federal government records
- Entered journal entries
- Processed invoices

The Forest Group, Brownsville, TX   *Fleet Manager*   **1994 –1995**
- Processed payroll
- Researched and maintained titles for all vehicles
- Set up data system for titles
- Communicated with insurance companies

Branco Marketing, College Station, TX   *Billing Clerk*   **1992 – 1994**
- Produced customer invoices
- Maintained inventory records

Engineer—Batteries to Energy Strategist

James Templin has had a long career in high tech, spending the last 10 years focused on the design and production of computer batteries and power supplies. He has won six patents for his company and is sought after for his expertise in battery design. With slower sales, however, his computer company is delaying the introduction of new products, so there is less design work overall for the company. James decides to apply for another position in the regulatory group. While things might be slow in batteries, energy regulations have actually increased—so this is an area of the company that may be safer from layoffs.

James has strong beliefs about energy conservation, government, politics, and public policy. He thinks the pivotal issue of energy conservation is getting control of large data centers, many of which consume as much energy as small cities. James begins to educate himself about data centers and energy efficiency.

James realizes that his work has given him a substantial background in energy conservation standards, government regulations, and intellectual property legal issues. James begins his job search inside the huge company where he works. He networks with coworkers in the regulatory group, hoping that a suitable position will open up. In addition, he builds his image on LinkedIn, reconnecting with college friends and former colleagues. In conversations only, by phone and in person, he delivers a consistent message: "I'm looking to move into energy policy, where I can use my engineering skills to make a difference."

Challenges to Making the Switch

James is known within his company as tough-minded and a doer. He has made some political errors in the past, expressing his strong opinions in the wrong settings. So, he may be viewed as not savvy enough to represent the company in delicate negotiations with the Environmental Protection Agency (EPA), Energy Star, and other regulatory bodies.

He is also at the senior engineer level, and the regulatory job requires a slightly higher pay grade. So James will have to convince the hiring manager that he is up to the management level of responsibility for his desired job. He will also have to highlight his leadership capabilities, because he is primarily known for his subject matter expertise in batteries.

Transferable Skills

Relationship building with regulators, manufacturing partners, and internal legal staff

Battery/power supply design and safety

Energy standards

Presentation skills/public speaking

Strategic thinking

Negotiation

Business partnerships in Asia, Europe, and Australia

Job Description
Energy Regulatory Strategist

- Assist in planning phase of new programs to identify legal requirements and key marketing requirements as they pertain to the regulatory environment

- Work on extremely complex problems where analysis of situations or data requires an evaluation of intangible variables

- Exercise independent judgment in developing methods, techniques, and evaluation criteria for obtaining results

- Outline required tests to ensure that company products are compliant with worldwide regulatory emissions, safety, and environmental regulatory agency requirements

- Develop and test methodologies as needed for evaluating additional features and needs based on lessons learned

- Prepare schedules, statements of work, and functional plans necessary to obtain required safety approvals for new products

- Work with regulatory investigations to review and analyze equipment that has failed in the field and that may have safety implications

---

Resume Makeover

James has created a combination resume that retains his technical achievements while emphasizing the skills needed for his next position.

1 "Energy Efficiency Strategist" is a close match to his desired position. With this headline, he says that he is qualified and interested.

2 His top achievements are selected based on the responsibilities of his new job.

3 After a rewrite, the Core Competencies section now matches the job requirements.

4 His current job achievements are expanded to highlight a special energy efficiency project he volunteered for in the past year.

5 He reframes his design achievements by adding the word "regulatory." In each statement, he refers to the regulatory challenges faced with each project.

6 His first two jobs from 1978 to 1984 are eliminated because of space.

7 The Education & Affiliations section now includes the Six Sigma Green Belt designation, which is much more powerful than a list of training classes on leadership and quality. He also sets the expectation that he will be able to represent the company based on speeches and presentations that he has already made.

James Templin

1234 Woodview Road   Houston, TX 77000 (713) 123-4567

EDUCATION

Texas A&M University, College Station, Texas
Bachelor of Science, College of Engineering, Engineering Technology, Electronics 1978

PROFESSIONAL EXPERIENCE

CC Computer Corporation - Houston, TX   September 1997 - Present
Development Manager – Batteries & Power Supplies

- Developed safety qualification process for Lithium Ion and Lead Acid batteries used in CC Computer Portable and Enterprise systems.
- Developed Roles and Responsibilities documenting cross line of business agreement of organizational tasks by Phase Review Process phase.
- Implemented tasking process and format for driving field defect root cause identification and closed loop corrective action.
- Developed input for OEM and commodity quarterly business reviews. Attended and led breakout sessions for OEM business reviews, and relationship team meetings.
- Represented Advance line of business on numerous core development teams.
- Worked with SQE group to audit and develop quality business contract goals for OEM suppliers. Supported Procurement on master purchase agreement.

AT&T, Marietta, GA   April 1990 - September 1997
Director of Engineering and Operations
Senior facility manager responsible for total manufacturing operations of satellite-based data communications equipment (VSATs).

- Cost management responsibility for $56 million material cost stream.
- Presented capability and technology briefing to customers. Reviewed contracts and provided direction and input to program management and product teams. This included software and hardware systems integration issues and resolution.
- Initiated and managed a program to improve supplier product quality by 200% while costs were reduced 10% or more per year.
- Provided reporting to the president and directed cross-functional quality improvement effort improving reliability by 300% in two years.
- Managed the design, development, systems integration, installation, profit and loss of software and hardware for a $24 million revenue business. Reduced product cycle time by half in two years.
- Responsible for transition to outsourced manufacturing and supply line process.
- Responsible for management of 63 employees, 16,000 square feet of manufacturing space and 25,000 square feet of distribution center.

Schlumberger Technologies, Orlando, FL   October 1984 - April 1990
Sales Engineer and Product Specialist

- Responsible for the attainment of a $2.7 million annual quota.
- Provided program management for multi-system deployments and systems integration of software, systems and network products.
- Coordinated deployments of equipment to out-source suppliers for production ramps, and source changes.
- Interviewed, analyzed, and provided advanced manufacturing processes and equipment to major electronic manufacturers in the southeast including AT&T, Harris, SCI, IBM, NCR, Westinghouse, Dictaphone, Hewlett-Packard, and DEC.
- Performed management and technical presentations, and assessed customer requirements.
- Acquired and evaluated competitive information and specifications; and provided strategy and insight to sales management.

Datapoint Corporation, San Antonio, TX   June 1982 - October 1984
Manager of Test Engineering

- Responsibilities included all production ATE and test equipment specified, built, and purchased for Datapoint.
- Maintained expense, capital, and NRE budgets and staff of twelve engineers and four technicians.
- Management of the 9725 Datapoint Manufacturing Information Systems operations.
- Administered multi-plant test apparatus such as component, in-circuit, functional, and systems level test.

Texas Instruments, College Station, TX   May 1978 - June 1982
Section Manager, Test Engineering

- Responsibilities included all production ATE and test equipment specified, built, and purchased for Texas Instruments.
- Responsible for updating and sustaining test equipment for the computer and peripheral product lines.
- Responsible for creating new tooling for all new products such as Winchester disk products, computer terminal, and peripheral equipment.

CORPORATE CITIZENSHIP AND ACTIVITIES:

- AT&T ISO 9000 Quality Systems Auditor.
- Participates regularly in internal AT&T ISO Audits of manufacturing facilities.
- MBNQA and President's Award AT&T site representative and team member.
- Reviewed other AT&T location's MBNQA and President's Award submissions for the team.
- Created and manages the Quality Data Center for Marietta.
- Member of AT&T Chief Engineer's and Quality Manager's Councils.
- Product Team member, responsible for generating quality plans, reliability assessments, introduction schedules, and product cost structure.

AWARDS:

VP Award CC Computer Corporation - October 1999
AT&T Business Communications Services Achievement Award - 1993

ADDITIONAL EDUCATION:

Leadership Development Program
    by AT&T Executive Education Development
    Corporate Education and Training Center
Lead Assessor of Quality Systems
    by Perry Johnson & Associates
Quality Assurance Auditing Techniques for ISO 9000
    by L. Marvin Johnson and Associates, Inc.
Quality Improvement Team Leader Training
    by AT&T Corporate Education and Training Center
Process Quality Management, and Improvement
    by AT&T Bell Laboratories
Management of Productivity and Quality
    by W. Edwards Deming
Quality, Productivity, and Competitive Position
    by W. Edwards Deming
Quality Improvement Through Defect Prevention
    by Phillip Crosby and Associates

JAMES TEMPLIN

1234 Woodview Road • Houston, TX 77000 • email@email.com • 713.123.4567 cell

(1)

ENERGY EFFICIENCY STRATEGIST

Regulatory Influence / Industry Leadership / Power Source Expert

(2)

- Known as a thought leader and outspoken advocate for efficient, pragmatic, and profitable solutions
- 20+ year record of success assisting multimillion-dollar sales deals with Fortune 500 accounts, while providing forward-thinking solutions that serve client needs
- Influential with all levels of the Energy Efficiency decision chain – governmental bodies; multi-company consortiums; and sales, marketing, and engineering organizations
- Adept at driving both practical and profitable solutions in the areas of Power, Enterprise, and Data Center Efficiency, and Energy Efficiency Standards
- Tenacious in building relationships with government regulators, technical and legal staff, and OEM vendors

Core Competencies

(3)

- Strategic positioning for multinational computer mfg.
- Building relationships with regulators
- Thought leader on enterprise energy management
- Battery technology expert – hold 6 patents
- Successful negotiation with EPA and the EU
- Advocate for efficiency AND profitability
- Shaper of policy and corporate strategy
- Powerful communicator of complex issues

PROFESSIONAL EXPERIENCE

Development Manager – Battery & Power Supplies
CC Computer Corporation – Houston, TX, 1997 – Present

Energy Efficiency Project

(4)

- Conceived, designed, and led a project to reduce energy use of CC Computer Corporation's on-site desktop computers by more than 30%.
- Saved the company $1.8 million per year in electrical power use, offsetting 8 tons of CO_2.
- Worked with software vendor to private label its innovative product for company's use with clients.
- Created a new profit center for CC services consulting group, generating $340K in consulting income during the first two quarters.

Regulatory/Design Achievements

(5)

- During fiscal years 1998 to present, have designed, managed, and produced numerous (approximately 45) battery and power supply improvements, leading to 10 patent disclosures, and 6 patents awarded at this time.
- Created an energy efficiency regulatory road map for delivering regulations ahead of schedule, while reducing the churn in the organization, maintaining total cost of ownership, and building market share.
- Developed safety qualification process for Lithium Ion and Lead Acid batteries used in Computer Portable and Enterprise systems.
- Developed Roles and Responsibilities documenting cross-line-of-business service level agreements of the battery and power supply development process.
- Implemented tasking process and format for driving root-cause identification and closed-loop corrective action for laptop computer power systems.
- Developed input and strategy for OEM and commodity quarterly business reviews. Attended and led breakout sessions for OEM business reviews, and relationship team meetings.
- Represented laptop lines of business on numerous core development teams.
- Worked with SQE (Supplier Quality) group to audit and develop quality business contract goals for OEM suppliers. Supported Procurement on master purchase agreements.

JAMES TEMPLIN

512.123.4567

Director of Engineering and Operations - AT&T - Marietta, GA, 1990 – 1997

- Senior facility manager responsible for total manufacturing operations of satellite-based data communications equipment (VSATs).
- Responsible for management of 63 employees, 16,000 square feet of manufacturing space and 25,000 square feet of distribution center.
- Cost management responsibility for $56 million material cost stream.
- Presented capability and technology briefings to customers. Reviewed contracts and provided direction and input to program management and product teams. Included software and hardware systems integration issues and resolution.
- Initiated and managed a program to improve supplier product quality by 200%, while costs were reduced 10% or more per year. Received Business Communication Achievement Award.
- Provided reporting to the president and directed cross-functional quality improvement effort, improving reliability by 300% in two years.
- Managed the design, development, systems integration, installation, profit and loss of software and hardware for a $24 million revenue business.
- Reduced product cycle time by half in two years.
- Responsible for transition to outsourced manufacturing and supply-line process.

Sales Engineer/Product Specialist - Schlumberger Technologies - Orlando, FL, 1984 – 1990

- Responsible for $2.7 million annual sales quota.
- Provided program management for multi-system deployments and systems integration of software, systems, and network products.
- Coordinated deployments of equipment to outsource suppliers for production ramps.
- Interviewed, analyzed, and provided advanced manufacturing processes and equipment to major electronic manufacturers in the Southeast, including AT&T, Harris, SCI, IBM, NCR, Westinghouse, Dictaphone, Hewlett-Packard, and DEC.
- Created and delivered management and technical presentations, and assessed customer requirements.
- Acquired and evaluated competitive information and specifications; providing strategy and insight to sales management.

EDUCATION & AFFILIATIONS

(6)

Texas A&M University, College Station, TX, 1978 - BS, College of Engineering
Green Belt - Six Sigma - Managed and mentored multiple projects
Speaker - Data Center Dynamics Tradeshow, November 2006
Speaker - AEA Conference, Brussels, June 2006

CORPORATE CITIZENSHIP & AWARDS

(7)

- AT&T ISO 9000 Quality Systems Auditor
- Participates regularly in internal AT&T ISO audits of manufacturing facilities
- MBNQA and President's Award AT&T site representative and team member
- Reviewed other AT&T location's MBNQA and President's Award submissions for the team
- Created and managed the Quality Data Center for Marietta
- Member of AT&T Chief Engineer's and Quality Manager's Councils
- VP Award CC Computer Corporation - October 1999
- AT&T Business Communications Services Achievement Award - 1993

Executive Development to Outplacement Consultant

Eileen O'Malley has had a focused career in executive development and organizational design. For the last three years, she has had a contract with a major university, helping its public radio station with a culture change. This process involves consulting, training, coaching, developing training materials, and delivery. With the new economy, however, culture-change work is considered a luxury—and her program is abruptly stopped.

She could go back to being a human resources professional. She has all the credentials. But with downsizing and layoffs, few firms have open positions in HR. She decides to go where her clients are—in coaching for outplacement, where executives are given assistance in finding their next position.

Challenges to Making the Switch

While Eileen's credentials in performance improvement and team effectiveness are substantial, she will have to revamp her resume to emphasize the more personal, one-on-one skills of a career counselor. She has never been a hiring manager, but she has researched their perspective and even created a course to help hiring managers select better candidates. She will have to shift her perspective from the employer's side to the job applicant's. By applying for a job with a large outplacement firm, she will also be able to use her training and design skills, creating workshops for groups of laid-off workers.

Eileen has not been laid off until now herself, so she will gain insights for her clients during her own job search. She also has substantial experience in networking, which is how she built her consulting practice.

Transferable Skills

Executive coaching

Knowledge of job responsibilities

Facilitation skills

Training design and delivery

Knowledge of hiring laws and practices

Writing

Networking and job search skills

Job Description
Outplacement Consultant

- Utilize career transition/job development techniques prescribed by company practice standards, nurturing client progression through regular contact and consistent attention to detail

- Knowledge about job search, business, and networking strategies with a keen ability to leverage the Internet

- Exceptional communication skills; adept at resume preparation and able to provide effective, productive editing services to clients throughout transition periods

- Able to impart pragmatic business judgment during one-on-one client consultations as well as small group training/facilitation

- Familiarity with various career transition strategies, including understanding of products and services in other company lines of business

- Quick study on technology usage; strong desire to embrace technology as a means for service improvement

- Unwavering client/customer service commitment

- Bachelor's degree in human resources, business administration, or any other closely related field

- Minimum 8 to 10 years professional business experience, including experience in a professional office environment

- Strong computing skills with proficiency in Lotus Notes and Microsoft Office are required

---

Resume Makeover

Eileen's resume is very content-dense with lots of terms that relate specifically to employee development. In the rewrite, most of the achievement statements have been simplified.

1 The look of the resume is updated with an Arial typeface, and the font size has been increased to 11 point in the Resume Billboard and skills summary. The rest of the resume is 10 point.

2 The Resume Billboard opens with a strong headline of Professional Development/Career Consultant. These four words express where she has spent most of her career, coupled with where she wants to go.

3 The Qualifications Summary includes only those experiences that have some bearing on job seeking and career counseling.

4 In the Relevant Skills and Accomplishments section, her most recent experiences are reframed and presented in the order of most relevance: coaching first, then training, then employee/executive development. The term "culture change" has been changed to employee/executive development because that is more relevant to the job search process.

5 Her achievement statements are shortened, eliminating about 18 lines of text. The result is a resume that is more inviting to the eye.

6 The Education and Professional Training & Other Affiliations sections are copied directly from her original resume. Her activities with ASTD, ISPI, SHRM, and IAF show a real commitment to her profession.

Eileen O'Malley, MA, SPHR

123 Any Street   Blacksburg, VA 24060   540-123-4567   email@email.com

Experience

2006–2009 Virginia Tech   Blacksburg, VA
Organization Effectiveness and Training
Design and implement organization development initiatives that support strategic goals of the College of Communication and WVTF Radio (NPR affiliate). This internal consultant position requires initiating and leading new programs, managing a budget and building relationships across the organization.

Culture Change
- Design and facilitate a participative, organization-wide culture change initiative for WVTF Radio including the strategic planning process. Enroll senior leaders and staff to identify their core values and competencies. Create competency-based development and performance management systems.
- Facilitate process improvement sessions for college administrative units based on Baldrige criteria with the goal of increasing focus and collaboration within each unit.
- Design and facilitate Appreciative Inquiry workshops with all staff to prepare for and respond to leadership transition.

Training
- Launch a performance management program and a personal learning plan program based on core competency development. Implement communication strategy, deliver training, and analyze program effectiveness.
- Design and deliver management skills training to all College and WVTF supervisors.
- Design and deliver diversity training to Virginia Tech staff community by request of the Associate VP of Human Resources. Received excellent feedback from participants at all levels of the organization.

Coaching
- Coach College leadership in addressing change management issues by communicating effectively to entire organization. Craft message and produce a multimedia means of delivering message.
- Coach radio station executives through culture change initiative.

2003–2006 Collaborative Consulting   Blacksburg, VA
Proprietor, Organization Development Consulting Practice
Helped clients work better together by developing individual communication and teamwork skills and fostering group collaboration. Grew business through networking and service activities.
- Coached director and executive-level management of a large retail employer by utilizing behavior-style assessments and 360 feedback process.
- Consulted to executive director of technology association to design an Executive Roundtable Program. Led a group of 6 consulting facilitators. Facilitated an ongoing roundtable of 12 Chief Information Officers in the Blacksburg technology industry to learn from each other by sharing their leadership experiences and challenges. Facilitated management and board retreats for non-profit organizations.
- Designed and delivered courses titled "Secrets of Collaborative Communicators" and "Leading When You Are Not in Charge" for both for-profit and non-profit sectors.
- Delivered management and professional development training to hundreds of participants for computer manufacturing corporation.
Clients include: Whole Foods Market, Dell Computer Corporation, IBM, Blacksburg Technology Council, Center for Tobacco Prevention, Theater Action Project, Virginia Tech/Pamplin College of Business, Center for Non-Profit and Community Based Organizations

2001–2003 PartnerSights, Inc.   Salem, VA
Consultant
- Lead consultant in diagnosing and analyzing organizational communication patterns, conducted focus groups and interviews, and presented recommendation to executive management that resulted in a series of executive management teambuilding events.
- Co-authored *Teamwork*, a book published in 2001 by Penguin that describes for consultants and professionals the power of responsibility-based team skills.
- Managed web content for the 3M Meeting Network, an online meeting resource with over 60,000 visitors

2001–2003 PartnerSights, Inc., cont'd   Salem, VA
Trainer
- Trained individuals and groups on personal responsibility-based team skills. Helped team leaders, project teams, and high-tech organizations create powerful, aligned teams through facilitating "Powerful Teams," a three-day seminar. Developed seminar business through managing print, web, and direct marketing strategies.
Clients included: Landmark Graphics, Concero, IBM, BMC Software, Condea Vista, 3M, Verizon Wireless, eLaw

1999–2001 Lee's Hardware   Renton, Washington
Human Resources Generalist/Training Manager
Designed a company-wide employee and management development program that supported the company's customer service mission and employee-centered management style appropriate to a distributed organizational structure.
- Worked closely with executive management team to identify and gain support for initiatives.
- Designed and implemented company-wide customer service initiative, including training all 300 employees, aligning management accountability, publishing ongoing communication, and implementing a service feedback system. The pilot program resulted in 62% increase of customer satisfaction.
- Developed manager training and learning activities congruent with culture and values.
- Coordinated an on-going calendar of product trainings and vendor site tours.

1995–1999
Human Resources Generalist
- Onboarded new employees, including recruiting, staffing, and delivering new employee orientation.
- Developed and administered performance management program for sales and administrative staff.
- Coached and trained store managers in addressing employee performance issues.
- Developed CDL drug testing and haz mat programs. Administered worker's compensation program.

1992–1995 Medallion Home Centers   Seattle, Washington
Human Resources Generalist/Compensation Specialist
- Coordinated salary administration and performance review process for 3,500 employees.
- Educated employees regarding benefit plans and FMLA, ADA, and corporate policies.

Education

Master of Arts, Whole Systems Design
1999   *Antioch University*   Seattle, Washington
Certification of Competency in Organization Development
- Co- taught graduate level course on Organization Diagnosis and Systems Theory
- Consulting practicum with National Marine Engineers' Beneficial Association, UN Conference for the Advancement of Women, and Terabeam, Inc.

Bachelor of Arts, Psychology
1992   *Northwestern University*   Evanston, Illinois
- Big-Ten Scholar Athlete, 1991

Professional Training and Other Affiliations
- Active membership: ASTD (former board member), ISPI (former board member), SHRM, IAF
- Senior Professional in Human Resources, 2002
- Certification in Human Resource Management - University of Washington, 1995
- Additional training: Lominger Leadership Products, Dialogue facilitation, Appreciative Inquiry, Seven Habits of Highly Effective People, Knowledge Team Effectiveness Questionnaire, Corporate Transformation Tools

Eileen O'Malley
email@email.com

Eileen O'Malley, MA, SPHR

123 Any Street   Blacksburg, VA 24060   540-123-4567   email@email.com

Professional Development / Career Consultant

- Expert resume preparation
- Executive coaching – 10 years
- Hiring practices subject matter expert
- Designed hiring manager training
- Coach on behavior style, strengths
- Power user: PowerPoint, MS Office, Lotus Notes
- Facilitated roundtable of CIOs, executive teams
- Keen understanding of performance metrics
- In-depth knowledge of job responsibilities
- Understand corporate organization models

RELEVANT SKILLS AND ACCOMPLISHMENTS

Coaching
- Coached college leadership in addressing change management issues by communicating effectively to entire organization. Crafted messages and produced multimedia delivery
- Coached radio station executives through culture change initiative

Training
- Launched a performance management program and personal learning plan program based on core competency development. Implemented communication strategy, delivered training, and analyzed program effectiveness
- Designed and delivered management training to 230 College and WVTF supervisors
- Designed and delivered diversity training to Virginia Tech staff community

Employee/Executive Development
- Designed a participative, organization-wide culture change initiative for WVTF Radio including the strategic planning process
- Enrolled senior leaders and staff to identify their core values and competencies. Created competency-based development and performance management systems
- Facilitated process improvement sessions for college administrative units based on Baldrige criteria with the goal of increasing focus and collaboration within each unit
- Designed and facilitated Appreciative Inquiry workshops with all staff to prepare for and respond to leadership transition

PROFESSIONAL EXPERIENCE

2006 – 2009   Virginia Tech   *Blacksburg, VA*
Organization Effectiveness and Training
- Design and implement organization development initiatives that support strategic goals of the College of Communication and WVTF Radio (NPR affiliate).
- Internal consultant position required initiating and leading new development and learning programs, managing a budget, and building relationships across the organization.

2003 – 2006   Collaborative Consulting   *Blacksburg, VA*
Proprietor, Organization Development Consulting Practice
- Coached director and executive-level management of a large retail employer by utilizing behavior-style assessments and 360 feedback process.
- Consulted to executive director of technology association to design an Executive Roundtable Program. Facilitated an ongoing roundtable of 12 chief information officers.
- Facilitated management and board retreats for non-profit organizations.
- Designed and delivered courses titled: "Secrets of Collaborative Communicators" and "Leading When You Are Not in Charge" for both for-profit and non-profit sectors.
- Delivered management and professional development training to hundreds of participants for computer manufacturing corporation.
- Clients included: Whole Foods Market, Dell Computer Corporation, IBM, Blacksburg Technology Council, Center for Tobacco Prevention, Theater Action Project, Virginia Tech.

2001 – 2003   PartnerSights, Inc.   *Salem, VA*
Consultant
- Analyzed organizational communication patterns, conducted focus groups and interviews, and presented recommendations to executive management.
- Co-authored *Teamwork* (Penguin, 2001) that describes for consultants and professionals the power of responsibility-based team skills.
- Managed web content for the 3M Meeting Network, an online meeting resource with over 60,000 visitors.

Trainer
- Trained individuals and groups on personal responsibility-based team skills.
- Facilitated "Team Power," a three-day seminar. Developed seminar business through managing print, web, and direct marketing strategies.
- Clients included: Landmark Graphics, IBM, BMC Software, I3M, Verizon Wireless, eLaw.

1999 – 2001   Lee's Hardware   *Renton, Washington*
Human Resources Generalist/Training Manager
- Designed a company-wide employee and management development program.
- Worked closely with executive management team to identify and gain support for initiatives.
- Designed and implemented company-wide customer service initiative, including training all 300 employees. The pilot program resulted in 62% increase of customer satisfaction.
- Developed manager training and learning activities congruent with culture and values.
- Coordinated an ongoing calendar of product trainings and vendor site tours.

1995 – 1999
Human Resources Generalist
- Onboarded new employees, including recruiting, staffing, and delivering new employee orientation.
- Developed and administered performance management program for sales and administrative staff.
- Coached and trained store managers in addressing employee performance issues.
- Developed CDL drug testing and haz mat programs. Administered worker's compensation program.

1992 – 1995   Medallion Home Centers   *Seattle, Washington*
Human Resources Generalist/Compensation Specialist
- Coordinated salary administration and performance review process for 3,500 employees.
- Educated employees regarding benefit plans and FMLA, ADA, and corporate policies.

EDUCATION

Master of Arts, Whole Systems Design, 1999   Antioch University   Seattle, Washington
Certification of Competency in Organization Development
- Co-taught graduate level course on Organization Diagnosis and Systems Theory
- Consulting practicum with National Marine Engineers' Beneficial Association, UN Conference for the Advancement of Women, and Terabeam, Inc.

Bachelor of Arts, Psychology, 1992   Northwestern University   Evanston, Illinois

PROFESSIONAL TRAINING & OTHER AFFILIATIONS

- Active membership: ASTD (former board member), ISPI (former board member), SHRM, IAF
- Senior Professional in Human Resources, 2002
- Certification in Human Resource Management – University of Washington, 1995
- Additional training: Lominger Leadership Products, Dialogue facilitation, Appreciative Inquiry, Seven Habits of Highly Effective People, Knowledge Team Effectiveness Questionnaire

141

Floral Designer to Office Administrator

When she was laid off from her floral design job, Carol Byrd knew it was time to retool her career and make a serious change. After nearly 26 years as a floral designer, Carol was still making minimum wage, working massive overtime before each holiday, and standing for hours on the job. She hopes to increase her income and move into office work, where she can return to a 40-hour, five-day work week.

Carol realizes that her computer skills need improvement to get an office job. Her niece, who is 15, introduced her to Microsoft Outlook and taught her how to attach files to e-mails. By writing cover letters, she brushed up on Microsoft Word. Then her sister taught her a little about QuickBooks, which she uses for her own home-based business. During the six weeks she was looking for a job, Carol also took a short course in Excel at the community college.

She is now ready to rewrite her resume using a functional approach to highlight her office skills.

Challenges to Making the Switch

Carol's work history is overflowing with floral design. Her many jobs, along with her statement of months and years, will likely red-flag her as a job-hopper. In order to show some real-world experience in office administration, she needs to state her work history back to 1990 or before. Because her office experience is so dated, she has to upgrade her skills a bit just to post resumes online and answer e-mails from prospective employers.

On the plus side, she has a good knowledge of retail activities such as displays, merchandising, inventory, stocking, and billing. She hopes to find an office job with a small company that will consider these traits an asset.

Carol has a large network of friends, vendors, former supervisors, and co-workers in the floral industry and virtually no other contacts. When she finds a job lead for office manager of a local floral distributor, she knows this is a great opportunity for her. She is hoping her rather weak office skills will be counterbalanced by her thorough knowledge of flowers and the floral industry.

Transferable Skills

Microsoft Office Suite software

Bookkeeping

Bank deposits, payroll

Customer service

Database use

Negotiation

Training

Floral industry knowledge

Job Description
Office Manager—Floral Wholesaler

- Record and bookkeeping involved with a floral distributor. Knowledge of flowers and experience in a floral shop a plus.

- Generate accurate documents and presentations. Must be good with Microsoft Office 2003 Professional, especially Excel. This position will use Outlook, Word, and occasionally PowerPoint.

- Answer phone inquiries and generate special orders in our proprietary order system.

- Check phone and e-mail messages from customers and vendors and respond to them within the same business day with specials, flyers, and other marketing information.

- For incoming shipments, photocopy and log each bill of lading as it arrives at the dock. Check shipments for quantity, accuracy, and quality of product.

- Maintain accounts receivable by invoicing customers, posting payment of invoices, and tracking non-routine and miscellaneous services.

- Account for petty cash transactions and reimbursements.

- Set up and maintain vendor and customer records in ACT! database.

- Budget for and purchase office items including hardware, software, services, and supplies.

Resume Makeover

Carol creates a functional resume to highlight her office experience.

1 The headline "Office Management" summarizes Carol's job objective. "Retail merchandise designer" is a term created to avoid using "floral designer" in her opening statement.

2 Responsibilities from all her jobs are divided into three main functional categories: Office/Bookkeeping, Customer Service, and Retail Management.

3 The Industry Experience section is designed to show that she has significant work experience outside the floral industry.

4 Carol's last 18 years are restated as if they were one job: "Floral Designer."

5 By including her work history all the way back to 1980, Carol shows significant responsibility in office environments.

6 Her Education section leads with her latest achievement—courses in Excel and PowerPoint—both of which are needed in her new position.

7 The Relevant Software & Equipment Use section allows her to restate these key words: Excel, Outlook, Word, PowerPoint, and QuickBooks. When posted online, her resume will be given a higher position because the key words match those in the job posting.

Carol Byrd
1234 Cannon Blvd. Apt. 806   Austin, TX 78700   512-123-4567   email@email.com

Education

Austin and Broward Community Colleges - Completed various courses
Texas A&M University - Texas Master Florist Certification

Employment History

Conner Hills Florist   **June 2003 – Jan. 2008**   **Austin, TX**
Floral Designer – Duties: Design Floral Arrangements, Sell and Design Wedding Flowers, Funeral Arrangements, Holiday Centerpieces and Decorations, Permanent Botanical Floral Arrangements, Customer Sales and Service, Place Orders for Flowers, Plants, and Supplies from Vendors

Becker Florist   **May 2002 – May 2003**   **Austin, TX**
Floral Designer – Duties: Same as above

Roses-R-Red-Florist   **Nov. 2000 – Apr. 2002**   **Ft. Lauderdale, FL**
Floral Designer – Duties: Same as above

Hargrove Florist   **Nov. 1990 – Oct. 2000**   **Ft. Lauderdale, FL**
Floral Designer – Duties: Same as above

Welton Industries   **Feb. 1989 – May 1990**   **Ft. Lauderdale, FL**
Administrative Assistant – Duties: Phones, Accounts Payable and Receivable, Bank Deposits, Invoices, Shipping and Receiving

Up-N-Coming Telcom, Inc.   **Aug. 1988 – Jan. 1989**   **Ft. Lauderdale, FL**
Receptionist/Bookkeeper – Duties: Payroll for 50, Gas Inventory, Profit & Loss Statement, Data Entry, Switchboard

Clayton Apartments   **Sept. 1987 – Aug. 1988**   **Ft. Lauderdale, FL**
Assistant Manager – Duties: Heavy Phone and Public Contact, Show Apartments, Collect Rent, Bank Deposits, Process Service Requests, Bookkeeping, Qualify Residents

Carol's Flower Affair   **June 1985 – Feb. 1986**   **Austin, TX**
Floral Designer – Duties: Design Floral Arrangements, Customer Service, Order Flowers and Plants, Delivery

Haytown Florist   **July 1982 – May 1985**   **Austin, TX**
Delivery Driver, Floral Designer

Hertz Rent-A-Car   **Jan. 1980 – Feb. 1981**   **Austin, TX**
Rental Representative, Title Clerk – Duties: Customer Service, Auto Rental and Return, Process Rental Contracts, Titles, Process Insurance on Accident Vehicles, Vehicle Registration

Carol Byrd

1234 Cannon Blvd. Apt. 806, Austin, TX 78700
(512) 123-4567 • email@email.com

❶ OFFICE MANAGEMENT

❷ Retail merchandise designer with 26 years in retail sales, customer service, merchandising, and production. Experience includes office management, customer service, inventory control, and bookkeeping. Competent in Outlook, Word, Excel, PowerPoint, and QuickBooks.

Office/Bookkeeping
- Served as office bookkeeper for a manufacturer, wholesaler, vehicle dealer, and telecom utility
- Responsible for accounts payable and receivables, invoicing, and reports
- Handled bank deposits, profit and loss statements, and inventory control
- Processed vehicles registrations and titles
- Tracked employee hours and processed payroll for 35-person dealership
- Familiar with QuickBooks; can generate custom reports

Customer Service
- As assistant manager, met the public and showed rental properties
- Qualified prospective residents; performed credit checks
- Collected rents, maintained books
- Processed service and maintenance requests

Retail Management
- Created merchandising displays throughout the store to increase sales
- Met with brides to plan wedding floral designs within a budget
- Planned and executed holiday decorations for homes and Governor's Mansion
- Negotiated rates with floral wholesalers
- Generated invoices on proprietary floral software
- Assisted customers with selection and design arrangements
- Created original and unique floral designs
- Supervised the decoration of churches and other facilities for weddings and events
- Kept an efficient and controlled work environment in the flower shop
- Trained co-workers in floral design, cash registers, invoicing, etc.

❸ INDUSTRY EXPERIENCE

Auto Dealership	Residential Rentals	Manufacturing
Car Rentals	Telecom Utility	Floral Retail Store

❹ PROFESSIONAL WORK HISTORY

Floral Designer   **1990 – PRESENT**

Connor Hills Florist	2003 – 2008	Austin, TX
Becker Florist	2002 – 2003	Austin, TX
Roses-R-Red-Florist	2000 – 2002	Ft. Lauderdale, FL
Hargrove Florist	1990 – 2000	Ft. Lauderdale, FL

Carol Byrd Resume – page 2

PROFESSIONAL WORK HISTORY Continued

Welton Industries   **1989 – 1990**   **Ft. Lauderdale, FL**
Administrative Assistant
Responsibilities: Phones, Accounts Payable and Receivable, Bank Deposits, Invoices, Shipping and Receiving

Up-N-Coming Telcom, Inc.   **1988 – 1989**   **Ft. Lauderdale, FL**
Receptionist/Bookkeeper
Responsibilities: Payroll for 50, Gas Inventory, Profit & Loss Statement, Data Entry, Switchboard

Clayton Apartments   **1987 – 1988**   **Ft. Lauderdale, FL**
Assistant Manager
Responsibilities: Heavy Phone and Public Contact, Show Apartments, Collect Rent, Bank Deposits, Process Service Requests, Bookkeeping, Qualify Residents

❺ Floral Designer

Carol's Flower Affair	1985 – 1986	Austin, TX
Haytown Florist	1982 – 1985	Austin, TX

Hertz Rent-A-Car   **1980 – 1981**   **Austin, TX**
Rental Representative, Title Clerk
Responsibilities: Customer Service, Auto Rental and Return, Process Rental Contracts, Titles, Process Insurance on Accident Vehicles, Vehicle Registration

❻ EDUCATION

University of Texas Informal Classes (Adult Education)
PowerPoint Intermediate and Excel Basics - 2008

Austin and Broward Community Colleges
Completed 32 hours in General Studies

Texas A&M University
Texas Master Florist Certification

❼ RELEVANT SOFTWARE & EQUIPMENT USE
- Intuit QuickBooks
- Microsoft Word, Excel, PowerPoint, Outlook
- Internet Explorer, AOL, e-mail, fax, copier
- Rosebud Point-of-Sale Software
- Teleflora Dove Point-of-Sale, Bookkeeping Software
- FTD Mercury

Graphic Artist to Sales Support

Carolyn Delgado has 14 years experience as a graphic designer and is currently working for a temporary service. She longs for a new career that will allow her to express her creativity while providing a dependable income and benefits. Graphic designer jobs in advertising agencies or marketing firms are scarce. Many other companies with creative departments are outsourcing work to India or Asia.

Carolyn's temporary service assigns her to a growing information company, screening calls for the sales team. She finds that she likes the customer contact and is quick to learn the business. The work environment suits her because the company is young, fast-paced, and growing.

She soon becomes aware of a job opening that would allow her to use her creativity in both copywriting and graphic design. She decides to revamp her resume and formally apply for the position.

Challenges to Making the Switch

Carolyn's work history is spotty; she has vacillated between survival jobs and her graphic design work. Even in graphic design, her longest tenure is three years; other jobs have lasted one year or less. A chronological statement of job history will make this fact glaringly obvious.

Her target job involves providing office support to the sales team. She does have some experience, but has never stated it on her graphic designer resume. She realizes she will have to add business activities such as office administration, invoicing, customer service, bookkeeping, and database management to her former jobs.

Carolyn has always developed creative concepts at the direction of her clients or supervisors. In her new role as sales support, she will be more autonomous in developing campaign ideas. Her resume needs to show the breadth of her creative work and prove that she has great ideas.

Transferable Skills

Sales

Customer service

Office administration

Multitasking

Creative copywriting

Graphic design/production

Desktop publishing

Job Description
Sales Support Coordinator

- Develop, coordinate, and implement sales contests, recognition events, and communication programs that boost effectiveness of sales representatives and their management

- Work to ensure sales employees' satisfaction, increase esprit de corps, and generate more sales and revenue by coordinating incentive programs

- Purchase required supplies, materials, and awards for recognition programs

- Develop and communicate information about rules and procedures to sales teams for contests and recognition programs

- Track, update, and publish the results for contests and incentive programs

- Plan, organize, and coordinate recognition events that acknowledge and reward excellence demonstrated by sales employees

- Collect and retain communication materials such as corporate policies, rules, dispute guidelines, sales scripts, presentation decks, training materials, contests, reporting, and all marketing literature

---

Resume Makeover

Carolyn's resume is expanded to two pages, allowing her to detail her creative work—because this will be part of her desired job.

1 The headline "Sales Support/Graphic Design" summarizes Carolyn's new job objective.

2 The Core Competencies listing allows her to show her breadth of experience. She reframes some of her experience into the language of the desired job description; for example, "Sales Tracking" and "Customer Databases."

3 Her extensive computer skills are given their own prominent section. She includes both graphic software and business software, such as Outlook, Word, and Excel.

4 Her work achievements are organized into five main categories, and each relates back to the target job. She expands the description of her work duties to emphasize her office administration skills.

5 Her survival job, working in a café, is reframed as customer service—adding to her attractiveness as an internal support employee.

6 Her work history is divided into graphic design and other experience. She showcases her 13 years of graphic design, while her survival jobs have been repositioned as sales and customer service positions.

7 Her numerous graphics projects are listed with client names that will be recognized by her interviewer.

CAROLYN DELGADO	P 512 123 4567 | email@email.net
	Austin, TX
	Web Site: www.name.net

PROFESSIONAL EXPERIENCE

Current — XYZ Online (Via Kelly Services) | Sales Phone Screening Team / Front Desk

2004 – 2005 — Nordstrom Café Bistro | Greeter/Cashier/Server
Freelance graphic designer and fine artist

2003 — XYZ CD Manufacturing | On-site Freelance Graphic Designer/Administrative Support
- Design and layout of music CD art; design of company print ads, direct mail
- Administrative functions as needed (updated database, inventory, front desk, phones)

2002 – 2003 — XYZ Telephone | Sales Representative, Outbound Call Center, Local Phone Service
- Used high-level customer service skills for needs assessment and product recommendation
- Multi-tasking of order entry and completion while following strict Required Follow Through

2001 – 2002 — XYZ Foods Group | Graphic Designer
- Designed point-of-purchase materials for national grocery chains (Kroger, Winn Dixie, Wal-Mart)
- Developed vendor relations; managed print production on time and within budget
- Managed inventory of all point-of-purchase materials; fulfilled merchant orders

2000 — XYZ Education Corporation, Houston | Registration Manager
- Accountable for registration in 3 major Texas cities; produced highest quarter since 1998
- Utilized high-level customer service/communication skills to discuss prospects' personal growth
- Facilitated 3-hour introductory presentations to potential participants

1999 – 2000 — Freelance Graphic Designer

1995 – 1998 — Agency Graphic Design Experience: XYZ Advertising | XYZ Creative

EDUCATION & TRAINING

Austin Community College, Austin, TX | Associate of Applied Science Degree | Commercial Art

Lamar University, Beaumont, TX | Certificate of Completion (1-year Program) | Office Administration

XYZ Education, Austin, Texas | Leaders Program
(6-month intensive leadership program focusing on communication, presentation, & public speaking)

COMPUTER SKILLS (PC AND MACINTOSH PLATFORMS)

QuarkXPress	Adobe Photoshop	Adobe ImageReady	Adobe Illustrator
Acrobat Distiller	Adobe GoLive	Adobe Streamline	PageMaker
Freehand	Beginning HTML	Act! Database	Filemaker
Microsoft Outlook	Microsoft Office (Word, Excel, PowerPoint)		

Web-based skills: General understanding of web design. I have designed and art directed the look and feel for 2 commercial clients, and I have built my own and a fellow artist's site using Adobe GoLive.

Carolyn A Delgado
1234 South Henderson • Austin, TX 78700
(512) 123-4567
email@email.com

(1) SALES SUPPORT/GRAPHIC DESIGN

Graphic Artist with experience in the creation of advertising, merchandising, point-of-purchase, and sales campaigns. Special talent for high-level sales, creative communication, and relationship management. Able to generate creative campaigns that produce sales team excitement and increased sales.

(2) CORE COMPENTENCIES

Sales Campaign Concepts	Vendor Relations/Sales Support	Sales Presentations
Graphic Design	Multi-tasking in Call Center Environment	Training Sales/Registration
Telephone Sales/Service	Creative Concepts – Ad Clients	Event Planning
Customer Databases	Sales Tracking	Multi-media art

(3) COMPUTER SKILLS (PC and Macintosh Platforms)

QuarkXPress	Adobe Photoshop	Adobe ImageReady	Adobe Illustrator
Acrobat Distiller	Adobe GoLive	Adobe Streamline	PageMaker
Freehand	Basic HTML	ACT! Database	Filemaker
Microsoft Outlook	Microsoft Word	Microsoft Excel	Microsoft PowerPoint

(4) PROFESSIONAL EXPERTISE

Sales/Sales Support
- Accountable for registration of training event in three major Texas cities; produced highest participation in two years
- Utilized high-level customer service/communication skills to discuss prospects' personal growth goals and register them into transformational training programs. Attained a 98% close rate by telephone. (XYZ Education)
- Facilitated a 3-hour introductory presentation to prospects for transformational training
- Used high-level customer service skills to assess client needs and make product recommendations (XYZ Telephone Outbound)
- In a busy Call Center environment, multi-tasked order entry and completion, while following strict follow-through procedures

Office Administration
- Created and updated customer database for CD manufacturing facility; included invoicing, shipping and inventory applications
- Tracked use of point-of-sale materials distributed to national grocery chains
- Opened and closed café business, including cash handling, preparation of deposits, etc.
- Competent in QuickBooks

Graphic Design/Production
- Designed point-of-purchase materials for food brokerage which were used in national grocery chains -- Kroger, Winn Dixie, and Wal-Mart
- Assembled mock-ups for sales presentations made by more than 35 brokerage reps to grocery store managers in six-state area
- Managed print production of point-of-sale materials; developed new vendor relationships; maintained tight budgets and schedules
- Met with musical artists to design CD art, along with website look, promotional brochures, postcards, and other direct mail

---

(5) Customer Service
- Greeted café customers and assisted with catering orders, answering questions, providing menu recommendations, and addressing special dietary needs
- Managed waiting line, seating availability and flow of customers in a 120-seat café; during peak times, we would serve 275+ customers during one meal cycle

Other Creative Accomplishments
- Created and produced multi-sensory art installation in conjunction with *Laughing at the Sun* Art Gallery to promote awareness of the beauty of all people, regardless of physical disabilities. Month-long fundraiser for the Texas School for the Blind and Visually Impaired.
- Copywriter and voice talent for 30-second radio spot "Dream Cars"
- Extra in full-length feature movie, *If a Man Doesn't Answer*
- Fine Art Showings in Austin, TX – XZY Java Company, Barnes & Noble, XYZ Coffee Shop, Amy's Ice Cream

(6) WORK HISTORY

GRAPHIC DESIGN

Freelance	1995–Present
XYZ CD Manufacturing, Austin, TX	2003
XYZ Foods Group, Austin, TX	2001–2002
XYZ Advertising, Austin, TX	1995–1998

SALES/CUSTOMER SERVICE

Hostess/Cashier	Nordstrom Café Bistro, Austin, TX	2004–2005
Sales Rep, Outbound Call Center	XYZ Telephone, Austin, TX	2002–2003
Registration Manager	XYZ Education, Austin, TX	2000

EDUCATION & TRAINING

Associate of Applied Science, Commercial Art
Austin Community College, Austin, TX

Office Administration Certificate
Lamar University, Beaumont, TX

(7) SELECTED FREELANCE GRAPHICS PROJECTS

Corporate Identity
Brochure & Email Templates
Training Posters
CD Covers/Inserts
Employee Direct Mail Brochure
Promotional Items
Campaign Invitation
Brochures
Feature Section Layout
T-Shirt Illustration

- XYZ Transformations, Inc. (National Trainer)
- XYZ Consulting, Inc. (International)
- Harold Johnson (Regional Sales Trainer)
- XYZ Executive Recruiting
- XYZ (National store chain)
- XYZ (Events Planner/Consultant)
- XYZ Rings
- XYZ CD (National CD Manufacturer)
- Acme Petroleum (Retail Fuel Dispensers)
- XYZ Computer
- March of Dimes, Texas Folic Acid Campaign
- Health Company International
- *Hearing Health Magazine*
- XYZ Little League Baseball Team

Loan Originator to Leasing Agent

During the last 10 years, Lindsay Haines has enjoyed her varied positions in sales and customer service. She enjoys working with people and obtains great satisfaction in finding viable solutions for her customers and clients.

However, her latest position as a loan origination officer was a real challenge. Strictly commission based, she had to generate all her own leads and customers. Due to the subprime lending mortgage debacle and the slowing of the real estate market, this has become a nearly impossible feat. Recently, when the mortgage company Lindsay worked for went out of business, Lindsay found herself unemployed. While not thrilled with the situation, she is happy to move on to something much less stressful.

Ideally, Lindsay would like to work a standard 8 A.M. to 5 P.M. job and have customers come to her. She becomes aware of a possible functional change to apartment leasing agent. In that position, she will be able to use much of her real estate background. She realizes that the pay may be less than what she's used to, but it will be much better than her income during recent months.

Challenges to Making the Switch

Lindsay is looking for something new and less stressful than mortgage banking. Being single, she would also like to have benefits. While she has never been a leasing agent before, she can market her experience in sales and customer service to show that she is a good match for this position.

While she is familiar with the real estate market, this shift will require her to learn more about the leasing market and leasing contracts. But Lindsay is a quick study and does not anticipate any major obstacles.

Transferable Skills

Customer service

People skills

Marketing and networking skills

Complaint and problem resolution

Financial applications, verification, and processing

Relationship building

Communication skills

Job Description

Apartment Leasing Agent

- Greet prospective tenants and determine their needs and preferences before showing them an apartment

- Professionally present the features and benefits of the apartment community

- Secure lease agreements and collect rental deposits from qualified persons

- Complete guest cards on all prospects, send thank-you notes, and perform visitor follow-up

- Ensure that "model" apartments are ready for show

- Address the needs of current residents

- Play an active role in the lease renewal process and assist in collecting back rent

- Complete and process all forms, agreements, and reports

- Maintain all resident and property files

- Conduct marketing outreach to local businesses to promote the property and increase visitor traffic

- Maintain an awareness of market conditions and trends and contribute ideas to the operations manager for improving tenant satisfaction

Resume Makeover

Lindsay's old-style resume, with the two-column format, reflects her work experience and highlights her many qualifications. She redesigns her resume to emphasize the skills and knowledge pertinent to the desired position of apartment leasing agent and expands it to two pages.

1 Lindsay's street address is eliminated to protect her identity when posting the resume online. Phone and email are enough for employers to reach her.

2 Lindsay eliminates the so-called qualifications on her original resume. These are primarily self-assessment. Instead, she will let her achievements speak for themselves.

3 Lindsay labels her resume with a headline that emphasizes her strengths: "Marketing and Sales."

4 She consolidates her qualifications into key words, which are much easier to read than long, italicized sentences.

5 In the Experience and Achievements section, she breaks down her experience into three major categories and bullets them, using an arrow bullet to highlight her achievements.

6 Her Work History section is simplified and listed after her Experience and Achievements section.

7 The Education section is moved to the end, and Lindsay eliminates the ICar certification that is not pertinent to the desired position.

Lindsay Haines

Sales, Marketing, Public Relations

4632 E. Michelle Drive
Phoenix, AZ 85032
(602) 123-4567

❷ Qualifications

➢ *Professional* with more than *ten years* of progressive work experience in diverse business environments.

➢ *Highly skilled* in client relations and needs assessment, sales/marketing strategies, account development, and administration, problem resolution, and staff training/supervision.

➢ *Expertise* in generating new business growth, promoting new products, increasing sales volume, and expanding market penetration.

➢ *Facilitate* a team approach to achieve organizational objectives, increase productivity, and enhance employee morale.

➢ *Proven ability* to effectively handle multi-task levels of responsibility.

➢ *Superior* communication, analytical, interpersonal, customer service, organizational, and leadership skills.

➢ *Thrive* in both independent and collaborative work environments.

➢ *Quick study* with the ability to easily grasp and put into application new ideas, concepts, methods, and technologies.

➢ *Energetic* and self-motivated team player/builder.

➢ *Proficient* in the use of various computer programs and software applications.

❼ Education/Licenses

Arizona Real Estate License
Arizona Mortgage License
Butler Community College, El Dorado
Pima Community College, Tucson
ICar certified

Employment Experience

Willow Creek Mortgage – Phoenix, AZ

Loan Officer, 1/07 – Present
Worked to further establish and grow a mortgage company throughout the state of Arizona. Participated in grass roots marketing and networking campaign within the real estate community. "Warm" called Realtors and offered assistance for their company/client needs, held social functions, offered prizes, designed and implemented marketing mailer, and attended numerous networking events. Achieved 120% of New Clients goal in an increasingly challenging and volatile market.

Wichita Trust Financial – Phoenix, AZ
Loan Officer, 10/03 – 1/07
Partnered in establishing a new brokerage firm. Instrumental in growing the company from three to twelve employees in the first six months. Recruited, interviewed, hired, and trained new employees. Identified, marketed, and developed referral sources throughout the real estate and financial community. Consistently closed five to six more loans on a monthly basis than eight other competing loan officers.

Jim Forrest Band – Phoenix, AZ
Manager, 3/01 – 10/05
Responsible for managing operations and marketing for an alternative country band. Networked extensively and attended national music conferences to market the band. Promoted the band through print advertisements, fliers, and radio. Actively sought out, interviewed, and hired music producer. Conducted fundraisers which led to the successful production of their initial CD. Booked the band at increasingly important venues such as the Governor's ball.

Business Software Associates – Phoenix, AZ
Sales Associate, 12/99 – 1/01
Solicited and secured business-to-business clients such as Frontier Airlines, Verizon, Bell Atlantic, Southwestern Bell, Triton, Brown & Williamson, and other Fortune 500 companies. Responsible for cold calling accounts and building relationships with key decision makers. Earned "top sales producer" within first six months of employment.

Bebedeaux Pontiac GMC – Tucson, AZ
Service Advisor, 5/97 – 7/99
Worked with customers to schedule service work and communicate additional service needed. Liaison between customer and technician in order to properly diagnose problems and communicate customer concerns. Facilitated customer complaints while maintaining high customer service satisfaction standards.

① Lindsay Haines   (602) 123-4567   email@email.com   Phoenix, AZ

Marketing and Sales

③④ CORE COMPETENCIES

Marketing outreach
Needs assessment
Client and community relations
Account development and administration
Property promotion
Market conditions and trend analysis
Leasing agreements

Management
Productivity improvement
Employee morale enhancement
Facilitation and training
Excellent oral and written communication skills
Strong presentation skills
Computer skills

⑤ EXPERIENCE and ACHIEVEMENTS

Marketing and Sales

- Identified, marketed, and developed referral sources throughout the real estate and financial community
  - ➤ On a monthly basis, consistently closed five to six more loans than eight other competing loan officers at a mortgage company
- Held social functions, offered prizes, designed and implemented a marketing mailer
  - ➤ Achieved 120% of new client goal in an increasingly challenging and volatile market
- Networked with local businesses
- Cold called accounts and built relationships with key decision makers
  - ➤ Secured business-to-business clients such as Frontier Airlines, Verizon, Bell Atlantic, Southwestern Bell, Triton, Brown & Williamson, and other Fortune 500 companies
  - ➤ Earned "top sales producer" within first six months of employment at a software company
- Promoted an alternative country band through print advertisements, fliers, and radio promotions
  - ➤ Conducted fundraisers which led to the successful production of their initial CD

Customer Service/Needs Assessment

- Worked with customers to schedule service work and communicate additional services needed
- Served as liaison between customer and technician in order to properly diagnose problems and communicate customer concerns
- Facilitated customer complaints while maintaining high customer service satisfaction standards
- "Warm" called Realtors and offered assistance for their company/client needs

---

Lindsay Haines   (602) 123-4567   email@email.com   Phoenix, AZ

Management

- Recruited, interviewed, hired, and trained new employees for a brokerage firm
  - ➤ Instrumental in growing the firm from 3 to 12 employees in six months
- Managed operations for an alternative country band
- Actively sought out, interviewed, and hired music producers

⑥ WORK HISTORY

Loan Officer	Willow Creek Mortgage, Phoenix, AZ	2007 – 2009
Loan Officer	Wichita Trust Financial, Phoenix, AZ	2003 – 2007
Manager	Jim Forrest Band, Phoenix, AZ	2001 – 2005
Sales Associate	Business Software Associates, Phoenix, AZ	1999 – 2001
Service Advisor	Bebedeaux Pontiac GMC, Tucson, AZ	1997 – 1999

⑦ EDUCATION and LICENSES

Butler Community College, El Dorado
Pima Community College, Tucson
Arizona Real Estate License
Arizona Mortgage License

Logistics to Sales Manager

Max Stover loves his expatriate lifestyle in picturesque Zhuhai, China, working for an American-based apparel supply chain. He hears rumors about possible layoffs because of declining sales, however, and is concerned that he may be on the short list because the manager who sent him to China has been replaced. Rather than waiting for the bad news, Max begins looking for opportunities with international and China-based companies.

He wants to stay in the apparel industry; however, he believes he can be more effective in sales management. He has a marketing degree and a natural affinity for sales but ended up in logistics because that was the only opportunity at the company where he did his college internship. Now, Max hopes to reposition himself in sales and use his logistics background to help him have a better understanding of products and all facets of manufacturing and supply chain management.

Challenges to Making the Switch

Max discretely conducts his job search during his spare time, hoping that management doesn't learn about his quest for another position. He faces stiff competition from professionals who prefer China's thriving marketplace rather than dwindling sales in their own country. Max realizes it will be difficult to cross over to sales because companies will be more inclined to select someone who has recent sales experience. He emphasizes his sales/marketing experience when he worked for an apparel trim supplier that purchased all products from China.

Max recognizes that China-based companies may be more inclined to hire Chinese nationals; however, he hopes his success in working for a large American merchandising office for two years will be impressive. He has learned the business culture in different provinces and knows how to maintain good relationships with Chinese citizens. Most importantly, he continues to take classes and study Mandarin and Cantonese in order to conduct business in two of China's primary languages.

Max begins making a list of potential companies that could hire him for sales. He learns as much as he can about them from talking to his contacts and reads expatriate magazines and blogs to be more familiar with their work. In the meantime, he saves as much money as he can in case he's laid off and needs reserve funds to stay in the country while he looks for work.

Transferable Skills

Sales

Marketing

Management

Presentation

Relationship-building

Mandarin and Cantonese languages

Customer service

Negotiation

Training

Job Description

China-Based Sales Manager

- More than five years experience in a garment exporting factory, including three years leading the department

- Bachelor's degree required

- Familiar with exporting workflow and foreign trade process

- Familiar with product orientation and ability to discuss development and concept of new products

- Knowledge of fabrics and ability to discuss customer's requirements

- Excellent English and Mandarin

- Skilled in planning, coordinating, and management

- Hard-working and good team spirit

Resume Makeover

Max's resume repositions him as an international sales manager based in China.

1 The contact information uses his address and phone number in Zhuhai, emphasizing that he is living in China and ready to go to work immediately for a Chinese company.

2 The International Sales Manager heading conveys his new focus.

3 The qualifications summary highlights his international experience in the apparel industry.

4 Selected key words are added in a three-column format to stand out and match terms in job descriptions.

5 The Professional Experience section leads off with references to his current base in China and extensive travel.

6 His Education section is expanded to include his consistent language studies and bicultural business training.

7 Personal information includes citizenship, birth date, and other information that is more common for resumes submitted to Chinese companies.

Max Stover

123 Pell St. #456, San Francisco, CA 94102
(415) 123-4567 Email: email@email.com
Website: www.linkedin.com/in/mstover

Seasoned supply chain professional seeking a sourcing management position. Excellent written and verbal communication skills. Strong negotiator and experienced in Asia-based production processes.

PROFESSIONAL EXPERIENCE

OAKRIDGE INC. – 1 ICON FOOTHILL RANCH, CA 92610
March 2007 – Present

APPAREL LOGISTICS COORDINATOR
January 2007 – August 2009 (Based out of Zhuhai, China)
- Responsible for Asian Sourcing Project focusing on the expansion of Oakridge's China-based merchandising office
- Responsible for identifying gaps in Oakridge's apparel supply chain and making appropriate suggestions as to how they should be managed
- Assist in trim and finished product factory analysis
- Material procurement analysis, WIP tracking, and vendor relations

LOGISTICS SPECIALIST – HOME OFFICE
February 2005 – January 2007
- Designed, developed, and implemented a billing automation project that streamlined Oakridge's apparel drop-ship process
- Created and maintained MS Excel and SAP-based reports measuring and quantifying historical and forecasted data
- Analyzed and streamlined processes in Oakridge's production, development, and logistics departments
- Performed continuous, internal audit to determine best practices
- Key presenter in special projects such as "Supplier Boot Camp," and "Doing business under the U.S. – China Textile agreement"
- Coordinated drop-shipments from Asia-based suppliers to Oakridge accounts in Asia, South America, Europe, and Australia
- Monitored supply against the ship-to-retail timeline of Oakridge's international customers
- Prepared training tools and played active role in training/mentoring of new employees
- Consistently led department in customer fulfillment rates for both production and sample seasons

PRODUCTION INTERN – HOME OFFICE
August 2004 – December 2004
- Worked with international suppliers to maintain production and supply chain calendar
- Created and maintained reports in MS Office, SAP, e-SPS
- Worked with other apparel departments to ensure on-time delivery of goods at competitive prices

TRACO USA, INC. – 123 CARNEVELD AVE, SAN FRANCISCO, CA 94066
December 2002 – Feb. 2004
MARKETING ASSOCIATE
- Provided excellent customer service to large volume apparel accounts such as The North Face, Jansport, and Pacific Sunwear.
- Responsible for creating new business in these areas through networking, attending trade shows, cold calls, and referrals
- Partnered with Asia-based customer care and manufacturing teams to ensure the best product possible to customers in the fastest amount of time, at competitive prices

EDUCATION

UNIVERSITY OF CALIFORNIA STATE UNIVERSITY OF LONG BEACH (CSULB)
(2001-2004) Graduated with a B.S .in Marketing. Coursework focused on marketing research, strategy, and promotions, as well as Management, International Business, Economics, and Information Systems

COLLEGE OF THE SISKIYOUS
(1999-2001) Completed over 60 hours of coursework focusing on Biology, Chemistry, Anatomy, and Physics

IRVINE VALLEY COLLEGE
(2006) Completed 3 units of Mandarin Chinese language

ZHUHAI, CHINA
(2007-Present) Twice-weekly Mandarin Chinese lessons from native speaker

OTHER RELEVANT EXPERIENCE AND SKILLS
- "7 Habits of Highly Effective People" Seminar
- "Doing Business under the US – China Textile Agreement" seminar
- International Travel and Expat. experience throughout Asia and South America
- Proficient in SAP, SharePoint, e-SPS, MS Word, Excel, Visio, and Outlook
- Excellent written and verbal communication skills, and command of the English language
- Excellent negotiation skills, especially for the nuances specific to the China market

PERSONAL
- Traveling – Currently living in Zhuhai, China, and have visited seven countries for either business or leisure
- Interests – Power lifting, boxing, basketball, hiking, camping, and reading
- Sports – Played basketball at the high school and junior college level

* Personal and business references available upon request or on LinkedIn website at top of resume

(1)

Max Stover
www.linkedin.com/in/name
email@email.com • 86-10-12345678
No.1234 East Yuehai Road, Gongbei District, Zhuhai, 519020

(2)

INTERNATIONAL SALES MANAGER

(3)

- 7+ years of apparel experience, including five years of overseeing accounts in China.
- Travel extensively throughout China for a Zhuhai-based merchandising office of an American company. Conduct business in Mandarin, Cantonese, and English.
- Excellent negotiation skills, especially for the nuances specific to the China market.
- Bachelor of Science Degree in Marketing and additional language courses in Mandarin and Cantonese Chinese.
- Proficient in SAP, SharePoint, e-SPS, MS Word, Excel, Visio, and Outlook.
- International travel and expat experience throughout Asia and South America.

(4)

Sales Forecasting	Business Development
Marketing Analysis	Customer Service
Management	Planning
Vendor Relations	
Exporting Workflow	
Foreign Trade Process	

(5)

PROFESSIONAL EXPERIENCE

OAKRIDGE INC., Zhuhai, China, and San Francisco, CA   **Aug. 2004 – Present**
Apparel Logistics Coordinator Jan. 2007 – Aug. 2009

Based out of Zhuhai, China, and travel extensively throughout the Guangdong, Shandong Jiangsu, Zhejiang, and Fujian provinces and to Shanghai

- Oversee Asian sourcing project focusing on the expansion of Oakridge's China-based merchandising office
- Identify gaps in Oakridge's apparel supply chain and make appropriate suggestions as to how they should be managed
- Assist in trim and finished product factory analysis
- Conduct material procurement analysis, WIP tracking, and vendor relations

Logistics Specialist, San Francisco, CA   Feb. 2005 – Jan. 2007

- Designed, developed, and implemented a billing automation project that streamlined Oakridge's apparel drop-ship process
- Created and maintained MS Excel and SAP-based reports measuring and quantifying historical and forecasted data
- Analyzed and streamlined processes in production, development and logistics. Performed continuous, internal audit to determine best practices
- Key presenter in special projects such as "Supplier Boot Camp," and "Doing business under the U.S. – China Textile agreement"
- Coordinated drop-shipments from Asia-based suppliers to Oakridge accounts in Asia, South America, Europe, and Australia
- Monitored supply against the ship-to-retail timeline of Oakridge's international customers
- Prepared training tools and played active role in training/mentoring of new employees
- Consistently led department in customer fulfillment rates for both production and sample seasons

Production Intern, San Francisco, CA   Aug. 2004 – Dec. 2004

- Contacted international suppliers to maintain production and supply chain calendar
- Negotiated costs and discussed schedules with other apparel departments to ensure on-time delivery of goods at competitive prices
- Created and maintained reports in MS Office, SAP, and e-SPS

TRACO USA, INC., SAN FRANCISCO, CA   **Dec. 2002 – Feb. 2004**
Marketing Associate

- Provided excellent customer service to large-volume apparel accounts such as The North Face, Jansport, and Pacific Sunwear
- Created new business in these areas through networking, attending trade shows, cold calls, and referrals
- Partnered with Asia-based customer care and manufacturing teams to ensure the best product possible to customers in the fastest amount of time, at competitive prices

(6)

EDUCATION AND LANGUAGE COURSEWORK

UNIVERSITY OF CALIFORNIA STATE UNIVERSITY OF LONG BEACH, 2004
Bachelor of Science in Marketing
Coursework focused on International Business, Marketing Research, Strategy and Promotions, as well as Management, Economics, and Information Systems

COLLEGE OF THE SISKIYOUS
Completed over 60 hours of coursework focusing on Biology, Chemistry, Anatomy, and Physics, 1999 to 2001

ZHUHAI, CHINA
Twice-weekly Mandarin and Cantonese lessons from native speaker, 2007 to present

IRVINE VALLEY COLLEGE
Completed 3 units of Mandarin Chinese language, 2006

SEMINARS
"Doing Business Under the US – China Textile Agreement"
"7 Habits of Highly Effective People"

(7)

PERSONAL INFORMATION

Citizenship: American, born in San Francisco, California, March 17, 1981
Gender: Male
Marital Status: Single, no children
Permanent Mailing Address: 123 Pell Street, Apt. 456, San Francisco, CA 94102
Current Residence and Travel: Live in Zhuhai, China, and have visited seven countries for either business or leisure
Interests: Power lifting, boxing, basketball, hiking, camping, and reading
Sports: Played basketball at the high school and junior college level

Max Stover/Page 2

Marketer to Project Manager

Natalie Wenzel has been working for a friend and business associate for more than two years doing research into accounting fraud. This is a sharp detour in her career, which has been in marketing, sales, and fundraising. She really considers herself a marketer but now has a resume that says, "Administrative Assistant." She knows she needs to go back to a more professional job in order to build her career.

Just as she is getting ready to move on, her friend fires her! It seems the investigations brought on by Sarbanes-Oxley legislation have decreased in number, and his consulting practice no longer needs a researcher. She is left with a less-than-great item on her resume and no prospects. She decides to rethink her career, stressing her marketing background and positioning herself for a new job in project management. Luckily, she has been networking with the local Project Management Professionals (PMP) chapter, has a PMP designation, and has done a few projects on the side.

Challenges to Making the Switch

Natalie's detour into the world of forensic accounting presents a confusing picture to future employers. A step back into an administrative role is not thought to be positive from the competitive world of marketing. She wants to be truthful about her work in research but realizes this item is holding her back.

Her background at Ford has given her some credibility as a project manager, but that experience is only three years. She decides to go with a strong marketing resume and position herself for a new career in project management, where her marketing background will likely be valued and she can utilize her substantial organization and research skills. The challenge is to convince the employer that she still has the drive and energy to make this functional switch at age 55.

Transferable Skills

Certified Project Management Professional (PMP)

Six-Sigma Green Belt

Web-based software integration

Managing an international team

Software creation and release

Designing and monitoring project scope

Job Description
Project Manager IT

- Project Manager who has at least five years experience managing software implementation and IT process improvement engagements

- Consulting background preferred along with financial service industry experience; PMP certification is a plus

- Experience managing one or more complex system integration projects with budgets greater than $1 million

- Experience organizing and determining a detailed approach for delivering both integration projects and programs

- Experience presenting project status to senior executives

- Ability to identify strategic integration needs, risks, and issues and devise well-thought-out strategies to solve them

- Motivating, evaluating, training, and coaching assigned staff

- Overseeing other consultants and subject matter experts as appropriate

- Defining project scope, planning major project phases, and establishing project success factors

- Developing and monitoring project budget; determining appropriate resource levels for projects

- Prioritizing issues for resolution, hold, or escalation

- Supervising the development of project work plans constructed from input provided by team leads and senior team members

Resume Makeover

Natalie's resume is revised, adding results statements and changing the focus from marketing to project management.

❶ Natalie adds her new PMP designation immediately after her name.

❷ A headline is created to match the position description: Project Manager. Opening statements detail her project manager successes.

❸ Core Competencies match, as nearly as she can, the requirements in the job description.

❹ She deletes her research job, deciding instead to include two minor project management contracts she has done under the banner of her own consultancy.

❺ Details are added to her achievement statements to give her resume a more businesslike and results-oriented feel.

NATALIE WENZEL, MBA

Miami, FL 33010   email@email.com   (305) 123-4567

Experience

Researcher/Administrative Assistant – ABC Consulting   Gainesville, 2007 - Present
Conducted research and created executive briefings for expert witness in forensic accounting
- Sifted through mountains of paperwork to find legally significant data to create detailed summaries of business events significant as evidence in civil lawsuits
- Manager of operations; arranged travel and personal assistance to company principal
- Managed office, invoiced clients, light bookkeeping, and hired temporary staff

Marketing Manager – Info Tech, Inc.   Gainesville, 2003 - 2007
Developed new markets for the leading Internet bidding and project management software used in the transportation construction industry
- Led cross-departmental teams for initial product deployment in international markets and at selected universities
- Developed and delivered product training and support programs for client installations
- Managed corporate conference and trade show marketing
- Created expert speaker program to build corporate and product brand leadership in new markets
- Initiated relationships with key contacts which resulted in product features in industry publications
- Evaluated competitive environment and ROI of market opportunities and product enhancements
- Led responses to RFPs to state and municipal transportation agencies
- Managed team budgets and resources efficiently

Project Manager - Ford Motor Company   Dearborn, 2000 - 2003
E-Business Strategy and Implementation, Global Purchasing
Developed and deployed global web-based system for managing supplier data, material, and financial transactions with more than 40,000 supplier firms
- Trained and supervised customer implementation training team
- Led cross-departmental international team to create interface with legacy system to Oracle
- Group leader for Six Sigma process to contain costs and minimize process time
- Managed development of project marketing materials and user support documentation

Director of Marketing and Member Services - University of Texas   Austin, 1992 - 1997
University Foundation and Alumni Association
Developed and managed corporate endorsements and sponsor programs
- Managed corporate partnership programs, increasing revenue
- Sourced, negotiated, and managed corporate contracts for affinity programs
- Developed long-range plan for corporate partnerships and revenue growth
- Trained and managed staff and alumni volunteers
- Developed marketing collateral and designed first web page
- Created public relations campaigns

NATALIE WENZEL, MBA   (305) 123-4567

Associate Director for the Capital Campaign – Philadelphia University   1990 - 1992
Developed and managed relationships and gift proposals with professional alumni, foundation, and corporate donors
- Achieved more than 200% revenue over plan
- Recruited and coordinated the charter Board of Directors
- Managed promotional events

Major Account Executive – Xerox Corporation   Boston, 1986 - 1989
Designed contracts for document outsourcing services
- Negotiated national contracts for Fortune 100 accounts and law firms in an extremely competitive environment
- Recognized as top regional performer

EDUCATION

MBA in Marketing and Finance, University of Florida
Attended practicum at Otto Beisheim Graduate School of Management, Koblenz, Germany

Paid Internships

Corporate Associate, Corporate Development and Strategy Department
Fannie Mae Corporation, Washington, DC

Project Associate, Strategy, Opportunity Identification and Policy Department
Blue Cross Blue Shield of Florida, Jacksonville, FL

Business Analyst Intern, State Commerce Department
Enterprise North Florida, Jacksonville, FL

BS in Business Administration, College of Notre Dame of Maryland

Project Management Professional (PMP), Project Management Institute, Pennsylvania

Coach University and IPEC Coaching, 2007 - Present

PROFESSIONAL AND COMMUNITY SERVICE

Junior Achievement	Council for the Advancement & Support of Education Member
United Way, Campaign	St. Vincent's Home for Children Events Volunteer
Junior League International Member	Big Brothers/Big Sisters - Fundraising and Mentorship
Corporate Adventures Inc. Team Leader	Gainesville Girls Club - Fundraising and Mentorship

❹

NATALIE WENZEL, MBA, PMP ❶

Miami, FL 33010 ■ email@email.com ■ (305) 123-4567

PROJECT MANAGER ❷

- MBA, Certified Project Manager, and Six Sigma Green Belt with management experience in software development, financial services, manufacturing, higher education, nonprofit, professional services support, and business services
  - Trailblazer – hired strategically and allowed to design and develop my positions
  - Proven track record in conceiving and executing IT product launch projects
  - Passionate and dedicated; a "cool head" in crisis, focused on budget and time constraints
  - Extensive experience managing International rollout of web-based CRM system
  - Creator of outside-the-box approaches and disciplined techniques to produce project results
  - Known for increasing revenue, developing new markets, and creating efficient processes

CORE COMPETENCIES ❸

- Market Expansion
- Leader for International IT Teams
- Million-Dollar Software Rollout
- Competitive Brand Analysis
- Staff and Vendor Training
- Software Integration Projects
- High-Impact Sales Presentations
- Client Relationship Expansion
- "C" Level Sales Presentations
- Expanding Customer Base
- Quality Improvement – Six Sigma Green Belt
- Staff Career Development

PROFESSIONAL EXPERIENCE ❹

Project Manager – Wenzel Project Consulting   Miami, 2007 – Present
Served as an ad-hoc project manager for local software firms

- Managed the rollout of AccountSoft v.3 to national markets: 9-month project resulted in 73% client renewals; and new product sales representing a 35% increase in client base.
- Project Manager for integration of financial client's new accounting software. Project involved coordinating the efforts of 10 Accounting Managers and 60 billing and AR clerks. Accomplished within budget and time parameters in 14 weeks.

Marketing Manager – SoftwareTech, Inc.   Miami, 2003 – 2007
Developed new markets for the leading Internet bidding and project management software used in the transportation construction industry

- Led cross-departmental teams for initial product deployment in international markets and at selected universities.
- Developed and delivered product training and support programs for client installations.
- Managed corporate conference and trade show marketing.
- Created expert speaker program to build corporate and product brand leadership in new markets.
- Initiated relationships with key contacts which resulted in products features in industry publications.
- Evaluated competitive environment and ROI of market opportunities and product enhancements.
- Led responses to RFPs to state and municipal transportation agencies.
- Managed team budgets and resources efficiently.

NATALIE WENZEL, MBA, PMP
Miami, FL 33010 ■ email@email.com ■ (305) 123-4567

NATALIE WENZEL, MBA, PMP   (305) 123-4567

Project Manager – Ford Motor Company   Dearborn, 2000 – 2003
E-Business Strategy and Implementation, Global Purchasing ❺
Developed and deployed global web-based system for managing supplier data, material, and financial transactions with more than 40,000 supplier firms

- Trained and supervised customer implementation team of 15 to roll out training of 40,000 vendor companies, including more than 500,000 persons.
- Led cross-departmental international team to create interface with legacy system to Oracle.
- Group leader for Six Sigma process to contain costs and minimize process time.
- Managed development of project marketing materials and user support documentation.

Director of Marketing and Member Services – University of Texas   Austin, 1992 – 1997
University Foundation and Alumni Association
Developed and managed corporate endorsements and sponsor programs ❺

- Managed corporate partnership programs, increasing revenue more than 300 percent in 5 years.
- Sourced, negotiated, and managed corporate contracts for affinity programs.
- Developed long-range plan for corporate partnerships and revenue growth.
- Trained and managed staff and alumni volunteers.
- Developed marketing collateral and designed first web page.
- Created public relations campaigns.
- Managed alumni and donor events.

Associate Director for the Capital Campaign – Philadelphia University   Philadelphia, 1990 – 1992
Developed and managed relationships and gift proposals with professional alumni, foundation, and corporate donors

- Achieved more than 200% revenue over plan.
- Recruited and coordinated the charter Board of Directors.
- Managed promotional events.

Major Account Executive – Xerox Corporation   Boston, 1986 – 1989
Designed contracts for document outsourcing services

- Negotiated national contracts for Fortune 100 accounts and law firms in an extremely competitive environment.
- Recognized as top regional performer.

EDUCATION

MBA in Marketing and Finance, University of Florida
Attended practicum at Otto Beisheim Graduate School of Management, Koblenz, Germany

Paid Internships
Corporate Associate, Corporate Development and Strategy Department
Fannie Mae Corporation, Washington, DC
Project Associate, Strategy, Opportunity Identification and Policy Department
Blue Cross Blue Shield of Florida, Jacksonville, FL
Business Analyst Intern, State Commerce Department
Enterprise North Florida, Jacksonville, FL

BS in Business Administration, College of Notre Dame of Maryland
Project Management Professional (PMP), Project Management Institute, Pennsylvania
Coach University and IPEC Coaching, 2007 – Present

PROFESSIONAL AND COMMUNITY SERVICE

Junior Achievement	Council for the Advancement and Support of Education – Member
United Way Campaign	St. Vincent's Home for Children – Events Volunteer
Junior League International – Member	Big Brothers/Big Sisters – Fundraising and Mentorship
Corporate Adventures Inc. – Team Leader	Gainesville Girls Club – Fundraising and Mentorship

Mortgage Underwriter to Bank Operations

Maureen Lang spent the last seven years as a mortgage loan underwriter. Two of her last four positions ended when her employer's company—moderately to heavily involved in subprime mortgages—went out of business. Although trained in conventional lending, she feels that mortgage lending is beyond her grasp because lenders are now seeking employees with FHA, VA, and DU designations. In addition, accounting-related positions now require accounting/finance or advanced degrees and a CPA. She has a total of 13 years experience in finance and wants to find a way to stay in banking. So she is currently looking to become a bank operations officer.

Challenges to Making the Switch

Hiring managers at banking institutions may be wary of anyone coming from the subprime mortgage lending environment. She will have to prove her dedication to quality lending and following guidelines.

With bank closings and mergers, the entire industry is slow to hire at this time. However, Maureen is encouraged by several local ads for positions in credit unions—a relatively stable part of the financial services industry. Maureen's experience in bank operations is limited to a consulting project when she first graduated, plus one year as an operations associate. She will have to show that she has some management-level experience, because bank operations officers nearly always supervise customer service and teller staff.

She resolves to study banking operations terminology and recent changes in the industry. Much of this is available in networking conversations and on government websites. She carefully revises her resume, emphasizing the compliance, management, and due diligence aspects of her finance positions.

Transferable Skills

Supervision, mentoring, and training

Risk evaluation

Customer service

Compliance with federal guidelines

Operations analysis

Problem resolution

Documentation

Job Description

Bank Operations Manager

- Ensure all internal and external customers' banking-related issues are efficiently handled by staff members

- Supervise daily activities of customer service representatives (CSR) and operational analysts; be able to perform all duties of a CSR and operational analyst

- Identify, recommend, and implement changes to improve productivity and customer service

- Assist team members with customer research and problem resolution; handle escalated issues

- Approve action items and resolution of daily reports (surveillance, NSF, and exceptions)

- Monitor interaction of CSRs with customers to ensure quality control; ensuring compliance with program and regulatory guidelines

- Hire, train, develop, and evaluate staff; ensure sufficient coverage with CSRs and operations analysts

- Demonstrate ability to exercise sound judgment and make decisions in line with company's guidelines

- Required: Bachelor's degree in business administration or related field; two years experience in banking operations; two years of managerial experience

Resume Makeover

Maureen's resume is rewritten to accentuate the experience she has had in banking operations.

1 The headline "Bank Operations" clearly states her objective. She follows this with eight statements that relate to the quality of her work, her management ability, and her sound judgment.

2 Her Skills Summary section is expanded to include terminology appropriate to bank operations. This section allows her to load the resume with words that will match bank operations job descriptions. If read by a machine, her resume will come to the top as a match.

3 Her mortgage experience is condensed into one item. She was performing the same tasks at each company, so one description works for all four jobs.

4 She ends the section with a bold statement that assures the reader that her underwriting judgment is sound, even though the companies are no longer in business.

5 The bank operations job is included on page one so that the quick reader will see a relevant job title.

6 Her six years of retail experience are left off so that all jobs on this resume relate to the financial industry.

Maureen Lang

1000 Haymaker Way, #60, Des Moines, IA 50310
512-123-4567 (cell)
email@email.com

PROFESSIONAL PROFILE

Accomplished mortgage underwriter with broad experience in credit analysis / review and operations with award-winning customer relations skills. Well organized with exceptional analytical and problem solving skills. Strong attention to detail and accuracy. Excellent communicator — verbal and written. Effective team builder / player / leader. Committed to total quality. Resourceful, dedicated, and responsible.

SKILLS SUMMARY

- Finance
- Credit and Ratio Analysis
- Regulatory Procedures and Compliance
- Problem Solving
- Reconciliation
- Customer Relations

MAJOR ACCOMPLISHMENTS

❖ Accurately underwrote up to 17 home equity mortgage credit applications daily.
❖ Successfully resolved issues with mortgage consultants / brokers and internal partners using communication and relationship-building skills.
❖ Acknowledged by Underwriting Manager and external Supervisors for being a team player and received multiple awards for exemplary customer service: New Century Mortgage; Finance America; *Legendary Service Award*, Wells Fargo Home Equity; and *Goodwill Ambassador*, Younkers Department Store.
❖ Effectively reduced 3rd quarter correspondent bank service charges 91% from 1st quarter and 98% from 2nd quarter.
❖ Identified serious Truth-in-Lending compliance issue and recommended viable solutions.
❖ Consulted on a cost reduction/revenue increasing project resulting in a 340% return on investment.

RELEVANT CAREER HISTORY

Underwriter, CIT Group, Des Moines, IA   2007

Underwriter I, New Century Mortgage, Denver, CO   2004 to 2007
Underwrote non-prime and Alt-A mortgage loan files with high degree of accuracy. Using problem solving skills and creativity, worked with internal Account Executives and Brokers to effectively restructure loans when necessary. Recognized multiple times for identifying fraud and misrepresentation.

Underwriter I, Finance America, Denver, CO   2003 to 2004
Assessed risk factors of sub-prime mortgage loan files and conditioned accordingly. Communicated with Account Executives and Brokers to resolve issues or offer alternatives. Was requested to be primary underwriter for highest-producing Account Executives.

Underwriter I, Wells Fargo Home Equity, Colorado Springs, CO   2001 to 2003
Underwrote prime paperless home equity loan applications for credit worthiness and soundness. Analyzed ratios and credit / risk factors using exception logic. Trained and mentored 3 new underwriters and approximately 10 team members from other departments.

Financial Operations Banking Associate, Vista Bank, Colorado Springs, CO   1996 to 1999, 2000
Responsible for correspondent bank cash management, buying / selling funds and reconciliations. Managed the wire department including wires in / out, ACH, tax payments, returns, and payroll files. Settled ATM transactions / reports. Processed Accounts Payable. Reconciled internal accounts.

Financial Officer and Office Manager, Trommer Law Firm
Oversaw financial and administrative operations. Managed three checking accounts, payroll, and accuracy of the trust account and client billing statements by posting costs / payments to client ledgers. Managed a $300K budget and supervised two employees.

Credit Union Examiner, State of Iowa   1994 to 1996
Examined (i) general ledger, (ii) loan and investment portfolios, and (iii) procedures to assess components of Capital, Assets, Management, Earnings, and Liquidity. Analyzed ratios for safety and soundness to prepare examination reports. Conducted meetings with Boards of Directors to review findings / recommendations.

Bank Consultant, Avery Lyons & Associates   1987
Formulated and implemented recommendations for procedural changes in all areas of banking, including teller / bookkeeper operations; personal, college, and commercial lending; insufficient funds; proofing; funds transfers; and correspondent banking. Also consulted on cost reduction and revenue increasing. Wrote consultant procedure / training manual.

OTHER EXPERIENCE

Assistant Manager, Johnston & Murphy Men's Shoe Store   1993 to 1994
Responsible for overall store management, merchandising, display advertising, and sales.

Sales Associate and Pacesetter, Younkers Department Store   1991 to 1994
Facilitated sales, merchandising, inventory management, and customer service. As Pacesetter, provided leadership and direction for associates of two departments.

Guest Relations, Best Western Bavarian Inn   1988 to 1991
Booked reservations and ensured guests' hospitality. Reconciled shift audits and assisted with night audit functions. Acted as relief Manager on Duty.

Assistant Manager, Bookkeeper, Buyer, Aunt Maude's Restaurant   1988 to 1989
Supervised operations and conducted inventory, ordering, and pricing functions. Reconciled guest checks, sales data, and remitted credit transactions.

EDUCATION and TRAINING

BBA, Iowa State University
Major: Management with Finance emphasis
Minor: Political Science

Additional coursework in: Masters Foundation Corporate Finance
Intermediate Accounting
Finance and Investments

Leadership: Landmark Education Corporation
Finance Team, 2006
Registration Fulfillment Team, 2001 – 2005
Leadership Program Coach 1997 – 2001 / Head Coach (1999)

Maureen Lang

1000 Waymaker Way #60, Des Moines, IA 50310   512.123.4567 (cell)   email@email.com

❶ BANK OPERATIONS

- Accomplished financial professional with broad experience in credit analysis, review and financial operations within regulatory, banking, and mortgage industries
- Earned reputation for ability to successfully de-escalate conflict leading to customer retention
- Recipient of many awards recognizing exceptional communication and customer service skills
- Achieved/exceeded goals while minimizing risk
- Highly organized and committed to the quality of my work
- Strong mentor, team builder, and leader
- Identified cost reduction/revenue enhancement opportunities to yield 340% return on investment
- Reduced avoidable cost/expense by more than 90% from prior two quarters within 90 days

❷ SKILLS SUMMARY

Finance	Risk Evaluation	Credit & Ratio Analysis
Cash Settlement	Problem Solving	Income Review & Asset Valuation
Customer Focus	Due Diligence	Fedline/Wire Transactions
Reconciliation	Vendor Management	ATM Transactions
Operation Analysis	CSR Management	Regulatory Guidelines
Proprietary Software	Debit Card Portfolio	Surveillance, NSF, Exceptions

❸ RELEVANT CAREER HISTORY

MORTGAGE UNDERWRITER   **2001–2007**

CIT Group	Des Moines, IA	2007
New Century Mortgage	Denver, CO	2004 to 2007
Finance America	Denver, CO	2003 to 2004
Wells Fargo Home Equity	Colorado Springs, CO	2001 to 2003

- Accurately underwrote mortgage loan applications while meeting or exceeding files-per-day standard
- Assessed credit/risk factors of prime retail home equity and subprime/Alt-A wholesale mortgage loan files for creditworthiness and soundness
- Coordinated with Account Executives and Brokers to resolve discrepancies or offer alternatives to restructure loans
- Reviewed/approved income, title, and collateral
- Recognized multiple times for identifying fraud and misrepresentation
- Successfully resolved issues with mortgage consultants / brokers and internal partners using communication and relationship-building skills

❹ *Achieved 99.8% underwriting accuracy as reviewed by Quality Assurance department (Wells Fargo).*

❺ FINANCIAL OPERATIONS BANKING ASSOCIATE   **2000**

Vista Bank   Colorado Springs, CO

- Responsible for correspondent bank cash management, buying/selling funds, and reconciliations between Federal Reserve, Federal Home Loan Bank etc.
- Managed the Fedline/wire department including wires in/out, ACH, tax payments, returns, and payroll files
- Settled ATM transactions reports; processed Accounts Payable; reconciled internal accounts

Reduced correspondent bank service charges by at least 90% from prior two quarters within 90 days.

Maureen Lang 512-123-4567

FINANCIAL OFFICER AND OFFICE MANAGER   **1996 to 1999**

Trommer Law Firm   Colorado Springs, CO

- Oversaw financial and administrative operations
- Managed three checking accounts, payroll, and accuracy of the trust account and client billing statements by posting costs/payments to client ledgers
- Managed a $300,000 budget and supervised two employees

Reduced outstanding long-term debt by 81% within 24 months.

CREDIT UNION EXAMINER   **1994 to 1996**

State of Iowa   Des Moines, IA

- Examined the areas of capital, assets, management practices, earnings, liquidity, and procedures for regulatory compliance and safety/soundness
- Wrote examination reports and conducted meetings with Boards of Directors to review findings and recommendations

Identified serious Truth-in-Lending compliance issue and recommended viable solutions.

PREVIOUS RELEVANT EXPERIENCE

BANK CONSULTANT   Avery Lyons & Associates   Emmetsburg, IA   **1987**

Formulated and implemented recommendations for procedural changes in all areas of banking, including teller/bookkeeper operations; personal, college, and commercial lending; insufficient funds; proofing; funds transfers; and correspondent banking

Consulted on cost reduction and revenue enhancement

Wrote client procedure/training manual.

Identified cost reduction / revenue enhancement opportunities to yield 340% return on investment.

❻ EDUCATION and TRAINING

BA, Business Administration, Iowa State University
Major: Management
Emphasis/Minor: Finance
Minor: Political Science

Masters Foundation Corporate Finance (8 hours)
Intermediate Accounting
Finance and Investments

LEADERSHIP
Landmark Education Corporation
Finance Team, 2006
Registration Fulfillment Team, 2001 – 2005
Leadership Program Coach 1997 – 2001 / Head Coach 1999

Pet Sitter to Veterinary Assistant

While her kids were growing up, Paula Brendle was happy to be a stay-at-home mom. She was an active participant in her kids' school activities and the Parent Teacher Organization (PTO). Her husband Tom's home construction business was very successful during the late 1990s and early 2000s, giving her the freedom to not have to work outside the home.

When her mother's health began to fail in 2006, Paula was able to provide full-time care without much impact on the family's income. In 2007, when her mother went into an intermediate care facility and their last child left for college, Paula started a pet sitting service. Because Paula likes animals, the business gave her something fun to do and provided her with a little extra spending money.

When the new housing market took a turn for the worse, Tom's business began to suffer. Tom has had to cut expenses, including health insurance. So Paula is looking for a steady paycheck with benefits.

If Paula has to get a steady job, she would like to work with animals. Fortunately, the animal care industry remains fairly steady. With her interest and experience in caring for animals and her ability to deal with people, Paula is well qualified to work as a veterinary assistant. The learning curve is relatively low, and many veterinary offices will train.

Challenges to Making the Switch

Paula has no real "paid" work history, and she took nearly two years to care for her aging mother. Her major achievements include volunteering at her children's schools, serving on the board of the PTO, and starting a pet sitting business. While Paula has not held any "real" jobs, her resume still shows that she was actively using her many skills and talents.

Paula hopes that her prospective employer will see her as competent, even though she doesn't have a documented job history.

Transferable Skills

Animal care (exercise, feeding, and grooming)

Animal behavior and training

Administration of medications

Administrative support

Customer service

Organization skills

Communication skills

Emergency management

Volunteer management

Fundraising

Community organizing

Leadership skills

Microsoft Office

Gregg shorthand

Job Description
Veterinary Assistant

- Provide health care to animals large and small
- Feed, exercise, and groom patients
- Clean and maintain holding areas and equipment
- Prepare and sanitize surgery suites
- Restrain and handle patients
- Customer service
- Clerical and administrative work
- Accept payments for services rendered
- Able to handle stress
- Professional and compassionate
- Good communication skills
- Ability to respond effectively in emergency situations

Resume Makeover

Paula's resume needs a complete overhaul. Using a different format, she finds a way to highlight her skills and strengths.

❶ She adds her target job title, veterinary assistant, so there's no doubt what job she's applying for.

❷ She lists her strengths and expertise at the top where they can be seen at a quick glance.

❸ Under Professional Accomplishments, her experience is better organized and easier to read.

❹ Work History is where she lists her most important "jobs" in reverse chronological order. She will have to address the gap in experience in her cover letter and interview. The simplest and most truthful explanation is, "I was caring for my ailing mother."

Paula Brendle
1234 Leebrad Street
Springfield, VA 22151
(703) 123-4567
email@email.com

OBJECTIVE: To care for animals in an environment where love, attention, and respect are mutually beneficial.

EMPLOYMENT:
2007 – Present **Pet Sitter:** Operated a pet sitting business. Supervised animals on an as-needed basis for clients. Responsible for walking, feeding, grooming, and administering medications if required.

2006 – 2007 **Caregiver:** Provided home/health care for my mother until she was placed into an intermediate care facility.

1992 – 2005 **Member and Officer PTO Board:** Fairfax County Public Schools: Volunteered in many capacities within the district. Areas of volunteering included: assisted teachers with games and socialization skills for students. **Tutored** 2nd-grade math students. **Safety Committee** worked with students to teach them about personal safety and also supervised their crossing guard assignments. **Fourth Grade Coordinator:** Planned field trips and recruited parent volunteers to accompany students. **Chairperson: Carnival Committee.** Supported and aided volunteers on the sales, food, games, prizes, decorating, and live entertainment committees. Responsible for securing city permits. Presided over volunteer meetings. **Auction Committees:** 6th and 7th grades. Responsible for securing location, heading meetings, aided volunteers in accruing items from local businesses in our community. **Food Committee:** Worked with community restaurants to purchase food and desserts, at large discount prices, to sell to students for a one-day change in their food choice each week. **8th grade Graduation Committee:** Implemented carnation sales event to raise money. Printed and sold tickets, developed theme, procured movie posters from area video stores, hired DJ. **Chairperson:** Decorating Committee for the 2004 and 2005 Homecoming Dances. **Head of Concessions:** Volunteered for Community Swim Team. **Nominated:** Volunteer of the Year 2003 by FCPS.

SKILLS: Microsoft Office; Keyboarding 50 wpm; Gregg Shorthand 50 wpm.

EDUCATION: LAMAR UNIVERSITY, Beaumont, TX
Business

PAULA BRENDLE

| (703) 123-4567 | 1234 Leebrad Street, Springfield, VA 22151 | email@email.com |

❶ VETERINARY ASSISTANT

Experienced and compassionate caregiver. ~ Loves and respects animals. ~ Communicates well with animals and humans.

❷ SUMMARY of QUALIFICATIONS

Key Attributes	Expertise	Office Skills

• Organized
• Hardworking
• Compassionate and caring
• Committed to the well-being of animals
• Calm during a crisis
• Great with animals
• Strong people skills
• Well known in the community
• Creative problem solver
• Desire to learn
• Able to multitask
• Strong attention to detail
	• Animal care (exercise, feeding, and grooming)
	• Administration of medications
	• Administrative support
	• Customer service
	• Emergency management
	• Business management
	• Volunteer management
	• Fundraising
	• Community organizing
	• Community liaison
	• Communication skills
	• Leadership skills
		• MS Office
		  Word
		  Outlook
		  PowerPoint
		  Excel
		• QuickBooks
		• Keyboard (50 wpm)
		• FAX, Scanner, Copier
		• Gregg Shorthand (50 wpm)

❸ PROFESSIONAL ACCOMPLISHMENTS

- Supervised animals for clients
- Walked, fed, and groomed animals
- Administered medications as needed
- Served on and managed numerous committees; secured meeting locations, facilitated meetings, recruited and managed volunteers, and engaged support and donations from local businesses
- As Carnival Committee Chairperson, secured city permits and managed volunteers
- Planned class field trips and recruited parent volunteers to accompany students
- Managed fundraising events
- Tutored second-grade math students
- Taught personal safety to and supervised student crossing guards
- Nominated as 2003 Fairfax County Public Schools Volunteer of the Year

❹ WORK HISTORY

Owner, Pet Sitting Business, Springfield, Virginia	2007 – Present
Board Member and Officer, Parent Teacher Organization Fairfax County Public Schools	1992 – 2005

EDUCATION

BBA – Management, Lamar University, Beaumont, Texas

Shipping Clerk to Sales

Michael Teague has been working for a firearms manufacturer in the shipping department for four years. He has an Associate's degree in music production, but his dream of being a rock star with his own band ended years ago. Meanwhile, he has been studying with an online university, gaining a four-year degree in information technology. He has a wife and a new baby son and is hoping to upgrade to a professional position. Then, word of layoffs hits the manufacturing plant. He learns that he is cut from the shipping staff but that a few positions have been opened in sales in an attempt to increase sales and help the plant recover. There are few jobs in his community, and the best ones are at this company. To salvage his job, he decides to make an attempt to move into sales.

Challenges to Making the Switch

The manufacturing plant where he works has more than 300 employees. Michael has thus far been invisible to management and has never met the vice-president of sales. He will have to approach this job as if he were an outside candidate. Although he lacks the Bachelor's degree required for this position, he is within six months of graduation. He also hopes that his information technology degree will be a special asset, as the company has just implemented new CRM software.

Michael's experience in sales is limited to a short time at Best Buy and working for a local auctioneer. On the plus side, he has been shipping his company's products for more than four years. Although there are 30,000 SKU numbers, he has trained himself to recognize many of them. The product catalog is his most important reference tool; he knows it from cover to cover. Because he has to interface with all the departments, he thoroughly understands the production process. By working directly with both retail and wholesale customers, he has a sense of what each segment cares about most.

He also has several friends in sales who will put in a good word for him because he has performed minor miracles in shipping their difficult orders. The actual interviewing process will be tough, though, because so many have applied for just one position.

Transferable Skills

Customer focus

Sales skill

Product line knowledge

Federal and international regulations

Computer networking/troubleshooting

Problem resolution

Billing, inventory systems

Documentation

Job Description

Product Specialist

- Direct marketer in the firearms industry providing quality merchandise through a portfolio of catalogs, e-commerce platforms, and fulfillment services; with more than 30,000 product SKUs, seeking an individual who can work successfully in a fast-paced and challenging environment

- Provide industry-wide perspective and insight in representing the sales and customer point of view that leads to effective plan development and execution

- Strong analytical skills with hands-on use of syndicated data, customer-specific information, and the ability to go beyond historical data interpretation and forecast future product trends

- Provide educational resources and information to brand marketing that aid in development of the annual business plan

- Identify category and account opportunities; initiate and implement projects that will result in increased sales

- BA in relevant academic discipline with five to seven years experience; understanding of firearms customer segments and a strong customer-focus orientation

- Excellent project management skills with demonstrated success in product launches and end-to-end execution of marketing strategies

- Enthusiasm for the firearms industry with knowledge of firearms, parts, and accessories

Resume Makeover

Michael's resume is completely rewritten to emphasize the skills and knowledge he brings as an internal candidate for a sales position.

1 Michael combines all his years of shipping and sales to come up with six years of experience he can claim serving customers.

2 He lists competencies mentioned in the job description and emphasizes his edge as an internal candidate for the job.

3 The Technical Knowledge section is moved up because it outshines his job experience in sales. He is hoping that the sales director will jump on the idea of a new salesperson who can also help out with computer and software troubleshooting.

4 The Professional Experience section is presented in a functional list. His shipping experience is framed as a customer service function.

5 The Job History section is simplified to play down the overlapping and part-time jobs common to young professionals' resumes. He also eliminates the term "clerk" in his current title.

6 He ends with an Education section featuring the IT degree he is about to complete. He leaves off the commercial music Associate's degree because it's not relevant to the job search.

Michael Teague
1234 Alberta Dr.
Ogden, UT 84201
(801) 123-4567

WORK EXPERIENCE

- **Best Buy** – Salt Lake City, UT: Sales Associate (01/03 – 07/03)
  Duties included: stocking, cashier, serving customers. Specialty knowledge of video games and cameras.
- **Luther Woltz Agency** – Salt Lake City, UT: Intern (08/03 – 12/03)
  Duties of sorting, filing, copying, and mailing of contracts and promo packs. Integration of news clippings into artist press packages.
- **Herald Rhoades Auction Service** – Brigham City, UT: Auction clerk (01/01 – 01/05)
  Auction preparation duties, bookkeeping during auction, and collection of buyer fees.
- **Aubrey Plumbing** – Ogden, UT, Asst. Warehouse Manager (02/05 – 06/05) Receiving, ordering stock, maintaining warehouse, and making deliveries.
- **Browning** – Morgan, UT: Shipping Clerk (08/05 – Present) Preparation and shipping of all domestic and international packages, warehouse organization, ordering of supplies, receiving.

EDUCATION

- **Bachelor of Science in Information Technology**
  Kaplan University (December 2009)
  - 4.0 GPA
  - Repeat Dean's List recipient
  - Studies include computer programming, networking and database management.
  - To Receive two certificates from the Committee on National Security Systems
    - Information Systems Security Professionals Certificate
    - Senior Systems Managers Certificate

- **6** • **Associate of Applied Science in Commercial Music**
  Salt Lake Community College   Salt Lake City, UT (2004)
  - 3.6 GPA
  - Phi Theta Kappa International Honor Society
  - Studies include music management, production, and recording; as well as composition, history, and psychology.

❸ TECHNICAL KNOWLEDGE
  - Computer troubleshooting, maintenance & repair
  - Visual Basic 2008
  - SQL Server 2008
  - Global – ERP Software
  - Peachtree Accounting
  - Microsoft Office: Word, Excel, Access, PowerPoint, Visio

Michael Teague

1234 Alberta Drive, Ogden, UT 84201 ♦ 801-123-4567 ♦ email@email.com

❶ SALES/CUSTOMER SERVICE SPECIALIST

Six years experience in serving targeted customers, matching products to customer needs, recommending alternatives, cashiering, billing, maintaining stock, and solving fulfillment/shipping issues. Four years experience gaining detailed knowledge of the Browning product line and an understanding of the company's market segments.

❷
- Customer focus and knowledge
- Problem resolution
- Excellent communication skills
- Firearms product knowledge
- Computer networking

- Coordination e-commerce & phone sales
- Computer programming & databases
- Ship 30,000 SKU products worldwide
- Know ATF & international shipping regulations
- Enthusiasm for firearms industry

❸ TECHNICAL KNOWLEDGE
- Computer troubleshooting
- Visual Basic 2008
- SQL Server 2008
- Global ERP Software

- Microsoft Office -- Word, Excel, Access, PowerPoint
- Visio
- Peachtree Accounting Software

❹ PROFESSIONAL EXPERIENCE

Sales
- For Best Buy, became a product specialist in digital products, serving clients with product selection, warranties, special orders, etc.
- For Herald Rhoades Auction Service, prepared items for auction, kept detailed records of sales, collected buyer fees, prepared bank deposits, and reconciled ledger.

Customer Service/Shipping
- For Browning, work with Account Executives in delivering large orders and staging shipping to serve client needs. Troubleshoot orders to 53 countries worldwide.
- Understand and communicate international shipping regulations to the sales staff, resolving problems.
- Worked directly with large-scale wholesalers, resolving order and shipping issues.

Inventory/Billing
- Maintained stock for commercial plumbing supply company with more than 45,000 parts
- Receiving, ordering, stocking the warehouse, making deliveries

❺ JOB HISTORY

Shipping	Browning, Morgan, UT	2005–2009
Auction Assistant	Herald Rhoades Auction Service, Brigham City, UT	2001–2005
Sales Associate	Best Buy, Salt Lake City, UT	2003
Intern	Luther Woltz Agency, Salt Lake City, UT	2003
Asst. Warehouse Manager	Aubrey Plumbing, Ogden, UT	2005

❻ EDUCATION

Bachelor of Science in Information Technology, Kaplan University (December 2009)
4.0 GPA, repeat Dean's List recipient
Studies include computer programming, networking, and database management.
To receive two certificates from the Committee on National Security Systems:
- Information Systems Security Professionals Certificate
- Senior Systems Managers Certificate

Social Worker to Program Manager

At the time Jennifer Verde accepted a job as a social worker, she was not sure what she wanted to do in public administration. She saw multiple openings for case workers for abused and neglected children and had no trouble landing a job in that capacity. Before long, she realized why the state agency had a high turnover rate—because of the difficulty in dealing with heart-wrenching situations. Jennifer decides to pursue other public sector work and takes time to determine what will be a better match for her. She enjoys positions that involve a variety of duties, including research, writing, and making presentations. She finds a position as a program manager at a state agency that provides services for businesses and job seekers. Jennifer has related experience, having worked at a federally funded workforce center. She hopes that her experience with training programs and knowledge of demand occupations, along with her bilingual skills, will help her transfer to a different agency.

Challenges to Making the Switch

Jennifer has never been a government agency program manager; however, she hopes her Master's degree and relevant work experience will compensate. Jennifer carefully customizes the state application that is required by all agencies and submits her resume to further highlight qualifications using key words from the job description. In a detailed manner, she pinpoints transferable skills in making presentations at work, along with her Toastmasters experience. She also stresses her research, analytical, and writing experience gained from a part-time research assistant position that she held while completing her degree. Although it has been five years since she worked in workforce development, she hopes that her familiarity with state agency training programs will be a big plus.

State agencies attract many more applicants these days. Those selected for interviews do the best job listing qualifications using key words from the job description. Jennifer takes pains to fill out her application and resume in a manner that will make it easy for a screener to understand her key qualifiers.

Transferable Skills

Project management

Presentation skills

Workshop materials development

Research

Analysis

Report preparation

Job Description

Public Program Manager

- Complete workforce business services projects, including assisting businesses with accessing state and local resources to meet their workforce training needs

- Work to target services and programs to meet the needs of employers for high-growth/demand occupations

- Assist with the development of outreach/action plans, marketing products, presentations, and workshop material

- Assist in managing projects with internal and external customers

- Serve as a liaison with employers, community and technical colleges, business service units of local workforce development boards, and other stakeholders

- Provide informational presentations at local and statewide venues and ongoing technical assistance and project development assistance for assigned geographic areas

- Assist with the preparation of administrative briefings, reports, and concept papers

- Research and evaluate information on service delivery methods, outputs, and activities in order to identify gaps in resources; prepare written recommendations for improvements

- Experience with project management, presentation preparation, public speaking, sales/marketing/outreach techniques, public relations, and grant proposal production and review

---

Resume Makeover

The resume has been expanded from a one-page resume with difficult-to-read, small type to a two-page resume with more details in bullet-point statements.

1 The headline "Program Manager Qualifications" is more specific than the reference in the original objective statement of a "challenging position within a public organization."

2 The Qualifications information is moved to the top and packed with key words, including an important reference to bilingual skills.

3 The Education section is streamlined to focus on key information, and the reference to the Dean's List is moved up to eliminate the Honors/Community Engagement section.

4 Under Professional Experience, the current job information is shortened because not all the bullet points are necessary.

5 Bexar County Workforce Center information is expanded to highlight experience that is directly related to the job description.

6 The Professional and Community Organizations section is expanded to include Toastmasters, other organizations, and a reference to grant-writing volunteer service.

Jennifer Verde

2487 Crowley Circle ♦ Austin, Texas, 78741 ♦ 512-123-4567 ♦ email@email.com

1 OBJECTIVE

Graduate of Master of Public Administration program seeking a challenging position within a public organization to apply my knowledge/skills in all aspects of organizational administration, policy research, finance, grant-writing, and public policy.

EDUCATION

December 2007 **Master of Public Administration**
Thesis: *Needs Assessment for a Ph.D. in Public Administration at Texas State University*
Texas State University - San Marcos, Texas
Major: General Public Administration **Cumulative GPA:** 3.62

August 1997 **Bachelor of Arts in Liberal Arts**, emphasis on Public Administration
Texas State University - San Marcos, Texas
Minor: History **Cumulative GPA:** 3.27 **GPA in Major:** 3.27

HONORS / COMMUNITY ENGAGEMENT

Scholarship: Memorial Presbyterian Foundation, Dean's List: Fall 2004, Spring 2005
Member of the *American Society of Public Administration*
Elected board member for Memorial Presbyterian Church, San Marcos, Texas, 2003 - 2006

EXPERIENCE

Conservatorship Specialist II: February 2008 - Present
Department of Children's Services
- Provide ongoing services to children in substitute care to meet specific needs; use appropriate resources to move toward uniting family and making other permanent plans for care.
- Initiate appropriate legal action and testify in court to achieve protection or permanent placement for children.
- Document case records by completing forms, narratives, and reports to form a written record for each client.
- Develop and maintain effective working relationships between Child Protective Services staff and law enforcement officials judicial officials, legal resources, medical professionals, and other community resources.
- Demonstrate appropriate respect for cultural diversity among co-workers and all work-related contacts.

Research Assistant: August 2006 - December 2007
Latinos and Media Project, School of Journalism & Mass Communication
- Gathered and analyzed Spanish-language print media to explore and describe levels of localism and quality of content delivered to Latino population in central Texas.
- Used SPSS program to conduct statistical analysis of newspaper contents to develop descriptive reports.
- Maintained correspondence with numerous media professionals for the Latinos and Media Project website.
- Developed an analysis of news content to explore the differences between corporate and non-corporate newspapers.

Instructional Assistant: September 2004 - June 2006
Texas State University, San Marcos, Texas
- Assisted professor with course development, classroom preparation, and management of student records.
- Developed lectures and test reviews for undergraduate government classes.
- Management of grades, research, and assignments of hundreds of undergraduate students.
- Schedule appointments and meetings with students.

Career Specialist: September 1997 - August 2004
Bexar County Workforce Center, San Antonio, Texas
- Responsibilities included case management, public speaking, and contacting employers.
- Assisted Business Services in making presentations at area schools, community functions, etc.

2 SUMMARY OF QUALIFICATIONS/SKILLS
- Knowledge of principles of Texas government, government agency policies, and procedures for public services.
- Research and development of reports on important topics for national, regional, and community development.
- Microsoft Windows, Excel, Word, PowerPoint, and Access; Statistical program experience; grant experience.
- Experience leading classes and workshops.
- Volunteering guru with a passion to use my talents to make a difference.
- Highly organized, detail oriented, and motivated team player.

Jennifer Verde
2487 Crowley Circle ♦ Austin, Texas 78741 ♦ 512-123-4567 ♦ email@email.com

① PROGRAM MANAGER QUALIFICATIONS

②
- Seven years workforce development experience with in-depth knowledge of training for demand occupations
- Fluent in English and Spanish. Made presentations in Spanish and translated documents from English to Spanish
- Managed training service projects with internal and external customers
- Extensive public speaking experience. Made presentations at colleges, community organizations, and for Toastmasters
- Prepared marketing brochures and workshop materials
- Researched and prepared reports to indentify gaps in service delivery
- Grant writing and statistical program experience

③ EDUCATION

Master of Public Administration   December 2007
Texas State University, San Marcos, Texas
Cumulative GPA: 3.62   Dean's List -- Fall 2004, Spring 2005

Bachelor of Arts in Liberal Arts, emphasis on Public Administration   August 1997
Texas State University, San Marcos, Texas
Cumulative GPA: 3.27

④ PROFESSIONAL EXPERIENCE

Department of Children's Services, Austin, TX   Feb. 2008 – Present
Conservatorship Specialist II
- Provide ongoing services for children in substitute care by using resources to reunite the family or make other permanent plans for children's care
- Initiate appropriate legal action and testify in court to achieve protection or permanent placement plans for children
- Document case records by completing forms, narratives, and reports to form a written record for each client

Texas State University, San Marcos, Texas   Aug. 2006 – Dec. 2007
Research Assistant
Latinos and Media Project, School of Journalism and Mass Communication
- Gathered and analyzed Spanish-language print media to explore and describe levels of localism and quality of content delivered to Latino population in Central Texas
- Conducted statistical analysis of newspaper contents to develop descriptive reports
- Maintained correspondence with numerous media professionals to gather information for the Latinos and Media Project website
- Assisted in writing the final report that explored the differences between corporate and non-corporate newspapers

Texas State University, San Marcos, Texas   Sept. 2004 – June 2006
Instructional Assistant
- Assisted professor with course development and classroom preparation
- Developed lectures and test reviews for undergraduate government classes
- Kept records of grades and assignments for more than 300 undergraduate students
- Scheduled appointments and meetings with students

⑤ Bexar County Workforce Center, San Antonio, TX   Sept. 1997 – Aug. 2004
Career Specialist
- Served as a case manager for more than 100 clients enrolled in Workforce Investment Act training programs for high-demand occupations
- Assisted Business Service Specialists in contacting employers to develop on-the-job training positions for case-managed clients
- Made informational presentations at community colleges, community functions, and at the workforce center
- Contacted area universities, community colleges, and private schools to determine suitable training for WIA clients

⑥ PROFESSIONAL AND COMMUNITY ORGANIZATIONS

Hispanic Women's Network of Texas
Vice Chair for Membership
Austin Chapter

Capital City Toastmasters
Vice President of Education

The Texas Children and Family Center Inc.
Volunteered to write grants

American Society of Public Administration
Travis County Chapter Member

Technical Writer to Financial Advisor

Michael Winchester was recently downsized from a software integration company where he had worked for eight years. The irony is that the company believed in his abilities so much, they financed half of his MBA studies at the local university.

Michael has long had an interest in investing and personal finance. He contributed the maximum to his company's 401(k), owned individual stocks, and took a few adult education courses in hedge funds and real estate investing. As the markets began recovering, he noticed that nearly every major investment house was hiring new financial advisors. Michael is drawn to this work because of his strong intellect and a core skill of analyzing vast amounts of information. He feels he is up to the challenge of learning a completely new profession.

Challenges to Making the Switch

Michael's resume is essentially a technical writer's story of success—working up from entry positions to a director managing a large technical writing staff. His knowledge base is primarily in technology, software integration, and product launches. While he has interfaced with customers in many companies, he has no direct sales experience. The challenge is to make his personal interest in finance and his new MBA the centerpieces of his new resume. To overcome his lack of sales experience, he stresses his customer analysis and communication skills. He lacks the designations of FINA Series 7 and 63, which are required for those who sell investment securities. In his cover letter, he will emphasize that he is willing to begin study for these tests immediately.

Transferable Skills

Oral and written communication	Customer service
Market/customer analysis	Influence with staff and clients
Feature/benefit analysis	Relationship building

Job Description

Financial Advisor

- Target prospective clients, identify their needs by analyzing their present income and asset situation, and recommend appropriate investment solutions

- Strong sales and communications skills and a genuine desire to help others

- BA/BS in business or finance; advanced degree/designation a plus (such as an MBA, CFP, CPA, QPA, and so on)

- FINRA Series 7, 63, and 65 or 66; or a willingness to complete these exams within the first year

- Excellent knowledge and communication of financial planning concepts and terminology

- Excellent knowledge and communication of products such as mutual funds, stocks, bonds, insurance, and annuities

- Firsthand knowledge of qualified plans, including plan design, plan administration, IRS regulations, retirement income planning, and fiduciary requirements

---

Resume Makeover

❶ The headline "Communications/Finance Professional" highlights his experience and recent education.

❷ In his Personal Statement section, Michael chooses to highlight his personal strengths rather than business achievements—most of which are not relevant to his new chosen profession. He begins with relationship and influence because the new job calls for substantial sales activities.

❸ The Core Competencies section allows him to show his breadth as a personal investor and his love for financial analysis.

❹ A one-line description of each company is included, helping the hiring manager understand the nature of his work.

❺ The work history detail is simplified; detailed dates (month and year) are removed. Promotions are condensed. He leads with the highest position achieved in each job.

❻ Each activity statement now tells a story of achievement.

❼ The Technical Skills section is left in. This special knowledge might prove useful because his co-workers will likely lack this depth of knowledge.

❽ The Education section includes his Master's project, which is in personal financial planning. Including his MBA three times in the resume is planned so that the reader comes away focused on this achievement.

MICHAEL WINCHESTER

1234 Townes Lane
Boston, MA 02100
h. 617 123 4567
c. 617 123 5555
email@email.com

Experience

❺

XYZ Software, Boston. December 2001 - 2009.
Director of User Interface Development. July 2007 - 2009.
Managed technical writing staff and GUI development staff ... Integrated team of 3 technical writers from Data Junction acquisition ... Selected and put in place new authoring tool set for technical writing team ... Managed customer incident escalations to Engineering ... Introduced paper prototyping process to GUI development ... Managed projects for SDK, Linux Requester, and Hot Fix deliverables, project team sizes up to 20 individual contributors ... Managed capital budget for Engineering department ... Developed software quality metrics used to evaluate quality of product releases.

Director of Technical Publications. July 2004 - July 2007.
Managed staff of 14 technical writers in Boston and Toronto ... Responsible for ~$1 million annual budget ... Developed and rolled out customer intimacy program for entire Engineering department ... Advised Globalization team on documentation translation issues ... Team won 3 Awards for Excellence from Society for Technical Communication in 1999 ... Improved customer satisfaction with product documentation 3 out of 3 years as reported by annual independent survey (Prognostics) ... Chairman of corporate charitable giving committee.

Manager of Documentation. December 2001 - July 2004.
Grew team from staff of 3 to staff of 14 ... Delivered world-class product documentation and online help for 4 major product releases and a host of service packs ... Modernized information resources from paper-only to a variety of convenient online delivery formats ... Developed and executed product vision for integrated online information resources ... Integrated geographically remote staff before, during, and after acquisition of Everyware Development in Toronto with zero employee turnover ... Established process for mining technical support database to quantify product "hot spots" ... Rolled out self-service center on the public website offering online books and information about bug fixes and available software patches.

XYZ Environment Corporation, Boston. June 1997 - December 2001. (Acquired by Norland, October 2001)
Principal Writer. Sydney, Australia. April 2001 - December 2001.
Managed adaptation of software product from 3rd party and product release ... Adapted manuals from 3rd party into HTML ... Wrote a 200-page manual from scratch ... Guided design of graphical interface for software product.

Manager of Documentation. February 2000 - March 2001.
Scheduled and managed 6 technical writers ... Responsible for $500K budget ... Successfully delivered complete context-sensitive Windows help, online manuals, and paper manuals (1400pp) for major product release on extremely tight schedule ... Designed and wrote automated online-help build system ... Managed on-time development and release of AppDesigner product ... Designed system of physical packaging, media labels, and documentation for software family with 48 different packages ... Coined "Entera" product name.

Lead Technical Writer. September 1998 - January 2000.
Supervised all aspects of documentation: system design through offset and on-demand production ... Scheduled staff of 3-4 writers ... Wrote high-level marketing material for many different products ... Managed packaging and documentation aspects of outsourced software manufacturing ... Helped make

---

Winchester   - 2 -

decisions regarding product features and release dates ... Managed numerous vendor relationships ... Tagged and compiled UNIX hypertext online manuals.

Technical Writer. June 1997 - August 1998.
First writer hired for start-up company ... Taught technical training courses ... Designed page layouts and content structure for documentation ... Wrote task-based users' guides and detailed functional reference information.

Williams College, Williamstown, MA.
Computer Center Consultant, Editor-in-Chief. September 1993 - May 1997.

Controllership Services, Littleton, CO.
Database Programmer. Part-time, 1992 - 1996.

Education

Boston University School of Management
Master of Business Administration. Class rank #1 as of January, 2009.

Williams College, Williamstown, MA
B.A. in English and History ... Concentration in Physics ... Computer Science courses in C and C++ ... Dean's List ... JV Soccer ... Outing Club ... Residential house vice-president... National Merit Scholar.

Skills

Financial, Technology, and Strategic Analysis ... Project Management ... Personnel Management ... Budget Management ... Audience Analysis ... Listening ... Perceiving ... Brainstorming ... Inquiring... Decision-making ... Writing ... Speaking.

Technical

SQL ... C++ (reading) ... Information Mapping™ ... UNIX shell ... Macintosh ... Windows Help ... Microsoft Project ... Excel ... Word ... PowerPoint ... Adobe FrameMaker ... Illustrator ... Photoshop ... Internet ... HTML ... version control systems ... open systems ... n-tiered client/ server ... web applications ... database concepts.

Personal

Heritage High School, Littleton, CO ... High Honors ... Graduated 7th in class of 460... Published 3 articles in *Astronomy* magazine ... Wrote 360-page techno-thriller novel ... Enjoy hiking, amateur soccer, basketball, travel, fiction.

MICHAEL WINCHESTER
1234 Townes Lane
Boston, MA 02100
H 617 123 4567 • C 617 123 5555 • email@email.com
Profile: www.linkedin.com/name

COMMUNICATIONS/FINANCE PROFESSIONAL

(1) Talented communications professional offering 12+ years of interpersonal and analytical success in software integration, operations, and general management. Eager to utilize my MBA with finance concentration in the role of Financial Advisor. Boston University School of Management MBA with finance honors – #2 in class. Team-oriented, entrepreneurial, self-motivated.

PERSONAL STATEMENT

(2) Among my strongest professional attributes are personal talents and characteristics that cannot be taught or learned. These characteristics differentiate me from other candidates with similar skill sets:

Strong relationship and influence skills as demonstrated by my superior customer satisfaction ratings and the longevity of my writing staff, in a high-turnover environment.
Ability to envision the links between financial models and the business environments they represent exceedingly quickly, developing a relatively deep understanding of financial offerings in a very short period.
Ability to assimilate large amounts of data, filter what is relevant and important, and make successful decisions based on the available data.
Superior communication skills, both oral and written, and an intense desire to help others through knowledge and analysis.
Strong intellect and intense personal motivation, as demonstrated by my MBA Executive Studies
Ability to comprehend new domains of knowledge extremely rapidly.
Natural leadership abilities and compassion, as shown by multiple promotions inside my former companies.

CORE COMPETENCIES
(3)
- Stock Brokerage Customer
- 401k Plan Experience
- Online Brokerage Customer
- Mutual Funds Investor
- Bond Fund Knowledgeable
- Hedge Fund Basics
- Financial Analysis
- Market/Customer Analysis
- Customer Intimacy
- Requirements Analysis
- Statistical Analysis
- Feature/Benefit Analysis
- Customer Communication
- Organizational Change
- Budget Management
- Performance Metrics
- Technology
- Public Speaking

EXPERIENCE

(4) **XYZ SOFTWARE**, Boston, MA
Data storage and data transformation software for the middle market.
Director of Technical Publications and User Interface Development (promoted from Manager) **(5)** 2001 - 2009

(6)
- Managed staff of up to 14 professional writers in Boston and Toronto and up to 4 software developers. Directly responsible for ~$1 million annual budget.
- Improved customer satisfaction with product documentation 3 out of 3 years, as reported by independent "Prognostics" survey.
- Reduced technical support case volume 14% by developing and executing a product vision for integrated online information resources, including self-service center on the public website offering online books and information about bug fixes and available software patches.
- Reduced lag time of International releases 66% (from 6 months to 2 months).
- Successfully integrated 6 writers through 2 acquisitions with no attrition.
- Project-managed 5 software application releases with project team sizes up to 20 individual contributors, all delivered on time and at or better than expected quality.

XYZ SOFTWARE, cont'd…
- Team won 3 Awards for Excellence from Society for Technical Communication in 2004.
- Improved predictability of release cycle and provided basis for continuous process improvement by developing software quality metrics used to evaluate quality of product releases.
- Chairman of corporate charitable giving committee including public relations and public speaking.

NORLAND (acquired Open Environment Corporation), Boston, MA, and Sydney   1997 - 2001
Multi-tier client-server middleware for large corporations.
Various Positions of Increasing Responsibility – Technical Writing, Communications, Management
- Managed up to 6 professional writers.
- Designed and wrote automated online-help build system, increasing writer productivity and eliminating human build errors.
- Developed complete Windows help, online and paper manuals (1,400 pages) for major product release.
- Designed system of physical packaging, media, and docs for software family with 48 variations.
- Wrote high-level marketing material for many different products.

TECHNICAL SKILLS **(7)**
- SQL
- C++ (reading)
- Information Mapping™
- UNIX Shell
- Macintosh
- Windows Help
- Database Concepts
- Microsoft Project
- Excel
- Word
- PowerPoint
- Adobe Framemaker
- Illustrator
- Photoshop
- HTML
- Version Control Systems
- Open Systems
- N-tiered Client/Server
- Web Applications

EDUCATION **(8)**
Master of Business Administration (MBA), Boston University School of Management, Boston, MA
Area of Concentration: Finance
Master's Project: Personal Financial Planning; Bond Fund Investing; Financial Modeling
Graduated with Honors, 2nd in class • Member of Beta Gamma Sigma • GPA 3.9/4.0

BA - English and History, Williams College, Williamstown, Massachusetts
Advanced Math and Physics courses • National Merit Scholar • GPA 3.8 in major

Trade Show Specialist to Grant Writer

Andrea Galloway got swept out of a great job when consumer spending took its first dive. Her company makes digital storage devices such as flash drives, memory cards for cameras, and music and video players. As a trade show specialist, she was responsible for coordinating hundreds of consumer and commercial shows each year. In the cutbacks, trade shows were the first to go.

Andrea has a long history of office management. While she enjoys the challenge, she is tired of corporate politics and the frantic pace. She considers going back to her original career, social work. The problem is that there are many things about the nonprofit world that also concern her—lower pay, insufficient budgets, work environments in poorer neighborhoods, and so on.

During her transition, she takes on a few writing projects and realizes that this is her true calling. She even teaches a course at the community college on grant writing and begins to network with nonprofit employees. She feels that if she can focus on writing and fund development, she will be comfortable going back to her former career in the nonprofit world.

Challenges to Making the Switch

Andrea's last formal experience with the nonprofit world was nearly 12 years ago as director of corporate development for a small public affairs forum. In order to show significant experience, she needs to include her executive director positions—both of which only lasted two years and were 21 to 25 years ago. Luckily, she does have a degree in social work and significant experience writing grants, supporting top executives, and managing nonprofits.

The main problem is Andrea's own ambiguity about re-entering the nonprofit world. She has an entire list of things she will not do: fund-raising, event planning, executive director role, and working in a poor or unsafe neighborhood. The only way to discover whether she can get a job that is pure grant writing is to revamp her resume and put it into the marketplace. Hopefully, she will find just the right spot in government or in a large nonprofit where she can focus on her first love: writing.

Transferable Skills

Grant writing

Knowledge of human services programs

Marketing savvy

Influence with community leaders

Needs assessments

Research skills

Training design and delivery

> ## Job Description
> # Grant Writer
>
> - Full-time grant writer to create funding proposals for new and existing programs
>
> - Experience in proposal/grant writing; budget preparation and needs assessment
>
> - One or more years experience and/or training; or equivalent combination of education and experience
>
> - Careful reading of RFPs issued by governmental funding agencies, working with program staff to design new services, and preparing well-written proposals that are consistent with RFP requirements
>
> - Familiarity with a variety of human services (for example, developmental disabilities, mental illness, drug and alcohol rehabilitation, homelessness, and employment), a demonstrated ability to facilitate decision-making around questions of program design, and ability to work independently
>
> - A writing sample (preferably a grant application) submitted along with a resume
>
> - Proficient computer, software, and organizational skills
>
> - Valid driver's license and insurability under the organization's motor vehicle policy
>
> - Bachelor's degree from a four-year college or university

Resume Makeover

Andrea's current resume is very content-dense with small type. The style needs to be updated and made more readable. The word "resume" is removed and the information is culled—highlighting only the most relevant experience.

1 The resume begins with a strong headline: "Director of Development/Grant Writer." These are the two positions Andrea would accept with a nonprofit.

2 The five achievement statements communicate her experience in the world of nonprofit funding.

3 The Core Competencies section is a mirror image of many of the grant-writing job descriptions she has collected from Internet job sites.

4 Her most important jobs are included on page one under "Relevant Professional Experience." Because they are so far in the past, she includes the years held rather than the calendar years.

5 "Other Experience" allows her to include three of her most important assignments as an office administrator. She includes her five years experience as trade show coordinator, which shows her stability in her last position. The other two jobs are selected in order to show that she has worked directly with high-level executives.

6 Her work history includes only title, company, and years. Included are two periods called "Contractor/Special Projects" to close any gaps in her work history. Her first two positions, 29 and 27 years ago, are left off the resume.

7 A Computer Proficiencies section is added. Andrea is a power user of social media, Macintosh-, and IBM-specific software. These experiences may give her an edge over other candidates.

8 In the Education section, she includes coursework related to business and accounting to show her interest in the finance side of nonprofits.

RESUME

NAME: Andrea Galloway
ADDRESS: 123 Cypress Lane
Redwood City, CA 94059

PHONE: 850-123-4567
EMAIL: email@email.com

EXPERIENCE

2004 – 2009
Flash Electronics
MARKETING/TRADE SHOW COORDINATOR: Coordinating trade shows, shipping out booth materials, communicating with show management the particulars of trade show participation, communicating with all departments, vendors, and distributors regarding the logistics of trade show participation. Follow up with the sales team post show. Entering all leads generated from trade show, creating and entering data into Excel spreadsheets for tracking purposes. Completing all required paperwork and administrative functions as it relates to trade show coordination, and providing administrative support to the marketing team.

1991 – 2004
OFFICE MANAGEMENT: Working as a contractor through employment agencies, set up and manage special projects and offices/departments for executives in a broad range of industries including:

Fast Help Corporation (Through Ann Wells Personnel Services, 1/01 – 9/01): Executive Assistant to President and CEO of $500M worldwide helpdesk and CRM company. Manage all office functions and provide support to both CEO and VP of Human Resources. Included extensive travel, calendar, special projects, follow up with direct reports. Assisted with executive searches, also provided intense support to joint working teams during acquisition of Remedy Corporation by Peregrine.

National Microproducts (Through Ann Wells Personnel Services, 11/99 – 1/01): Executive Assistant to Senior Vice President of Commercial Sales of $1B worldwide distribution company. Comprehensive support position with heavy work in design, research, development, and maintenance of financial and performance reports using Excel as well as company databases. Calendar, Travel, Supplies, Contracts oversight and planning. Event management including quarterly and regional meetings for staff and vendors. Training and coordination of regional directors, administrative assistants and salespeople and executives joining the team. Coordination with Marcom, Sales, vendor and customer executive teams to assure maximum benefit to vendors and customers of available training and development opportunities.

Exodus Communications (Through Ann Wells Personnel Services, 7/99 – 10/99): Executive Assistant to Executive Vice President of Customer Service of worldwide ISP. Provided travel and calendar management. Monitored estimates, purchase orders and invoice process to assure prompt reimbursement. Worked with regional directors to coordinate regional visits, meetings, weekly updates, and field support. Provided liaison and training to regional administrative assistants in division.

Tandem Computers (Through Interim Personnel, 7/96 – 10/97): Administrative Assistant to Director of Worldwide Professional Services. Major focus on design and production of presentations utilizing PowerPoint, Excel, Word. Included gathering, collating, and analyzing needed information on project progress. Also provided support to 15 other people on the team worldwide including travel, phone, MIS, office equipment/supplies/access.

SEGA (Through Wollberg Michelson): Supported Director of Creative Services: Travel, calendar management, correspondence, developing and managing a purchase order issuance and tracking process/database, vendor relations, orientation, inventory.

Bank of America (Through Wollberg Michelson, 1/91 – 10/93): Due Diligence financial analysis of over 3,000 contracts during merger. Supported Vice President of Short Term Asset Sales, then Sr. Vice President of Credit. Included calendar, travel, meeting management, correspondence.

1990 – 2004
CONSULTANT: Target and carry out short- and long-term projects both as employee and independent subcontractor. Primary projects have centered around needs assessments, research, analysis, project design/development, proposals and management assistance to businesses, government, and nonprofit corporations. Includes:

MARKETING/SALES (1999): Community and market research, marketing plan, and development of materials for a community-based music conservatory. Aided process and prepared tax exemption applications for nonprofit status. Facilitated board development and planning.

DIRECTOR OF CORPORATE DEVELOPMENT (1997 – 98): The Trenton Club, Campbell, CA. Design and implement development program to grow and strengthen corporate relationships and support for leading nonpartisan public affairs forum focusing on Silicon Valley issues. Activated Corporate Development Committee. Restructured member fees and benefits. Developed new marketing materials and strategy. Recruited and placed record number of corporate sponsors in high-visibility events. Track and analyze corporate membership usage. Researched potential donor, foundation, and corporation support. Initiated newsletter corporate column. During tenure, tripled corporate membership revenue and increased event sponsorships by 50%.

SPECIAL CONTRIBUTOR/MEMBER REPRESENTATIVE, PRODIGY INTERNET SERVICES (1991 – 1999): As Member Expert, founded the Domestic Violence bulletin board with record response nationwide including coverage by both AP and Gannett both for effectiveness and as the first formal board in cyberspace to work with domestic violence.

OWNER: Transition Adults International, Los Gatos, CA. Online workshops, discussions, humor, referrals, consultation, and support groups for adults going through transitions in their lives.

1988 – 1990
EXECUTIVE DIRECTOR: Career Strategies, San Francisco, CA. CEO of corporation providing employment preparation and placement of youth with physical disabilities. Responsible for all phases of management including Personnel, Risk Management, Finance, EEO/AA, CAL-OSHA, Contracts, Planning and Fund Development. During tenure: Designed and directed ongoing workshops as well as special joint series with Mayor's office on Earthquake Preparedness/Access to Safety. Increased corporate revenues by 50% through successful marketing, proposal writing, and fundraising. Hired, trained and supervised staff of 15 including staff, volunteers, and contractors. Established new pilot employment program as a separate profit making enterprise.

1985 – 1987
EXECUTIVE DIRECTOR: Eastside Counseling Center, San Jose, CA. As CEO of multicultural counseling/training corporation, managed staff of 70 employees/subcontractors providing 24-hour crisis counseling, training, therapy to over 4,000 families/year. During tenure: Development and marketing increased income by 62%. Designed state-of-the-art computerized accounting and management information system. Working with staff/management teams, revised and upgraded job descriptions, personnel policies, evaluation procedures, and compensation structure. Implemented compliance and monitoring of all risk management as well as saving over $30,000 by independent research and negotiation of insurance coverage plans and rates. Planned, secured funding, and supervised ongoing series of workshops on family health issues, staff professional development, and cultural awareness and drug abuse prevention.

1982 – 1984
SENIOR PROGRAM PLANNER: Iowa Governor's Office, Des Moines, Iowa. Development and implementation of $3.5 million federal block grant program. Contract negotiation, technical assistance, development of regulations, monitoring of 19 agencies with total funding of $39 million/year. Authored annual report earning award by National Governor's Association.

1980 – 1982
PLANNER/GRANT WRITER: Woodbury Community Action Agency, Sioux City, Iowa. During tenure, grant writing brought in over $5 million in annual government, foundation, and contract funding.

COMPUTER PROFICIENCIES

Advanced: Microsoft Office: Word, PowerPoint, Excel, Outlook
WordPerfect, Lotus 1-2-3, Lotus Notes
MAC , PC, Networked systems, Windows, Internet Research and Utilization

Typing: 80 wpm

EDUCATION

Augustana College: Bachelor of Arts, Social Work. Extensive training in Accounting, Business Administration, Marketing/PR, Human Resources, Business Law, Contracts

ANDREA GALLOWAY

123 Cypress Lane, Redwood City, CA 94059 • email@email.com • 850-123-4567 cell

DIRECTOR OF DEVELOPMENT/GRANT WRITER

Strategic Planning/Collaboration/Program Design

- Consistent achievement in creating funding proposals for new and existing programs
- Firsthand experience with RFPs issued by governmental funding agencies
- Significant management experience in human services including domestic violence, multicultural counseling, mental health, life transitions, drug and alcohol rehabilitation, and public affairs
- Effectively collaborate with corporate givers; ability to approach and influence community leaders
- Marketing savvy – capable of understanding ideas that will "sell" in the funding marketplace

Core Competencies

- Grant/proposal writing
- Facilitate discussion for program strategies
- Direct and indirect sales; influence key thought leaders
- Develop own leads for funding sources
- Community/need assessments
- Training design & delivery
- Powerful communicator
- Excellent computer skills

RELEVANT PROFESSIONAL EXPERIENCE

DIRECTOR OF CORPORATE DEVELOPMENT
The Trenton Club, Campbell, CA, 1 year
Design and implement development program to grow and strengthen corporate relationships and support for leading nonpartisan public affairs forum focusing on Silicon Valley issues
- Activated Corporate Development Committee
- Restructured member fees and benefits
- Developed new marketing materials and strategy
- Recruited and placed record number of corporate sponsors in high-visibility events
- Tracked and analyzed corporate membership usage
- Researched potential donor, foundation, and corporation support
- Initiated newsletter corporate column
- During tenure, tripled corporate membership revenue and increased event sponsorships by 50%

EXECUTIVE DIRECTOR
Career Strategies, San Francisco, 2 years
CEO of corporation providing employment preparation and placement of youth with physical disabilities
- Responsible for all phases of management including Personnel, Risk Management, Finance, EEO/AA, CAL-OSHA, Contracts, Planning and Fund Development
- Designed and directed ongoing workshops as well as special joint series with Mayor's office on Earthquake Preparedness/Access to Safety
- Increased corporate revenues by 50% through successful marketing, proposal writing, and fundraising
- Hired, trained, and supervised staff of 15 including full-time employees, volunteers, and contractors
- Established new pilot-supported employment program as a separate profit making enterprise
- Developed consortiums of agencies, networks, and youth

EXECUTIVE DIRECTOR
Eastside Counseling Center, San Jose, 2 years
CEO of multicultural counseling/training corporation providing 24 hour crisis counseling, training, and therapy to over 4,000 families/year
- Managed staff of 70 employees/subcontractors
- During tenure development and marketing increased income by 62%
- Designed state-of-the-art computerized accounting and management information system
- Working with staff/management teams, revised and upgraded job descriptions, personnel policies, evaluation procedures, and compensation structure
- Implemented compliance and monitoring of all risk management as well as saving over $30,000 by independent research and negotiation of insurance coverage plans and rates
- Planned, secured funding, and supervised ongoing series of workshops on family health issues, staff professional development, and cultural awareness and drug abuse prevention

---

OTHER EXPERIENCE

MARKETING/TRADE SHOW COORDINATOR
Flash Electronics, 5 years
Support to sales staff of international manufacturer of consumer electronic storage devices
- Communicating with show management the particulars of trade show participation, communicating with all departments, vendors, and distributors regarding the logistics of trade show participation
- Follow up with the sales team post show: entering all leads generated from trade show, creating and entering data into Excel spreadsheets for tracking purposes
- Managing budget and completing all required paperwork and administrative functions related to trade shows

EXECUTIVE ASSISTANT
National Microproducts, 14 months
Executive Assistant to Senior Vice President of Commercial Sales of $1B worldwide distribution company
- Comprehensive support position with heavy work in design, research, development and maintenance of financial and performance reports using Excel as well as company databases
- Calendar, travel, supplies, contracts oversight and planning
- Event management including quarterly and regional meeting for staff and vendors
- Training and coordination of regional directors, administrative assistants, sales people, and executives joining the team
- Coordination of sales, vendor, and customer executive teams to assure maximum benefit to vendors and customers of available training and development opportunities

DUE DILIGENCE, FINANCIAL ANALYSIS
Bank of America, 1-1/2 years
- Due diligence and financial analysis of over 3,000 contracts during merger
- Supported Vice President of Short-Term Asset Sales, then Sr. Vice President of Credit
- Included calendar, meeting management, correspondence

WORK HISTORY

Marketing/Trade Show Coordinator	Flash Electronics, Redwood, CA	2004–2009
Contractor/Special Projects	Various Employment Agencies	2000–2004
Marketing/Sales	Community Music Conservatory	1999
Director of Corporate Development	Trenton Club, Campbell, CA	1997–1998
Contractor/Special Projects	Various Employment Agencies	1991–1996
Executive Director	Career Strategies, San Francisco, CA	1988–1990
Executive Director	Eastside Counseling Center San Francisco, CA	1985–1987

COMPUTER PROFICIENCIES

- Microsoft Office: Word, PowerPoint, Excel, Outlook
- WordPerfect, Lotus 1-2-3, Lotus Notes
- MAC, PC, Networked systems, Windows
- Internet research and utilization
- Social Media: Twitter, Facebook, LinkedIn, etc.

EDUCATION

Bachelor of Arts, Social Work -- Augustana College, Sioux Falls, SD

Accounting	Business Administration	Marketing/PR
Human Resources	Business Law	Contracts

Trainer to Systems Consultant

Catherine Lawrence graduated with a degree in history and promptly found a job in a major corporation teaching classes to employees. She enjoyed the work and was popular with her students. Unfortunately, when the company decided to cut costs, one of the first things to go were internal classes in "frivolous" subjects such as time management and team-building, and Catherine's job was eliminated.

She quickly discovered that every other corporation in town had made the same cutbacks, and there were no jobs in her field. In fact, the market was flooded with other people who had the same background and more experience.

Catherine loves to travel and enjoys meeting new people. Furthermore, she has always been good at managing interpersonal relationships and navigating politics in the workplace—so she is ideally suited for a consulting role where she would have the opportunity to use and develop those skills.

Challenges to Making the Switch

Catherine's experience is limited to one role at one company. Although she taught classes in a variety of topics and even designed some of the classes herself based on the needs identified by management, her resume does not showcase her best asset, which is her ability to manage information and communicate effectively.

She has no technical or computer background required for jobs today—other than minimal expertise in word processing, spreadsheets, and slide decks. Because the majority of consulting jobs are in IT consulting, she appears to be completely unqualified for the work.

On the other hand, she has talked with consultants in a variety of technical specialties and has learned that there are many roles on a typical IT consulting project that do not require in-depth systems knowledge. A willingness and ability to learn about the client company's business processes, listen to the requirements and concerns of the employees, and effectively communicate information is much more important. The same skills and personality traits that made her a popular trainer will make her a productive and successful consultant.

Transferable Skills

Public speaking and presentation skills

Quickly master new information

Ask questions and listen effectively

Communicate complex information clearly

Produce accurate documentation

Teach adults in a corporate environment

Word, Excel, PowerPoint, and Visio skills

Job Description

Systems Consultant

- Conduct interviews with users to identify business requirements

- Document requirements and obtain approval

- Collaborate with team members and users to develop new business processes and generate user documentation

- Develop test scenarios and sample data based on the new business processes

- Assist with system testing and document test results, including error reporting and development of workarounds for unresolved issues

- Assist users with preparing for the transition and act as help desk support/backup during the period immediately following implementation

- Participate in team meetings

- Issue weekly status reports and update project plans in a timely manner

- Outstanding communication and interpersonal skills

- Full-time travel required

Resume Makeover

Catherine's resume has focused too much on what she did and too little on the skills required to be successful in the desired role. By changing the format of her resume to highlight her skills, she is able to show that she is fully qualified for this job.

1 She adds an e-mail address on her resume, which is required for any job applicant today.

2 She eliminates the list of class titles and topics she taught, which are not relevant to the job she wants.

3 While her title in her previous job was not "consultant," her job actually included many tasks that can be described as "consulting." She adds "Internal Consultant" to her last job title.

4 Upon reflection, she realizes that her daily tasks in her job included many activities beyond simply teaching classes. By listing these activities, her resume now closely parallels the job description for a functional IT consultant.

5 Her degree is in a completely unrelated field, so she eliminates all unnecessary detail—leaving only the details that will appeal to an employer.

6 "References Available upon Request" is deleted because it's assumed the applicant can provide references.

Catherine Lawrence
10601 Cascade Drive
Houston, Texas 77043
(713) 123-4567

Experience:

7/2002 to 5/2009   ExxonMobil Corporation   Houston, Texas
Trainer

On-staff instructor for employee development classes including:

❷

Time Management
Team-Building
Organizing Presentations
Conducting Performance Reviews
Email Etiquette
Employee Travel and Expense Policy Guidelines
New Hire Orientation

Education:

1998 to 2002   University of Texas at Austin   Austin, Texas
❺   Bachelor of Arts, 2002

Major: History
Minor: Elementary Education
GPA: 3.92/4.0

Groups and Affiliations:

American Society for Training and Development
Society of Human Resource Professionals
Texas Exes – Houston Chapter

❻   References Available Upon Request

Catherine Lawrence
Consultant
10601 Cascade Drive
Houston, Texas 77043
(713) 123-4567
email@email.com

❶

Professional Experience

❸ 2002 to 2009   ExxonMobil Corporation   Houston, Texas
Internal Consultant/Trainer

Responsible for development and delivery of internal training programs. Activities included:

❹
- Conduct interviews with employees and management to identify opportunities for improvement
- Research topics and identify resources for developing course material
- Make recommendations for additional classes based on analysis of requirements, cost, available resources, and potential return-on-investment for the organization
- Produce training documentation and prepare presentations
- Present training material in formal classroom and informal conference formats
- Conduct follow-up evaluations to determine effectiveness of training and adjust course material as appropriate
- Prepare weekly reports on training activities for management review
- Collaborate with other training development experts to ensure that training content and materials meet the requirements of the organization

Consistently received top ratings from training attendees and management for exemplary performance of all tasks.

❺ **Education**   University of Texas at Austin   Austin, Texas
B.A., 2002

Additional Skills

Proficient in Microsoft Word, Excel, PowerPoint, and Visio.
Excellent communication and presentation skills.

Part 4

Career Transitions: Changes in Function and Industry

Analyst to Community Relations; Aviation to Light Rail

Tamara McGraw has been part of the Washington, D.C., consulting crowd for the last five years. When she loses her job due to contract losses, she decides to ply her skills in another market. She has a long history with aviation and is even a trained pilot and flight instructor. The entire aviation industry is in turmoil, however, and the jobs are few and far between. She is reluctant to dive back into the Washington scene because the long hours and extreme pressures have taken a toll on her health. She soon becomes aware that light rail is an industry that is still hiring in many metropolitan cities across the United States. The new administration policies may also provide financial incentives for this industry because it represents a shift in energy consumption.

Tamara has had consulting experience that is mostly support to high-level government contractors. She understands the process of creating policy, proposing legislation, and reacting to Washington mandates. She is really confused about which direction to go until she analyzes what she actually did on the job—researching, writing, facilitating meetings, developing policy statements, and preparing various documents for the public and for management. It occurs to her that a public relations job for a transportation company might be ideal for her skills and background.

Challenges to Making the Switch

Working for a Washington contractor is unlike nearly any other professional experience. Tamara finds it hard to drop the "inside-the-Beltway" terminology and really *explain* what her responsibilities are. In order to get more familiar with public relations and the demands of that profession, she will need to attend some local Public Relations Society of America (PRSA) meetings and conduct information interviews.

Another issue is tenure: her first three jobs in Washington lasted a year or less. She will need to have good explanations why she jumped from one job to the next so quickly.

Her primary barrier to her new career will be translating her "support" activities to the world of public relations, where many professionals must make their own policy decisions with little management oversight. She will also need to convince prospective employers that her aviation industry experience has prepared her to quickly understand railroad issues and terminology. This is a huge leap for her professionally, but at the core, she has all the skills she needs. Tamara will have to rely on her influencing skills to present her case.

Transferable Skills

Writing

Project management/organization

Meeting facilitation

Presentation skills

Researching leading-edge technology

Strategic planning

Knowledge of homeland security issues

Job Description

Community Relations—Light Rail

- Minimum of a Bachelor's degree in English or mass communications

- At least seven years of public affairs experience with two years demonstrated experience working for federal, state, or local government clients or a corporate consulting firm

- Strong writing, media relations, and event facilitation experience

- Must possess a good understanding of community outreach and government relations

- Excellent written and oral communication skills and the ability to communicate and interpret technical information to a variety of stakeholders using various communication vehicles

- Detailed-oriented, organized, demonstrated initiative; ability to multitask

- Able to create informational materials such as brochures, newsletters, fact sheets, fliers, and web content

- Implementation of public affairs, community outreach, government relations, and media relations strategic plans

- Building strong relationships with local elected officials and key community leaders, implementing media campaigns

- Coordinating and helping to facilitate stakeholder meetings and workshops; client base includes federal, state, and local government sectors as well as private industry

Resume Makeover

Tamara creates a resume that calls out her primary professional skills.

1 She adds the headline "Public Affairs/Community Relations" under her name.

2 The Key Achievements format allows her to call out what she considers her primary professional skills. For each one, she describes a recent project she led or completed on her own.

3 The Core Competencies section mirrors some of the tasks in the job description. She includes homeland security and disaster recovery—both important issues in any transportation company.

4 She removes her first two jobs as ramp agent and dispatcher. They have no bearing on her job search in public affairs.

5 She includes her Bachelor's degree but does not state her major (Spanish) and minor (psychology) because neither contributes to this job search.

6 Her commercial pilot and flight instructor designations are given less prominence than her degree.

Tamara McGraw
202-123-1234 (cell)
email@email.com
Profile: www.linkedin.com/name

Program Management Analyst, *Lighthouse, Washington, DC*   2005-2009
Provided support to The Joint Planning and Development Office (JPDO), a federal policy office, including representatives from NASA, FAA, DOD, TSA, DOC, DOT, and The White House Office of Science and Technology Policy, and the private sectors.

- Managing day to day tasking
- Researching leading edge technology
- Acting liaison between agencies
- Assisting executive level management
- Contributing to strategic planning
- Participating on the policy team
- Ensuring communications between external and internal customers
- Assisting with the development of best business practices and methodologies
- Managing special projects
- Technical writing
- Writing reports for management
- Market research
- Analyzing airline statistics airport
- Coordinating technical papers, reports, documents, and other deliverables with clients
- Support for office management
- Problem solving and quick action tasks associated with a small business

Program Management Analyst, *Steed Consulting, Washington, DC*   2005-2006
Provided support to The Joint Planning and Development Office (JPDO), a federal policy office, including representatives from NASA, FAA, DOD, TSA, DOC, DOT, and The White House Office of Science and Technology Policy, and leaders in the private sectors.

Consultant, *Community Resources Inc, Washington, DC*   2004-2005
Provided support to the United States Department of Agriculture (USDA)

- Responsible for business continuity research, data collection, and writing recommendations
- Researching and writing disaster recovery and preparedness plans
- Developing solutions for government agency communication and coordination
- Developing recommendations for compliance with Homeland Security guidelines
- Preparing reports and presentations for USDA upper management
- Participating in emergency preparedness table top exercises

Program Management Analyst, *ABC System, Washington, DC*   2004
Provided support to Federal Aviation Administration (FAA) Surveillance Implementation Lead.

- Assisting with implementing radars into the National Airspace System (NAS)
- Performing research and data analysis
- Assisting with acquisition and cost analysis
- Acting liaison between FAA headquarters and regions

University Instructor, *Mount Hood Community College, Mt Hood, WA*   2003
Taught college-level courses including Careers in Aviation, Private Pilot, and Aviation Business

Flight Instructor   2001-2004
The Flight Shop and Austin Academy of Aviation, Oregon and Texas
Taught flight lessons

- Instructing private through commercial and instrument students
- Flying sightseeing tours
- Flying small charter
- Flying the pipeline
- Scheduling and coordinating charters and student flights
- Mentoring students
- Marketing

Ramp Agent, *Airborne Express, Austin, Texas*   2002

Dispatcher, *Air Tahoma, San Diego, CA*   2001

EDUCATION

- Commercial Pilot with a Certified Flight Instrument Instructor (CFII) Rating
- Texas State University, San Marcos, Texas
  B.A. Spanish, Minor: Psychology
- Studied at the University of Salamanca in Salamanca, Spain

1

TAMARA MCGRAW

PUBLIC AFFAIRS / COMMUNITY RELATIONS

C: 202-123-1234 ▪ H: 202-123-5678 ▪ email@email.com

2

KEY ACHIEVEMENTS

- **Public Affairs:** Five years experience working for Washington, D.C., transportation consultants and public policy agencies. Have successfully coordinated projects at the level of the Joint Planning and Development Office (JPDO), NASA, FAA, DOD, TSA, DOC, DOT, and the White House. Able to liaise with multiple interests and keep projects moving forward.
- **Leadership:** Created and led a team of government contractors from multiple companies that resulted in the first MS Project schedule and developed a draft process for risk mitigation. The client later chartered the team.
- **Organization and Influence:** During a contract transition, assumed the role of Acting Program Manager. Within three weeks, the 24-member team was reenergized, a draft organization chart had been created, and a road map for near- and long-term activities was established.
- **Writing and Communication:** For the USDA, researched, wrote, and developed local, state, and federal communication plans during a large foodborne outbreak. Coordinated media strategy.
- **Content Creation:** While working as a university instructor, created, wrote, and taught college courses by envisioning the needs, coordinating technical and academic requirements with school officials, and creating course curricula. The courses were later incorporated into the program and used by other instructors.

CORE COMPETENCIES

3

- Writing & researching
- Media relations
- Strategic project planning
- Facilitating stakeholder consensus
- Reports & presentations to governmental leaders
- Disaster recovery and preparedness
- Homeland security issues related to transportation
- Materials acquisition and cost analysis

PROFESSIONAL EXPERTISE

Program Management Analyst, *Lighthouse, Washington, DC*   2005-2009
Provided support to The Joint Planning and Development Office (JPDO), a federal policy office, including representatives from NASA, FAA, DOD, TSA, DOC, DOT, and the private sectors. Office of Science and Technology Policy, and the private sectors.

- Managing day-to-day tasking
- Researching leading-edge technology
- Acting liaison between agencies
- Assisting executive-level management
- Contributing to strategic planning
- Participating on the policy team
- Ensuring communications between external and internal customers
- Assisting with the development of best business practices and methodologies
- Managing special projects

Program Management Analyst, *Steed Consulting, Washington, DC*   2005-2006
Provided support to The Joint Planning and Development Office (JPDO), a federal policy office, including representatives from NASA, FAA, DOD, TSA, DOC, DOT, and The White House Office of Science and Technology Policy, and leaders in the private sectors.

Tamara McGraw   202-123-1234

Consultant, *Community Resources Inc, Washington, DC*   2004-2005
Provided support to the United States Department of Agriculture (USDA).

- Responsible for business continuity research, data collection, and writing recommendations
- Researching and writing disaster recovery and preparedness plans
- Developing solutions for government agency communication and coordination
- Developing recommendations for compliance with Homeland Security guidelines
- Preparing reports and presentations for USDA upper management
- Participating in emergency preparedness table-top exercises

Program Management Analyst, *ABC System, Washington, DC*   2004
Provided support to Federal Aviation Administration (FAA) Surveillance Implementation Lead.

- Assisting with implementing radars into the National Airspace System (NAS)
- Performing research and data analysis
- Assisting with acquisition and cost analysis
- Acting liaison between FAA headquarters and regions

Analyst, *Erie Innovations, Bend, Oregon*   2003
Provided support to President/CEO for an aviation-consulting firm.

- Technical writing
- Writing reports for management
- Market research
- Analyzing airline statistics airport
- Coordinating technical papers, reports, documents, and other deliverables with clients
- Support for office management
- Problem solving and quick action tasks associated with a small business

University Instructor, *Mount Hood Community College, Mt Hood, WA*   2003
Taught college-level courses including Careers in Aviation, Private Pilot, and Aviation Business.

Flight Instructor   2001-2004
The Flight Shop and Austin Academy of Aviation, Oregon and Texas
Taught flight lessons.

- Instructing private through commercial and instrument students
- Flying sightseeing tours
- Flying small charter
- Flying the pipeline
- Scheduling and coordinating charters and student flights
- Mentoring students
- Marketing

5 EDUCATION

- Bachelor's Degree, Texas State University, San Marcos, Texas

6
- Studied at the University of Salamanca in Salamanca, Spain
- Commercial Pilot with a Certified Flight Instrument Instructor (CFII) Rating

Construction Supervisor to Energy Auditor; Homebuilding to Public Utility

Miguel Zapata has been a successful homebuilder and construction manager for 11 years. The new housing market is in a shambles, with beautiful new homes standing idle while homeowners wait for financing. He considers home remodeling, but compared to new construction, remodeling work is hard to get, smaller in scope, and requires patience to work around owners in occupied spaces. He needs to find a steady source of income fast.

Miguel goes to a networking event and learns that the local utility company is actually adding staff. It seems they are expanding an energy conservation program for commercial customers. They need to hire energy auditors who can evaluate possible energy-saving situations, make recommendations, and then inspect the work before a rebate is given to the customer. He is excited about the work—but most of all excited at the prospect of having a steady paycheck with a stable company.

Challenges to Making the Switch

The hiring manager at the public utility may have a bias that construction workers have a "get-it-done" attitude and can be sloppy about details. Miguel is going to have to show how important quality, energy efficiency, and compliance issues are to him.

Miguel has solid experience in homebuilding but very little exposure to commercial construction. He will need to stretch the concept a little to claim that multi-family jobs—apartment buildings—even qualify as commercial work. The shift from outdoor construction work to office work will be a huge change for him. He knows he will need to brush up on his computer skills, which are very basic.

On the other hand, he has managed construction projects and understands the importance of heating, ventilation, and air-conditioning (HVAC). His own custom building company offered warranties to new homeowners. He knows that when homeowners are dissatisfied, it almost always involves heating and cooling equipment. Over the years, he has become savvy about choosing quality equipment with high energy efficiency ratings—sized correctly for the space.

Miguel also has a keen familiarity with insulation techniques, insulated windows, and energy-saving doors. He has built "green," using straw-bale techniques on several custom homes going back to 1998.

A great asset working in his favor is his ability to speak and read Spanish, because many of the customers in Texas are Hispanic.

Transferable Skills

Construction management

Customer service

Compliance with building codes and OSHA

Communication and persuasion skills

Site inspection

Cost/benefit analysis

Report writing

Job Description

Energy Auditor

- Assist in the investigation, analysis, and documentation of energy conservation and utility cost-reduction measures

- Provide site walk-through assessments

- Collect detailed information (utility data, equipment and building data, operational characteristics, temperature, flow and pressure measurements, and so on)

- Conduct technical research assisting with the identification and evaluation of energy efficiency measures, calculation of potential energy savings, and audit report preparation

- Conduct engineering studies and investigations to determine that jobs are complete, accurate, in accordance with good engineering practices and within contract constraints

- Certified Energy Manager (CEM) certification or have the ability to obtain such certification within one year

- Knowledge of HVAC, lighting and heating/cooling plant equipment

- Well-developed verbal and technical report-writing skills

- Working knowledge of standard office computer software (Excel, Word, PowerPoint, and so on)

- Bachelor's degree or equivalent experience

Resume Makeover

Miguel's resume is expanded to two pages in order to add information about energy efficiency equipment and practices.

1 The headline "Energy Efficiency Construction Manager" allows him to state who he is now and how he feels about the value of building green.

2 His first seven statements are designed to focus attention on any knowledge he currently has about energy efficiency.

3 The Core Competencies list allows him to portray his compliance with standards and his keen sense of getting the job done right.

4 For each job, he emphasizes his role as business manager. Here, he focuses on written records and purchase orders.

5 For Premiere Homes, he adds a line about high-efficiency homes and that he has experience with cost/benefit calculations.

6 For Eagle Homes, he includes the line, "One of the first builders to experiment with straw-bale construction." This positions him as forward-thinking and thinking green, even 12 years ago.

7 He adds his two-year college experience, hoping that he won't be cut because he lacks a four-year degree.

Miguel Zapata

123 Lariat Circle, Liberty Valley, TX 78600
email@email.com (512) 123-4567

PROFILE

Results-oriented, dedicated construction professional with 11+ years expertise of management and development in the Residential and Commercial industry. Successful completion of multi-million-dollar projects through coordinating trades, developing partnerships, and building positive rapport with architects, engineers, local officials, vendors, and clients while maintaining costs. Exceptional abilities in contract negotiations, project estimating, impending design issues, building code and regulations, material purchasing, team building, and site management.

EMPLOYMENT HISTORY

PROJECT MANAGER   2007 - 2009
Arcadia Properties, Leander, TX
Plan, organize, schedule, and manage all activities on site for commercial project of 20-unit apartment complex. Control overhead while maintaining written records and verifying purchase orders. Responsibilities include: supervise crews of all trade workers, manage all construction activity, review of design and blueprint, analysis of project, permitting, budget analysis, quality control, safety and compliance, managing vendors and materials, all estimations and job costs, troubleshoot for structural issues during construction, critical path project management, building code compliance, and certificates of occupancy.

SUPERINTENDENT   2005 - 2007
Premiere Homes, Cedar Ridge, TX
Supervised and directed all aspects of construction from start to finish of homes. Planned, scheduled, and managed vendors. Continually monitored and inspected all work of subcontractors to ensure quality. Submitted purchase orders and other related information for tracking of budget. Provided exceptional customer service through buyer orientation and walk-throughs. Maintained successful communication between corporate and field representatives.

OWNER   2004 - 2005
Zapata Custom Builders, San Marcos, TX
Directed all aspects involved in building quality custom homes from start to finish, including take-offs, budgeting, scheduling, inspections, and all facets of construction. Supervised all vendors and trades to ensure timely finish and quality of jobs. Provided superior customer service and managed warranty service.

CO-OWNER   1998 - 2004
Eagle Homes / Dale Wayne Homes, Corpus Christi, TX
Directed all aspects involved in building quality residential homes from start to finish, including development, take-offs, inspections, and all facets of construction. Communicated with all vendors and subcontractors to ensure quality, timely finish of jobs, as well as compliance to building codes and regulations. Maintained all paperwork and coordinated invoices for payment to vendors to maintain budget. Provided superior customer service and managed warranty service.

SKILLS

- 11+ YEARS CONSTRUCTION SUPERVISION & MANAGEMENT
- 9+ years Warranty Management
- Superior Customer Service skills
- Excellent Time and Project Management skills
- Superior Communication skills and Problem Solving abilities
- Bilingual (Spanish)

MIGUEL ZAPATA

123 Lariat Circle • Liberty Valley, TX 78600 • email@email.com • 512-123-4567 cell

❶ ENERGY EFFICIENCY CONSTRUCTION MANAGER

HVAC / Residential & Commercial / Client Relationships

❷
- Known as a premier Project Manager for residential and multi-family projects
- Experienced in HVAC contracting and warranty work
- Cost/benefit analysis for homeowners considering high-efficiency construction products and techniques
- Specified and managed installation of high-efficiency windows, doors, and lighting
- Adept at communicating with customers, managing subcontractors, and writing reports
- Bilingual – Spanish and English
- Competent in office PC applications – Word, Excel, PowerPoint, etc.

Core Competencies

❸
- Management and oversight of commercial construction
- Supervision of all construction trades
- Construction safety and OSHA compliance standards
- Critical path project management
- Building code compliance
- Buyer orientation/warranty service
- Budget tracking: JIT materials delivery
- Powerful communicator

PROFESSIONAL EXPERIENCE

❹ PROJECT MANAGER 2007 - 2009
Arcadia Properties, Leander, TX – Commercial Building Project
- Plan, organize, schedule, and manage all activities on site for commercial project of 20-unit apartment complex.
- Control overhead while maintaining written records and verifying purchase orders.
- Responsibilities include:
Supervise crews of all trade workers, manage all construction activity, review of design and blueprint, analysis of project, permitting, budget analysis, quality control, safety and compliance, managing vendors and materials, all estimations and job costs, troubleshoot for structural issues during construction, critical path project management, building code compliance, and certificates of occupancy.

❺ SUPERINTENDENT 2005 - 2007
Premiere Homes, Cedar Ridge, TX – Homebuilding
Involved in all aspects of planning and specifying materials for custom, high-efficiency homes.
- Supervised and directed all aspects of construction from start to finish of homes. Planned, scheduled, and managed vendors.
- Continually monitored and inspected all work of subcontractors to ensure quality. Submitted purchase orders and other related information for tracking of budget.
- Provided exceptional customer service through buyer orientation and walk-throughs.
- Maintained successful communication between corporate and field representatives.

OWNER 2004 - 2005
Zapata Custom Builders, San Marcos, TX - Homebuilding
- Directed all aspects involved in building quality custom homes from start to finish, including take-offs, budgeting, scheduling, inspections, and all facets of construction.
- Supervised all vendors and trades to ensure timely finish and quality of jobs. Provided superior customer service and managed warranty service.

MIGUEL ZAPATA 512.123.4567

❻ CO-OWNER 1998 - 2004
Eagle Homes / Dale Wayne Homes, Corpus Christi, TX
- One of the first builders to experiment with straw-bale construction. Successfully built more than 10 custom homes using this innovative technique.
- Directed all aspects involved in building quality residential homes from start to finish, including development, take-offs, inspections, and all facets of construction.
- Communicated with all vendors and subcontractors to ensure quality, timely finish of jobs, as well as compliance to building codes and regulations.
- Maintained all paperwork and coordinated invoices for payment to vendors to maintain budget.
- Provided superior customer service and managed warranty service.

SKILLS

- 11+ YEARS CONSTRUCTION SUPERVISION & MANAGEMENT
- 9+ years Warranty Management
- Superior customer service skills
- Excellent time and project management skills
- Superior communication and problem-solving abilities
- Bilingual (Spanish)

EDUCATION

❼ Dade County Community College
Completed 2-year program in Law Enforcement

Consultant to Sales Manager; Outsourcing to Health Care

Hailey Rogers has spent the last two years working herself out of a job. She is a manager with a huge consulting agency that helps American businesses outsource business functions to other countries. She has worked with businesses in Panama, the Philippines, and India, helping them create infrastructure and systems to meet the service expectations of her Fortune 100 clients. She has enjoyed the fast pace, the problem solving, and the constant need to keep an eye on the success of each of her large contracts. Now, she is being laid off herself. The companies she has developed as vendors are now working directly with their American partners, and her consulting contracts are ending.

By networking, she becomes aware that hospitals—especially the for-profit ones—are still hiring. She looks into several positions and finds one of interest: physician sales director. This is essentially a marketing job designed to encourage physicians to refer more patients to the hospital system. While titled very differently, the challenges of this job are similar to her old one. She would be working with the hospital management to create care protocols that satisfy both patients and their referring physicians. She would also be working on marketing and business development strategies—functions that are second nature to a consultant.

In her research prior to her first interview, she finds herself getting excited about the position and about the industry of health care. She spends hours reading online about the health-care industry. As she studies the business, she begins to see how her consulting skills are transferable.

Challenges to Making the Switch

Hailey lacks several of the key qualifications for this position: 7 to 10 years of sales management experience and a health-care background. She will have to convince the hiring manager that her marketing and program management experience are equivalent to experience in sales. She has worked with some of America's largest companies, helping roll out marketing and sales campaigns, and managed a large-company merger. She understands corporate cultures and is an expert in predicting the consequences of change. She also has a finely honed sense of what will work and how much quality it takes to satisfy demanding customers. She feels that her experience dealing with CEOs, CFOs, CTOs, and other top-ranking executives will translate nicely to the physician market.

Hailey is also worried about her four-year gap in employment. During that time she did a little consulting but also had a bad experience with a franchise business she started. She is concerned about how and even whether she should include this on her resume.

Transferable Skills

Understanding clients' needs

Business process architecture

Project/program management

Creating infrastructure

Client satisfaction research

Managing work process

Sales and marketing savvy

Influence with decision makers

Job Description

Physician Sales Director

- Seven to 10 years experience in sales in a health-care environment

- Direct the day-to-day operational activities of the sales and customer service functions, serving key target customers: physicians, employers, consumers, and payers

- Develop, manage, and motivate sales staff to fulfill customers' acquisition, retention, and growth strategies and objectives

- Develop and evaluate sales and facility staff to achieve measurable sales objectives

- Work with hospital management teams and division management to develop annual organizational and individual hospital sales plans

- Meet with targeted physicians as needed, but at least quarterly for retention of current business and development of new business

- Oversee recruitment, selection, and training of all new sales representatives

- Partner with marketing to develop sales materials and strategies to be used by sales representatives

- Ability to establish and commit to a long-range goal or vision after analyzing factual information and assumptions

- Ability to manage staff and resources consistent with organization goals

Resume Makeover

Hailey's resume is very good but needs focus and changes in terminology.

1 "Marketing/Sales Management" is added as a headline under Hailey's name. These are the first words read and the impression she wants to make.

2 The subtitle "Customer Acquisition/Sales Strategies/Mobilizing Resources" contains terms that describe her former job in the language of health-care marketing.

3 The Professional Competencies section is loaded with key words from the job description.

4 Her job history remains in the more-accepted chronological format.

5 Hailey adds a line to explain the work her current company does. This is especially important because she is changing industries.

6 Her achievement statements already contain many documented outcomes of costs reduced, percentage improvement, and revenue earned. This is the language of sales.

7 She includes her two-year sabbatical, calling it "Independent Contractor" and detailing her professional achievements during that time.

8 Volunteer and Education sections are simplified to conserve space. She leaves in her extensive work with the YMCA because it shows her leadership ability.

Hailey Rogers
1234 Ferris Dr.
Dallas, Texas 97300

(503) 123-5678
email@email.com

PROFILE

Professional career reflects 15 years experience and success working in fast-paced environments requiring strong interpersonal, organizational, and technical skills. Key industry experience includes: telecom, health insurance, and computer hardware service providers. Core competencies include:

- Project/Program Management
- Contract Negotiations
- Client Account Management
- Vendor Selection and Management

- Employee Lifecycle Management
- Workforce Planning
- Process Architecture
- Operational Leadership

PROFESSIONAL EXPERIENCE

XYZ Consulting, Inc.   2007-present
Manager, Business Processes Outsourcing (2008-present)
Contractor, Business Processes Outsourcing (2007-2008)

Leading projects and process change initiatives for multiple clients. Responsibilities include: sales process support, cost estimation and proposal development, mobilization, and process architecture projects. Directing international teams in a heavily matrixed environment. Facilitating negotiation between executives who represent diverse workstreams and agendas.

- Analyzed drop in customer satisfaction scores for key client. Designed and implemented improvement initiative delivering 19% improvement in Customer Satisfaction scores within 60 days. Solution is projected to reduce costs by $553M within 9 months.
- Developed contact center solution required for support of new Medicare product. Introduced upgrades in core technical, administrative, and membership accounting technology. Organization supported provider and member solutions in 24 states.
- Managed execution of new contract requirements in Panama & the Philippines that will deliver $12 M in revenue for XYZ Consulting, Inc.

ATT Wireless Services   1994-2003
Program Manager, Market Transformation, National Operations (2000-2003)

Strategy development and implementation of initiatives including marketing, sales support, brand transition, training, organizational staffing redesign, and reductions and systems integration. Led leadership team of 30 program managers.

- Delivered new product launches in 24 ATT Wireless markets with +2,900 points of sales distribution.
- Guided integration of acquired company netting an additional 1M customers, 618 employees, +360 points of sales distribution.
- Exceeded corporate financial goals for the acquisition project by more than $40 M.

Hailey Rogers   page 2

National Vendor Manager, Call Center Operations (1998-2000)

Led national call center organization and administered contracts in excess of $700 M. Integrated 5 separate regional operations into one national organization. Delivered improved staffing utilization and increased customer satisfaction.

- Directed 12-month project resulting in workforce capacity expansion of an additional 8 call centers located in 4 time zones staffing 3,000 FTEs.
- Contributed to negotiation of vendor contracts producing a 30% savings.
- Recaptured $1M in late fees by strengthening alliances with external suppliers.

Call Center Operations Manager, National Customer Operations (1997-1998)

Served in a headquarters staff position tasked with improving key performance indicators in call centers. Strategically planned for integration of regional activation call centers and supported systems into cohesive, national business unit with shared objectives and financial accountability. Managed three million new customer activations per year with an annual budget exceeding $125M.

Customer Care Supervisor, Dallas District (1994-1997)

Responsible for hiring, training, supervising, scheduling, and motivating employee performance in 200-seat inbound call center. Special projects included retail store training and alignment, and a monthly newsletter distributed to +280K customers. Team performance: 120% of objective.

Selected Volunteer and Community Service Work

Women's Shelter (2002-2007)

- Courtroom Advocate

YMCA of Greater Dallas (2000-2002)

- YMCA Committee Chair-Child Development
- YMCA Metro Board Member
- YMCA Gold Award Winner 2000
- YMCA "Super Quota Buster" Award Winner for 2001 & 2002

Education and Certifications

Degree:

Dallas Baptist University, Dallas, Texas
Bachelor of Business Studies-Management, 2003

❶

HAILEY ROGERS
MARKETING / SALES MANAGEMENT
1234 Ferris Dr. ▪ Dallas, TX 97300 ▪ Home 503-123-1234 ▪ Cell 503-123-5678 ▪ email@email.com

❷

CUSTOMER ACQUISITION/SALES STRATEGIES/MOBILIZING RESOURCES

Seasoned marketing and business development professional, directly responsible for landing and servicing multi-million-dollar contracts with Fortune 100 companies. Accountabilities include analyzing outsourcing needs, developing proposals, creating infrastructure to serve clients needs, and monitoring programs for effectiveness, customer satisfaction, and retention. Key industry experience includes: telecom, health insurance, and computer hardware service providers.

❸

PROFESSIONAL COMPETENCIES

- Business development
- Project/program management
- Strategic marketing and branding
- Contract negotiations
- Account management
- Infrastructure development
- Executive/CEO influence

- Recruitment & workforce training
- Product/service line launches
- Process architecture
- Operational leadership
- Sales reporting processes
- Vendor selection & management

CAREER HIGHLIGHTS

❹

XYZ Consulting, Inc.   **2007 - present**
A global management consulting, technology services, and outsourcing company

❺

Manager, Business Processes Outsourcing (2008 - present)
Contractor, Business Processes Outsourcing (2007 - 2008)

Simultaneously lead projects and process change initiatives for multiple clients. Responsibilities include: sales process support, cost estimation and proposal development, mobilization, and process architecture projects. Direct international teams in a heavily matrixed environment. Facilitate negotiation between executives who represent diverse workstreams and agendas.

❻

- Analyzed drop in customer satisfaction scores for key client. Designed and implemented improvement initiative delivering 19% improvement in Customer Satisfaction scores within 60 days. Solution is projected to reduce costs by $553M within 9 months.
- Developed contact center solution required for support of new Medicare product. Introduced upgrades in core technical, administrative, and membership accounting technology. Organization supported provider and member solutions in 24 states.
- Managed execution of new contract requirements in Panama & the Philippines that will deliver $12M in revenue for XYZ Consulting, Inc.

Independent Contractor   **2004 - 2006**

Conducted business development activities related to franchise opportunities, independent consulting firm, and nonprofit organizations. Additional experience includes a 6-month assignment as Assistant Manager of high-end retail clothing store producing $4M in annual revenue.

❼

- Evaluated franchise opportunities in automotive, business services, and healthcare industries.
- Provided solution and subject matter expertise for private clients focused on supply chain process improvements, fundraising, post-merger integration, recruiting, and disaster recovery.
- Completed Dallas' Smart Start Entrepreneurship program.

HAILEY ROGERS   EMAIL@EMAIL.COM

1994 - 2003

ATT Wireless Services

Program Manager, Market Transformation, National Operations (2000 - 2003)

Strategy development and implementation of initiatives including marketing, sales support, brand transition, training, organizational staffing redesign and reductions, and systems integration. Led leadership team of 30 program managers.

- Delivered new product launches in 24 AT&T Wireless markets with +2,900 points of sales distribution.
- Guided integration of acquired company netting an additional 1M customers, 618 employees, +360 points of sales distribution.
- Exceeded corporate financial goals for the acquisition project by more than $40M.

National Vendor Manager, Call Center Operations (1998 - 2000)

Led national call center organization and administered contracts in excess of $700M. Integrated five separate regional operations into one national organization. Delivered improved staffing utilization and increased customer satisfaction.

- Directed 12-month project resulting in workforce capacity expansion of an additional 8 call centers located in 4 time zones staffing 3,000 FTEs.
- Contributed to negotiation of vendor contracts producing a 30% savings.
- Recaptured $1M in late fees by strengthening alliances with external suppliers.

Call Center Operations Manager, National Customer Operations (1997 - 1998)

Served in a headquarter staff position tasked with improving key performance indicators in call centers. Strategically planned for integration of regional activation call centers and supported systems into cohesive, national business unit with shared objectives and financial accountability. Managed 3 million new customer activations per year with an annual budget exceeding $125M.

Customer Care Supervisor, Dallas District (1994 - 1997)

Responsible for hiring, training, supervising, scheduling, and motivating employee performance in 200-seat inbound call center. Special projects included retail store training and alignment, and a monthly newsletter distributed to +280K customers. Team performance: 120% of objective.

SELECTED VOLUNTEER & COMMUNITY SERVICE WORK

❽

Women's Shelter (2002 - 2007) — Courtroom Advocate

YMCA of Greater Dallas (2000 - 2002)
YMCA Committee Chair-Child Development   YMCA Metro Board Member
YMCA Gold Award Winner 2000   YMCA "Super Quota Buster" Award Winner, 2001 - 2002

EDUCATION

Bachelor of Business Studies–Management — Dallas Baptist University, Dallas, Texas, 2003

Human Resources Manager to Office Administrator; Wholesale to Health Care

Rhonda Fletcher had a great seven-year run in human resources when a move and a health crisis derailed her career. First, she was downsized; then, she experienced the onset of a chronic illness that took her out of the job market for nearly two years. She later moved with her husband as he pursued a doctoral degree in another city. She is now ready to go back to recruiting, but most HR professionals are now in the business of laying off workers, not recruiting. She decides to reposition her experience as office management and seek a job in one of the few industries that are hiring right now: health care.

Challenges to Making the Switch

Rhonda's confidence is low. For the last several years, she has worked a few temporary jobs—but every one resulted in a termination. She feels confused and vague about her future. She wants to re-ignite her career and take a less demanding job so that she can work a regular schedule and maintain her good health status. Her doctors tell her specifically that she must limit the stress in her life. Her experience in the health-care field is limited to her own personal experience as a patient. While she feels this is important, she does not want to reveal her chronic illness to a prospective employer.

Rhonda is also concerned about the gaps in her employment and about how to answer the objection that she is overqualified for the office management job she really wants. She is hoping that her HR skills will actually put her at the top of the stack of candidate resumes. As a former HR professional, she can easily take on a higher level of responsibility—including employee policies, hiring, and benefits.

Transferable Skills

Reception

Office software

Employee records

Bookkeeping

Benefits administration

Database management

Correspondence

Report writing

Customer surveys

Job Description

Office Administrator—Health Care

- Variety of duties related to the authorization and recertification of insurance for the patients of the care center and their physicians

- Use fax, Internet, e-mail, written log books, computer, and patient charts; answer telephones, route calls, schedule patient appointments, and greet patients and visitors

- Collect data essential to the hospital registration and billing process, enter patient charges, schedule ancillary testing, assemble patient charts, and file patient charts

- Use QuickBooks to create reports of interest to the care center management

- Normal maintenance of office equipment

- Ability to present information in one-on-one and small group situations

- Order office supplies and some medical supplies as directed

- Assist in preparation of periodic reports on programs and operations

- Assist in marketing initiatives and maintaining website information

- Assist in the design and collection of customer surveys and the interpretation of results

- BA degree required

Resume Makeover

Rhonda's resume is changed to a functional style to de-emphasize her tenure in HR jobs.

1 Her headline "Office Administrator" matches the job description. The opening statement avoids the words "human resources" and instead speaks in terms of employee records, policies, and recruiting.

2 The Core Competencies section allows her to use many of the key words in the job description while still being accurate to her experience.

3 By leading with Relevant Software & Equipment Use, she is acknowledging that she understands this is a clerical position.

4 Her achievement statements are copied directly from her original resume. She deletes the higher-level activities to play down the fact that she is overqualified.

5 Customer Relations is the second grouping, because she knows patient relations will be very important in her new job.

6 By including Benefits Administration, she proves her familiarity with health insurance—which is critical in health-care office administration.

7 The Industry Experience section shows that she is flexible and able to work in many different environments.

8 Her work history is simplified to play down the level of jobs she has held in the past.

9 Her Master's degree is eliminated because this work is not relevant. An advanced degree will likely fuel the overqualified interpretation.

RHONDA FLETCHER
1234 Oakhaven Drive
North Andover, MA 01810
(978) 123-4567
email@email.com

OBJECTIVE
Opportunities to utilize my seven years of Human Resources experience to help an organization successfully implement change in employee development, training, benefits, and recruitment.

SUMMARY OF QUALIFICATIONS
- HR Generalist with an emphasis on employee relations, recruiting, and performance management
- Experienced in high-volume recruiting for new and growing businesses
- Proficient in the use of Microsoft Office Suite as well as Internet applications

PROFESSIONAL EXPERIENCE

VOLT SERVICES   North Andover, MA   3/06-3/07
Recruiting Coordinator (contract employee)
- Supported four recruiters with the recruiting/interview process
- Assisted candidates with successfully applying for positions via a new online application system
- Responsible for all correspondence sent to applicants regarding their applications and interviews
- Scheduled interviews for the executive team via MS Outlook
- Monitored and processed candidate expense reimbursements

MIDDLESEX COMMUNITY COLLEGE   Middlesex, MA   2/05-4/05
Human Resources Administrative Assistant
- Maintained job applicant database and sent out correspondence to all applicants
- Served as a receptionist in a fast-paced Human Resources department assisting visitors and answering telephone calls
- Processed new hire orientation paperwork
- Prepared and maintained personnel files and records
- Reviewed and forwarded employment and payroll documents for appropriate signatures

TEMPLE EMANUEL   Worchester, MA   3/04-2/05
Part-time Receptionist/Office Assistant
- Answered telephones and greeted and assisted congregation members with various needs
- Performed general office duties including the processing of donations

STANBROOK DISTRIBUTION SERVICES, INC. Leicester, MA   4/02-6/03
Human Resources Representative
- Recruited for both non-exempt and exempt positions for the entire Northeast territory
- Acted as the primary contact on benefit-related inquiries for the Northeast sales field
- Completed and processed the necessary paperwork on COBRA
- Created various staffing and benefit reports using ReportSmith

---

RHONDA FLETCHER   Page 2

STANBROOK DISTRIBUTION SERVICES, INC. Leicester, MA   4/02-6/03
Cont'd
- Assisted in the planning of employee functions such as children's holiday party and the United Way Campaign

BLUEBAR ELECTRIC   Northboro, MA   2/99-12/01
Human Resources Generalist
- Trained and counseled managers on employee development issues, including documenting employee performance, writing performance reviews, taking appropriate corrective action, and handling workplace diversity issues
- Investigated and resolved immigration matters, allegations of sexual harassment and racial discrimination, and other potential legal issues
- Successfully recruited for various positions via media sources, job fairs, college postings, state employment agencies, and minority organizations
- Administered the employment screening process which included reviewing resumes and applications, interviewing, testing, and conducting all background checks
- Functioned as the main contact with employment agencies to review contracts, place new orders for temporary employees, evaluate their work performance, and resolve issues between the agencies, temporary employees, and the managers
- Conducted orientations for new employees
- Researched and managed all workers' compensation and disability claims
- Organized and implemented activities and programs to aid in the retention of employees
- Maintained all personnel files

MANPOWER, INC.   Waltham, MA   9/97-2/99
Recruiting Coordinator/Service Representative
- Researched and implemented various recruiting plans and strategies to form and maintain a pool of qualified employees for all skill areas
- Enhanced retention rates through the implementation of the referral bonus and company award program
- Recruited, interviewed, and assessed candidates for temporary and temp-to-hire assignments
- Coached and counseled temporary employees on job-related issues to ensure quality performance and job satisfaction
- Administered the training of temporary employees to upgrade their skills in current software applications and operating systems
- Conducted service calls to ensure quality customer service and expand business
- Implemented corporate initiatives to improve service delivery to customers and temporary employees including ISO 9000 compliance, training in equal opportunity employment, and unemployment compensation

EDUCATION
INDIANA UNIVERSITY   Bloomington, IN   1997
Master of Sciences, Elementary Education
CLARK UNIVERSITY   Worchester, MA   1993
Bachelor of Arts, Geography/Environmental Studies

9

Training/Employee Relations
- Created and launched employee functions such as the children's holiday party and the yearly United Way Campaign.
- Organized and implemented activities and programs to aid in the retention of employees at a 250-person facility.
- Enhanced retention rates at Manpower, Inc. through implementation of the referral bonus and company award program.
- Administered the training of temporary employees to upgrade their skills in current software applications and operating systems.
- Trained and counseled managers on employee development issues, including documenting employee performance, writing performance reviews, taking appropriate corrective action, and handling workplace diversity issues.
- Created and conducted new hire orientations for warehouse, office, and sales employees.

Employment/Security Issues
- Administered the employment screening process, including conducting reference and background checks.
- Discovered, researched, and resolved I-9 documentation errors and omissions in more than 500 employee records.
- Investigated and resolved immigration matters, allegations of sexual harassment and racial discrimination, and other potential legal issues.
- Managed the background and credit check process – gathered information, asked applicants for clarification, worked with security, and informed applicants of hiring decision.

7 INDUSTRY EXPERIENCE

Staffing Agency   Electric Wholesale   Higher Education
Food and Health   High Tech

8 RELEVANT WORK HISTORY

Office Temporary	Various Assignments	North Andover, MA	2007 – Present
Recruiting Coordinator	Volt Services	North Andover, MA	2006 – 2007
HR Administrator	Middlesex Community College	Middlesex, MA	2005
HR Representative	Stanbrook Distribution Services	Leicester, MA	2002 – 2003
HR Generalist	Bluebar Electric	Northboro, MA	1999 – 2001
Staffing Consultant	Manpower, Inc.	Waltham, MA	1997 – 1999

9 EDUCATION

BA, Geography/Environmental Studies – Clark University, Worcester, MA 1993

Rhonda Fletcher

1234 Oakhaven Drive ◆ North Andover, MA 01810 ◆ (978) 123-4567 ◆ email@email.com

1 OFFICE ADMINISTRATOR

Office professional with 7 years experience in employee records, policies, and recruiting. Created and maintained databases, handled performance issues, administered employee benefits. Knowledgeable about health insurance terminology, and payment requirements. Works well in a team environment, with varied responsibilities and a fast pace.

2 CORE COMPETENCIES

Reception – greet, serve, schedule   Benefits administration
Employee records/databases   Office equipment contracts
Data collection & retrieval   Report writing & analysis
QuickBooks – Intermediate user   Correspondence
Temporary employee contracting   Employee relations

MS Office Suite
Customer surveys
Customer billing issues
Employee policies
Orientation & training

3 RELEVANT SOFTWARE & EQUIPMENT USE

- MS Word, Internet Explorer, Outlook, Excel, Access
- ADP ReportSmith software
- QuickBooks
- Various company-specific staffing/employment databases

4 Office Administration
- Served as a receptionist in a fast-paced HR department of 7, assisting visitors and answering telephone calls.
- Scheduled interviews for a team of 6 executives via MS Outlook, coordinating schedules of the executives and applicants in different locations and time zones.
- Responsible for negotiating and administering an on-site temporary employment agency vendor and contract, lowering the hourly bill rate by 15% on 150 temporary positions.
- Functioned as the main contact with employment agencies to review contracts, place new orders for temporary employees, evaluate their work performance, and resolve issues between the agencies, temporary employees, and their managers.
- Responded and managed unemployment claims, researching and providing management with details for hearings.
- Supported 4 recruiters with the recruiting/interviewing process.
- Responsible for all correspondence sent to applicants regarding their application and interviews.
- Maintained job applicant database in Access for community college with approximately 150 employee positions.

5 Customer Relations
- Conducted weekly in-person service calls for Manpower, Inc. to ensure quality customer service, increase temporary job orders, and expand the business relationship.
- Implemented corporate initiative to improve service delivery to customers and temporary employees including ISO 9000 compliance, training in EEO, and unemployment compensation.
- Created, delivered, and analyzed customer and employee surveys.

6 Benefits Administration
- Acted as the primary contact on benefit-related inquiries for approximately 200 employees, with a variety of health and dental plans.
- Completed and processed the necessary paperwork for FMLA and COBRA benefits.
- Created various staffing and benefit reports for management using ReportSmith.

Meeting Planner to Business Development; Arts to Architecture

Mary Kovar has spent the last seven years struggling to keep a performing arts center in the black. She has been a one-woman show—attracting talent, promoting the event to the public, and doing all the behind-the-scenes production. In the process, she has learned how to stage weddings, plays, musical performances, and even art exhibits. She is masterful at keeping all the artists and vendors producing for her. Even with her nonprofit clients, she has been able to keep costs low and generate the maximum profits for their fundraising events. The economic times have finally caused the Winfield Center for the Performing Arts to fold, however.

During the last few years, Mary has picked up valuable skills in meeting planning. She also has experience in sales, promotion, and office management. For this career change, she wants to dedicate her work life to green energy. She soon finds a job lead from her sister for business development director of an architectural firm that is big in the green building industry.

Challenges to Making the Switch

Mary does not have one of the key requirements: a college degree. She is hoping that her combined years in business will make up for this fact. She is also eager to show her recent training as a meeting planner as evidence of her willingness to grow in her career.

The trick will be convincing the principal at the architectural firm that she has key industry knowledge necessary to operate in the world of design and construction. If she can position the arts center and comedy club years as business development (10), plus her years of direct selling (3), she can actually claim that she has been doing the required activities for a long time. In addition, she has a connection to construction. She worked in her husband's real estate business some 17 years. Even though this experience was from 1982 to 1999, she decides to add it to her resume because it shows her knowledge of building practices.

Transferable Skills

Building client/vendor relationships

Sales skills

Community relations

Market research

Proposal writing

Presentation skills

Strategic planning

Event planning

Trade show planning

Job Description
Business Development—Architecture

- Identify and establish relationships with potential clients, maintain and expand relationships within existing client organizations, develop market networks, and position the firm for potential opportunities

- Work with business development and marketing leadership within the firm and establish the strategic plan, goals, and objectives to grow the business in green design and construction

- Use market data and other business information to develop lists of appropriate potential clients

- Analyze and qualify potential clients in terms of professional and financial value to the firm

- Identify and contact key decision makers

- Work directly with market sector leaders, project directors, project managers, and other firm leaders in the pursuit of new opportunities

- Work directly with marketing services in the preparation of brochures and proposals

- In collaboration with the project director, develop proposal and interview strategies and guide the team through these processes

- Participate in conferences, professional associations, and other external organizations to develop business contacts

- Maintain client relationships during project delivery to assure client satisfaction

- Excellent written and verbal communication skills

- Bachelor's degree required (business, marketing, architecture, or engineering); minimum five years business development and/or marketing experience

Resume Makeover

Mary's goal is to reposition her sales, marketing, and promotion experience into language appealing to the profession of architecture.

1 The headline "Business Development Professional" says exactly what she is looking for.

2 She opens with seven career achievements that tie directly into the language of the job description. She has bulleted these items to make them easier to read than paragraph style.

3 Her Core Competencies list is formulated specifically to respond to the job description. She puts her most important skills—product and services marketing, developing contacts through networking, and creating brochures, ads, and promotional material—in the left column.

4 Rather than a laundry list of activities, each of her positions details accomplishments, with results in percentages or dollars when possible. She highlights her business development responsibilities by leading with these.

5 She changes her title at the comedy club to more closely reflect her responsibility for building the business. She contacts the former owner to be sure he is aware of this change, should he be called for a reference.

6 She also adds a listing for her bookkeeping and payroll experience with her husband's business—Newland & Company. She reports her title as "Manager" to accurately reflect her extensive responsibilities. Because this was a family business, there is no downside to changing her title.

7 She adds in an education listing for event planning, which has some relevance to her desired job.

Mary Kovar
1234 Norman Trail
Omaha, NE 68100
402-123-4567
email@email.com

SUMMARY OF EXPERIENCE
Self-motivated, proactive, and accomplished Administrator/Meeting & Special Events Director, with experience in directing, managing, coordinating in the public and private sectors; organizing and managing special projects, charity fundraisers, corporate meetings, trade shows, and weddings. Industry recognition for being a talented, valuable asset with independent work abilities requiring minimal supervision.

CONTINUING EDUCATION & TRAINING
2006   Metropolitan Community College   Event and Meeting Management Program
Completed Courses: Introduction to Hospitality Management; Introduction to Convention and Meeting Planning, Exhibition and Trade Show Operations Management; Honor Roll
- Studying for CMP Certification - Meeting & Event Planning
- International Meeting Planning, Convention, Trade Show Planning

Languages: Spanish, German
Computer Skills: Microsoft Word & Excel, Microsoft Power Point

DETAILED PROFESSIONAL EXPERIENCE

Winfield Center -- Performing Arts & Event Facility, Omaha, NE   11/02 – 01/09
Meeting & Special Events Director
- Arrange and meet with clients
- Follow through with all client correspondence and phone calls
- Maintain calendar
- Complete and negotiate client contracts
- Type reports and memos
- Coordinate client meetings, events, conferences
- Oversee setup of all aspects of meetings and events
- Plan/create menus for meetings/events
- Market/promote Center through industry meetings, networking, continuing education
- Hire staff and security
- Recommend hotels
- Arrange transportation when needed
- Schedule maintenance and repairs for facility
- Buyer of all commodities
- Wedding ceremony and reception coordinator
- Set up and work trade shows
- Provide outstanding customer service

Greater Kansas City Corridor Council, Kansas City, MO   2002
Office Manager (on Contract)
- Screened all incoming calls, type reports, memos, brochures, and correspondence
- Management of the President's electronic mail and all correspondence related to his office
- Liaison between board and committee members
- Coordinated board and committee meetings and materials
- Created projected cash flow and expenditure projection chart for Council's bank line of credit and accounts payable
- Worked with Board Members and all committees on projects, corresponding, and attending meetings and workshops
- Maintained and disbursed membership packets to prospective members

Kenley Group, Omaha, NE   1999 – 02
Field Sales Manager
- Field Sales Manager for seven gift manufacturers
- Territory - Austin, Waco, San Marcos, Kerrville, Fredericksburg, and surrounding towns
- Shipped over $600,000 in first year with a 50% annual increase in sales
- Responsible for developing and increasing sales volume in the Central Texas region
- Opened new accounts, expanded existing accounts, increased retention
- Assisted new businesses in creating displays, inventoried and restocked merchandise

Comedy Tonight, Omaha, NE   1988 – 91
Manager/Coordinator/Controller
- Designed Club Layout
- Managed day-to-day operations
- Finished out space, purchased equipment and furnishings
- Decorated club, commissioned artists for design work
- Booked talent, coordinated travel and hotel accommodations
- Procured alcohol, condiments, and refreshments
- Managed work schedules and payroll
- Created promotional campaigns and handled all catering
- Responsible for group and individual sales
- Wrote press releases/worked with media on advertising campaigns
- Coordinated special events

ASSOCIATIONS
Member of Meeting Professionals International - Kansas City Chapter
Member of Women in Film
Member Professional Convention Management Association

PUBLIC SERVICE AND CIVIC AFFAIRS
Regional President & Executive Officer of WRJ Organization – Nebraska & Kansas
National Board Member

ZONTA - Professional Women's Organization

Mary Kovar
1234 Norman Trail, Omaha, NE 68100   402-123-4567   email@email.com

Business Development Professional

❶
- Self-motivated, proactive, and accomplished Business Developer.
- Adept at identifying, qualifying, and approaching potential business clients.
- More than 12 years experience in creating and promoting public events.
- Expert at writing proposals and coaching business presentations.
- Experienced in planning and participating in trade shows for maximum monetary value.
- Skilled at directing, managing, and coordinating vendors for special projects, charity fundraisers, and corporate meetings.

❷
- Recognized for being a talented, valuable asset, working independently and requiring minimal supervision.

❸ CORE COMPETENCIES

Product & services marketing	Proposal writing	Trade shows
Developing contacts through networking	Presentations	Fundraising
Brochures, ads, promotional material	Contract negotiations	Event planning
Community relations	Team building/leadership	Customer retention
Direct sales experience – 12 years	Budget/payroll/billing	Strategic planning
Analyzing & qualifying opportunities	Vendor management	

PROFESSIONAL EXPERIENCE

❹ Managing Director, Business Development
Winfield Center -- Performing Arts & Event Facility, Omaha, NE   2002 - 2009
- During the first 18 months, increased overall sales over 65%
- Built event bookings from 15% to 89% of the total revenue by creating events with partnering non-profits, performing artists, associations and organizations
- Attended industry meetings, continuing education, and trade shows to build contacts and create venture partners
- Successfully planned and produced nearly 200 events each year
- Director of Catering, Bar Service, and Maintenance: creation of menus, coordinating seating, working with vendors, hiring staff
- Buyer of all commodities: scheduled maintenance inside and outside of facility, hired security for all events
- Meeting/Event Planner: coordinated all aspects of meetings, breakout rooms, arrangements for equipment, food, beverage service
- Wedding Planner: ceremony and reception coordinator, meetings with bride and family

Office Manager (On Contract)
Greater Kansas City Corridor Council, Kansas City, MO   2002
- Screened all incoming calls, created reports, memos, brochures, and correspondence
- Management of the President's electronic mail and all correspondence related to his office
- Liaison between board and committee members
- Coordinated board and committee meetings and materials
- Created projected cash flow and expenditure projection chart for Council's bank line of credit and accounts payable
- Worked with Board Members and all committees on projects, corresponding and attending meetings and workshops
- Created, maintained, and disbursed membership packets to prospective members

Field Sales Representative
Kenley Group (Sales Representative), Omaha, NE   1999 - 2002
- Field Associate Sales Representative for 7 gift manufacturers
- Territory – Omaha, Lincoln, Kansas City, Des Moines, and surrounding towns
- Shipped over $600,000 in first year with a 50% annual increase in sales
- Responsible for developing and increasing sales volume in the Central Texas region
- Opened new accounts, expanded existing accounts, increased retention
- Assisted new businesses in creating displays; inventoried and restocked merchandise

❺ Manager/Promoter
Comedy Tonight, Omaha, NE.   1988 - 1991
- Responsible for group and individual sales, planned events while coordinating with wait staff and management, wrote press releases, worked with media on advertising campaigns
- Design, management, and day-to-day operations of comedy club
- Finished out space, bought equipment, and furnished in the creation of comedy club in Omaha, NE. Decorated club, interviewed artists who created artwork of comics for club, worked with booking agents in making arrangements for talent
- Coordinated travel and hotel accommodations
- Procured alcohol for bar, condiments, and refreshments for club
- Managed work schedules and payroll for bartenders and wait-staff, took reservations, hosted and seated customers
- Created promotional campaigns and handled all catering for guest parties
- Coordinated special events while maintaining Real Estate and Land Development Company

❻ Manager
Newland & Company, Omaha, NE   1982 - 1999
- Contract Administrator preparing lease agreements and all related documentation for vendors/suppliers and subcontractors
- Managed and maintained residential and commercial office leases and residential lot sales
- Showed properties, developed lease agreements and purchases
- Managed the hiring of subcontractors, oversaw maintenance and repairs of rental properties
- Received and tracked all payments for rental homes and commercial properties
- Reconciled bookkeeping, AR & AP

ASSOCIATIONS
Member of Meeting Planners International – Kansas City Chapter
Member of Women in Film
Member Professional Convention Management Association

❼ CONTINUING EDUCATION & TRAINING
Event and Meeting Management Program, Metropolitan Community College   2006
Completed Courses: Introduction to Hospitality Management; Introduction to Convention and Meeting Planning, Exhibition and Trade Show Operations Management

Nurse to Administrator; Hospital to Home Health Care

Kathie Bryson has spent the last two years working herself out of a job. Because of her experience in building treatment methodologies, she was hired to collaborate with a medical director in setting up a diagnosis treatment unit of a major hospital. After 24 months, the policies, procedures, and staff are in place, and she is the first to be let go in a cost-cutting measure.

Kathie has substantial experience as a business owner and entrepreneur. The risk and insecurity associated with owning and managing a private practice has increased with the economic downturn, however, and she wants to move into a management role in an insurance company or major corporation where she can exercise her health-care supervisory and management abilities without the pressures of running a small business. Her goal is to find a position where she can coach and manage a staff of nurses so that she can focus on the quality of care provided and on general administration. One of the first positions she becomes aware of is administrator for home health care, a fast-growing segment of the health-care industry.

Challenges to Making the Switch

Kathie's home health-care experience dates back to her early nursing days—before 1996. Much has changed in the industry since then. Several positions ask specifically for home health-care expertise. Her business experience is limited to a small coaching practice, a selection company, and managing her own psychotherapy practice. While significant, she has never managed business facilities nor been responsible for profitability in a large enterprise. She is hoping that her substantial experience in marketing will overshadow this issue. In addition, her experience as a coach and therapist will be invaluable as she takes on another managerial role. She will need to further document her management successes in preparation for an interview.

Transferable Skills

Nursing

Management

Marketing through sales and networking

Caseload management

Treatment design and delivery

Collaboration with medical professionals

Oversight of patient care

Supervision and management

Staff screening and selection

Job Description
Home Health-Care Administrator

- Accountable for the overall business management of two branches, including development of new programs to meet the needs of the community

- Develop and implement short- and long-term strategic plans that support quarterly business plans

- Secure business growth by developing sales and marketing strategies for obtaining revenue goals

- Successful financial operation of the branches, development of the operating budget, and the establishment of plans to meet or exceed financial goals

- Oversight of patient/client care services delivered and implementation of plans for improvement of customer satisfaction

- Selection and supervision of branch associates, providing development opportunities, instruction, guidance, and counseling

- Ability to apply to daily operations JCAHO standards, federal, state, and county rules and regulations; ensure the branch's compliance for licensure

- Three to five years proven management experience

- Understanding of reimbursement patterns for Medicare and other payers

- Strong people management and leadership skills

- Excellent communication, interpersonal, and negotiation skills

---

Resume Makeover

Kathie's resume needs to emphasize her management, coaching, and supervisory skills.

1 The Resume Billboard begins with "Healthcare Administrator"—a close match to the job description.

2 The nine achievement statements emphasize her management, marketing, and business savvy. She is also able to highlight her creativity in designing new care programs. She adds numbers to give her prospective employer a sense of the scope of her supervisory experiences.

3 The Core Competencies section allows her to highlight specific experiences that are included in the job description.

4 Each job begins with her title to emphasize her role, rather than the business entity.

5 She includes greater detail for various Registered Nurse (RN) jobs between 1982 and 1996 to highlight her range of experience in health care.

6 She adds references to Coach University, "Certified Professional Behavior & Values Analyst," and "Leadershiip Program" to her education and certifications. While not as important in a pure nursing resume, they add to her image as a management professional.

Kathie Bryson

1234 Any Street
Dallas, Texas 75201
(214) 123-4567
email@email.com

Objective: A healthcare professional seeking a position in a corporate environment where I can excel using my healthcare, communication, and management skills.

Professional Experience

Methodist Hospital, Dallas, TX   2007-2009
Unit Manager
Acute Care Inpatient Psychiatric Facility / Dual Diagnosis Unit

- Collaborate with the Medical Director to open a Dual Diagnosis Treatment Unit.
- Manage clinical staff of nurses and mental health technicians.
- Responsible for developing unit policies and procedures.
- Responsible for scheduling to cover unit 24 hours/day.
- Responsible for preparing hospital staff for JCAHO review.
- Responsible for development of unit programming.

Freedom Counseling, Inc., Dallas, TX   2002-2007
President and Psychotherapist
Founder of a private coaching and psychotherapy practice treating patients suffering with chemical dependency and mental health problems.

- Collaborated with a local psychiatrist and developed a thriving practice within 6 months.
- Once running, responsible for all aspects of running and delivering care in a private practice setting.
- Marketed various services to local psychiatric facilities as well as to other practitioners.
- Partnered with other psychiatrists in developing and delivering comprehensive care to their patients.

PerfectFit, Inc., Austin, TX   1998-2002
Consultant and Coach
Co-founder of company providing online pre-screening assessment tools and processes to assist technology companies to hire properly to build high-performing sales, customer service, and product development teams.

- Responsible for business development and sales through cold calling C-Level decisions makers.
- Account Executive role nurturing existing and up-selling established accounts.
- Presented comprehensive results of team analyses to management teams.
- Performed 1:1 profile debriefs and coached managers and employees for performance improvement.

Target market was technology companies. Some customers included: Pervasive Software, Dazel, ETI, Sprint PCS.

Success Process, Austin, TX   1996-1998
Executive Coach
Founder of professional coaching practice working with executives and middle- to upper-management individuals committed to personal and professional improvement and advancement.

- Developed clientele through extensive networking.
- Worked one-on-one with individual corporate executives, managers, and employees using various behavioral assessments for performance improvement as well as career development and succession planning.
- Conducted weekly coaching calls in an effort to distinguish performance issues and to strategize for rapid growth and movement toward a sense of life/work balance initiatives.

Steinbach & Associates, Austin, TX   1994-1996
Psychotherapist and Registered Nurse
Outpatient methadone clinic for the treatment of patients with opioid dependence.

- Role as RN and LPC to manage caseload of addiction and psychotherapy clients.
- Worked with individuals, couples, and families to overcome various psychological and family issues.
- Emphasis was on medication management for various physical and mental health problems.

Registered Nurse   1982-1996
Worked in various healthcare settings including hospitals, clinics, psychiatric facilities, and home healthcare.

Education

Master of Science, Counseling Psychology, Our Lady of the Lake University, San Antonio, TX
Bachelor of Science, Nursing, University of Texas Arlington
Associates in Nursing, Delaware Technical and Community College, Newark, DE

Certifications

RN, Registered Nurse
LPC, Licensed Professional Counselor/Analyst

Kathie Bryson
214.123.4567

CONSULTANT & COACH
Perfect Fit, Inc., Austin 1998 - 2002
Co-founder of company providing online pre-screening assessment tools and processes to assist technology companies to hire properly to build high-performing sales, customer service, and product development teams
- Responsible for business development and sales through cold-calling C-Level decisions makers.
- Account Executive role nurturing existing and up-selling established accounts.
- Presented comprehensive results of team analyses to management teams.
- Performed 1:1 profile debriefs and coached managers and employees for performance improvement.
- Target market: technology companies. Customers included: Pervasive Software, Dazel, ETI, Sprint PCS.

EXECUTIVE COACH
Success Process, Austin, TX 1996 - 1998
Founder of professional coaching practice working with executives and middle- to upper-management individuals committed to personal and professional improvement and advancement
- Developed clientele through extensive networking.
- Worked one-on-one with individual corporate executives, managers, and employees using various behavioral assessments for performance improvement as well as career development and succession planning.
- Conducted weekly coaching calls in an effort to distinguish performance issues and to strategize for rapid growth and movement toward a sense of life/work balance initiatives.

PSYCHOTHERAPIST/REGISTERED NURSE
Steinbach & Associates, Austin, TX 1994 - 1996
Outpatient methadone clinic for the treatment of patients with opioid dependence
- Role as RN and LPC to manage caseload of addiction and psychotherapy clients.
- Worked with individuals, couples, and families to overcome various psychological and family issues.
- Emphasis was on medication management for various physical and mental health problems.

REGISTERED NURSE 1982 - 1996
Worked in various healthcare settings including hospitals, clinics, psychiatric facilities, and home healthcare.
Responsible for both management and staff nursing roles in the following areas:
- Surgical ICU
- Emergency Room
- Medical ICU
- Coronary ICU
- Inpatient Mental Health
- Outpatient Mental Health
- Internal and Family Medicine

Education
Master of Science, Counseling Psychology, Our Lady of the Lake University, San Antonio, TX
Bachelor of Science, Nursing, University of Texas Arlington
Associate in Nursing, Delaware Technical and Community College, Newark, DE
Graduate of Coach University
Graduate of Landmark Education's Leadership Program

Licensures and Certifications
RN, Registered Nurse
LPC, Licensed Professional Counselor/Analyst
CPBVA, Certified Professional Behavior & Values Analyst
Introduction Leader for Landmark Education

KATHIE BRYSON, RN, LPC

1234 Any Street
Dallas, TX 75201

Phone: 214.123.4567
email@email.com

Healthcare Administrator

- Seasoned nurse and LPC with 15 years experience in management and business administration
- Proven track record of building practices through community outreach, networking, and marketing
- Developed a thriving psychiatric practice for chemical dependency within 6 months
- Collaborated with psychiatrists and other professionals to design new comprehensive care program
- Responsible for preparing hospital staff of 245 for JCAHO review
- Managed clinical staff of 45 nurses and 14 mental health clinicians
- Led entrepreneurial executives in strategic planning for business growth
- Direct experience in sales – built successful coaching and selection businesses 1996 - 2002
- Staff selection expert, trained as a coach and behavior analyst

Core Competencies

- Strategic planning
- Marketing and sales plans
- Community networking
- Staff screening and selection
- Oversight of patient care
- JCAHO standards
- Medicare/insurance reimbursements
- Strong communication skills
- Proven management experience
- Caseload management
- Mental health practice standards
- Drug, alcohol addiction therapies
- Surgical, coronary ICU
- Medication management

Professional Experience

UNIT MANAGER
Methodist Hospital, Dallas, TX 2007 - 2009
Acute Care Inpatient Psychiatric Facility / Dual Diagnosis Unit
- Collaborated with the Medical Director to open a Dual Diagnosis Treatment Unit.
- Managed clinical staff of 45 nurses and 14 mental health technicians.
- Responsible for developing unit policies and procedures.
- Responsible for scheduling to cover unit 24 hours/day.
- Designed and delivered a process to prepare hospital staff for JCAHO review.
- Responsible for development of unit programming.

FOUNDER
Freedom Counseling, Inc., Dallas, TX 2003 - 2008
Founder and manager of a private coaching and psychotherapy practice treating patients suffering with chemical dependency and mental health problems

PRESIDENT & PSYCHOTHERAPIST
- Collaborated with a local psychiatrist to develop a thriving practice within 6 months.
- Responsible for all aspects of running and delivering care in a private practice setting, including staffing and scheduling, conflict resolution, problem solving, and interpersonal skills.
- Partnered with other psychiatrists in developing and delivering comprehensive care to their patients.
- Developed a unique recovery coaching model and delivered in one-to-one and group settings.
- Marketed the Coaching Model program to build the practice.

Project Manager to Career Counselor; Software to Staffing

Julia Jennings has worked in high tech for several years as a program manager. With the economic downturn and employee cutbacks, however, the stress to do more with less time and fewer resources is really taking its toll on her. Adding to the stress is her concern that her job could be cut next. While she's still employed, Julia is being proactive and looking for a new job outside the technology field.

At a previous job, Julia worked as a career counselor in a campus environment. She really loved working with people and helping place them in good jobs. With current graduating classes facing the worst economy since the 1970s, universities are beefing up their career counseling services for new grads and alumni—providing a great opportunity for Julia.

Challenges to Making the Switch

Julia has spent the last four-plus years in marketing and project management for large companies. Previously, however, she was a career development specialist with a local university, so the leap is not that great. In addition, her IT background can help candidates interested in high-tech jobs, and her corporate experience can be a plus when coaching candidates seeking corporate positions. While the switch may mean a lower salary, the position is more stable and much less stressful than her current position.

Transferable Skills

Customer service

Interpersonal skills

Presentation skills

Organizational skills

Communication skills

Project management

Interviewing skills

Job Description

Career Counselor

- Assist recent graduates, alumni, and current students with career placement

- Conduct seminars on resume creation, interviewing, and job search skills

- Help coordinate and participate in job fairs, career fairs, portfolio nights, and other student activities and events

- Research and analyze employment trends at the local and national level

- Accumulate and maintain information for employment statistics

- Establish and maintain relationships with potential employers to obtain job listings

- Maintain placement information and student placement files

- Develop and maintain a current job list for graduating students and alumni

- Interview students and graduates to assist in strategizing for their professional job search

- Provide reports to management on employment progress of specific classes

---

Resume Makeover

Julia's resume is revised to highlight the skills, knowledge, and experience pertinent to her desired position.

1 Julia follows the advice of several career experts and eliminates her street address from her new resume to deter identity theft.

2 Her career counselor qualifications are showcased at the top, listing many of the competencies outlined in the job description.

3 In the Accomplishments section, Julia focuses on the parts of her previous experience that are pertinent to the job. Her skills are organized under three categories: Marketing/Outreach, Relationship Management, and Coaching/Training.

4 She excludes much of her more recent and nonpertinent accomplishments as a program manager so she does not appear overqualified.

5 Her job history is consolidated and shortened under Work History.

6 She ends with an Education section that shows her Bachelor's degree. She mentions her telecommunications major and business minor because these might be important to the university hiring manager.

Julia Jennings

1306 Rydam Circle, Atlanta, GA 78745, 404-123-4567 email@email.com

Experience 4/07 – Present	**Vision Corporation** Atlanta, GA

4

Alliances Program Manager
- Launch and manage global alliances program including worldwide marketing and operations initiatives for 180 partners and a 15-person field team in EMEA, APAC, LATAM, and US
- Develop new processes for partner contracts and fee program, collaborating with Legal, Finance, and Sales Operations teams, resulting in consistency and quality control of contracts and payment of fees
- Key contributor on core teams for corporate-wide initiatives including product launch teams and CRM selection and implementation, providing input on partner needs and requirements
- Manage creation of partner marketing tools including enablement collateral, recruitment guides, product overviews, and sales workbook
- Collaborate with channel marketing manager, driving extranet overhaul, MDF program development, website updates, and field marketing support
- Create and implement worldwide partner enablement plan including technical and sales enablement
- Manage partner leads and pipeline, reporting quarterly and annual results to senior leadership
- Manage relationships with Strategic Partners with a focus on business development and go-to-market initiatives resulting in better tracking of key wins and lead generation
- Led partner sponsorship of annual customer conference, exceeding revenue target by 32%

12/04 – 3/07   **International Micro Devices (IMD)**   Austin, TX

4

Brand & Programs Manager, Server/Workstation Division
- Collaborated with internal teams and hardware partners including IBM, HP, and Sun on branding initiatives and launches including training on nomenclature, messaging, and planning and executing product launch events; Managed "Shop IMD" web presence for Partners HP and Sun
- Provided messaging and demonstration input for server/workstation presence at trade shows and conferences, working closely with internal teams as well as hardware and software partners to build compelling and interesting demos for attendees

Marketing Manager, North America Commercial Marketing
- Collaborated with team to develop demand generation programs with partners with a focus on seminars and events with end-users and partner sales organizations
- Defined and developed a 22-city road show, resulting in expansion of end-user awareness
- Managed vendor relations efforts in the strategy definition, implementation, oversight, and desired metrics for a new lead generation system resulting in 500 Enterprise-level leads
- Part of core events teams that managed IMD's presence at major industry trade shows and events

6/01 – 11/04   **Texas State University, McCoy School of Business**   San Marcos, TX

Associate Director, MBA Career Services
- Served as main internal and external contact for MBA Career Services; managed 6-member team
- Developed and implemented student outreach/tracking program increasing graduation placement rate

Career Development Specialist
- Built and maintained relationships with corporate managers to understand hiring needs and processes to prepare students, resulting in improved yields for companies and increased opportunities for students
- Coached marketing and consulting candidates on job search strategy and execution including analyzing core competencies, strengths, and weaknesses, and developing action plans and deliverables
- Conducted training presentations to groups of employers and students ranging from 10 to 400

8/99 – 1/01   **Premier Technology Partners** – *Campus Recruiter*   Chicago, IL

4

- Created marketing, communication, and event plans to target candidates and build brand recognition on campuses resulting in increased awareness and better yields on offers; collaborated with multi-level internal teams to assess recruiting needs; established budgets for 5 programs

2/97 – 8/99   **Anderson Consulting** – *Campus Recruiting Manager*   Chicago, IL

- Created marketing plans for two top-tier MBA programs including messaging, events, presentations, and interview days for up to 180 candidates

Education   **Indiana University,** Bloomington, IN; Bachelor of Arts, Telecommunications, Business Minor

Julia Jennings

 404-123-4567~ email@email.com ~ Atlanta, GA

Career Counselor

Marketing / Relationship Management / Training

- Consistent achievement in student outreach and tracking programs
- Effective coaching of job search candidates
- Skillful delivery of training presentations
- Successful use of marketing tools and communications
- Expert management of team and community relationships

CORE COMPETENCIES

Leadership
Well organized
Project/program management
Event planning/coordination
Client/relationship management
Business development
Marketing
Training

Networking
Management
Interviewing
Coaching
Oral and written communication skills
Strong presentation skills
Creative problem solver
Computer skills

ACCOMPLISHMENTS

Marketing/Outreach

- Created marketing plans for two top-tier MBA programs including messaging, events, presentations, and interview days for up to 180 candidates

- Developed marketing, communication, and event plans to target candidates and built brand recognition on campuses resulting in increased awareness and better yields on offers; collaborated with multi-level internal teams to assess recruiting needs; established budgets for five programs

- Prepared and implemented student outreach/tracking program, increasing graduation placement rate

- Managed creation of partner marketing tools including enablement collateral, recruitment guides, product overviews, and sales workbook

Relationship Management

- Served as main internal and external contact for MBA Career Services, managing a six-member team

- Built and maintained relationships with corporate managers to understand hiring needs and processes necessary to help prepare students prepare for the job search, resulting in improved yields for companies and increased opportunities for students

Coaching/Training

- Coached marketing and consulting candidates on job search strategy and execution, including analyzing core competencies, strengths, and weaknesses, and developing action plans and deliverables

- Conducted training presentations to groups of employers and students ranging from 10 to 400

WORK HISTORY

2007 – 2009   *Alliances Program Manager* ~ Vision Corporation ~ Atlanta, GA
2004 – 2007   *Brand & Programs Mgr, Server/Workstations* ~ International Micro Devices ~ Austin
              Marketing Manager, North America Commercial Marketing
2001 – 2004   *Associate Director, MBA Career Services* ~ Texas State University, McCoy School of
              Business ~ San Marcos, TX
1999 – 2001   *Campus Recruiter* ~ Premier Technology Partners ~ Chicago, IL
1997 – 1999   *Campus Recruiting Manager* ~ Anderson Consulting ~ Chicago, IL

EDUCATION

Indiana University, Bloomington, IN; Bachelor of Arts, Telecommunications, Business Minor

Retail Sales to Business Development; Housewares to Elder Care

After five years working in retail, Christine Kelleher has been fired from her job. The store is responding to the economy and cutting staff. Being fired was almost a relief, because she had mentally resigned from the company about six months before.

At 60, she found it physically difficult to do the climbing, lifting, and spending long days on her feet. She was also tired of working weekends and evenings. She knows that she must find a less physically demanding job. Christine is reeling from her job loss in the face of a very tight economy. To make matters worse, she is still grieving her mother's recent death.

Out of these seemingly disastrous events, Christine begins to get ideas for her next career. She spent considerable time and energy caring for her mother and later visiting her daily in a nursing home. Although this was unpaid work, she realizes that she has an affinity for seniors and enjoys serving their needs. She also loves organizing events with groups of friends and remembers fondly her time organizing golf tournaments at work. On reflection, she also sees that her most enjoyable work was early in her career as she used her journalism degree and her marketing savvy.

Challenges to Making the Switch

Christine wants to execute a "boomerang" career change—going back to her original training as a journalist and marketer. The problem is that her last marketing job was seven years ago! She is also lacking confidence when competing with the 20-something crowd. She knows that a high-profile, fast-paced career is not for her. She also needs a new resume that doesn't lead with retail. A functional resume will go a long way toward helping her present her marketing experience.

Transferable Skills

Marketing know-how

Event planning

Customer service

Copywriting

Job Description

Business Development Director—Audiology

- Be a consummate and credible professional capable of establishing new partnerships in the senior market in order to reach an ever-expanding client base with hearing products and services

- Develop new business relationships; generate and negotiate new income for the company to an agreed annual target, to increase year after year

- Present to potential clients through direct communication in face-to-face meetings, telephone calls, and e-mails

- Spend 80 percent of the time out of the office in meetings with partners and potential clients; travel is limited to within the metro area, with no overnight travel

- Identify and manage health fair and trade show participation, creating ways to capture and follow up on prospective clients

- Create and manage events that educate potential clients and cement relationships with nursing and retirement homes

- Create and be accountable for all client proposals, contracts, and any further documentation, following company procedures

- Create sales materials, brochures, and educational presentations as necessary to expand awareness in the community

---

Resume Makeover

The challenge is to reformat her resume, which is chronological, into a resume that highlights marketing job performance dating back 10 to 26 years.

❶ Christine brings her resume up to date by adding an e-mail address. She practices e-mail and computer skills that have grown rusty during her retail years.

❷ The headline "Business Development Professional" indicates her target job or objective.

❸ The Resume Billboard area is filled with competencies that match the desired job description.

❹ Direct mailing experience is expanded into an achievement statement that indicates the scope of the project and results.

❺ The golf tournament experience is upgraded to reflect the results achieved for the organization.

❻ The work history section is abbreviated to play down her last two nonmarketing positions.

❼ Employment in teaching and insurance are eliminated because they are not relevant.

❽ University graduation dates are eliminated to help this job candidate seem younger.

Christine Kelleher
1234 81st Street
Des Moines, IA 50300
515-123-4567

Experience
Sales Associate
Bed, Bath & Beyond   2004 - 2009
- Maintained displays in the "hard goods" of small appliances
- Responsible for stocking, marking, and inventory in my department
- Responded to customer questions, assisted with special requests

Food Demonstrator
Dahl's Food Store   2002 - 2004
- Worked in various departments demonstrating products and selling to customers

Associate Director, Annual Fund Programs
Drake University, Des Moines, IA   1999 - 2002
- Managed the development and oversaw mailing of all Annual Fund solicitation letters
- Coordinated direct mail annual fund programs targeting alums, parents, grandparents, alums in reunion years, and "Friends of Drake Arts"
- Set fundraising goals for reunion years – 3 out of 5 classes reached their goal
- Coordinated large annual mailing for 40,000 alums, both donors and non-donors, segmented by school
- Planned meeting and events for "Friends of Drake Arts"
- Acted as staff liaison between the Annual Funds Office and Parents Association
- Coordinated matching gift program
- Represented Drake for 3 years on Iowa College Foundation calls in northwest Iowa

Director, Membership Services
Iowa Grocery Industry Association   1984 - 1999
- Assisted members in relations with government agencies, association board, and other trade associations
- Negotiated discounted services for members from allied companies, including insurance and telephone
- Performed research for members regarding government rules, regulations, and procedures
- Represented Iowa Grocery Industry Association at trade shows, including making arrangements, setting up booth, and interacting with attendees
- Edited bi-monthly magazine; sold advertising space in magazine
- Wrote press releases as needed
- Designed and wrote brochures, fliers, letters for all association activities
- Planned convention, in conjunction with committee, including contracting with speakers and creating registration materials
- Organized golf tournaments and related activities – prizes, gifts, lunch, dinner
- Planned annual awards banquet and related activities – sponsor recognition, emcee, registration
- Set agendas, made arrangements, and compiled materials for committee and board meetings

Other Employment
❼
Teacher – Montessori School of Fargo and Wausau	1976 – 1981
Physicians Mutual Insurance Company	1971 – 1975

Education
❽
- Bachelor of Science, Marketing, Drake University, Des Moines, IA 1984
- Montessori Teaching Certificate, Twin Cities Montessori, St Paul, MN 1976
- Bachelor of Arts, Journalism, Creighton University, Omaha, NE 1971

Christine Kelleher

515-123-4567

1234 81st Street, Des Moines, IA 50300

email@email.com ❶

❷ Business Development Professional

Marketing and communications professional with a desire to work in a professional setting, preferably in elder care. Experienced in business development, fundraising, account management, and client service.

❸
- Client Development/Relations
- Direct Marketing
- Event Planning
- Sales & Educational Presentations

- Customer/Client Service
- Promotional copywriting
- Trade Shows, Conventions
- Create ads, brochures, press releases

Professional Accomplishments

Business Development

❹
❺
- Managed and oversaw annual fundraising campaign to more than 40,000 alums, generating an average of $3.5 million per year
- Created and organized Annual Golf Tournament, including sponsorships, gifts, and prizes, generating $65,000 or more in revenue each year for our association
- Negotiated discount services with national vendors such as AT&T, FedEx, and Office Max to enrich our "member services" package
- Planned Annual Convention as both a fundraiser and membership builder; made all arrangements, contracted for speakers, sold sponsorships; coordinated volunteers

Client/Customer Services
- Worked directly with retail customers -- special orders; gift registry
- Assisted Grocery Association members in relations with governmental agencies
- Served large-dollar donors, providing information and recognition
- Acted as a liaison between university staff and parents association
- Researched government rules, regulations, and procedures for members

Marketing Communications
- Wrote and edited a bi-monthly magazine distributed to 3,600 members statewide
- Designed and wrote press releases, brochures, fliers, and letters for member campaigns
- Organized industry trade shows including displays, giveaways, volunteers, lead generation, follow-up, and ROI assessment

❻ Work History

Sales Associate	Bed, Bath & Beyond	2004 - 2009
Food Demonstrator	Dahl's Food Store, Des Moines, IA	2002 - 2004
Associate Director, Annual Fund Programs	Drake University, Des Moines, IA	1999 - 2002
Director, Member Services	Iowa Grocery Association, Des Moines, IA	1984 - 1999

Education

❽
BS, Marketing	Drake University, Des Moines, IA
BA, Journalism	Creighton University, Omaha, NE

Retail Sales to Engineer; Clothing to Government

Elaine Mitchell is a stay-at-home mom who has spent nearly 15 years raising her three children. Her volunteer work includes a community playground and some water resources work for her local township. While she kept the books for her husband's small business, her only paid work in the last decade has been as a retail clerk. She wants to boost her family's lifestyle by putting her degree in civil engineering back to work.

Environmental preservation is Elaine's passion. Her perfect job would be a water resources engineer with a civil engineering firm, doing public projects such as dams, wetlands, preservation, and so on. While her college work included this specialty, she has only volunteer work in this field.

Challenges to Making the Switch

Elaine starts her job search by interviewing a few friends who are in the field. Her hopes of working for a private civil engineering firm are diminished as she learns that funding for public works is stalled due to the economy. Her lack of a Professional Engineer (PE) designation might limit her growth inside an engineering firm, anyway.

Her fear that she will have to start over as a rookie engineer is confirmed, but she also finds out that engineering graduates are highly prized because there is a shortage in the field. She decides to try for a government engineering job, where she can learn the ropes again and not have to focus on studying for her PE license.

Transferable Skills

Drafting/designing

Knowledge of engineering/construction principles

Permitting for public works projects

Project management

Proposal writing

Client contact/customer service

Business management

Staff supervision

Bookkeeping

Job Description
Air Quality Engineer

- Work with environmental staff and inspect client facilities to support the state's air quality program

- Monitor compliance with all state, local, and federal regulations governing facility operations, air quality and environmental compliance, permitting, and remediation

- Utilize technical writing, communication, and organizational skills in preparing reports and responses to air permitting requests

- Conduct air quality compliance and engineering tasks in support of a Title V air quality management program

- Perform emission calculations, permitting, rule analysis, and compliance tasks for manufacturing facilities

- Conduct workplace inspections to ensure compliance with air quality requirements

- Required: Bachelor's degree in environmental science, chemistry, engineering, physical, or biological science

Resume Makeover

Elaine's resume is completely revamped to highlight her engineering experience, even though it goes back 15 years.

1 The Executive Summary allows her to include all the engineering experiences she has had, even though several were volunteer.

2 She specifies that she expects to start over at entry level, acknowledging her rusty experience.

3 The Skills Profile allows her to include all of her primary engineering competencies.

4 She presents her engineering experience first, even though it is the first work she has done.

5 "Field Experience" allows her to summarize all the on-the-job skills she gained in her early years.

6 She presents her Volunteer Work section next because it is engineering related.

7 Her current job experience is presented last because it is not relevant to this search.

Elaine Mitchell

1234 Lakeway Drive, Georgetown, TX 78600 ◆ 512-123-4567 Cell ◆ email@email.com

QUICK SIGNS, INC., Georgetown, TX   2006-Present
Co-Owner/Office Manager
- Manage the flow of jobs, creating worksheets and invoices
- Generate billing and actively monitor collections
- Supervise bookkeeping and manage office paperwork

JC PENNEY, Round Rock, TX   2005-Present
Associate
- Customer service; some training and mentoring
- Cashier
- Zoning and replenishing

NJ CAP – New Jersey Child Assault Prevention Program, Phillipsburg, NJ   2005-2006
Facilitator (Grades K-6)
- Completed special Child Assault Prevention training
- Role Player Facilitator in classroom skits demonstrating child assault prevention scenarios

HOPE TOWNSHIP BOARD OF EDUCATION – Playground Committee   2002-2006
Chairperson
- Successfully wrote and won grants totaling $30,000
- Led fundraisers that resulted in an additional $10,000
- Tested playground equipment, creating a cost-effective and kid-friendly design
- Managed vendors and suppliers to our limited budget

HOPE TOWNSHIP ENVIRONMENTAL COMMISSION   2002-2006
Commission Member
- One of eight-member Commission
- Monitored construction activities for environmental issues such as water run-off, erosion, and pollution
- Conducted Limestone Inventory for Hope Township to ensure safe groundwater resources
- Successfully re-designed a 20-acre park in order to protect the lake and native plant species

QUINN, SMITH & ASSOCIATES, Pompano Beach, FL   1992-1994
Consulting Engineers – Land Development
Engineer, Project Manager, and Design Engineer
- Coordinated all permitting for the firm
- Certified projects to the various agencies where permits were held
- Prepared all legal documents for project close-outs
- Inspected job sites as the client representative

HARRY A. THOMAS & ASSOCIATES, Pompano Beach, FL   1987-1992
Consulting Engineers, Planners & Surveyors
Design Engineer – Land Development Department
- Approved shop drawings; some drafting
- Coordinated as-built work
- Coordinated permitting

Education
Florida Atlantic University, Boca Raton, FL, 1988-1989
Master's Degree Program in Environmental & Water Resources Engineering (Civil Engineering Program)
Completed courses in Marine Reinforced Concrete Design, Water Resources System Engineering, Dynamic Hydrology, and Water Quality and Treatment

Texas A&M University, 1986
Bachelor of Science, Maritime Systems Engineering, Specializing in Ocean Engineering

Elaine Mitchell

1234 Lakeway Drive, Georgetown, TX 78600   512-123-4567 Cell   email@email.com

Executive Summary

Engineering graduate with experience in land development, parks, playgrounds, and water resources. Adept at construction services and client representation. Seasoned volunteer with experience in grant writing, committee leadership, coordination, and environmental issues.

Ideal job – entry level position in engineering or related field, utilizing background in client representation on environmental issues, land utilization, and urban development.

Skills Profile

- Civil Engineering with Water Resources Emphasis
- Construction Services
- Permitting & Certifications
- Grant Writing
- Small Business Bookkeeping
- Business Process Management
- Supervision of Hourly Employees
- Community Leadership

Engineering Experience

QUINN, SMITH & ASSOCIATES, Pompano Beach, FL, 1992 - 1994
Consulting Engineers – Land Development
Engineer, Project Manager, and Design Engineer

- Coordinated all permitting for the firm
- Certified projects to the various agencies where permits were held
- Prepared all legal documents for project close-outs
- Inspected job sites as the client representative
- Conducted job coordination and pre-construction meetings
- Working knowledge of contract documents and specifications, invitations to bid, and proposals
- Conducted field site inspections

HARRY A. THOMAS & ASSOCIATES, Pompano Beach, FL, 1987 - 1992
Consulting Engineers, Planners & Surveyors
Design Engineer – Land Development Department

- Drafting
- Approved shop drawings
- Coordinated as-built work
- Coordinated permitting
- Certified projects to the various agencies where permits were held
- Prepared all legal documents for project close-outs
- Processed pay applications
- Conducted job coordination and pre-construction meetings

Field Experience

- Water pressure tests
- Sewer inspections
- Inspections on underground utilities
- On-site meetings
- Bridge construction – project management; inspection
- Concrete slump tests
- Asphalt and concrete tests
- Park re-design

Elaine Mitchell

Volunteer Work

HOPE TOWNSHIP SCHOOL BOARD OF EDUCATION – Playground Committee, 2002 - 2006
Chairperson

- Successfully wrote and won grants totaling $30,000
- Led fundraisers that resulted in an additional $10,000
- Tested playground equipment, creating a cost-effective and kid-friendly design
- Managed vendors and suppliers to the limited budget
- Successfully managed three phases of a community build; managing approximately 100 volunteers

HOPE TOWNSHIP ENVIRONMENTAL COMMISSION, 2002 - 2006
Commission Member

- One of eight-member Commission
- Monitored construction activities for environmental issues, such as water runoff, erosion, and pollution
- Conducted Limestone Inventory for Hope Township to ensure safe groundwater resources
- Successfully re-designed a 20-acre park in order to protect the lake and native plant species

Recent Professional Experience

QUICK SIGNS, INC. Georgetown, TX, 2006 - Present
Co-Owner/Office Manager

- Manage job scheduling, creating supporting work orders and invoices
- Manage accounts receivables and actively monitor collections
- Supervise bookkeeping and manage office paperwork

JC PENNEY, Round Rock, TX, 2005 - Present
Associate

NJ CAP – New Jersey Child Assault Prevention Program, Phillipsburg, NJ, 2005 - 2006
Facilitator (Grades K-6)

Education

Florida Atlantic University, Boca Raton, FL, 1988 - 1989
Started Master's Degree Program in Environmental & Water Resources Engineering
Completed courses in Marine Reinforced Concrete Design, Water Resources System Engineering, Dynamic Hydrology, and Water Quality and Treatment

Texas A&M University, 1986
Bachelor of Science – Maritime Systems Engineering, specializing in Ocean Engineering

Computer Skills

Microsoft Word   Microsoft Excel
Cyrious – POS Management Software   Intuit QuickBooks

Retail Sales to Contracts Manager; Hardware to Software

Nadine Simpson has a solid background in accounting, auditing, and finance. After being fired from her university position as business manager, she felt the need for a fresh start near her family. She moved to California and took a job that would be fun and creative—window and blinds consultant for a national hardware store. Now, after two years in retail, she is being downsized.

Nadine was depressed about her job loss at first because she dreaded going back to accounting as a profession. Through coaching, however, she was able to see what parts of her former jobs she truly liked: business management, client and vendor contact, and working in a dynamic, fast-paced office. She also remembered how much she enjoyed creating systems to capture and monitor information. She is ready to go back to her old career, accounting and office management. If she can find the right environment, she will likely enjoy it again.

While looking for an accounting position, she discovers a job description for contracts manager and realizes that she has the qualifications. By creating a functional resume, she was able to highlight the skills most critical for the job.

Challenges to Making the Switch

Nadine has some experience with contracts from her business management days, but that was more than five years ago. She certainly has never written contracts nor even had to revise them. She will need to emphasize her quick learning skills in the interview.

The job requires knowledge of CostPoint software, which she does not have. She plans to research the software and its capabilities so she can talk about it in the interview. She will also describe how she has tackled new software and applications in the past.

Nadine is naturally a reserved, shy person. The contracts manager job will demand that she relate to all the company departments, plus all its clients and vendors. Luckily, she has been meeting the public, discerning their needs, and resolving any issues that came up with custom orders. She will describe her new skills in the interview.

It has been nearly five years since Nadine has worked in an office and as an accountant. The contracts manager job will require her to be far more detail-oriented than she has been of late. She is also a little concerned about sitting behind a desk all day.

Transferable Skills

Accounting, auditing, compliance, contracts

Vendor relations

Managerial skills

Negotiations

Customer service

Exacting written and oral communication

Collection letters and phone calls

Job Description
Contracts Manager

- Seeking a contracts manager with a Bachelor's or higher degree in accounting, business, contracts, or finance

- Responsible for administration of multiple contracts of varying size and complexity using internal and external consultants

- Maintain and update consultant time sheet software, keeping a close eye on budgets and alerting team leaders to overages in a timely way; CostPoint software experience a plus

- Assist in preparing and negotiating subcontracts, ensuring compliance with prime contract terms and conditions to include flow-down provisions

- Interface with customers, internal consultants, and external contractors for negotiation and contract administration, change order management, and adherence to contract terms and conditions

- Interface with both the client and internal team leaders on the status of contract completion and alert management to any service deficiencies or other client concerns

---

Resume Makeover

Nadine's resume has been expanded to two pages in order to provide more detail about her responsibilities and achievements that relate to the contracts manager job.

1 The resume title highlights her former business manager position and includes the targeted job, contracts administration.

2 In the Core Competencies section, she emphasizes her proficiency in technical applications and client/vendor contact. The key words CostPoint, vendor, contract, and negotiations are included to match the job description.

3 Because business software will be a big part of her next job, it is given its own section.

4 The new functional organization of experience allows Nadine to direct attention to business/contract management, technology, and vendor/customer relations—all of critical importance in her target job.

5 Nadine's accounting/audit background is relegated to the end of the functional skills on page two.

1234 Stromley Avenue, San Jose, CA 95100
408-123-4567 Home 408-123-5555 Mobile
email@email.com

Nadine Simpson

Experience   4/2006–present   Home Depot   Campbell, CA
Sales Associate, Decor Department

- Sell in-stock and special-order window coverings and wallpaper to designers, contractors, and DIY customers
- Educate customers about features of various types of window and wall coverings and methods of installation

6/2003–10/2005   University of Colorado   Boulder, CO
Business Manager, Student Media Department

- Responsible for all aspects of billing and accounts receivable for advertising in the student newspaper. Yearly sales over $750,000
- Supervised human resources and payroll function for over 125 hourly employees
- Performed other accounting functions including purchasing, accounts payable, travel, budgeting, and financial analysis
- Managed office operations including ordering office supplies, supervising receptionists, and distributing mail
- Managed distribution of newspapers and supervised student delivery personnel

10/1998–4/2003   University of Iowa   Iowa City, IA
Internal Auditor, Office of Internal Audit

- Planned and conducted audits of various University departments and functional areas; duties included writing audit programs, performing audit procedures, monitoring compliance with University policies, and financial analysis
- Made oral and written presentations of audit findings to various levels departmental and administrative management
- Developed and maintained a MS Access database of audit reports and findings as well as the office web page

1/1996–10/1998   Union Pacific Corporation   Omaha, NE
Senior Auditor, Corporate Audit Staff

- Planned and conducted all phases of financial and operational audits of subsidiary companies
- Made oral and written presentations of audit findings to various levels of financial and operating department management
- Supervised and evaluated the performance of staff auditors, responsible for training auditors, assigning subordinates to specific review areas, and monitoring audit progress to ensure timely completion of assignments

Education   1991–1995   University of Iowa   Iowa City, IA
Bachelor of Business Administration - Accounting
Graduated with High Distinction

Skills   Passed Certified Public Accountant Examination in May 1995
Proficient in QuickBooks and Microsoft Office applications such as Word, Excel, Access, Outlook, and PowerPoint
Continuing studies in C++ and MS Access programming

NADINE SIMPSON

BUSINESS MANAGER/CONTRACTS ADMINISTRATION

1234 Stromley Ave.   San Jose, CA 95100   H: 408-123-4567   C: 408-123-5555   email@email.com

FINANCIAL ANALYSIS/CONTRACT ADMINISTRATION/BUSINESS MANAGEMENT

CPA-certified Staff Accountant with 10 years experience in financial analysis, business management, budgeting, forecasting, internal audits, and contracts. Especially proficient in accounting and database software. Continuing studies in C++ and MS Access Programming.

CORE COMPETENCIES

- MS Access Database Proficient
- Managed Vendor Relationships
- Oversaw Ad Revenue Accounting
- Presentations to VP-Level

- CostPoint Experience
- Contract Negotiations
- Annual Budgeting
- Forecasting

- Consolidated Financial Statements
- Monitoring Internal Controls
- Knowledgeable in GAAP
- Planned and Led Internal Audits

BUSINESS & ACCOUNTING SOFTWARE

Excel	Word	Great Plains	FrontPage
CostPoint	Outlook	QuickBooks	HTML
Access	PowerPoint		

PROFESSIONAL EXPERTISE

Business/Contract Management

- Responsible for all aspects of billing and account receivables for advertising in the student newspaper of Colorado State University. Yearly sales: $750,000.
- Managed office operations in an office with 8 full-time professional employees and more than 100 student journalists, technical and advertising sales staff.
- Negotiated contacts and managed a group of 14 student delivery personnel, who distributed 15,000 copies each weekday.
- Supervised and evaluated the performance of staff auditors.

Technology

- Designed and implemented an Access Database to consolidate and analyze common audit findings. Published reports on internal University website in order to share best practices.
- Customized and maintained timesheet software for hourly professional employees and 100 student journalists, technical, and advertising sales staff.
- Designed the first departmental website for Iowa State University's Internal Audit group. Self-taught in FrontPage.

Vendor/Customer Relations

- Sourced special-order window coverings and wallpaper for designers, contractors, and do-it-yourself customers. During my tenure of 2 years, my store increased window and wall orders by 15%.
- Researched and invoiced over $27,000 in uncollected revenue from a major advertising agency. Brought account up-to-date and retained the advertising clients.

Communication Skills

- Made oral and written presentations of audit findings to various levels of departmental and administrative management.
- Provided business forecasts and financial analysis to VP-level executives.
- In retail career, educated customers and designers about features of window and wall coverings and explained installation techniques.

Accounting/Audit

- Planned and conducted all phases of financial and operation audits of subsidiary companies of the Union Pacific Corporation, the nation's largest railway.
- Planned and conducted audits of various University of Iowa departments and functional areas.
- Performed accounting functions including purchasing, account payable, travel, budgeting, and financial analysis for a $750,000-income student newspaper.
- Wrote audit programs, performed audit procedures, monitored compliance with policies, financial analysis.
- Led auditing teams, assigning subordinates to specific review areas, monitoring audit progress to ensure timely completion of assignments.

PROFESSIONAL WORK HISTORY

Sales Associate, Décor Department		
Home Depot	Campbell, CA	2006 - Present
Business Manager, Student Media Department		
University of Colorado	Boulder, CO	2003 - 2005
Internal Auditor		
University of Iowa	Iowa City, IA	1998 - 2003
Senior Auditor		
Union Pacific Corporation	Omaha, NE	1996 - 1998

EDUCATION AND PROFESSIONAL DEVELOPMENT

Bachelor of Business Administration – Accounting   University of Iowa, Iowa City, IA   1995
Graduated with High Distinction
Certified Public Accountant Examination – Passed in May 1995
Continuing Studies in C++ and MS Access programming

Recruiter to Administrator; Staffing to Information Technology (IT)

Kay Peterson was working for a small staffing firm where she was responsible for placing office and temporary workers. She enjoyed interviewing candidates and helping them prepare for interviews. When the volume of job orders dropped off due to changes in the economy, however, she moved into sales and business development where she was under a great deal of pressure to produce. After months of struggling to meet quota, she was dismissed. During that time, she also lost her husband to cancer. As a result, Kay realized that she needs to make a change in order to reclaim her life balance. She wants to go back to an administrative role that has regular hours and less stress but where her talents for organization and customer service will be valued. She has her eye on a program coordinator position with a local company that provides services and support for computing tasks on a mainframe system.

Challenges to Making the Switch

Kay has worked as a recruiter for the last three years, which demands a high level of customer service and people orientation but does not showcase her talent for organization and coordinating tasks. She has taken classes and achieved several certifications in this field, which demonstrates her commitment to excellence in recruiting. Her administrative experience took place earlier in her career, so a potential employer may fear that she sees this move as a step backward.

Kay's challenge is to convince the employer that her reasons for making the change are legitimate and permanent and that her achievements in recruiting will enhance her ability to perform administrative tasks effectively.

The administrative position she is seeking includes interaction with customers and internal staff, so her experience as a liaison between candidates and employers naturally applies.

Transferable Skills

Customer service

Problem-solving skills

Multitasking in a stressful environment

Task coordination and organization

Documentation and reporting

Job Description

Administrative Program Coordinator

- Position requires a broad base of knowledge and skills with a focus on customer satisfaction and quick response/solutions to problems; activities include a high degree of customer interaction, thus requiring a customer-oriented employee with good people skills

- Monitor call center mailboxes for tech support, billing questions, and usage requests daily (three- to six-hour shifts)

- Analyze requests from vendors and dispatch to one of 23 technicians according to system and issue; make initial e-mail or voicemail contact and dispatch calls to technicians for resolution; follow up with requester for further response needed (average 1 to 20 issues an hour)

- Process paperwork related to support issues and resolutions, obtain management signatures, make copies, and distribute to customers and files

- Perform system administration tasks in various systems to resolve support issues, coordinate requests with technicians and solution developers, and notify customers of solutions

- Requires a high degree of organization and the ability to management complex tasks involving multiple required steps in a timely and customer-focused manner

---

Resume Makeover

Kay's executive assistant and task coordination skills are moved to the top of her resume to highlight her ability to perform these tasks.

❶ The Executive Summary of her original resume is replaced by a Skills Summary featuring experience specifically related to the role of office administrator. The third-person language (which uses "she") is replaced by the more current first-person language (which uses "I").

❷ Relevant administrative jobs are moved to the Career Highlights section so that they are listed before the more recent recruiting experience, which appears first in the Chronological Experience section.

❸ Specific details are added to each of Kay's recruiting and administrative jobs in her Chronological Experience section to emphasize results.

❹ Each job description is expanded to include the customer service or executive assistant tasks that were included. She retains the month/year style in order to showcase short-term jobs that were administrative in nature.

❺ Every temporary or contract position is listed with a short description to demonstrate Kay's flexibility and willingness to learn new tasks. Evidence of success is included to show her ability to master those tasks quickly.

Kay Peterson

512. 123.4567
email@email.com

Executive Summary

A results-oriented professional with over 4 years in the staffing industry in Dallas and Austin. Her customer focus is proven by her success in developing and maintaining business partners like Microsoft, Peterbilt, IBM, TRW, and Advanced Micro Devices. Her demonstrated strengths are developing strong business relationships and building a strategic network of clients and candidates in the local community.

Professional Experience

DIVERSIFIED SOURCING SOLUTIONS, Fort Worth, Texas   July 2008 to May 2009
Human Resources Recruiter responsible for recruiting in six branch offices in Dallas and Fort Worth. Activities included screening candidates, marketing to client organizations, and negotiating contracts.

JPS HEALTH NETWORK, Fort Worth, Texas
June 2008 to July 2008
Human Resource Assistant, contract, responsible for coordinating New Hire documentation for health professionals, employment verification, and conducting pre-screening interviews by telephone.

MANPOWER NORTH AMERICA, Irving, Texas   December 2007 to May 2008
Human Resource Recruiter, corporate employee.

TRIAD FINANCIAL CORPORATION, Dallas, Texas   August 2007 to November 2007
Human Resource Assistant, contract. Project: Recruited and processed over 900 applicants to fill 46 positions within 4 weeks, including a successful job fair. Positions were Customer Care and Collections requisitions. Tracked candidates from Internet's ADP contact management database. Created offer letters for new employees and coordinated documents for new hires. Scheduled interviews and follow-ups using Microsoft Office Outlook calendar function.

AUSTIN 3-1-1 CALL CENTER, Austin, Texas   January 2007 to July 2007
Executive Assistant to Director of Call Center, contract

IBM, Austin, Texas   July 2006 to December 2006
Executive Assistant, contract. Supported Program Director and 7 managers for IBM's Industry Solutions Software Group. Consistently set up 15-plus US and International conference meetings using IBM Lotus Notes 7 database on a daily basis. Confirming attendance of major key players.

KEY DIRECTIONS, Austin, Texas   2001 to 2005
Creating curriculum and presenting training workshops for communication and career enhancement for Austin Energy Laboratories, First Magnus Financial, Texas Legal Partners, University of Texas, Austin Community College, and local associations in Austin.

THOMSON LEARNING, DRAKE BEAM MORIN INC, Austin, TX   August 2001 to 2004
Thomson, an $8 billion business: Leading provider in knowledge transfer in the medical and educational fields which merged with Drake Beam Morin, the national outplacement service with over 200 offices nationally.
Trainer and Career Consultant
Creating and facilitating career-oriented workshops for Applied Materials and Motorola clients, and coaching individuals on resume development, interviewing skills, and career search strategies.
- Generated business job leads from experience in staffing industry and community network which resulted in 30% placement during economic technical downturn in Austin in 2001.
- Managed and coached 154 diverse clients from Applied Materials in career search strategies.
- Developed new curriculum and facilitated weekly interactive Career Strategy workshops using PowerPoint.

Kay Peterson   512-123-4567

VOLT SERVICES, Technical Division, Austin, Texas   June 2000 to August 2001
National contingency staffing firm with 300 offices nationally.
Technical Recruiter
Proactively added to the business client base and provided contract and direct hire technical staffing solutions for project managers, software developers, database administrators, technical writers, desktop and network support engineers for businesses in the Austin community. Some of the established clients included Advanced Micro Devices.
- Recruited and qualified first placement in 2½ weeks after starting with Volt.
- Qualified and placed 20 technical and management contractors and direct employees in the first 6 months.
- Developed new business relationships from proactively networking in the community including volunteer position as Ambassador for Technical Business Network organization in Austin.

BUSINESS CONTROL SYSTEMS, Austin, Texas   June 1999 to June 2000
Technical Recruiter
Demonstrated ability to meet immediate and long-term Information Technology staffing solutions for state and public client base as well as corporate clients. Staffing solutions included these skills: Project Managers, software developers, desktop and network engineers.
- Developed and maintained new and existing business relationships.
- Identified, screened, and presented qualified applicants to clients and negotiated contract rates.

EUROSTAFF; Division of EUROSOFT, Austin, Texas   September 1998 to March 1999
Account Manager
Promoted to Account Manager as point of contact for the National Health Insurance Corporation (NHIC) account, division of Electronic Data Systems. Our division met and exceeded our customers' expectations:
- Tripled branch's candidate placements: **3 to 15** per week.
- Increased billing hours from **1,000 to 3,300** weekly.
- Interviewed, tested, and qualified up to 40 applicants a month for **NHIC** managers.

Technical Recruiter
Marketed and established professional relationships with department managers in Austin's technical market, including state and local offices, SWBell, EDS, and IBM. Interviewed, screened, and presented prospective applicants to clients. Using Word, Excel, and Fox Pro database.

SNELLING SEARCH, Denton, Texas   November 1997 to June 1998
Recruiter, Technical Division
Marketed technical and network support engineers for diversified customer base including: **Microsoft, Peterbilt, and First State Bank.**

PERSONNEL CONNECTION, Las Colinas, Texas   August 1997 to November 1998
Clerical and Technical Staffing Recruiter - Contract
Screened, interviewed, and tested clerical and technical (bench technicians) applicants. Counseled employees on performance issues. Used Caldwell Spartin's Tempware 5 software to query database and match skilled applicants with open orders.

Education and Training

Associates Degree in Business, American Institute of Commerce, Davenport, Iowa
Certified Technical Recruiter, Snelling University, Dallas, Texas

Professional Organizations

National Speakers Association (Local and National membership)
Toastmasters International, CTM, public speaking organization
Women's Chamber of Austin
Executive Women International
National Business Exchange (Business Entrepreneur Association)

Kay Peterson, PHR

512.123.4567

email@email.com

① SKILLS SUMMARY

- 6 years Executive Assistant with Fortune 500 corporations
- Legal/Executive Secretary (63 Hrs) Diploma – Kaplan University
- Associate Arts, Business – Graduate December 2009

Ability to prioritize within critical timelines	Proficient in drafting/editing documents
Strong customer service orientation	Prepared and audited expense reports
Ability to manage multiple priorities and complex tasks efficiently	Effective liaison between direct reports and management
MS Outlook, Word, Excel, PowerPoint	1.5 years using Lotus Notes 7 Database

② CAREER HIGHLIGHTS – OFFICE MANAGEMENT

IBM, contract in Austin, Texas

Executive Assistant

- Supported Financial Program Director and 7 managers for IBM's Financial Solutions.
- Consistently set up 15 plus U.S. and International conference meetings and conference calls using IBM Lotus Notes 7 database on a daily basis. Confirming attendance of major key players and coordinating schedule of each was set for calls. Additionally, made travel arrangements for executives for national and international conferences.
- Drafted and edited correspondence for director and managers.
- Coordinated resources, catering, and audio-visual equipment for conferences.

AUSTIN 3-1-1 Call Center, Austin, Texas

Executive Assistant to Director of Call Center, contract

- Temporary assignment while Executive Assistant was on extended leave.
- Coordinated schedule for Director and conferences in center.
- Assisted supervisors by conducting telephone and personal interviews to screen customer service candidates, ensuring quality candidates were selected for ongoing new hire classes.
- Left to relocate to Fort Worth, Texas, after contract was completed.

CHRONOLOGICAL EXPERIENCE

Diversified Sourcing Solutions, Fort Worth, Texas   07/2008 to 10/2008

Human Resources Recruiter

Full Desk Recruiting for 6 branch offices in Dallas and Fort Worth.

- First placement brought in $5,100 after 2 weeks on the desk.
- Marketing candidates by calling decision makers and negotiating contracts.
- Screening candidates to match open job orders.
- Left due to financial down-turn and re-organizational downsizing by seniority.

③ JPS Health Network, Fort Worth, Texas   06/2008 to 07/2008

Human Resource Assistant, contract

- Coordinating New Hire documentation for Allied Health Professionals
- Calling to verify education and past employment
- Candidate pre-screening telephone interviews
- Left for full-time position

Manpower North America, Irving, Texas,   12/2007 to 5/2008

Human Resource Recruiter, corporate employee

Full Desk Recruiting: Client development, sourcing, screening, and placing business professionals in the Dallas area.

- Placements increased branch office billings $100,000 in 8 weeks.
- Marketed staffing service to corporate hiring managers.
- Negotiated fees and contracts for staffing services.
- Generated management reports in MS Excel and MS Word.

Kay Peterson, PHR

512-123-4567

④ Triad Financial Corporation, recruiting project   8/2007 to 11/2007

Human Resource Assistant, contract

- **Project:** Recruited and processed over 900 applicants to fill 46 positions within 4 weeks, including a successful job fair. Positions were Customer Care and Collections requisitions.
- Tracked candidates from Internet's ADP contact management database.
- Created offer letters for new employees and coordinated documents for new hires.
- Scheduled interviews and follow-ups using Microsoft Office Outlook calendar function

AUSTIN 3-1-1 Call Center, Austin, Texas   1/2007 to 7/2007

Executive Assistant to Director of Call Center, contract

- Temporary assignment while Executive Assistant was on extended leave.
- Coordinated schedule for Director and conferences in center.
- Assisted supervisors by conducting telephone and personal interviews to screen customer service candidates, ensuring quality candidates for ongoing new hire classes.
- Left to relocate to Fort Worth, Texas, after contract was completed.

④ IBM, Austin, Texas   7/2005 to 12/2006

Executive Assistant, contract

Supported Program Director and 7 managers for IBM's Industry Solutions Software Group.

Executive Assistant

- Supported Program Director and 7 managers for IBM's Industry Solutions Software Group.
- Consistently set up 15 plus U.S. and International conference meetings using IBM Lotus Notes 7 database on a daily basis. Confirming attendance of major key players.

⑤ Key Directions, Austin, Texas   6/2003 to 7/2005

Human Resource Consultant

Marketed communications training classes to corporate clients in Austin and Fort Worth.

Created curriculum and facilitated training workshops. Clients included:

Austin Energy Laboratories, First Magnus Financial, and University of Texas.

Thomson Learning, DBM Inc, Human Resource Mgt, Austin, Texas   8/2001 to 6/2003

Thomson: an $8B business, a national outplacement/Human Resource Management organization.

Human Resource Career Consultant, contract

- **Created** and facilitated career-oriented workshops for Applied Materials and Motorola clients and coached individuals on resume development, interviewing skills, career search strategies, and salary negotiations.
- **Generated** management reports for tracking progress in MS Excel and follow-up with clients and their ongoing career search and attendance to educational workshops.

⑤ Volt Services, Technical Staffing, Austin, Texas   6/2000 to 8/2001

Recruiter and Account Manager

Marketed, screened, and placed top-quality candidates for short- and long-term technical projects for hiring managers in Austin, including IBM and Advanced Micro Devices.

⑤ Relevant Experience:

Executive Assistant to Director of Sales for Marriott Park Central, Dallas, Texas	1991 – 1993
Executive Assistant to Telops Manager for GTE Telops, Irving, Texas	1994 – 1996

EDUCATION AND TRAINING

Human Resource Professional Certification (PHR) University of Texas, Austin

Associate of Arts - Business, Tarrant County Community College (Graduate December 2009), Fort Worth, Texas

Legal/Executive Assistant Diploma, Kaplan University, (63 hours), Davenport, Iowa

Society of Human Resource Management Association, National and Fort Worth Member

Toastmasters International, Public Speaking Organization

Retired to Mortgage Administrator; Library to Banking

Kathleen Winkelman and her husband have retired twice: once when they sold their bookstore business and a second time when her husband was offered an early retirement package at his financial services company. They once thought they were set for life and were through working. They even bought property in France and lived there for a number of years. Then, the financial markets crashed—and their retirement income decreased by 80 percent.

Kathleen's husband suffered a heart attack last year and is struggling to find a job in his former career as an insurance executive. She decided to go back to work full-time to restore their monthly income.

Challenges to Making the Switch

Kathleen has a very spotty work history. While she was raising her children, she worked now and then at mostly hourly jobs without a lot of responsibility.

Her major achievements are volunteer work for the local entrepreneurs association and the YMCA. She managed to secure federal funding for a beautification project led by the entrepreneurs in the Old Town District in downtown Madison, Wisconsin. She has also been a business owner and has a very independent spirit. Her original resume reflects this attitude. The emphasis on retirement and half-time work, however, portrays her as someone who really doesn't want to work.

Ironically, the mortgage industry crisis provides her the perfect entry back into the work world. When she reads the job ad for mortgage administrator, she realizes the duties are very similar to her work in the Dane County Attorney's office. Although the environments are completely different, the same detail orientation and devotion to rules and legal nuances are required. She updates her resume to specifically reflect these duties.

Transferable Skills

Customer service

Inbound and outbound phone contact

Verifying documentation

Resolving documentation issues

Researching legal details

Counseling customers

Online processing of transactions

Communication skills

Job Description

Mortgage Administrator

- Perform a variety of loan servicing tasks within a banking environment

- Handle inbound and outbound customer calls

- Provide customer account updates, verify loan documentation and credit information

- Resolve problems regarding documentation issues

- Assist in researching and resolve discrepancies

- Update and counsel borrowers on the status of their file, provide options, and walk them through the process

- Process routine to complex transactions online

- Resolve routine to moderately complex problems and inquiries, and refer difficult problems to specialists

- Must have six months experience, preferably in legal, banking, customer service/call center, loss mitigation, mortgage industry, sales, or collections environment

- Outstanding communication skills

- Professional demeanor

Resume Makeover

Kathleen's resume needs a complete overhaul. Using "Resume of" is extremely old-style. She finds a Microsoft Word template that helps her upgrade the style, typefaces, and organization.

1 She minimizes her recent part-time job at the library. While current, it is far less important than her former experience at the County Attorney's office.

2 The headline "Office Administrator" is designed to match, as nearly as she can, the title "Mortgage Administrator."

3 Her wide-ranging experience is simplified into three functional categories, and each one represents one to three jobs.

4 Her office experiences at the Dane County Attorney's office match quite closely to her desired work as a loan administrator. These duties are placed at the top of the accomplishments under the functional title "Legal Research/Case Specialist."

5 Her Education and career history items are separated so they can be understood more easily.

6 In Career Highlights, she includes her most important jobs in reverse chronological order. She will have to address the gaps in employment in her cover letter and interview. The simplest and most truthful explanation is, "I was raising my family and being a homemaker."

7 Under Education, her legal assistant certificate is placed first because that knowledge will play an important role in the mortgage administrator job.

Resume of

Kathleen Winkelman
1234 Maple Street, Madison, WI 53701

email@email.com; Cell: 708-123-4567

Objective: Clerical and/or customer service work in downtown area.

Recent Experience:
❶ Half-time Customer Service Clerk, Madison Public Library, May 2006-November 2008

Checking materials in/out; issuing library cards; collecting fines; processing, and shelving

Customer Service, Dorothy's Dress Shop, Madison, November 2005-May 2006

Opening shop; serving customers; operating cash register; maintaining health standards

Skills:
Communications: Greeting customers; handling telephones; writing, copy reading and proofreading; editing newsletters; developing training materials; facilitating workshops; interviewing for hiring, feature writing and legal documents

Computer Operations: Data entry/retrieval; inventory management; word processing

Retail Operations: Customer service; cash register and credit card machines; ordering, shipping and receiving

❺ **Education and Career History:**
B.A. Political Science, University of Wisconsin, Madison, 1981
Human Resources in Insurance, Human Services, and City Government; 1981-1991
Legal Assistant Certificate of Specialization, Madison Area Technical College, 1993
Retired from Dane County Attorney's Office, Madison, WI, June 1996
Volunteered for YWCA Women Against Violence Program
Organized Old Town Residents, Neighbors, and Friends
Freelance writer for *Old Town Encounter*
Owned and operated Old Town Book Cellar, Madison, WI, 2000-2002
Retired to Menton, France, and Naples, Florida 2003-2005

MATURE ▪ RESPONSIBLE ▪ FLEXIBLE ▪ PUNCTUAL

Kathleen Winkelman
1234 Maple Street, Madison, WI 53701

Cell: 708-123-4567
email@email.com

❷ Office Administrator

Seasoned, responsible office professional. Wide range of experiences. Flexible in work schedule, punctual, and hard-working. Enjoys providing excellent customer service.

Core Competencies

- Data entry, retrieval
- Word processing
- Inbound and outbound calls
- Resolving documentation issues
- Researching legal issues

- Counseling public on rights and procedures
- Resolving record discrepancies
- Recording transactions in proprietary system
- Creation and revision of legal documents
- Legal database research

❸ Professional Accomplishments

❹ Legal Research/Case Specialist

- Maintained and updated records of children in protective custody and teenage delinquents
- Researched legal procedures
- Counseled minors and parents on their rights, responsibilities, and procedures of the court
- Responsible for accurate recording of all transactions – fees and fine paid, community service performed, documents filed, etc.

Customer Service

- Greeted and served library customers
- Learned how to locate books and other materials
- Handled walk-in traffic at busy County Attorney's office

Retail Operations

- Owned and operated *Old Town Book Cellar* for 2 years
- Sales associate in dress shop; serviced public; stocked; tracked inventory
- Cash register and credit card machines
- Ordering merchandise, shipping and receiving

❺ Career Highlights

❻ **Madison Public Library**	Customer Service Clerk	2006 - 2008
Old Town Book Cellar	Owner, operator	2001 - 2003
Case Specialist/Researcher	Dane County Attorney's Office	1991 -1996
Human Resources Specialist	XYZ Insurance Company	1981 -1991

Education

❼ **Legal Assistant Certificate**	Madison Area Technical College	1993
BA, Political Science	University of Wisconsin, Madison	1981

Sales to Fundraiser; Telecommunications to Nonprofit

Diane Preston has a big heart and derives her greatest satisfaction from nonprofit volunteer work. She is having difficulty generating sufficient income from her telecommunications sales consulting work, however, because of the decline in the economy. After her husband is laid off from a defense contract, she needs a staff position that provides steady income and group health benefits for her family, which includes a disabled son with Cerebral Palsy.

Diane knows that it will be difficult to compete with others for manager-level telecommunications positions. That prompts her to take a leap of faith and apply for nonprofit fundraising positions. She has no problem asking for support from wealthy donors and believes her sales and marketing background will be an asset at a nonprofit organization. She hopes her MBA, volunteer background, and grant-writing experience will help her cross over into a director-level position.

Challenges to Making the Switch

Diane's nonprofit experience is limited to volunteer work and contract grant writing, and she knows that some organizations hesitate to hire people who made considerably more money at for-profit businesses. Most of the development director positions require several years of nonprofit staff experience; however, Diane is reluctant to apply for an entry-level position and appear overqualified. Diane decides to emphasize her success as a nonprofit fundraiser and effective manager who devises innovative ways to help businesses boost income. In her resume, she highlights her successes and Master's degree, hoping they will be considered in lieu of paid nonprofit experience.

Nonprofit organizations benefit from experienced individuals who can wear many hats. Diane's versatility and past successes will be reflected in letters of recommendation from nonprofit executive directors. When she submits her resume and cover letter, she will include copies of several recommendation letters.

Transferable Skills

Fundraising	Special event coordination
Marketing	Relationship building
Grant writing	Program development
Management	Volunteer training

Job Description

Development Director

- Four-year degree, Master's/MBA strongly preferred; at least two years of nonprofit development experience

- Direct development programs, including promotions, collateral materials, grant writing, and other fundraising activities

- Plan and manage all appropriate events and activities, including donor recognition, cultivation, stewardship, and so on

- Build meaningful relationships with individuals, businesses, corporations, and foundations for the purpose of meeting philanthropic needs

- Manage the maintenance of fundraising records, including prospect assignments, cultivation and solicitation status, gift and recognition records; ensure that the database and donor management information is appropriate and updated

- Manage gift acknowledgement

- Recruit, train, and oversee volunteers involved in annual fundraising campaigns

---

Resume Makeover

1 The headline "Development Director" provides a focus that is lacking in the original objective statement with general information.

2 The subhead "Fundraising/Grant Writing/Volunteer Management" contains key words taken from the job description.

3 Seven bullet point statements reinforce qualifications and references to results and successes as a fundraiser and grant writer.

4 The Core Competencies section is loaded with key words for nonprofits, and no references are made to skills that pertain exclusively to the telecommunications industry.

5 To emphasize nonprofit background, volunteer work is moved up to the first item under Professional Experience.

6 Additional grant writing and nonprofit experience is added to the first item.

7 More details are included in the fundraising work for hurricane evacuees to further enhance her diverse nonprofit experience.

DIANE PRESTON
1234 Southside Drive
Dallas, TX 75208
(214) 123-4567
email@email.com

OBJECTIVE

Challenging position that will take full advantage of my diverse experience to enhance positive growth for a developing organization.

SUMMARY OF QUALIFICATIONS

- Results-oriented professional with extensive and broad-based experience in business management, marketing, new business development, and building customer relations.
- Noted for initiative, dependability, organization, integrity, motivation, and strong positive relationships with others.
- Strengths include effective communication, team building, added value management, customer service, motivation, and professionalism.
- Productive, resourceful employee with experience across multiple industries.
- Working knowledge of Microsoft Office with emphasis in Excel and QuickBooks Pro.

PROFESSIONAL EXPERIENCE

TELECOMMUNICATIONS CONSULTANT   Dallas, TX 2002 – Present
D. Preston & Associates

Serve clients in sales, training and customer-retention projects

- Enable organizations to improve telecommunications systems toward meeting goals
- Third-party oversight of sales proposals
- Problem/resolution covering the full gamut of the sales operation
- Support for every stage of the sales cycle
- Monitoring sales staff/sales observations
- Using best-practices-based analysis and processes to help achieve cost-effective solutions

STRATEGIC ACCOUNT MANAGER   Kansas City, MO 2000 – 2002
Horizon Inc.

Initiated sales leads and qualified sales leads. Secured the accounts of desired leads and executed excellent customer service. Managed and cultivated existing accounts and built strong customer relationships.

- Responsible for many facets of operations
- Supervised the fulfillment of customer needs through the entire supply chain process

SENIOR ACCOUNT MANAGER   Dallas, TX/Overland Park, KS 1998 – 2000
Teligese Inc.

Marketed local, long distance, and Internet services over digital wireless microwave networks and fiber optic networks. Success in meeting and exceeding presented goals. Promoted from position of Account Manager to Senior Account Manager.

- "Top Performer in the Southwest Region" in 1999
- Served as both a sales and corporate trainer to Account Representatives
- Ability to develop successful relationships with key decision-makers

SALES MANAGER   Irving, TX 1996 – 1998
Publications of America

Developed both domestic and foreign markets for the distribution of video and book publications. Successful in developing leads, exceeding sales goals and customer service goals.

- Ranked #1 in sales for 1998
- Organized and represented the company at industry trade shows

SALES REPRESENTATIVE   Irving, TX 1990 – 1996
GTS Directories

Marketed and sold websites designed to promote and advertise businesses on the Internet and marketed traditional yellow page advertising to new and existing accounts. Exceeded sales goals in a deadline-oriented business environment.

- Consistently in the top 10% of Sales Representatives
- Selected to train staff in both sales and corporate programs

Volunteer Experience

DEVELOPMENT/GRANTS COORDINATOR   Dallas, TX 2006 – Present
The Hartford Avenue Contemporary

Volunteered to assist with fundraising, grant writing and coordination of special events and projects for a not-for-profit arts organization.

- Solicit donations at special events and grant writing
- Provide support to patrons and artists
- Collaborate for membership drives and annual renewals

OPERATIONS/DIRECTOR OF MEALS   Dallas, TX 2005
Saint Joseph Community Center

Managed the acquisition of meals for Hurricane Katrina evacuees from Dallas-area institutions and restaurants. Number of individuals served ranged from 200–600 people.

- Maintained strict adherence to health department regulations

Additional volunteer experience includes serving as a Cerebral Palsy Association Board Member. Contract grant-writing assignments for Any Baby Can of Dallas from 2002-2008

EDUCATION

MBA   2005
Tacoma University

BS Psychology/Sociology   1989
Northwest State University

DIANE PRESTON

1234 Southside Drive ■ Dallas, TX 75208 ■ 214-123-4567 ■ email@email.com

DEVELOPMENT DIRECTOR
Fundraising / Grant Writing / Volunteer Management

- More than five years of proven fundraising experience. Increased donations by 35 percent in two years.
- MBA degree in Business Management and Bachelor's Degree in psychology/sociology.
- Recruited and managed up to 20 volunteers. Conducted training prior to annual fundraising campaigns.
- Proven track record in staging and managing successful events – charity balls, donor dinners, music and theatre performances, and educational programs.
- Influential with all levels of the decision chain — work collaboratively with C-level clients and donors.
- Successful grant-writing experience. Researched and wrote four grants that generated $3.5 million.
- Productive, resourceful, energetic employee with experience in non-profits, publishing, the arts, and telecommunications.

Core Competencies

- Proven Fund Raiser
- Grant Writing
- Volunteer Management
- Special Events Coordinator
- Marketing
- Program Development
- Project Management
- Creating Collateral
- Non-Profit Experience
- Training and Mentoring
- Developing Gifting Programs
- Microsoft Office/QuickBooks

PROFESSIONAL EXPERIENCE

Development Coordinator – The Hartford Avenue Contemporary Gallery, 2006 – Present
Dallas, TX
Art Exhibits, Annual Meetings, Theater & Music Performances, Educational Programs

Achievements
- Assist in developing special events to solicit donations, which boosted funding by 35 percent.
- Collaborate on membership drives and annual renewals. Involved in creating collateral and acknowledging major donors.
- Recruit and coordinate volunteer staff with up to 20 people. Train and mentor volunteers.
- Serve as a docent for art exhibits. Create and conduct educational programs for children.

Additional non-profit experiences from 2006 to 2008 includes contract grant-writing for Any Baby Can of Dallas, which generated $3.5 million in funding.

Served as a Board Member of the Cerebral Palsy Association of Dallas from 2002 to 2008.

Telecommunications Consultant – D. Preston & Associates, 2002 – Present
Dallas, TX
Serving clients in sales, sales training, and customer retention projects

Services
- Assist organizations in improving telecommunications systems and retaining customers
- Provide third-party oversight of sales proposals
- Offer problem/resolution covering the full gamut of the sales operation
- Facilitate customized sales staff training sessions and monitor new employees
- Using best-practices-based analysis and processes to help achieve cost-effective solutions

Fundraiser/Director of Meals – Saint Joseph Community Center, 2005
Dallas, TX

Achievements
- Managed the acquisition of donated meals from Dallas-area institutions and restaurants
- Created operations system for mealtime schedules, donor information, and food deliveries
- Procured donated meals for Hurricane Katrina evacuees for 21 days
- Served up to 600 people at each meal
- Maintained strict adherence to health department regulations

---

DIANE PRESTON

Strategic Account Manager – Horizon Inc., 2000 – 2002
Kansas City, MO

Achievements
- When local service was launched by AT&T, developed and closed the largest sale in AT&T's Central Region to a multi-million-dollar retailer.
- Secured the accounts of desired leads and executed excellent customer service.
- Managed and cultivated existing accounts and built strong customer relationships.
- Responsible for many facets of service delivery – engineering, customer service support.
- Project Manager for complete telecommunications installations.
- Supervised the fulfillment of customer needs through the entire supply chain process.

Senior Account Manager – Teligese Inc. 1998 – 2000
Dallas, TX/Overland Park, KS

Achievements
- Marketed local, long distance, and Internet services over digital wireless microwave networks and fiber optic networks
- Project Manager for complete telecommunications installations
- Successful in meeting and exceeding company sales goals
- Promoted from Account Manager to Senior Account Manager in less than two years
- Rated "Top Performer in the Southwest Region" in 1999
- Served as both a sales and corporate trainer to other Account Representatives
- Successfully developed relationships with key decision-makers on accounts believed to be "unworkable"

Sales Manager – Publications of America 1996 – 1998
Irving, TX

Achievements
- Developed both domestic and foreign markets for the distribution of video and book publications
- Successful in developing leads, exceeding sales goals and customer service goals
- Ranked #1 in sales for 1998
- Organized and represented the company at industry trade shows

Sales Representative – GTS Directories, 1990 – 1996
Irving, TX

Achievements
- Marketed traditional Yellow Page advertising to new and existing accounts
- Upsold the relatively new concept of websites and ecommerce to Yellow Page advertisers
- Acquired new business by selling to advertisers in a competitor's directory
- Exceeded sales goals in a deadline-oriented business environment
- Consistently in the top 10% of Sales Representatives in the nation
- Selected to train staff in both sales and corporate programs

EDUCATION & TRAINING

MBA in Business Management – Texas State University 2005
BS Psychology/Sociology – Northwest State University, Maryville, MO
Grant Writing Certificate Course – El Centro Community College, Dallas, TX

Teacher to Trainer; Education to Oil and Gas

Brad Hinson worked as a retail manager for a decade before the events of September 11, 2001, prompted him to go back to school and finish his Bachelor's and Master's degrees. He thought he could make a difference in the world as a public school science teacher but feels burned out after three years. Brad enjoys creative aspects of developing educational programs and recalls how much he liked training new retail employees and managers. He decides he will be more effective as a corporate trainer and explores opportunities in that field. His keen interest in natural science helps him target the oil and gas industry, which has expanded opportunities. Brad hopes to parlay his education, teaching, and training experience to make a second career change.

Challenges to Making the Switch

Brad has limited training experience; however, he hopes that his advanced degree, teaching experience, and knowledge of the oil and gas industry will help him make the transition to corporate training. He transforms his teacher-oriented resume into a version that is more common in the training field. Because most of the postings specify at least two years experience, Brad expands on what he did while training retail employees and demonstrating computers. He also adds part-time computer skills instruction that he did during the summer school break. Brad joins the American Association for Training and Development and schedules informational interviews to receive advice on how to break into corporate training. He asks several professionals to critique his resume to help him fine-tune it before he applies for openings.

Corporate training has attracted many former public school teachers who prefer working with adults. Brad hopes to ease his transition by reading oil and gas journals, along with other information, to update his knowledge of the field.

Transferable Skills

Training for diverse groups

Product training

Presentation skills

Curriculum development

Program design

Managing budgets

Computer/technical skills

Program evaluation

Job Description

Oil and Gas Company Trainer

- Five or more years of operations and/or maintenance training or related experience in oil- and gas-related operations or similar industrial environment

- Bachelor's degree preferred; major discipline: instructional technology

- Computer proficiencies: Microsoft Word, Excel, and PowerPoint

- Collaborate with and provide training support for on-site training personnel at domestic and international field locations

- Design, develop, and implement programs using the Instructional System Design process to meet competency requirements for operations and maintenance positions, petro-technical staff, and support organizations

- Develop and coordinate the distribution of training information and materials to promote standardization throughout the organization

- Collaborate with Learning Services Group to design, develop, and administer computer-based training applications as needed

- Evaluate deliverables throughout the design, development, and implementation of training projects to ensure consistent quality and to facilitate continuous improvement

- Manage the technical training development budget

Resume Makeover

1 The headline "Oil & Gas Training and Development" conveys a corporate training focus.

2 The subhead "Training/Curriculum Development/Budget Management" contains key words from the job description.

3 The seven bullet points showcase relevant training experience and a reference to an advanced degree in a related field.

4 The Core Competencies section is loaded up with key words found in the job description.

5 Under Professional Experience, training and technology consultant is listed first to highlight adult training experience.

6 Public school teaching experience details are limited.

7 The research field assistant reference is expanded to include teaching skills.

8 Store manager experience includes information about product demonstrations and training employees and managers.

9 "References available upon request" is deleted, since this is always assumed.

Brad Hinson

1234 Collins Street
Auburn, NY 13021
Home (315) 123-4567
Cell (315) 123-5555
email@email.com

CERTIFICATION: Adolescent Education, Earth Science, grades 7-12, with grades 5-6 extension, New York State Initial Certification September 2007

EDUCATION:

Master of Arts in Teaching, Adolescent Education, Earth Science, May 2006
SUNY Cortland, Cortland, NY, January 2005 – May 2006

Bachelor of Science, Geology, December 2004
SUNY Cortland, Cortland, NY, January 2002 – December 2004

Associate of Science, December 2002
Cayuga Community College, Auburn, NY, January 2002 – December 2002

TEACHING EXPERIENCE:

Teacher, Middle School Science (7th Grade Life Science, 8th Grade Physical Science)
Skaneateles Middle School, Skaneateles, NY, August 2006 – present

Substitute Teacher (various subjects)
Skaneateles Central Schools 2005 – 2006
Marcellus Central Schools 2005 – 2006
Homer Central School 2005 – 2006

Student Teacher, Physical Science, 8th Grade
Homer Junior High School, Homer, NY, Spring 2006

Student Teacher, Regents Earth Science, 8th Grade Physical Science
Marathon High School, Marathon, NY, Spring 2006

Student Observer, Life Science, 7th Grade, (25 hours)
Homer Junior High School, Homer, NY, Fall 2005

Student Observer, Physical Science, 8th Grade, (25 hours)
Camillus Middle School, Camillus, NY, Fall 2005

Student Observer, Regents Earth Science, Student Observer (25 hours)
Skaneateles High School, Skaneateles, NY, Spring 2005

Student Observer, Regents Earth Science, Student Observer (25 hours)
Marcellus High School, Marcellus, NY, Spring 2005

RELATED EXPERIENCE:

Master's Thesis, Spring 2006 – Focused on using inquiry methods in science outside the classroom. Researched the popularity, use, and perceived success of using field experiences in the secondary science curriculum. Polled 14 Central New York secondary science educators on their use of field experiences in their curriculum.

Teaching Assistant, Geology Department, Geomorphology Lab
SUNY Cortland, Fall 2005

Tutor, math and science
Private, 2003 – present
Peer Tutor, Academic Support Center, Cayuga Community College, Auburn, NY

ADDITIONAL EXPERIENCE:

Employee Training Consultant
Manufacturers Representative and Employee Trainer
Channel You Inc., 2008 – Present

Skills Alliance
Software training, material development 2008 – Present

Computer, Consumer Electronics and Technology Consultant
MTN Computing: Owner and sole proprietor. Personal computer consulting, teaching and training, repair, home network design and implementation, network and entertainment system integration. 2003 – Present

Research Field Assistant, Geology Department
SUNY Cortland, 2004 – 2006
Scholars Day Poster Presentation, Fall 2005

Marketing and Retail Management
Various employers since 1987

TECHNOLOGY EXPERIENCE:

Familiarity with both Microsoft and Apple platforms

Software:
- Windows: high proficiency with Microsoft Windows 95, 98, ME, NT, 2000, XP, Vista, Windows 7 beta (limited), Word, Excel, PowerPoint, Outlook and Outlook Express, Adobe Photoshop, Premier, Acrobat, Mozilla Firefox.
- Apple: beginning familiarity with Mac OS. X, iTunes, iMovie, iDVD, iPhoto, Garage Band, MS Office for Mac.

Hardware:
- Experience with hardware: Desktops (internal and external hardware), laptops, tablet PCs, smartboards, PDAs, PMP (MP3 & MP4) players, inkjet printers, photo printers, laser printers, scanners, networking (wired and wireless), digital cameras and digital photography, web cams.

SKILLS:

Teaching and Training
Conducted training for employees for more than 50 locations
Selected as Regional Trainer for seven-state region
Management and Leadership
Directed up to 60 salespeople representing seven departments
Increased department profitability from -10% to +35% in first month in position
Research and Laboratory
Selected to travel to Alaska to work as field research assistant
Worked as a laboratory teaching assistant teaching undergraduate students

ORGANIZATIONS:

EarthWorks
New York State Science Teachers Association
Sports Car Club of America

REFERENCES:

Available upon request

❾

Brad Hinson
email@email.com
1234 Collins Street   Auburn, NY 13021
Home (315) 123-4567   Cell (315) 123-5555

OIL & GAS TRAINING AND DEVELOPMENT
Training/Curriculum Development/Budget Management

- More than five years of relevant experience, including providing employee, manager, product, and technical training
- Master of Arts degree in Education and Earth Science
- Developed curriculum and materials for classroom training and computer-based training applications
- Selected to travel throughout the U.S. and conduct training at 50 sites
- Regularly evaluated training programs and modified presentations
- Monitored budgets and helped company reduce training costs by 20 percent
- Computer Skills: Microsoft Word, Excel, PowerPoint, Outlook and Outlook Express, Adobe Photoshop, Premier, Acrobat, Mozilla Firefox

CORE COMPETENCIES

Training	Oil & Gas Knowledge	Evaluations
Curriculum	Field Training	Orientations
E-Learning	Budget Management	Demonstrations

PROFESSIONAL EXPERIENCE

Training and Technology Consultant   2008 – Present
- Conducts summer software adult training classes for Skills Alliance, including Word, Excel, Access, PowerPoint, and Adobe Photoshop
- Develops instructional materials and facilitates classes with up to 20 students
- Repairs hardware; designs and installs network and entertainment systems integration

Physical Science and Life Science Teacher   2006 – Present
Skaneateles Middle School, Skaneateles, NY
- Teaches 7th Grade Life Science and 8th Grade Physical Science
- Oversees student teachers in the classroom

Research Field Assistant, Geology Department   2004 – 2006
SUNY Cortland, Cortland, NY
- Selected to work as a field research assistant in Alaska
- Provided instruction on research methods for undergraduate students

Store Manager   1993 – 2003
Kell Computers, New York, NY
- Advanced from entry-level sales associate to store manager. Supervised 60 salespeople representing seven departments
- Increased department profitability from -10% to +35% during the first year as manager in 1997
- Traveled to 50 locations throughotte U.S. and conducting employee and manager training
- Assisted in developing the company's first computer-based training programs used for orientation and ongoing employee training
- Frequently demonstrated computers, software, and other technical products

EDUCATION

Master of Arts in Teaching, Adolescence Education, Earth Science 2006
SUNY Cortland, Cortland, NY

Bachelor of Science, Geology 2004
SUNY Cortland, Cortland, NY

Associate of Science, 2002
Cayuga Community College, Auburn, NY

ORGANIZATIONS
EarthWorks, Sports Car Club of America

Technical Manager to Consultant; Telecommunications to Consulting Agency

After a long career as a software engineer and technical manager in the telecommunications industry, Janice Roginski felt burned out in her current role. Having started with the company only a year after the breakup of Bell Systems, she has endured many corporate transformations and acquisitions during her tenure. Although her resume shows only one employer since 1985, she has worked under at least five corporate structures, names, and cultures.

When the company started layoffs, she was glad to take an attractive severance package based on her 20-plus–year history with the company. With the downturn in the economy, however, she realizes she needs to go back to work to supplement her pension and investment income.

Janice's strengths as a manager were in coaching and mentoring her team, and she feels that these same attributes will translate nicely to a consulting role. Her passion is organizational design (OD), which involves developing processes, roles, and reporting relationships within an organization. She is enthusiastic about applying her experience as a technical manager to new challenges.

Challenges to Making the Switch

Janice is in her mid-50s and wants the security of a regular salary from a solid, respected company. Most consulting firms offer contract work, but she is looking for full-time, salaried pay. She will need to apply her engineering and management skills within a large, established consulting organization. Because her expertise in OD comes from experience on the job instead of a university program, she is prepared to accept a consulting position that focuses on project management. She hopes to get her foot in the door and understands that the plum OD projects will come after she has proven herself as a consultant on more technical assignments.

Janice is extremely outgoing. By networking with former colleagues, she was able to find a job lead at a consulting firm that serves her former employer. Although she lacked the consulting experience required for the position, her technical background and knowledge of the client company culture made her an attractive hire.

Transferable Skills

Software development

Project management

Process and quality improvement

Employee development/mentorship

Strategic planning

Job Description

Engineering Consultant/Project Manager

- Responsible for coordinating all aspects of a project, including strategic planning, resource allocation, task assignment, tracking and reporting progress, and obtaining signature approval of finished product

- Supervise the daily activities of project team, which may include up to 60 professional engineers and developers

- Coordinate process improvement initiatives

- Act as liaison between project team and corporate management to facilitate communication

- Report status of project, including budget and timeline changes, to executive steering committee

- Provide technical supervision and support to all project team members, including participation in project tasks where needed, to ensure that project is completed in accordance with contract requirements

- Minimum 10 years of consulting experience required

- At least five years of project management experience or PMI certification required

---

Resume Makeover

Janice's long career as an engineer is reframed into functions that fit the consulting industry.

1 Focus attention on the leadership development and mentoring aspect of her experience in the first paragraph.

2 In the Competencies section, she has incorporated key words from the job description: process improvement, strategic planning, project management, and liaison/advocate/spokesperson.

3 Janice's notable, measurable achievements as technical project manager—process improvements and employee development success—are highlighted in the Professional Expertise section.

4 All achievement statements are simplified, stripping away much of the engineering and company-specific jargon.

5 Her 20-year career in telecommunications is collapsed into one entry but retains the years at each level to show consistent career growth.

6 Early jobs as software engineer and development engineer are eliminated because the technology is obsolete, making them less relevant.

JANICE ROGINSKI

1234 Foxridge Court
Arlington, TX 75603
Home: (972) 123-4567   *email@email.com*

SUMMARY

Over 20 years engineering and management experience in telecommunications/high-tech industry. Extensive experience with all aspects of software development, quality, and process improvement, project management, and product management. Enthusiastic, energetic, and innovative, with the ability to attract, develop, and retain highly talented and motivated engineers. In five years, had 4 engineers from group of 12 promoted to Distinguished Member of Technical Staff, a promotion awarded to approximately 1% of the technical population annually.

PROFESSIONAL EXPERIENCE

AT&T MOBILITY / CINGULAR WIRELESS / SOUTHWESTERN BELL, Dallas, TX   **1985 – 2005**

Smart Networking Systems Engineer   2002 – 2005
- Chaired cross-organizational architecture board.
- Authored high-level and detailed requirements specifications.
- Spearheaded reduction in Systems Engineering Process Documentation from over 300 pages to less than 80 pages.
- Worked toward a Level 2 and Level 3 Systems Engineering Process as evaluated using the Software Engineering Institute's (SEI) Capability Maturity Model Integration (CMMI) standards.

Smart Networking Technical Manager   1998 – 2002
- Managed group of 5-12 engineers responsible for systems engineering and architecture for the Smart Networking group enhanced Control Server, enhanced Media Resource Server, and group of developers responsible for providing application infrastructure software to facilitate both internal and third party application development.
- Built group into one of the most respected in the organization; four members promoted to Distinguished Member of Technical Staff (approximately 1% of the technical population receives this award annually), and one to Technical Manager.
- Provided system overview presentations to customers and worked closely with them to better understand both their technical requirements and review process needs.
- Ensured high quality requirements were provided for over 100 features per year.
- Helped drive over ten major platform architectural initiatives from conception to implementation, one of which won the 2000 Bell Labs President Award.

Customer Market Development   1996 – 1997
- Developed strategic market direction for customers in the local connectivity arena with particular emphasis on broadband data for online services.
- Evaluated Asynchronous Digital Subscriber Loop technology for the competitive local access market focusing on proposed internal developments and overall industry direction.
- Created an end-to-end architectural vision for the local access market by working closely with architects from the Access, Switching, and Data product realization centers.
- Clarified and focused definition of this Internet server product offering by working cross-organizational contract issues and creating customer-focused marketing materials.

Product Management / Systems Engineering   1993 – 1996
- Provided customer support to sales teams for the Automatic Call Distribution product including development of pricing efforts.
- Created and delivered product presentations to customers both onsite and on the customers' premises.
- Created and chaired product architectural board which processed 58 action items and resolved 23 in five months.
- Improved product requirements process by creating product-specific Feature Specification Document (FSD) template.
- Lead author for largest FSD ever produced for subcontractor's requirements; pioneered process and delivered approved FSD on schedule.
- Enhanced relations with a difficult customer.

JANICE ROGINSKI   PAGE TWO

Chair, Software Design Process Management Team   1990 – 1993
- Baselined existing software design processes into a single, flexible ISO-certified software design process used by approximately 2000 developers across the entire 5ESS project; created and delivered training to the development community.
- Created and delivered original moderator training course and organized weekly meeting for information dissemination.
- Originated and evaluated three software design process Quality Improvement Proposals; two were adopted to enhance the quality of the Software Design and Document Review processes.

Software Development Lead Engineer   1988 – 1993
- Lead engineer on 50-plus technical headcount feature.
- As key requirements reviewer, identified over 10% of all issues at initial review and 14% of all issues at acceptance review; worked closely with systems engineering to resolve all issues and continued as critical reviewer of all requirements issues raised throughout the product development.
- Led requirements analysis effort employing Object Oriented Analysis techniques and mentored team in the application of these techniques.
- Led team of eight software developers and coordinated software design, implementation, and testing of 273 tagged requirements addressing call processing feature interactions for an Automatic Call Distribution system.

5ESS Software Project Planner   1988
- Instrumental in defining group charter.
- Expedited identification of feature owners and developers.
- Organized first estimation meeting held for project.
- Initiated the inaugural meeting of project management groups across product releases and coordinated ongoing monthly meetings.

Software Development Engineer   1985 – 1988
- Researched, designed, and held first department call scenario code walkthrough and presented approach and metrics to the department.
- Edited and contributed key sections to ISDN conference/transfer feature high-level design development.
- Presented conference/transfer call feature call scenarios on training videotape.
- Reviewed all Feature Requirements Documents for department.

⑥ E-SYSTEMS, INC., Garland, TX   1983 – 1985

Software Engineer
- Developed functional and detailed design changes for a signal processing system implemented on five Hewlett-Packard computers.
- Implemented touch-screen interface on an existing multiple-terminal display system.
- Prepared and delivered formal presentations to government customer.

⑥ EASTMAN KODAK, Rochester, NY   1980 – 1983

Development Engineer
- Analyzed, designed, and implemented Ektachem E400 Blood Analyzer microprocessor software in a multi-computer real-time system.
- Analyzed data tracking needs for a high-speed, large-volume film-processing center.

EDUCATION
- Completed 16 hours of graduate classes in Management and Organizational Behavior, Benedictine University, Lisle, IL
- **BS**, Electrical Engineering, Purdue University, West Lafayette, IN, 1980
- Completed degree and over 16 months co-op experience with DuPont within four years
- National Merit finalist

JANICE ROGINSKI
ENGINEERING CONSULTANT
1234 Foxridge Court • Arlington, TX 75603 • H: 972.123.4567 • email@email.com

TECHNICAL CONSULTING / PROJECT MANAGEMENT / ENGINEERING

① Engineering Consultant with extensive background in technical management, system and process engineering, project management, and end-to-end software development. Capable of building underperforming organizations into highly effective ones, as well as leading organizations through accelerated growth or rapid change.

COMPETENCIES

②
- Software Development
- Process Improvement
- Quality Management
- Strategic Planning

- Project Management
- Product Development
- Liaison / Advocate / Spokesperson
- Creative Problem Resolution

- Organizational Design
- Client Needs Analysis
- Team / Workshop Facilitation
- Employee Development

PROFESSIONAL EXPERTISE

Process/Quality Improvements

③
- 17 years experience in creating process improvement initiatives. Initiated process improvement trials to adopt a systematic approach to process improvement.
- Transformed two separate existing software design processes into a single, flexible ISO-certified software design process used by 2,000 developers, a project second to only the Space Shuttle in number of lines of code.
- Streamlined process documentation by 66%. Standardized ad hoc document review processes. Created and delivered training for documentation review facilitators.

Technical Management

④
- Directed 5-12 engineers determining and implementing software, hardware, and protocol requirements for the Intelligent Network platform (AT&T – Technical Manager).
- Assumed responsibility for software development; obtained incremental funding to include macros as part of the engineering program.
- Drove 10+ major platform architectural initiatives from conception to implementation. Provided high quality requirements for 120+ features per year. Provided expertise to other projects to foster teamwork throughout the organization.
- Successfully gathered requirements from 100+ customers and allowed them insight into product road maps to maintain excitement and interest.

Organizational Development
- Rebuilt a group devastated by previous downsizing and restructuring efforts into one of the most respected work groups in the organization.
- Chaired the AT&T Intelligent Network and ACD Architecture Boards. Recruited global experts to sit on the boards to review and approve major feature sets. Resolved problems and ensured field input was incorporated into new product requirements.
- Proposed and led a single group overseeing all 5ESS product releases. Defined the charter, identified feature owners and developers, organized the inaugural meeting; coordinated monthly and release commitment meetings.

Employee Development
- Attracted top talent to the AT&T team with challenging work and cross-functional training.
- Secured promotions for 1 team member to Technical Manager and an unprecedented 4 members to Distinguished Member of Technical Staff (generally awarded to 1% of the technical population annually).

JANICE ROGINSKI

- Garnered team recognition for the development of a salable, innovative, scalable device to meet capacity demands, yielding multifold ROI in less than 12 months.
- Acknowledged by Director and VP for creating one of the top teams in the 500+ member division.

PROFESSIONAL HISTORY

⑤ **AT&T Mobility / Cingular Wireless / Southwestern Bell, Dallas, TX   1985 – 2009**
A 20-year engineering/management career with consistent and substantive promotions.

Systems Engineer, Smart Networking	2002 – 2005
Technical Manager, Smart Networking	1998 – 2002
Customer Market Development	1996 – 1997
Product Manager/Systems Engineer	1993 – 1996
Chair, Software Design Process Management Team	1990 – 1993
Lead Engineer, Software Development	1988 – 1993
Project Planner, 5ESS Software	1988
Engineer, Software Development	1985 – 1988

EDUCATION AND PROFESSIONAL DEVELOPMENT

Management and Organizational Behavior, Benedictine University, Lisle, IL
Completed 16 hours of graduate classes

BS, Electrical Engineering, Purdue University, West Lafayette, IN
Completed degree and 16+ months of co-op experience with DuPont within 4 years

Trainer to Customer Support; Software to Office Equipment

Keith Como received his walking papers from a software company just as unemployment hit 9.1 percent. His job loss was a trickle-down effect of the construction industry bust. His position selling and implementing hardware store software was eliminated as several large hardware retail chains failed. He is in his late 40s and doesn't want to go back to the high pressure of commission sales.

When Keith lost his job, he went through a period of confusion and depression. He has the talent to be in sales but really lacks the heart for it. When he finally acknowledged to himself that his first love is training and working with customers, his job search became focused.

Challenges to Making the Switch

Keith realizes he is a trainer at heart, just when training jobs are being cut from nearly every company. Training positions are scarce, but luckily Keith is skilled at training customers—one of the few training positions still considered critical to business success.

Because he doesn't want a sales position, he will need to recast his recent experience as account manager—emphasizing the customer service aspects and playing down the sales activities.

Transferable Skills

Software implementation/training

Project management

Customer service

Sales support

e-learning/Web-based training applications

> ## Job Description
> ## Service Support/Product Trainer
>
> - Conduct post-sale product training to the end users on specific business system products and services, including black-and-white and color printers and copiers, facsimile equipment, document management solutions, and related software
>
> - Conduct training sessions (classroom and non-classroom) for sales personnel on equipment operations, maintenance, and troubleshooting as assigned
>
> - Required: Bachelor's degree or equivalent field-related experience
>
> - Strong communication, presentation, and organizational skills
>
> - Knowledge of PC and/or Macintosh applications
>
> - Experience working with end users in a support and/or training capacity

Resume Makeover

Keith chooses to create a functional resume so that he can de-emphasize his sales background.

1 The headline "Service Support/Product Trainer" matches the job description perfectly.

2 The bulleted copy summarizes his most relevant experience in just six lines.

3 The "Customer Service/Sales Support" achievements section is placed at the top because this experience is most relevant to the targeted job. If he applies for project management or technical positions, he can lead with a different skills section.

4 His 10-year history with ABC Software Solutions is described with detail featuring his four main job titles. He changes the titles slightly to communicate his responsibilities more accurately. By using bullets within the paragraphs, he can provide a lot of detail in a small space.

5 By combining his two account manager positions at ABC Software, he de-emphasizes his sales goal of $43,000, which appeared at the top of his old resume.

6 His first three positions are deleted because they do not contribute to this job search.

7 Because the job description calls for a strong computer background, Keith's skills in this area are given their own section.

8 His year of graduation from college is removed. Combined with item 6, he has the opportunity to appear six years younger.

9 Keith leaves in his substantial work with the Boy Scouts because he feels it clearly communicates his commitment to mentoring and training.

Keith Como
123 Horizon Trail, Round Rock, Texas 78600
512-123-4567 email@email.com

Work Experience

ABC Software Solutions, Direct Account Manager   2008-2009
ABC Software Solutions Inc., Los Gatos, CA—Customer Account Management and Upgrade Sales for Ace Hardware Stores and Lumber Yards

Responsible for generating $43,000 per month in gross margin sales of hardware and software add-ons and upgrades to an existing client base of 160 Ace Hardware stores and lumber yards in the Midwest, Southeast, and Northeast U.S. Proficient in the use of the SalesForce Customer management program.

Implementation Coordinator   2006-2008
ABC Software Solutions Inc., Los Gatos, CA—Eagle Professional Services Group

Responsible for coordinating the implementation of all new Eagle Small Store Systems (SE) and some Key New Accounts. This includes working with customers to determine scheduling needs and expectations, ensuring shipping, installation, training, and post Go Live commitments are met. Other responsibilities include managing the company Small Store Sharepoint site and other SE reporting, conducting a weekly Status Meeting wherein all aspects of the Eagle SE systems are discussed, and monitoring the resolution of SE issues to ensure they are being addressed. Overall I am the "Throat to Choke" for all things SE. I manage my time effectively in a solo environment in order to keep up with the constant flow of requests for assistance and my regular work responsibilities.

eLearning Specialist   2004-2006
ABC Software Solutions Inc., Austin, TX—Hardware Store and Home Center Group Education

Responsible for training ABC customers on the use of several components of the ABC Eagle Retail Management Software including Point of Sale, Accounts Receivable, Purchasing, Inventory, and a variety of other specialized Software via telephone and via Microsoft Office LiveMeeting. Using my excellent communication skills I helped our customers learn to use their systems to maximize their profits in mostly retail environments. I was the company Subject Matter Expert for the TimeClock Plus integration with the Eagle System.

Senior Customer Business Representative   2001-2004
ABC Software Solutions Inc. (formerly TRIAD), Austin, TX—Order Management and Customer Service

Responsible for training Order Management Team Members on departmental policies and procedures. Oversaw the Order Management of all orders involving the Credit Authorization products and for several Key New Account Sales Specialists. Developed new policies and procedures for the Order Management Department and was involved with Oracle ERP Transition Project. As a senior member of the team I managed my time effectively.

Triad Direct Sales Specialist   1999-2001
TRIAD Inc., Livermore, CA—Computer System Upgrade Sales for Hardware Stores and Lumber Yards

Responsible for generating $39,000 per month in gross margin sales of hardware and software add-ons and upgrades to an existing client base of 225 hardware stores and lumber yards in Northern California, Pennsylvania, and Canada. I trained other team members in the features and benefits of the Eagle for Windows Suite of Software and used Placeware for conducting On-Line Demonstrations for customers. I qualified for Gold Club 2000.

Technical Sales Associate   1996-1999
Test & Manufacturing Resources, Los Gatos, CA—Computer Aided Semiconductor Test Equipment Sales

I was primarily responsible for Burn-in Board Tester Line, generating revenue of $500K per year. Provided installation, training, and applications support to new and existing customers in Northern California. I was also responsible for a Probe Card Analyzer Line, assisting in sales of over $1.9 million in 1996, $3.4 million in 1997, and $1.8 million in 1998. I completed Applied Precision Inc.'s Field Service Engineer Training in order to provide customer technical service and applications support for their Probe Card Analyzers.

Corporate Automation and Training Specialist   1989-1996
Premier Travel Center, San Francisco, CA—Largest Independent Travel Agency in San Francisco

I was responsible for all aspects of Travel Agent Automation Training and Agency Automation. I customized software programs to assist agents with difficult and repetitive accounting procedures as part of agency's transition from commission only to fee for service.

Retail Sales Associate   1990-1991
Crate and Barrel, San Francisco, CA—Home Furnishings

Performed all tasks required during seasonal holiday employment, including cashiering, stocking, keeping store facings looking good, and helping customers.

Corporate Travel Advisor   1987-1989
Equitec, Oakland, CA—Property Management Corporation

I focused on Corporate Travel arrangements for Equitec's personnel and clients. I was responsible for training agents on new software enhancements as a SAABRE Key Coordinator.

Telemarketing Team Coordinator   1985-1987
Stephen R. Covey and Associates, Provo, UT—Personal and Professional Productivity Consultants

I managed a telemarketing team offering Covey's "Masters of Executive Excellence" and "Seven Habits of Highly Effective People" courses to top-level executives.

Education

Business Professional's Course   March 2000
Hecht and Associates, Sunnyvale, CA

Product and Industry Course   August 1999
TRIAD Inc., Livermore, CA (Received Top Performer Award)

Field Service Level 1 Course   September 1998
Applied Precision Inc., Issaquah, WA

B.S. in Travel and Tourism: minor in Italian   1986
Brigham Young University, Provo, UT

Skills

Microsoft Office Suite – I am especially proficient at Microsoft Excel, and using Outlook for scheduling my time.
Eagle System – I am familiar and comfortable with teaching others to use basic Eagle System programs.
SalesForce – I am familiar and comfortable using SalesForce.com Web Application for customer management.
Oracle – Proficient in the use of Oracle for Order Management and limited use of the ECO, Purchasing, and Accounts Receivable Modules.
Guardian, GTWeb, Triton, Take Control – Proficient in the use of these tools as they relate to Order Entry, Customer Billing, and Order Management.
Discoverer Report Writing – I have written several Discoverer Reports for extracting Data from Oracle's Order Management Module, including the Field Engineer Installation checklist used by the Order Management Group to advise the Education Department of new orders.
Languages – I am proficient in Italian and some Spanish.

Interests

Boy Scouts of America, Camping, and Dutch Oven Cooking – I have held several leadership positions in the BSA. I am currently Scoutmaster of Troop 200 in Cedar Park, Texas, building boys into men with character and integrity.

Keith Como   512-123-4567 · email@email.com   Pg. 2

ABC SOFTWARE SOLUTIONS INC. continued…

eLearning Specialist, Eagle Professional Services (2004-2006)
Delivered web-based training to customers and co-workers in use of software. • Developed, refined, and updated training curriculum and PowerPoint Presentations for web-based training. • Participated on-site at go-live events as hands-on software trainer. • Developed training for top tier user group conference. • Scheduled training sessions using ViewCentral for online registration. Recorded training sessions for 24-hour web-based access. • Became company subject matter expert for third-party software programs, TimeClock Plus, and Total Rental. • Promoted to Implementation Coordinator.

Senior Customer Business Representative (2001-2004)
Trained order management team members on departmental policies and procedures. • Oversaw the order processing of complex orders from top salespersons. • Developed new policies and procedures for the Order Management Department. • Involved directly with Oracle ERP Transition Project. Promoted to eLearning Specialist.

⑤ Account Manager, ABC Software Direct (1999-2001 & 2008-2009)
Trained sales team in the features and benefits of Eagle for Windows Software. • Responsible for generating $43,000 per month in gross margin sales of add-ons and upgrades to client base of 160 Ace Hardware stores and lumber. • Conducted on-line demonstrations of software for customers. • Assisted co-workers in the use of SalesForce.com to manage customers and create mass mailers.

⑥ TEST & MANUFACTURING RESOURCES, Los Gatos, CA   1996-1999
Customer Support/Sales for Computer Aided Semiconductor Test Equipment
Provided installation, training, and applications support to new and existing customers. Generated revenue of $500K per year in Burn-in Board Tester Sales.

PREMIER TRAVEL, San Francisco, CA   1989-1996
Corporate Travel Agent Trainer, Quality Assurance, and Travel Policy Compliance
Trained travel agents in use of Computer Reservation System. • Customized software programs to assist agents with Quality Assurance and compliance with varied Corporate Travel policies.

⑦ <u>COMPUTER SKILLS</u>

Word	PowerPoint	SharePoint
Excel	Access	LiveMeeting
Outlook		

⑧ <u>EDUCATION AND PROFESSIONAL DEVELOPMENT</u>
Bachelor of Science, Travel & Tourism, Minor in Italian, Brigham Young University, Provo, UT
Business Professional's Course, Hecht and Associates, Sunnyvale, CA
Training Design and Teleclass Leader Training, Friesen, Kaye and Associates
Prove-It! Spanish Comprehension Test – 86% Correct

⑨ <u>COMMUNITY SERVICE</u>

Boy Scouts of America   Eagle Scout Mentor (mentor 20 candidates)
Scoutmaster, Troop 185   Merit Badge Counselor
New Scout Leader Trainer

Training the Boys of Today to Become the Men of Character and Integrity of Tomorrow

---

❶ Keith Como
123 Horizon Trail · Round Rock, TX 78600
512-123-4567 · email@email.com

❷ SERVICE SUPPORT/PRODUCT TRAINER

- Trained varied audiences in wide-ranging topics including software, policies, and procedures
- Developed training curriculum for new products and policy guidelines
- Managed detailed implementation projects from end to end, involving multiple departments
- Delivered eLearning/web-based training using web conferencing services
- Guided teams to creatively solve problems
- Bilingual: Certified by Prove-It! Spanish Comprehension test, with 86% correct

❸ RELEVANT SKILLS AND ACCOMPLISHMENTS

Customer Service/Sales Support
- Mentored and trained team of five order entry specialists, helping to reduce errors on over 60 major orders per week with average price of $30K and average of 20 line items
- Managed relationships with 160 hardware store accounts, resulting in sales of over $35K per month in add-on and upgrade sales, winning Top 10% of Sales force award
- Achieved recognition for exceptional customer service to internal and external customers

Training
- Delivered software training to more than 75 customers per week via web conferencing, reducing the need for onsite trainers and saving the company approximately $2,000 per new installation
- Developed training for specialized software, standardizing content delivery, and improved customer satisfaction
- Created PowerPoint presentations using proven best practices to maximize student retention of course content

Implementations and Project Management
- Coordinated training and implementations of 100+ new Eagle retail system projects within two years, increasing customer satisfaction from 20% to over 80%.
- Refined processes for information flow between training, development, distribution, and sales, resulting in reduction of duplicate efforts and weekly time savings of over 20 man hours.
- Led, organized, and conducted weekly project status meetings. Facilitated the resolution of issues by leveraging the resources of more than 15 core team members.

Technical Skills
- Participated in Oracle transition of order management software, allowing company to retire older software programs and eliminate duplicate systems
- Trained customers and co-workers in the following Business Management Solutions Software: ABC Software Eagle, ViewCentral, TimeClock Plus, Total Rental, Salesforce.com, and IssueTrak

❹ EMPLOYMENT EXPERIENCE

ABC SOFTWARE SOLUTIONS INC. Los Gatos, CA, and Austin, TX   1999-2009
Project Manager, Eagle Small Store Edition (2006-2008)
Managed Implementations and Training of new computer systems, coordinating end-to-end activities including: Shipping, On-site Installation, Training, and Post Go-live follow-up. • Provided single point of contact for all aspects of implementation projects. • Maintained SharePoint Database of over 100 projects. • Conducted weekly status and issue resolution meetings. • Reported weekly to upper management overall progress of all implementations. • Developed training curriculum for new products. • Tested and refined training processes before distribution to training staff.

Career Resources

Workforce Agencies by State

Each state operates an agency that is in business to help job seekers quickly find work. These agencies are also host to local Job Clubs, usually a weekly gathering of job seekers. Job Clubs provide job leads, ideas for your search, networking opportunities, and training in resume writing and interviewing skills. If you have an interest in retraining for a new career, these agencies will provide details and applications for state and federal jobs training grants. Most if not all of these services are free to state citizens. Your local workforce agency is the place to start and end your job search.

Alabama Office of Workforce Development: www.owd.alabama.gov/

Alaska Dept. of Labor & Workforce Development: labor.state.ak.us/

Arizona Dept. of Commerce: www.azcommerce.com/Home

Arkansas Dept. of Workforce Services: www.arkansas.gov/esd/

California Labor & Workforce Development Agency: www.labor.ca.gov/

Delaware Economic Development Office: dedo.delaware.gov/

Hawaii Dept. of Labor & Industrial Relations: hawaii.gov/labor/wdd

Indiana Dept. of Workforce Development: www.in.gov/dwd/

Iowa Workforce Development: www.iowaworkforce.org/

Kansas Dept. of Commerce: www.kansascommerce.com/

Kentucky Workforce Investment: workforce.ky.gov/

Louisiana Workforce Commission: www.laworks.net/

Maine Workforce Development: www.maine.gov/labor/workforce_dev/index.html

Maryland Dept. of Labor, Licensing & Regulation: www.dllr.state.md.us/county/harford/

Massachusetts Labor & Workforce Development: www.mass.gov/?pageID=elwdhomepage&L=1&L0=Home&sid=Elwd

Michigan Career, Education & Workforce Programs: www.michigan.gov/mdcd

Minnesota Workforce Center System: www.mnworkforcecenter.org/

Mississippi Dept. of Employment Security: www.mdes.ms.gov/wps/portal#null

Missouri Division of Workforce Development: ded.mo.gov/WFD/

Montana Workforce Center Directory: wsd.dli.mt.gov/service/officelist.asp

Nebraska Workforce Development: www.dol.state.ne.us/nwd/center. cfm?PRICAT=1&SUBCAT=1Z

Nevada: nv.gov/WorkingHere_Nevada.htm

New Hampshire Dept. of Employment Security: www.nh.gov/nhes/

New Jersey Workforce Public Information Network: lwd.dol.state.nj.us/labor/wnjpin/wnjpin_index.html

New Mexico Dept. of Workforce Solutions: www.dws.state.nm.us/

New York State Dept. of Labor: www.labor.state.ny.us/

North Carolina Workforce Services: www.nccommerce.com/en/WorkforceServices/

North Dakota State Government: www.nd.gov/

Ohio Office of Workforce Development: jfs.ohio.gov/owd/

Oklahoma Workforce: www.workforceok.org/

Oregon Dept. of Community Colleges & Workforce Development: www.oregon.gov/CCWD/

Pennsylvania Workforce Development: www.paworkforce.state.pa.us/paworkforce/site/default.asp

Rhode Island Dept. of Labor & Training—Workforce Development: www.dlt.ri.gov/wfds/

South Carolina Workforce Development: www.sccommerce.com/scworkforce/WorkForceDevelopment.aspx

South Dakota Dept. of Labor: dol.sd.gov/

Tennessee Dept. of Labor & Workforce Development: www.tennessee.gov/labor-wfd/cc/

Texas Workforce Commission: www.twc.state.tx.us/

Utah Dept. of Workforce Services: jobs.utah.gov/jobseeker/dwsdefault.asp

Vermont Dept. of Labor: www.labor.vermont.gov/

Virginia Employment Commission: www.vec.virginia.gov/vecportal/

Washington Development Councils: www.wa.gov/esd/wdc.htm

West Virginia Workforce Development: www.wvdo.org/workforce/index.html

Wisconsin Workforce Development Association: www.wwda.org/

Wyoming Workforce Development Council: wyowdc.org/

Internet Job Search Boards

When you're looking for a job, which websites come to mind? Probably CareerBuilder.com and Monster.com. They are the best known and promoted names in online job boards. While they may be the most widely used by job seekers, not all employers use these services to search for new hires. It is costly to list jobs, and some hiring managers prefer to post on boards that are specific to an industry or function. In fact, some job seekers purposely search and post on the lesser-known sites in order to have a competitive edge. Here are some to consider:

- **Indeed:** This job search engine consolidates all the job listings from major job boards (including Monster and CareerBuilder), newspapers, associations, and company career pages. Just enter a key word and city, state, or ZIP code to search available openings.

- **Simply Hired:** Similar to Indeed, this site crawls job boards and company sites to find local jobs, identify trends, and research salaries.

- **Yahoo! HotJobs:** Much like Monster and CareerBuilder, you can search for jobs or upload your resume and let search agents find you.

- **Job Search USA:** Offers job listings from various organizations, including not-for-profits, small businesses, corporations, and educational institutions.

- **SnagAJob.com:** Features job listings for part-time and hourly positions.

- **mediabistro.com:** This is mostly an online meeting place for creative professionals, but it also features job postings that are ideal for anyone who creates or works with content or noncreative professionals who work in a content-related industry. You have to register (for free) to view detailed job listings.

- **Talent Zoo:** This is another niche site that serves the advertising, marketing, and media industries.

- **Dice.com:** This technology-focused site features opportunities for qualified technical and engineering professionals.

- **NursingJobs.org:** This nursing-specific job site lets you search for nursing jobs by specialty and location or for travel nursing. This is just one example of dozens of profession-specific job boards.

To find an industry-specific job board for your field, do an Internet search (for example, search for a term such as "accounting job boards").

If you've been using Monster or CareerBuilder but aren't satisfied with the results, you should expand your resources and search as many job boards as you can.

Most career experts believe that only a fraction of available jobs are listed online. To conserve hiring dollars, some companies will post one job title, when five or six similar positions at various levels are available. So don't get discouraged if your perfect job isn't listed. If you have most of the qualifications and are truly interested, post your resume and give it a shot. Many job seekers find the perfect position by interviewing for a different one. Get in the job search game and market yourself freely.

Books About Career Changing

Since the 1970s, there have been hundreds of books written about finding your passion and changing to a career that suits you. In books, you can discover your strengths and get guidance on your true path. Here are some books that I consider especially helpful:

Beck, Martha. *Finding Your Own North Star.* Three Rivers Press, 2001.

———. *Steering by Starlight: The Science and Magic of Finding Your Destiny.* Three Rivers Press, 2009.

Bolles, Richard. *What Color Is Your Parachute? 2009, A Practical Manual for Job-Hunters and Career-Changers.* Ten Speed Press, 2009.

Bridges, William. *Transitions, Making Sense of Life Changes—25th Anniversary Edition.* Da Capo Press, 2004.

Buckingham, Marcus, and Donald O. Clifton. *Now, Discover Your Strengths.* Free Press, 2001.

Dychtwald, Ken. *Age Power: How the 21st Century Will Be Ruled by the New Old.* Tarcher, 2000.

Harkness, Helen. *Don't Stop the Career Clock.* Davies-Black Publishing, 1999.

Jewell, Catherine. *The Career Passion Test™.* Success Address Press, 2005. Also available from www.CareerPassionCoach.com.

———. *STAR Performance.* Success Address Press, 2002. Also available from www. CareerPassionCoach.com.

Sher, Barbara. *I Could Do Anything If I Only Knew What It Was.* Delacorte Press, 1994.

Sinetar, Marsha. *Do What You Love and the Money Will Follow.* Dell Publishing, 1987.

Yate, Martin. *Knock 'em Dead Resumes, Eighth Edition.* Adams Media, 2008.

Resume Resources

Transferable Skills

Throughout your career, you have learned how to perform tasks and procedures at work. Over time, you master the task and can truthfully say that you have built a skill. These job skills are often transferable to other job functions or to the same function in another industry. Transferable skills are the key to finding a new career.

Presented here are the transferable skills mentioned in the 50 career-changer profiles in this book. This is by no means an exhaustive list, however, because there is no limit to the number of ways to describe your personal work abilities. This list is organized by function. Use it as a thought-starter for your own unique resume.

Administrative/Customer Service/Operations

Accounting	Filing
Accurate record keeping	Graphic design/production
Audit procedures	Gregg shorthand
Auditing	Inbound and outbound phone contact
Bank deposits	Keyboarding
Benefits administration	Management
Bookkeeping	Math knowledge
Client management	Medical terminology
Communicating in a foreign language	MS Office Suite software
Communication skills	Multitasking
Computer software skills	Negotiating
Creative copywriting	Office administration
Data analysis	Office software
Database management	Payroll
Database use	Planning
Desktop publishing	Presentations to management
Documentation	Problem solving
Employee records	Purchasing

Reception

Recommending corrective actions

Relationship building

Report writing

Scheduling

Scheduling, cross-checking calendar dates

Strategic thinking

Sourcing

Verbal and written communication skills

Word, Excel, PowerPoint, Visio skills

Compliance/Engineering

Auditing

Benefits administration

Bid/analytical calculations

Business process architecture

Community liaison

Community organizing

Compliance with building codes and OSHA

Compliance with federal guidelines

Construction knowledge

Construction management

Creating strategic customers

Customer service

Design knowledge

Preparation and review of documentation

Documentation and reporting

Electrical system design

Emergency management

Employee records

Energy standards

Engineering/construction principles

Equipment selection and installation

Executive interface

Federal and international regulations

Fraud investigations

Homeland security issues

HVAC knowledge

Inbound and outbound phone contact

Instrumentation

Inventory systems

Knowledge of hiring laws and practices

Knowledge of construction

Management

Marketing

Math knowledge

Meeting facilitation

Multitasking

Multitasking in a stressful environment

Needs assessment

Negotiation

Operations analysis

Outside sales

Permitting for public works projects

Planning

Presentation skills

Problem resolution

Problem-solving skills

Product line knowledge

Product presentations

Project management/organization

Strategic planning

Relationship building with regulators

Strategic thinking

Researching leading-edge technology

Substation power plant systems

Risk evaluation

Supervision

Sales

Task coordination and organization

Scheduling

Writing

Information Technology

Asking questions and listening effectively

Planning and analysis

Communicating complex information clearly

Presentation skills

Computer networking/troubleshooting

Problem resolution

Coordinating cross-functional groups

Process design

Customer focus

Producing accurate documentation

Database use

Product line knowledge

Documentation

Quickly mastering new information

E-learning

Software implementation/training

Federal and international regulations

Strategic thinking

Help desk experience

System modeling

IT hardware, software, and programming

Technical support

MS Office Suite software

Web-based training applications

Multitasking

Management

Accurate documentation

Collaboration with medical professionals

Active listening

Commitment to quality

Asking questions and listening effectively

Communicating complex information clearly

Behavior management

Communication skills

Benefits administration

Counseling

Business process architecture

Creating infrastructure

Call center background

Customer focus

Caseload management

Customer service

Client satisfaction research

Database management

Database use

Detail orientation

Documentation

Effective communicator

Emotionally composed

Employee development

Employee records

Grading tests

Inbound and outbound phone contact

Influence

Influence with decision makers

Interpersonal skills

Lesson planning

Managing work process

Marketing through sales and networking

Math knowledge

Mentorship

MS Office Suite software

Multitasking

Negotiation

Office software

Oversight of patient care

Payroll

Preparation and review of documentation

Presentation skills

Problem solving

Producing accurate documentation

Project/program management

Public speaking

Quickly mastering new information

Sales and marketing savvy

Staff screening and selection

Strategic thinking

Supervision and management

Supervision of personnel

Technology skills

Treatment design and delivery

Understanding client needs

Manufacturing/Products

Accounting

Auditing

Bid/analytical calculations

Certified project manager

Compliance with federal guidelines

Computer skills

Construction supervisor

Cost-reduction skills

Creating strategic customers

Customer requirements and communication

Design and launch of new products

Designing research questionnaires

Designing and monitoring project scope

Preparation and review of documentation

Drafting

Electrical system design

Emergency management

Engineering/construction principles

Equipment selection and installation

Executive interface

Federal and international regulations

Instrumentation

Interpersonal skills

Inventory systems

Managing an international team

Managing research projects

Master carpenter

Math knowledge

Moderating focus groups

Multicultural program management

Multitasking

Opening new markets

Operations analysis

Permitting for public works projects

Plumber

Presentation skills

Problem resolution

Process improvement

Producing accurate documentation

Product line knowledge

Product road-mapping

Purchase orders—place, track, and expedite

Qualitative research design

Relationship building with manufacturing partners

Relationship building with regulators

Reviewing and analyzing records

Risk evaluation

Six-Sigma Green Belt

Software creation and release

Strategic thinking

Supervising hourly workers

Training

Training design

Vendor evaluation and negotiation

Web-based software integration

Marketing/Public Relations/Advertising

Administrative support

Billing, invoicing and tracking expenses

Business development

Client correspondence

Client management

Cold calling

Communication skills

Community liaison

Community organizing

Coordinating high-level meetings

Creating strategic customers

Creative copywriting

Customer service

Customer/client communication

Database use

Desktop publishing

Editing, revising, and proofing legal documents

Event planning

Fundraising

Grant writing

Graphic design/production

Inbound and outbound phone contact

Influence skills

Influence with community leaders

Interpersonal skills

Knowledge of human services programs

Liaising with legislative staff

Market research

Marketing savvy

Marketing—print and Internet

Microsoft Office Suite software

Multitasking

Needs assessments

Negotiation

Organization

Presentation skills

Problem resolution

Proposal writing

Public speaking

Research skills

Sales skills

Strategic planning

Strategic thinking

Trade show planning

Training design and delivery

Verbal and written communication skills

Volunteer management

Purchasing

Accounting

Auditing

Computer skills

Cost-reduction skills

Customer focus

Database use

Documentation

Federal and international regulations

Influence skills

Interpersonal skills

Inventory systems

Math knowledge

Microsoft Office Suite software

Multitasking

Negotiation

Operations analysis

Problem resolution

Process improvement

Produce accurate documentation

Product line knowledge

Purchase orders—place, track, and expedite

Reviewing and analyzing records

Risk evaluation

Strategic thinking

Supervision

Vendor evaluation and negotiation

Sales

Account forecasting

Account planning

Accurate measuring and ordering

Client management

Closing

Cold-calling

Commitment to quality

Communicating in a foreign language

Communication skills

Consultative sales

Creative copywriting

Customer service

Database use

Desktop publishing

Detail orientation

Documentation

Graphic design/production

Inbound and outbound phone contact

Leadership

Management

Managing hourly workers

Marketing and networking skills

Merchandizing, product placement

Microsoft Office Suite software

Multitasking

Negotiating

Negotiation skills

Outside sales

People skills

Pipeline management

Presentation

Presentation skills

Problem solving

Prospecting

Public speaking

Reading and creating blueprints

Relationship building

Research, reporting, and trend analysis

Retail management

Sales skills

Strategic thinking

Supervising and mentoring sales staff

Training a field sales force

Vendor relationships

Verbal and written communication skills

Training/Development

Asking questions and listening effectively	Math knowledge
Business process architecture	Mentorship
Communicating complex information clearly	Motivating special needs students
Communication skills	Microsoft Office Suite software
Computer/technical skills	Multitasking
Creative copywriting	Networking and job search skills
Curriculum development	Organizational skills
Customer service	Presentation skills
Database use	Producing accurate documentation
Desktop publishing	Product training
Documentation	Program design
E-learning	Program evaluation
Employee development	Project management
Executive coaching	Public speaking
Facilitation skills	Quickly mastering new information
Grading tests	Software implementation/training
Graphic design/production	Teaching adults in a corporate environment
Interpersonal skills	Training design and delivery
Interviewing skills	Training for diverse groups
Knowledge of hiring laws and practices	Web-based training applications
Knowledge of job responsibilities	Word, Excel, PowerPoint, and Visio skills
Lesson planning	Workshop materials development
Managing budgets	Writing

Creating Your e-Resume

Virtually all companies today use the Internet as a primary means of recruitment. Because you will be asked to submit your resume as part of online applications, you need a version that strips out the formatting and is plain text, or ASCII format. This explanation will walk you through the process of converting a Microsoft Word document to plain text.

Converting to ASCII or Plain Text

The purpose of this step is to produce a document that can be read by all operating systems, all Internet service providers, and resume-tracking software systems.

1. Make sure your formatted resume is saved. A good format is: Name Name - Job Title.doc.

2. Use the "Save As" feature and create a new name such as: Name Name – Job Title eResume.

3. In "File Type," scroll to and select "Plain Text." Click Save.

4. In the menu box, make sure that "Insert Line Breaks" is *not* checked. Make sure that "Allow Character Substitution" *is* checked.

5. Click "Save," then close the document. Your new document will be saved as a .txt file.

You should read your document and then clean it up in the next step.

Cleaning ASCII Documents to Optimize Readability

1. Open your resume .txt file from "My Documents" (not inside Word).

2. Go to "File, Page Setup" and set the page to portrait. Set margins to one inch left, two inches right, and one inch top and bottom. Align all information to the left.

3. Make sure your name and contact information are copied from the original document. If these were in a header, you will likely have to retype them.

4. Check for strange characters (such as dollar signs). Usually the substitutions are asterisks, which are fine. Make changes as appropriate.

5. Correct any strange line breaks.

6. Where you have tables, you will want to delete the boxes that indicate cells. Create line breaks between items so that your table information is in the form of a list aligned to the left.

7. Separate sections using all-caps headings and lines composed of keyboard characters such as asterisks, hyphens, equals signs, tildes, and so on.

8. Save the file. Make sure "Insert Line Breaks" is *not* checked and that "Allow Character Substitution" *is* checked.

You now have a document you can use to cut and paste into an e-mail or online application. If you find that your text looks crazy in some applications, you will want to go on to the next step.

Creating a Cut-and-Paste Resume

1. Open your .txt resume file.

2. Click "Save As" and then call the document "Name Name cutnpaste Resume.txt."

3. Make sure both "Insert Line Breaks" and "Allow for Character Substitution" are checked.

4. Because you already set the margins in an earlier step, your resume is formatted at 65 characters, the standard width of e-mail windows and a standard screen shot.

Use this version when you insert your resume into an e-mail or when you fill out online applications.